Amos Users' Guide
Version 3.6

James L. Arbuckle

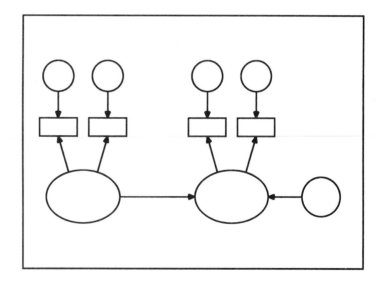

For more information, please contact:

Marketing Department
SPSS Inc.
444 North Michigan Avenue
Chicago, IL 60611
Tel: (312) 329-2400
Fax: (312) 329-3668
URL: http://www.spss.com

SmallWaters Corporation
1507 E. 53rd Street, #452
Chicago, IL 60615
Tel: (773) 667-8635
Fax: (773) 955-6252
URL: http://www.smallwaters.com

Amos User's Guide Version 3.6
Copyright © 1997 by SmallWaters Corporation
All rights reserved.
Printed in the United States of America.

1 2 3 4 5 6 7 8 9 0   03 02 01 00 99 98 97

ISBN 1-56827-125-5

Library of Congress Catalog Card Number:96-070421

Contents

Introduction

Amos implements the general approach to data analysis known as structural modeling, analysis of covariance structures, or causal modeling. This approach includes as special cases many well known conventional techniques, including the general linear model and common factor analysis. Structural modeling is sometimes thought of as an esoteric method that is difficult to learn and use. This is a complete mistake. Indeed, much of the importance of structural modeling lies in the ease with which it allows nonstatisticians to solve estimation and hypothesis testing problems that once would have required the services of a specialist. Amos was originally designed as a tool for teaching this powerful and fundamentally simple method. For this reason, every effort has been made to see that it is easy to use. The program also incorporates the results of extensively testing a variety of numerical algorithms. The methods implemented in Amos are believed to be the most effective and reliable ones now available.

Features

Amos provides the following methods for estimating structural equation models: maximum likelihood, unweighted least squares, generalized least squares, Browne's asymptotically distribution-free criterion, and scale-free least-squares.

Amos has a number of distinguishing features in addition to the usual capabilities that are also found in other structural equation modeling programs. Amos can compute full information maximum likelihood estimates in the presence of missing data. The program can analyze data from several populations at once. It can estimate means for exogenous variables, and intercepts in regression equations.

Bootstrapped standard errors and confidence intervals are available for all estimates, as well as for sample means, variances, covariances and correlations. Percentile intervals and bias-corrected percentile intervals (Stine, 1989) are implemented. Bollen and Stine's (1992) bootstrap approach to model testing is also incorporated.

Multiple models can be fitted in a single analysis. Amos examines every pair of models in which one model can be obtained by placing restrictions on the parameters of the other. The program reports several statistics appropriate for comparing such models. A test of univariate normality is provided for each observed variable, as well as a test of multivariate normality. An attempt is made to detect outliers.

Amos accepts a path diagram as a model specification, and displays parameter estimates graphically on a path diagram. The path diagrams used for model specification, as well as those that display parameter estimates, are of presentation quality. They can be printed directly, or imported into other applications, such as word processors, desktop publishing programs, and general-purpose graphics programs.

New features added in Release 3.5

Many new features have been added to Amos since Release 3.1.

- The Users' Guide has been rewritten.

- The reference section of the Users' Guide is also available on line.

- Several new goodness-of-fit measures have been added, so that all well-known fit measures are now reported.

- The graphical interface has been greatly enhanced in response to suggestions from users of Release 3.1. All fit measures can now be displayed on the path diagram. The new release provides more control over the appearance of the path diagram, including the placement of arrows and the format of parameter estimates. The ability to select or deselect all objects at once is now included. Pop-up menus are now provided as an alternative method for choosing drawing operations.

- Amos now keeps multiple backup copies of .AMW files.

- The graphical interface permits automatic estimation of means and intercepts.

- The graphical interface is now capable of recognizing latent variables, indicator variables and residual variables. It is possible to draw a latent variable with all of its indicators and associated residual variables in a single operation. You can rotate the indicators of a latent variable and reflect them through a horizontal or vertical axis. If you move a latent variable, Amos will (at your option) move its indicators and residual variables also.

- A new drawing operation is provided to automatically attach a residual variable to an existing variable.

- Amos now attempts to preserve any symmetries that are present in a path diagram. That is, roughly speaking, if you make a change in your path diagram that would destroy some symmetry, Amos will (at your option) try to change the rest of the path diagram in order to restore the symmetry.

Two new features will be especially useful in teaching structural modeling:

- You can display the degrees of freedom for a model at any time during the course of drawing its path diagram. Thus you can recalculate the degrees of freedom after adding new elements to the path diagram or after changing the model constraints.

- The *modeling laboratory* allows you to enter an arbitrary choice of parameter values, and then observe the resulting implied moments and the resulting value of the discrepancy function. The modeling laboratory allows a student to try out one set of parameter values after another in an attempt to make the implied moments resemble the sample moments.

New features added in Release 3.6

Amos Release 3.6 has added support for reading raw data in these binary database formats:

- SPSS .SAV files

- dBase III and IV

- Foxpro 2.0 and 2.5

- Microsoft Access 1 and 2

In addition to the standalone Amos package published by SmallWaters, a customized version is also distributed by SPSS. *SPSS Amos* is functionally equivalent to the standalone version, except that it installs itself into the SPSS Statistics menu and expects an SPSS working file as default data input.

About this manual

This Users' Guide contains 21 examples that constitute an introduction to structural modeling as well as to the use of Amos. Examples 1 through 4 show how you can use Amos to do some conventional analyses— analyses that could be done using a standard statistics 'package'. These examples show a new approach to some familiar problems while also demonstrating all of the basic features of Amos. There are sometimes good reasons for using Amos to do something simple like estimating a mean or correlation, or testing the hypothesis that two means are equal. For one thing, you might want to take advantage of Amos's ability to handle missing data. Another reason would be to use Amos's bootstrapping capability, particularly to obtain confidence intervals.

Examples 5 through 8 illustrate the basic techniques that are commonly used nowadays in structural modeling.

Example 9 and those that follow demonstrate advanced techniques that have so far not been used as much as they deserve. These techniques include a) simultaneous analysis of data from several different populations, b) estimation of means and additive constants in regression equations, c) maximum likelihood estimation in the presence of missing data, and d) bootstrapping to obtain estimated standard errors. Amos makes these techniques especially easy to use, and I hope that they will become more commonplace.

Program development and maintenance

No computer program is ever finished as long as people keep using it. I am already working on the next version of Amos. Your suggestions would be appreciated. SmallWaters intends to port Amos to other operating systems whenever there is sufficient demand. If you would like to use Amos on another operating system, please let SmallWaters know what your needs are.

A last word of warning: While the people at SmallWaters and I have engaged in extensive program testing to ensure that Amos operates correctly, all complicated software, Amos included, is bound to contain some undetected bugs. SmallWaters and I are committed to correcting any program errors. If you encounter any odd-looking or seemingly erroneous results, please report them to the SmallWaters technical support staff.

Other sources of information

Although the Users' Guide contains a good bit of expository material, it is not by any means intended to be a complete guide to the correct and effective use of structural modeling. Bollen's (1989) comprehensive text is an important reference that can also serve well as an introduction to structural modeling. Loehlin's (1992) text has the advantage of not being tied to the use of any particular computer program. You can use it as a guide to the use of Amos or any other structural modeling program. The book also contains a useful introduction to exploratory factor analysis, which is often used in the early stages of an investigation, before an Amos analysis is appropriate.

Structural Equation Modeling: A Multidisciplinary Journal contains methodological articles as well as applications of structural modeling. It is published by

> Lawrence Erlbaum Associates, Inc.
> Journal Subscription Department
> 10 Industrial Avenue
> Mahwah, NJ 07430
> phone: 201-236-9500
>   fax: 201-236-0072

An electronic mailing list called Semnet was established by Carl Ferguson and Edward Rigdon to provide a forum for discussions related to structural modeling. Comprehensive information about joining and searching Semnet, plus how-to instructions for unsubscribing from the list, can be found on the world wide web at

> `http://www.gsu.edu/~mkteer/semnet.html`

In short, to subscribe to Semnet, send the message

> `subscribe semnet` *`firstname lastname`*

to `listserv@ua1vm.ua.edu`. For example, I would subscribe by sending the message

> `subscribe semnet James Arbuckle`

After subscribing, you will receive messages that are distributed to all subscribers to the list. You will also be able to send messages that will be seen by other subscribers.

Edward Rigdon also maintains a list of frequently asked questions (FAQs) about structural equation modeling. That list is located on the world wide web at

> `http://www.gsu.edu/~mkteer/semfaq.html`

Acknowledgments

Many people contributed to the development of Amos. Morton Kleban and Rachel Pruchno were two early Amos users who helped to influence the development of the program. Jonathan Brill is a frequent source of good advice. Michael Friendly used several versions of the program and provided useful feedback. Amos has had the benefit of extensive testing by Christopher Burant and David Burns, two active structural modelers who generously took the time to report their experiences. Kenneth Bollen made a number of valuable suggestions, including the idea of a one-step procedure for drawing latent variables along with their indicators and residual variables. Many subsequent enhancements to the graphics interface flowed from this single idea. Students in my structural modeling class have been a perennial source of feedback and new ideas.

At SmallWaters, Eveline Murphy provided proofreading and expert advice on English grammar and page layout. Neil Lane did an excellent job testing the program and drafting most of the new material in the Examples section. Jeremy Staum and Hongwei Zhang tested Version 3.6. Werner Wothke edited the Amos Users' Guide extensively with respect to both style and content. Werner also redesigned the menu structure of the graphical interface and provided guidance on various statistical and programming issues. Many portions of the Users' Guide were substantially rewritten at SmallWaters, including the first nineteen examples.

David Marso and Michael Woods of SPSS provided essential guidance for the Version 3.6 interface, and Hyunjung Bae contributed her organizational skills to keeping the Version 3.6 deployment on track.

Although Amos introduces some new techniques, the program is primarily the implementation of other people's ideas. I would like to mention that I relied heavily on the chapter by Browne (1982). This document helped to shape my view of the field of structural modeling, as well as serving as a blueprint for the numerical portions of Amos.

Finally, I wish to take note of the singular role of Karl Jöreskog in demonstrating that structural modeling, as we now know it, is possible, and in persuading people that the method is useful. Developing a program like Amos is made immeasurably easier by the knowledge that one is dealing with a problem that is both soluble and worthwhile.

James L. Arbuckle

Ambler, Pennsylvania   July, 1996

Installation instructions

Software requirements

The **Amos standalone** package, Version 3.6 or later, runs on Intel-compatible PCs, under the Windows dialects:

- MS-Windows 3.1 (with Win32s)
- Windows 95
- Windows NT 3.51
- IBM OS/2 Warp (WIN-OS/2 with Win32s, in full-screen mode)

On Macintosh and UNIX systems, Amos can be run through the use of Windows emulators, such as the *SoftWindows 95* program distributed by *Insignia Solutions* (web page: http://www.insignia.com).

SPSS Amos runs on the same operating systems as the standalone version. The two Releases of Amos are functionally equivalent. However, technical support is limited to genuine Microsoft Windows dialects.

32-bit operations

Amos Release 3.6 is compiled as a 32-bit program in order to handle large computational problems at high speeds. It requires a version of Windows which supports 32-bit computing, such as Windows 95 and Windows NT, or Windows 3.1 and IBM OS/2 Warp with the Win32s system patch installed.

Note: Microsoft Windows 3.0, the WIN-OS/2 box in IBM OS/2 2.11 (or earlier) and Insignia Solutions SoftWindows 3.0 (or earlier) are inherently 16-bit and do not support Amos 3.6.

Hardware requirements

Intel compatible PC with a 386, 486 or Pentium CPU and a mouse or equivalent pointing device. Amos requires 6.4Mbyte disk space; the Win32s support kit, when needed, uses an additional 1.6Mbyte. A numeric coprocessor is recommended.

RAM requirements vary by operating system. A minimum of 4 Mbyte RAM is required to run Amos under Windows 3.1. However, suggested RAM is 6 Mbyte (or more), especially for modeling larger problems, or for running Amos in parallel with other programs.

Minimum RAM requirements for OS/2 and Windows 95 are in the 8-16 MByte range. Windows NT definitely requires a minimum of 16 Mbyte RAM.

Amos installation

Installation under Windows 95

Standard installation is from the Windows 95 **Start** menu:

1. Insert Amos 3.6 Disk 1 (of 2) in your 3.5 inch drive (presumably the `A:` drive).

2. Open the **Start** menu.

3. Click on **Run**.

4. Specify `a:\setup` as the program you want to run.
   Hit *<Enter>*.

The setup program will guide you through the installation procedure. You will see information displays, such as

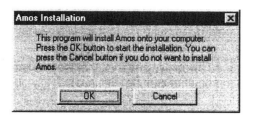

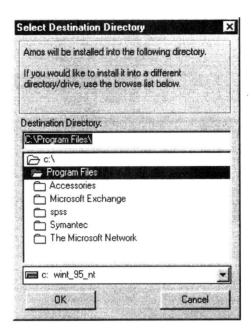

Follow these instructions.

Installation on a Windows NT 3.51 workstation

1. Log on to Windows NT 3.51.

    *   If Amos is to be used by a single user only, log on using that user's ID.

    *   If Amos is to be used by more than one users, log on as the system administrator. For reasons of file security and integrity, Amos should be installed on an NTFS drive.

2. To install Amos on the NT system, locate the diskette titled

    Amos 3.6x   Disk 1 of 2

    and insert it in drive **A:** (presumably a 3.5 inch drive).

3. From the Windows Program Manager's **File** menu, choose **Run ....** Then type

        a:\setup

    and hit *<Enter>*.

4. The setup program will guide you through the rest of the installation procedure, presenting you with various information displays and queries, similar to those given under Windows 95. Follow these instructions.

    If you logged on at step 1 as an individual user, or if you decided not to install Amos on an NTFS drive, this completes the Amos installation.

5. *File security and integrity on multi-user systems*: If you logged on at step 1 as the system administrator and installed Amos on an NTFS drive, the Amos files can be protected from accidental overwrites. Complete the installation as follows.

    *   Set access permissions for the Amos program directory and all its files and subdirectories.

        In the NT **File Manager**, select the Amos program directory. From the **Security** menu, click on the **Permissions** command. The **Directory Permissions** dialog will be displayed.

        Remove existing directory permissions for Amos, if any.

        Click on the **Add** button. The **Add Users and Groups** dialog will be displayed. Set **Administrator** permissions to **Full Control (All)** , and Amos user permissions to **Read (RX)**. Click on **OK**.

Back in the **Directory Permissions** dialog window, select the check boxes for **Replace Permissions on Subdirectories** and **Replace Permissions on Existing Files**. Click on **OK**.

- Instruct Amos users to initialize the environment variable AMOS in their NT User Environment:

    Open the Windows NT **Control Panel**.

    Open **System**.

    Go to the section titled **User Environment Variables for ...** and answer the two queries

    Variable: AMOS

    Value: %HOMEDRIVE%%HOMEPATH%

    Click on **OK.**

    When set to this value, the AMOS variable ensures that separate personal copies of the Amos initialization files are being maintained in the users' home directories. *Note*: You might want to check that all personal home directories have indeed been created on the NT workstation.

- Inform the users that the Amos EXAMPLES and TUTORIAL subdirectories are write-protected. The example and tutorial files should be copied over to personal working directories before being used with Amos.

Installation under Microsoft Windows 3.1

Under Windows 3.1 and Windows for Workgroups 3.11, the Win32s system patch provided by Microsoft is needed to run Amos 3.6 or later.

For installing the Microsoft Win32s patch, locate the diskette titled

Win32s   Disk 1 of 2

and insert it in drive A:

From Program Manager's **File** menu, choose **Run ...** . Then type

    a:\setup

The setup program installs the Win32s Release 1.20, unless a version of Win32s is already present on the system. The next step will be to install Amos 3.6.

To install Amos on your system, locate the diskette titled

Amos 3.6x   Disk 1 of 2

and insert it in drive **A:**

From the Windows Program Manager's **File** menu, choose **Run ...** .

Then type

```
a:\setup
```

The setup program will guide you through the installation procedure. You will see information displays and queries, similar to those given under Windows 95. Follow the instructions displayed by the setup program.

Installation under IBM OS/2 Warp (with WIN-OS/2)

IBM OS/2 Warp supports Amos in *full-screen* WIN-OS/2 sessions.

Installing Amos in WIN-OS/2 should be identical to installation under Windows 3.1. Regrettably, the tense competition between IBM and Microsoft has rendered the initial configuration of Win32s under OS/2 harder than it should be. Perhaps, Win32s support will become easier with subsequent releases of OS/2, but at the time of this writing (Summer 1996), some system configuration "by hand" is still required.

It turns out that OS/2 Warp needs a device driver named `vw32s.sys`. The problem is that the version of `vw32s.sys` which ships with (the 1995 release of) OS/2 Warp supports the MS-Win32s only up to release 1.10, while Microsoft has now (early 1996) issued Release 1.30 of Win32s.

SmallWaters has found a workable solution for IBM OS/2 Warp using Win32s Release 1.20 which is bundled with Amos. The following instructions are perhaps a wee bit technical, but will get you going:

1.   Download the upgraded `vw32s.sys` device driver and the file `vw32s.txt` from `ftp://hobbes.nmsu.edu/os2/patches` by binary *ftp*. Alternatively, if there is a file named `win32s.zip`, you may download that instead. If these files are dated 10-14-95 or later, they will support Win32s up to Release1.25-b or later.

     Follow the instructions in `vw32s.txt` to install the patch.

2.   In the OS/2 `CONFIG.SYS` file, configure the `vw32s.sys` device driver with the switches

```
device=C:\os2\mdos\vw32s.sys 1,20,100
```

     This is different from IBM's official instructions, but seems to work.

3.   Open a full-screen session of WIN-OS/2 and follow the instructions on page 11 for installing **Win32s** and **Amos** under Windows 3.1.

Uninstalling Amos

A utility on the Amos distribution package makes it easy to remove the program from the hard disk. The utility will also remove all references to Amos from the Windows system configuration files.

> *Note:* Uninstalling Amos may erase all work files located in the Amos directory. Be sure to save all needed files and datasets before proceeding.

The procedure for uninstalling Amos depends on the operating system:

1. Remove any write-protection of the Amos files and directories.

2. On Windows 3.1, IBM OS/2 Warp (WIN-OS/2) or Windows NT 3.51 platforms, locate the Amos Program Group and double-click on the **Uninstall Amos** icon. Follow the instructions displayed by the uninstall program.

3. In Windows 95, program deinstallation is through the Windows 95 Control Panel.

    - Open the Windows 95 **Start** menu and select the **Settings** submenu.

    - Open the **Control/Panel**.

    - Open **Add/Remove Programs**; the **Install/Uninstall** panel should be in the foreground.

    - Select **Amos** from the list of installed programs, displayed in the lower section of the panel, and click on the **Add/Remove** button.

Follow the instructions given by the uninstall program.

Network and multi-user support

Amos Version 3.6 is network aware. For network use, Amos should be installed in a dedicated directory on the file server. After installation, this directory, the two subdirectories underneath it, and all files in these directories should be marked *read-only* for regular users. If possible, depending on the type of network, all program files in the Amos server directory should be marked *execute-only* as well.

Amos maintains two configuration files, `config.amd` and `amos.ini`, to store information about the user's last analyses and preferred working style. Amos looks for the configuration files in two directories: first, in the working (data) directory and, second, in the path given by the AMOS environment setting (*cf.*, **$Include** command, described in the *Amos Text*

Reference Guide). If Amos cannot find the configuration files in those directories, the program will initialize from the read-only configuration files located in the Amos program directory. On exit, Amos will replace (or create) the configuration files in the path given by the `AMOS` environment setting, if any, or in the user's working (data) directory.

Amos uses the value of the environment variable `TEMP` to determine the directory for temporary files. "`TEMP`" directories should be located on the client workstations, not on the server, in order to avoid file corruption or sharing violation messages. Thus, on each client workstation, edit the `AUTOEXEC.BAT` file so that the `TEMP` variable points to a local directory, for instance,

```
SET TEMP=C:\WINDOWS\TEMP
```

Example files

When you install Amos, all files used in the Examples section of the Amos Users' Guide are placed in the **EXAMPLES** subdirectory, below the Amos program files. To read any of these examples, press or choose the menu item **File|Open**.

The files used in the Tutorial Section of the Amos Users' Guide are placed in the **TUTORIAL** subdirectory.

Technical support

A web page discussing standard technical support issues involving Amos can be found at

```
http://www.smallwaters.com/amos/support
```

For additional technical support of the **Amos standalone version**, contact the SmallWaters technical support line at

voice:	USA-773-667-8635
fax:	USA-773-955-6252
Internet:	support@smallwaters.com

Twenty-four-hour turn-around time can usually be maintained on the Internet connection. Technical support by phone or fax can be speeded up when you leave both your day and evening phone numbers.

For technical support of **SPSS Amos**, contact your local SPSS office or

voice:	USA-312-329-3410
fax:	USA-312-329-3668
Internet:	support@spss.com

Tutorial: Getting started with Amos Graphics

Purpose of this tutorial

This tutorial will get you started using **Amos Graphics** under Microsoft Windows. It will not demonstrate all of Amos's features, nor does it try to teach you how to interpret the results of an Amos analysis. The purpose of the present document is merely to guide you through your first Amos analysis. Once you have worked through the example presented here, you can turn to the Amos Reference Guide. Additional worked examples of statistical applications are presented in the Examples section of this Users' Guide.

Note: For the **Amos standalone** version, the results of this tutorial exercise are given in the file `getstart.amw`, located in the `TUTORIAL` subdirectory, below the Amos program files. **SPSS Amos** requires minor changes, implemented in the file `startsps.amw`, also located in the `TUTORIAL` subdirectory.

Prerequisites

This tutorial assumes that Amos has been installed on your computer (see: Installation, *p.* 7). Also, it assumes that you already have some experience in using a Windows program other than Amos, so that you are familiar with operations like selecting an item from a menu, moving the mouse pointer, clicking and double-clicking the mouse, and so on.

The data

Hamilton (1990) provided several measurements on each of 21 states. Three of the measurements will be used for the present example: 1) average *SAT* score, 2) per capita income expressed in $1,000 units, 3) median education for residents 25 years of age or older. The data, from the file `hamilton.amd` in the TUTORIAL subdirectory, are:

Table 1		
SAT	Income	Education
899	14.345	12.7
896	16.370	12.6
897	13.537	12.5
889	12.552	12.5
823	11.441	12.2
857	12.757	12.7
860	11.799	12.4
890	10.683	12.5
889	14.112	12.5
888	14.573	12.6
925	13.144	12.6
869	15.281	12.5
896	14.121	12.5
827	10.758	12.2
908	11.583	12.7
885	12.343	12.4
887	12.729	12.3
790	10.075	12.1
868	12.636	12.4
904	10.689	12.6
888	13.065	12.4

A model

The path diagram in Figure 1 shows a model for these data. It is a simple regression model in which one observed variable, *SAT*, is predicted as a linear combination of the other two observed variables, *Education* and *Income*. As with nearly all empirical data, the prediction will not be perfect. The latent variable *Other* therefore serves to absorb random variation in the *SAT* scores and systematic components for which no suitable predictors were provided.

Each single-headed arrow represents a regression weight. The number "1" in the figure specifies that *Other* must have a weight of one in the prediction of *SAT*. Some such constraint must be imposed in order to make the model *identified*, and it is one of the features of the model that must be communicated to Amos.

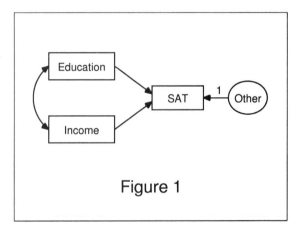

Figure 1

You need to provide Amos with information about both the model (in Figure 1) and the data (in Table 1).

Specifying the model

When you start **Amos Graphics** (by double-clicking on the **Amos Graphics** icon), you will see a window like the following, containing a large rectangle and several menu titles:

The Opening and Toolbox Windows when a new path diagram is created.

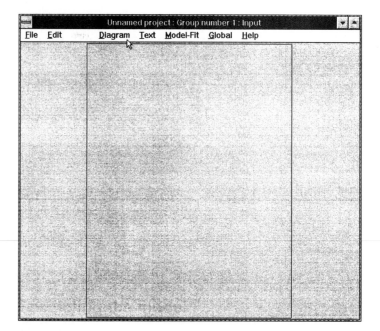

The large rectangle (in the center of the window) represents a sheet of paper. Its shape depends on how your printer is set up. In this example the printer is set up in *portrait* mode, and the rectangle is taller than it is wide. If your printer is set for *landscape* printing, the rectangle will be wider than it is tall.

In addition to the **Amos Graphics** main window, Amos displays a toolbox window with "button" commands which may be used as shortcuts for drawing and modeling operations.

The purpose of this exercise is to draw a replica of Figure 1 within the boundaries of the big rectangle. Your tools are the mouse, the menu and button commands, and occasionally the keyboard.

Drawing the variables

Tools for drawing the path diagram can be chosen from the **Diagram** menu or by clicking on the appropriate button in toolbox 1 (most drawing tools are loaded in toolbox 1 when **Amos Graphics** is installed). The next two pictures show how the commands are selected:

Click on the **Draw Observed** *command from the* **Diagram** *menu to draw boxes for the observed variables or ...*

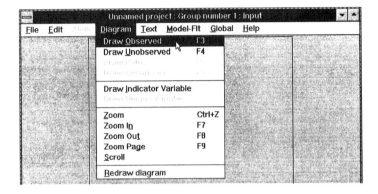

... select the **Draw Observed** *button from toolbox 1 to draw boxes for observed variables. (Temporarily-inactive buttons are darkened).*

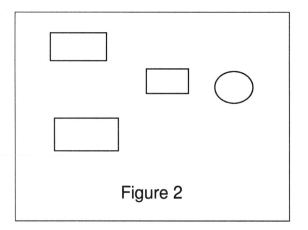

Begin the construction of your path diagram by drawing three rectangles to represent the three observed variables in the model. First, click on the **Draw Observed** button (or select the **Draw Observed** command from the **Diagram** menu). The button will change in appearance, so that it looks as if it is illuminated. Then move the mouse pointer to the place where you want the *Education* rectangle to appear. Don't worry too much about the exact placement of the rectangle. You can move it later on. Once you have picked a spot for the *Education* rectangle, press the left mouse button and hold it down while making some trial movements of the mouse. Movements of the mouse will affect the size and shape of the rectangle. When you are satisfied with its appearance, release the mouse button. You don't need to be too picky. You can change the rectangle's size and shape later. Having completed the *Education* rectangle, use the same method to draw two more rectangles for *Income* and *SAT*. As long as the **Draw Observed** button is illuminated a new rectangle will appear every time you press the left mouse button and move the mouse.

Next, draw an ellipse to represent *Other*. Ellipses are drawn the same way as rectangles, except that you begin by clicking on the **Draw Unobserved** button. After drawing the ellipse, your screen should look more or less like Figure 2.

Figure 2

Naming the variables

To assign names to the four variables, click on the **Text (Enter/Edit)** button. Then use the mouse pointer to pick one of the objects in the path diagram—the ellipse or one of the rectangles. It doesn't matter which object you start with, but say you start with the rectangle that is supposed to represent *Education*. Move the mouse pointer to the *Education* rectangle. (The rectangle will change color.) Click the left mouse button, and the following dialog will appear:

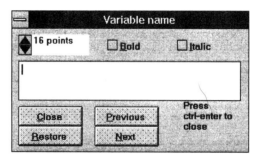

Type the name *Education* in the space provided and press the "Enter" key. Follow the same procedure to name the remaining three variables. The path diagram should end up looking something like Figure 3.

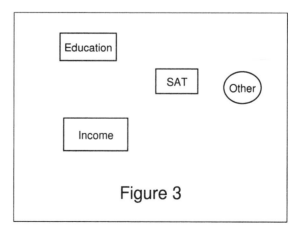

Figure 3

Drawing arrows

To draw the single-headed arrows in the path diagram, start off by clicking on the **Draw Path** button. Then, to draw an arrow from *Education* to *SAT*, go through the following steps: 1) Move the mouse pointer to the *Education* rectangle. 2) Press the left mouse button and hold it down. 3) While holding down the left mouse button, move the mouse pointer to the *SAT* rectangle. 4) Release the mouse button. Repeat this procedure for each of the remaining single-headed arrows.

Drawing double-headed arrows is similar to drawing single-headed arrows except that you begin by clicking on the **Draw Covariance** button. Then, to draw the double-headed arrow connecting *Education* and *Income*, go through the following steps: 1) Move the mouse pointer to the *Income* rectangle. 2) Press the left mouse button and hold it down. 3) While holding the left mouse button down, move the mouse pointer to the *Education* rectangle. 4) Release the mouse button. Your path diagram should then resemble Figure 4.

Note: *The initial curvature of the two-headed arrow follows an arc drawn in clockwise direction. When the arrow is drawn from Income to Education, the curvature will be to the left. When we draw in the other direction, going from Education to Income, then the curvature will be to the right.*
*The curvature of any two-headed arrow can be changed later with the **Shape** command.*

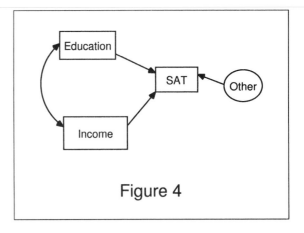

Figure 4

Constraining a parameter

In order to identify the regression model, the scale of the latent variable *Other* must be defined. You can do this by fixing either the variance of *Other* or the path coefficient from *Other* to *SAT* at some positive value. Suppose you want to fix the path coefficient at unity. To do so, first click on the

Parameter Constraints button. Then move the mouse pointer to the arrow that points from *Other* to *SAT*. Click the left mouse button, and the following dialog box will appear:

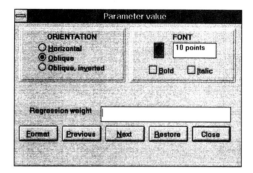

Using the keyboard, type the value "1" in the space provided and press the **Close** button. The path diagram should then look like Figure 5. This completes the path diagram except for any changes you might want to make to improve its appearance.

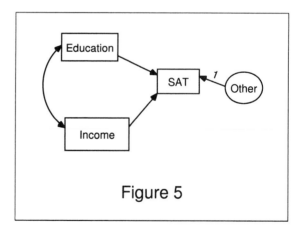

Figure 5

Improving the appearance of the path diagram

You can change the appearance of your path diagram by moving objects around, and by changing their sizes and shapes. Such changes do not affect the meaning of a path diagram. That is, they do not change the model specification. To move an object, first press the **Move** button. Then point to the object with the mouse pointer and press the left mouse button. With the left mouse button held down, you can drag the object to its new location simply by moving the mouse. **Amos Graphics** will automatically redraw all connecting arrows.

To change the size and shape of an object, first press the **Shape** button. Then point to the object with the mouse pointer and press the left mouse button. While the left mouse button is being held down, moving the mouse will change the size and shape of the object.

No matter how carefully you try to adjust the size, shape and location of individual objects in your path diagram, the path diagram as a whole will probably end up looking slightly out of kilter. You might, for example, want the *Education* and *Income* rectangles to look exactly alike, but it is very hard to accomplish this by adjusting one rectangle at a time. Amos provides tools for achieving this and other aesthetically desirable effects, but these are fine points that will not be pursued here.

Printing the path diagram

To print the path diagram, click on the **Print** button in toolbox 1. When the following dialog box appears, click on **Print**:

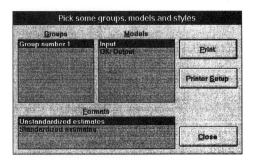

Entering the data

To enter the data in Table 1, begin by clicking on the **$ command** button. A window will appear with the title **"$" commands: Group number 1**. Type the following lines in this window:

```
$Smc
$Standardized
$Sample size = 21
$Input variables
     SAT
     Income
     Education
$Raw Data
     899    14.345    12.7
     896    16.370    12.6
     897    13.537    12.5
     889    12.552    12.5
     823    11.441    12.2
     857    12.757    12.7
     860    11.799    12.4
     890    10.683    12.5
     889    14.112    12.5
     888    14.573    12.6
     925    13.144    12.6
     869    15.281    12.5
     896    14.121    12.5
     827    10.758    12.2
     908    11.583    12.7
     885    12.343    12.4
     887    12.729    12.3
     790    10.075    12.1
     868    12.636    12.4
     904    10.689    12.6
     888    13.065    12.4
```

The first two lines are optional. **$Smc** requests a squared multiple correlation for each endogenous variable. (There is only one endogenous variable in this example—*SAT.*) **$Standardized** requests standardized parameter estimates. **$Smc** and **$Standardized** are just two of many optional commands that are documented in the **Amos Text Reference Guide** and that can be entered in the **"$" commands** window.

It is not necessary to duplicate the indentation and spacing shown above. Just make sure that every pair of adjacent numbers is separated by at least one space. In the last line, for example, there must at least one space between "888" and "13.065". Apart from this requirement, spaces are ignored.

After all data have been entered, close the **"$" commands** window, either by pressing <ctrl>-D or by selecting the **Diagram** command from the **File** menu.

Reading data from an SPSS system file

Note: *SPSS system files support variable names of up to eight characters. In the SPSS data set **HAMILTON.SAV**, used in this example, the variable name* Education *has therefore been shortened to* Educatn. *Remember to change the path diagram accordingly.*

As an alternative to ASCII (or text) based data input, Amos Graphics, Version 3.6 or later, supports input of several binary database formats, including SPSS `*.SAV` files. In addition, SPSS Amos can also read the data of the current SPSS working file, when Amos is started directly from the SPSS Statistics menu (*See* **Specifying the source of data in SPSS Amos** on page 51).

For associating a saved binary input file with the path diagram, follow these steps.

1. In the Amos **File** menu, click on **Binary Data File ...**

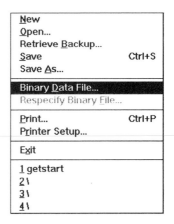

This will bring up a dialog box for specifying the binary data file.

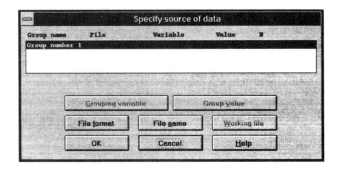

Click on **File format.**

2. A list of supported binary database formats is presented:

Select **SPSS** and click on the **OK** button.

3. Amos shows the names of all SPSS .SAV files in the current working directory. Select the file hamilton.sav in the TUTORIAL subdirectory, below the Amos program files, and click on **OK**.

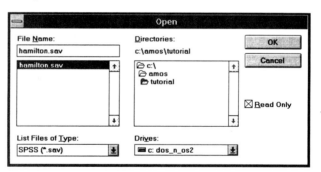

4. In the last dialog, Amos reports the file HAMILTON.SAV to be associated with the current path model (there is only one group of data). To accept, click on OK.

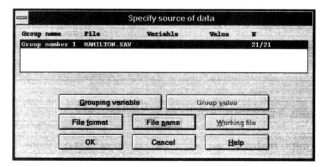

Performing the analysis

Clicking on the **Calculate Estimates** button will cause Amos to save the problem setup to a file, and to carry out the analysis. If no filename has yet been associated with this problem, Amos will prompt for one.

While Amos is calculating the model estimates, a small window is displayed to keep you informed about the progress of Amos's computations:

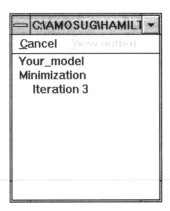

Viewing text output

When Amos has finished the analysis, the text output file with the results is presented in the foreground. If you have made any mistakes in entering the model or the data, an error message will be located at the end of this file.

Assuming that the analysis was performed as expected, the text output file will look about like this:

Iterations converged.

Chi-square test of restrictions imposed on the implied covariance matrix. No such restrictions found in this model!

These maximum likelihood estimates are identical to the standard least-square solution for regression coefficients. Amos standard errors (S.E.) are asymptotically correct. The Critical Ratio (C.R.) is defined as

C.R.=Estimate/S.E.

```
Minimum was achieved


Chi-square =     0.000
Degrees of freedom =     0
Probability level cannot be computed

Maximum Likelihood Estimates
- - - - - - - - - - - - - - - - - - - - - - - - - - -


Regression Weights:           Estimate      S.E.      C.R.      Label
- - - - - - - - - - - - - -    - - - - - - -  - - - - -  - - - - -  - - - - -

    SAT <--- Education        136.022     30.555     4.452
    SAT <------ Income          2.156      3.125     0.690


Standardized Regression Weights:      Estimate
- - - - - - - - - - - - - - - - - - - - - - - - -    - - - - - - -

          SAT <----- Education         0.717
          SAT <-------- Income         0.111


Covariances:                  Estimate      S.E.      C.R.      Label
- - - - - - - - - - - -        - - - - - - -  - - - - -  - - - - -  - - - - -

  Education <--> Income         0.127      0.065     1.952


Correlations:                         Estimate
- - - - - - - - - - - -                - - - - - - -

      Education <------> Income        0.485


Variances:                    Estimate      S.E.      C.R.      Label
- - - - - - - - - -            - - - - - - -  - - - - -  - - - - -  - - - - -

            Education        0.027      0.008     3.162
               Income        2.562      0.810     3.162
                Other      382.736    121.032     3.162


Squared Multiple Correlations:        Estimate
- - - - - - - - - - - - - - - - - - - - - - - - -    - - - - - - -

                    SAT        0.603
```

Viewing graphics output

To view the path diagram along with Amos' parameter estimates, click on the **Groups/Models** button. The following dialog box will appear:

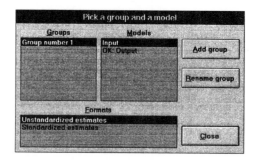

The **Models** list box contains two items—"Input" and "OK: Output". If you choose "Input", Amos will display the path diagram exactly as you entered it, without the Amos parameter estimates. You should, instead, choose "OK: Output". You can choose between unstandardized and standardized estimates by clicking on the appropriate item in the **Formats** list box. Then click on the **Close** button.

If the **Models** list box does not contain an "OK: Output" item, this means that parameter estimates aren't available. This could be because an error occurred while Amos was running. Of course it could also mean that you just forgot to run Amos by clicking on the **Calculate estimates** button. *You have to re-run Amos after every change to the model or the data in order to keep the parameter estimates up to date.*

If you selected "Standardized estimates", and assuming that you used the optional Amos commands **$Smc** and **$Standardized**, a path diagram similar to Figure 6 should appear on your screen.

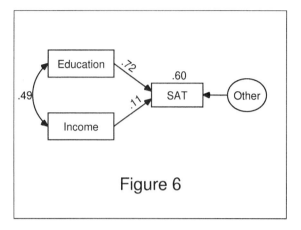

Figure 6

The value .49 is the correlation between *Education* and *Income*. The entries .72 and .11 are standardized regression weights. The number .60 is the squared multiple correlation of *SAT* with *Education* and *Income*.

Printing the parameter estimates

To print the path diagram along with Amos's parameter estimates, click on the **Print** button. When the following window appears: 1) Choose "OK: Output" from the **Models** list box. 2) Select either unstandardized or standardized estimates from the **Formats** list box. 3) Click on the **Print** button.

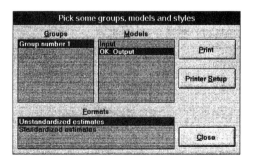

Tutorial: Getting started with Amos Text

Purpose of this tutorial

This tutorial will get you started with **Amos Text** under Microsoft Windows. While the primary use of **Amos Text** is as a computing engine for **Amos Graphics**, it may sometimes be more convenient to use **Amos Text** directly, without going through the graphical interface at all. For instance, it may be easier in **Amos Text** to specify particular, very large models or to conduct simulation studies on the statistical properties of parameter estimates.

The remainder of this section will guide you through a first-time use of **Amos Text**. Once you have worked through the section, you can turn to the Amos Reference Guide.

Note: The results of this tutorial exercise are given in the file `getstart.ami`, located in the `TUTORIAL` subdirectory, below the Amos program files.

Additional worked examples of statistical applications can be found in the Examples section of this Users' Guide.

Prerequisites

This tutorial assumes that Amos has been installed on your computer. If not, install it now (see: Installation on *p.* 7). You should also be fairly familiar with both text and graphics operations under the Microsoft Windows operating system, and should know how to select an item from a menu, use the mouse, and edit plain text files with a system editor such as Microsoft Notepad.

Data and Model

Hamilton's (1990) data, discussed on page 16, are used in this example. We will consider the path model from page 17, which may be expressed as a traditional regression equation of the *SAT* deviation scores:

$$SAT = b_1 \cdot Education \ + \ b_2 \cdot Income \ + \ Other$$

You should provide **Amos Text** with information about both the data and this structural equation.

Specifying the model

When you start **Amos Text** (by double-clicking on the Amos Text icon), you will see a dialog box with the following options:

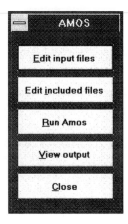

Click on the **Edit input files** button. Amos will display the Notepad file-opening dialog:

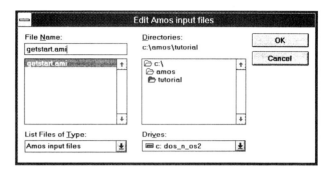

If the file `getstart.ami` was installed in the Amos **TUTORIAL** directory, open it now. Otherwise, fill in the filename here and press the **OK** button to open a new file in which to enter the **Amos Text** commands and data from scratch. In either case, you should arrive in a Notepad editing session with the following file contents:

Input data set supplied here: sample size, names of observed variables, and raw data.

Regression model: Path coefficient of residual error must be fixed at unity.

```
Education, Income (in 1K units) and SAT
Data from Hamilton (1990)

$Smc                    ! Compute R-square and
$Standardized           ! standardized solution

$Sample size = 21
$Input variables
    SAT
    Income
    Education
$Raw Data               ! 21 data records follow
    899    14.345   12.7
    896    16.370   12.6
    897    13.537   12.5
    889    12.552   12.5
    823    11.441   12.2
    857    12.757   12.7
    860    11.799   12.4
    890    10.683   12.5
    889    14.112   12.5
    888    14.573   12.6
    925    13.144   12.6
    869    15.281   12.5
    896    14.121   12.5
    827    10.758   12.2
    908    11.583   12.7
    885    12.343   12.4
    887    12.729   12.3
    790    10.075   12.1
    868    12.636   12.4
    904    10.689   12.6
    888    13.065   12.4
$Structure
    SAT = Education + Income + (1) Other
```

Alternatively, the regression model could have been stated in path notation:

```
$Structure
     SAT <--- Education
     SAT <--- Income
     SAT <--- Other (1)
```

Amos Text employs the default assumptions that the *latent* exogenous variable **Other** is uncorrelated with any other exogenous variable, and that the two *observed* exogenous variables, **Education** and **Income,** are correlated with each other. These are the standard assumptions of ordinal least-squares regression. Therefore, this example does not require any explicit covariance specifications.

After you finish entering the commands and data, save the file to disk and exit the Notepad editor.

Performing the Analysis

Clicking on the **Run Amos** button will cause Amos to interpret the command file and data. A small window will appear and keep you informed about the progress of the computations:

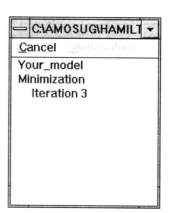

Viewing text output

When Amos has finished the analysis, the text output file will be displayed immediately in the foreground. If you have made any mistakes in entering the model or the data, an error message will be located at the end of this file.

Assuming that the analysis was performed as expected, the pertinent section of the text output file will look about like this:

These maximum likelihood estimates are identical to the standard least-square solution for regression coefficients. Amos standard errors (S.E.) are asymptotically correct. The Critical Ratio (C.R.) is defined as

$$C.R.=Estimate/S.E.$$

```
Maximum Likelihood Estimates
- - - - - - - - - - - - - - - - - - - - - - - - - - - -

Regression Weights:            Estimate     S.E.      C.R.      Label
- - - - - - - - - - - - - - -   - - - - - -   - - - - -   - - - - -   - - - - -

    SAT <--- Education         136.022     30.555     4.452
    SAT <------ Income           2.156      3.125     0.690

Standardized Regression Weights:    Estimate
- - - - - - - - - - - - - - - - - - - - - - - -      - - - - - - - -

           SAT <----- Education        0.717
           SAT <--------- Income       0.111

Covariances:                   Estimate     S.E.      C.R.      Label
- - - - - - - - - - -           - - - - - -   - - - - -   - - - - -   - - - - -

   Education <--> Income          0.127      0.065     1.952

Correlations:                              Estimate
- - - - - - - - - - - -                     - - - - - - - -

      Education <------> Income        0.485

Variances:                     Estimate     S.E.      C.R.      Label
- - - - - - - - - -             - - - - - -   - - - - -   - - - - -   - - - - -

               Education         0.027      0.008     3.162
                  Income         2.562      0.810     3.162
                   Other       382.736    121.032     3.162
```

If the input file was named `getstart.ami`, then text output can be found in a file named `getstart.amo`. The contents of this file may be displayed, edited, and/or printed as needed.

Amos Graphics Reference Guide

Drawing operations

Amos provides many operations for drawing path diagrams and for improving their looks. For example, you can

- Draw an ellipse to represent an unobserved variable
- Move the ellipse from one place to another
- Make an ellipse bigger or smaller, or change its shape.

These are only three examples of drawing and modeling operations; there are about eighty others. Amos provides four different ways to pick the operation you want to perform:

- Using the mouse to press a button in a toolbox
- Using the mouse or the keyboard to select an item from a menu
- Pressing a "hot key" on the keyboard (for some operations)
- Using the second mouse button to select an item from a pop-up menu (for some operations).

These four methods of selecting an operation are described in the following sections.

Using toolboxes

You can choose an operation by pressing a button in an Amos toolbox. That is, you move the mouse pointer over the appropriate button in the toolbox and click the left mouse button. Amos provides two toolboxes that can be customized. Here is what their default versions look like:

Toolbox 1 has most of the buttons necessary for creating a path diagram and for model fitting. Toolbox 2 has useful functions for fixing up existing path diagrams. The toolboxes shown here contain only 39 buttons each, but you can make the toolboxes bigger or smaller, and fill them with your own selection of buttons (see page 165).

Only one toolbox at a time is visible. You can toggle between the two toolboxes by pressing ⟡ (see page 166).

Using menus

To initiate an operation, you can also choose an item from the Amos menu. Here is what the menu looks like when you indicate that you want to draw an ellipse:

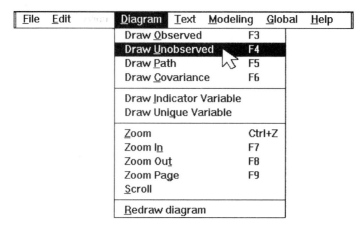

Menu items can also be selected from the keyboard. Instead of using the mouse to select Draw Unobserved from the Diagram menu, you could instead hold down the ALT key and press the D key followed by the U key.

Using hot keys

Special "hot keys" are provided for a few common operations. For example, you can indicate that you want to draw an ellipse by pressing the <F4> key. When a hot key is available for an operation, the hot key is shown on the menu

Using pop-up menus

Once you have drawn a path diagram, or drawn it partially at least, you can use one additional method of choosing further operations on the path diagram. You can move the mouse pointer over any object in the path diagram (that is, any rectangle, ellipse, arrow or caption), and click the *second* mouse button. Then Amos will display a menu of operations that can be performed on that object. For example, using the second mouse button to click on an ellipse will pop up a menu of things that you can do to ellipses. Hot keys are also documented in the section **Catalog of drawing operations** beginning on page 44.

Getting help

Finding out what a toolbox button does

To get a one-line explanation of what a button does, place the mouse pointer over the button. A brief description of its function will appear in the title bar of the Amos window. For a more complete explanation, press the <F1> function key.

Finding out what a menu item does

To get an explanation of a menu item, point to the menu item. *Hold down* the left mouse button (don't release it) and press the <F1> key. For an alternative method see

 Get help for a single button or menu item on page 170.

Catalog of drawing operations

This section of the Users' Guide explains each of the Amos drawing operations.

▫ Start a new path diagram

Menu: **File|New**

Pressing ▫ starts a new path diagram. If you are already working on a path diagram when you press ▫, you will be asked if you want to save it before starting a new one.

☞ Read an old path diagram from disk

Menu: **File|Open...**

Pressing ☞ allows you to retrieve a path diagram that you saved previously.

Related commands:

🖫 **Save a path diagram** on page 48

Retrieve a previous backup

Menu: **File|Retrieve Backup...**

Pressing allows you to choose from a list of previously backed up path diagrams:

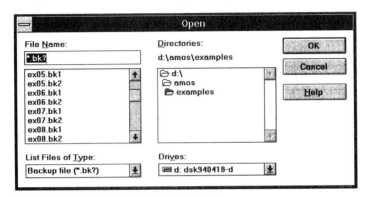

To see how the backup capability works, suppose you have made several changes to a path diagram called alpha, saving the path diagram (using) periodically. Then the most recently saved version of the path diagram will have the name **alpha.amw**. The version before that will be called **alpha.bk1**. The version before **alpha.bk1** will be called **alpha.bk2**. And so on. You can specify as many as nine backups (the oldest version would then have a name that ends with **.bk9**), or you can specify that no backups be kept. Use to specify how many backups to keep.

Related commands:

 Choose miscellaneous options on page 159

 Save a path diagram on page 48

⊞ Save a path diagram

Menu: **File|Save**
Hot key: **Ctrl-S**

Pressing allows you to save the path diagram on disk. The first time you save a path diagram, you will be asked to give it a name. If you subsequently make changes to the path diagram and press again, the updated version will replace the original version.

Note: If you want to save a path diagram under a new name (avoiding replacement of an earlier version) use instead.

Related commands:

Read an old path diagram from disk on page 46

Save a path diagram with a new name on page 49

Save a path diagram with a new name

Menu: **File|Save As...**

To save a path diagram without destroying an earlier version, you need to save the new version under a new name. To do so, press 🖪.

Related commands:

🖫 **Save a path diagram** on page 48

Binary data file ...

Menu: **File|Binary Data File** ...

Beginning with Release 3.6, Amos supports these **binary database file formats**.

- dBase III and IV
- Foxpro 2.0 and 2.5
- Microsoft Access 1 and 2
- SPSS

For ASCII (or text) based data input, the **original Amos data format**[1] is supported as well.

The approach for specifying a binary data source depends on whether you are using the standalone version of Amos or the SPSS version.

Specifying the source of data in Amos (standalone version)

The original state of the **File** menu in the standalone version of Amos is shown in the following illustration.

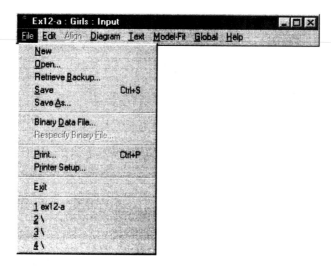

---

[1] The original Amos data format uses the following "$" commands to describe the data to be analyzed.

$Correlations, $Covariances, $Include, $Inputvariables, $Means, $Missing, $Rawdata, $Samplesize, $Standarddeviations

These commands are described in the Amos Text Reference Guide. They may not to be used when analyzing data in a binary database file.

Notice that **Binary Data File** does not have a check mark next to it. In this state, Amos reads data in the original Amos data format.

To analyze data in supported database files, select **Binary Data File**. A dialog will guide you through the choices required to specify the source of your data. Afterwards, the **File** menu will appear as shown in the following illustration.

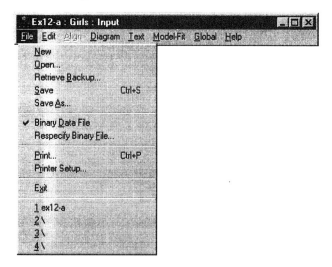

In this illustration, **Binary Data File** is checked to indicate that data are to be read from a database file (and not in the original Amos data format).

To respecify which database file to use as the source of data, or to restrict the analysis to a subset of observations, choose **Respecify Binary File**.

Remember that, if **Binary Data File** has a check mark next to it, you have to remove the check mark in order to go back to using the original Amos data format. (Choose the **Binary Data File** item once to remove the check mark if one is present.)

Specifying the source of data in SPSS Amos

When Amos is started from the SPSS Statistics menu, Amos uses the current SPSS working data set by default.

Note: If changes are made to the SPSS working data set after SPSS Amos has been started, the running copy of Amos will not automatically take those changes into account. This is because when Amos is started from the SPSS Statistics menu, it creates a snapshot of the current SPSS working data set and uses the data in that snapshot. The new working data set can be used after closing and restarting SPSS Amos.

The initial state of the SPSS Amos File menu is shown in the following illustration.

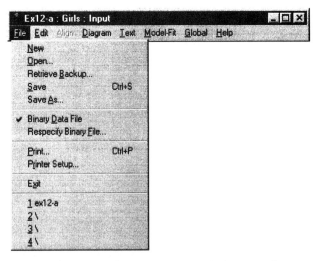

The **Binary Data File** and **Respecify Binary File** menu choices permit you to specify alternative sources of data or to restrict the analysis to a subset of observations. If you wish to treat the entire SPSS working data set as a single sample in your analysis, no steps are required to specify the source of data.

In order to do a multiple-group analysis, or to analyze data from an alternative SPSS data file (.sav file), or to read data in **some other database**, choose **Respecify Binary File** from the **File** menu. A **dialog box** will guide you through the choices required to specify the source of your data.

To analyze data in the **original Amos data format**, remove the check mark from **Binary Data File** on the File menu. (Clicking on **Binary Data File** will toggle the check mark.)

Specify source of data

This dialog box allows you to specify the database file (or files) to be analyzed. It also allows you to restrict the analysis to a subset of the observations in a data set.

In a multiple-group analysis:

- Data for all the groups can reside in a single data file, with group membership determined by the value of one of the variables in the data file.

- Data for each group can come from a different data file.

The following illustration shows the initial state of the dialog box using the standalone version of Amos to carry out the analysis of Example 12-A in the *Users' Guide.* The list box shows that the

![Groups/Models] button has already been pressed to specify that there are two groups called "Girls" and "Boys".

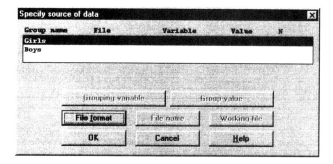

When using the SPSS version of Amos, the dialog box appears as shown in the following illustration. The list box shows that the current working SPSS data set is to be used for both girls and boys. (To be more precise, Amos will use the data set that was the current working data set at the time that Amos was started from the SPSS "Statistics" menu.)

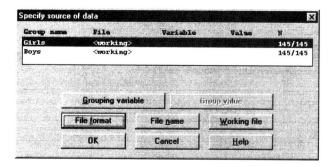

File format Specifies the data file format for the group that is selected in the list box. In a multiple-group analysis, the data from each group can be in a different format.

File name Specifies the data file for the group that is selected in the list box.

Working file In SPSS Amos, the **Working file** button specifies that the SPSS working data set is to be analyzed.

Grouping variable Allows you to choose a variable to be used for determining membership in the group that is selected in the list box. For example, if the data set contains a **GENDER** variable that takes on values "male" and "female", the choice of **GENDER** as a grouping variable would allow the restriction of group membership to males only or to females only.

Group value Allows you to specify the value that the grouping variable takes on for the group that is selected in the list box.

OK Closes the dialog box and saves any changes you have made.

Cancel Closes the dialog box and discards any changes you have made.

Choose a data file format

This dialog box allows you to select a data file format.

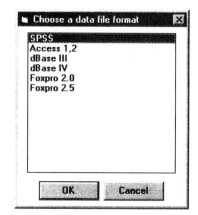

OK   Closes the dialog box and saves any change that you have made.

Cancel   Closes the dialog box and discards any change that you have made.

Choose grouping variable

This dialog box allows you to choose a variable to be used for determining group membership. This grouping variable can be either numeric or character-valued, and must identify each group with a single, unique value.

In the following illustration, taken from Example 12-A of the *Users' Guide,* the variable **GENDER** has been selected. (**GENDER** takes on values "male" and "female", so that the **Choose value for group** dialog box can be used to restrict group membership either to males or to females.)

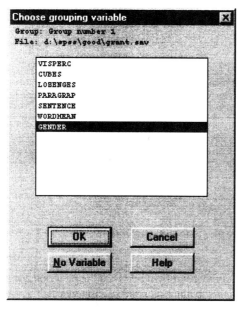

No Variable	Disables subset selection for group membership. Group membership is extended to all observations in the data set.
OK	Closes the dialog box and saves any changes you have made.
Cancel	Closes the dialog box and discards any changes you have made.

Choose value for group

This dialog box allows you to specify a value for the grouping variable. In the following illustration, taken from Example 12-A of the *Users' Guide,* the variable **GENDER** has previously been selected as the grouping variable.

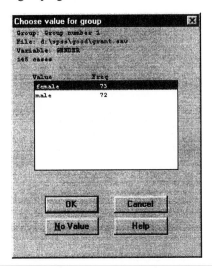

The list box displays a frequency distribution of the values of **GENDER**. In the illustration, the "female" row has been selected, restricting group membership to the 73 females.

No Value   Disables subset selection for group membership. Group membership is extended to all observations in the data set.

OK   Closes the dialog box and saves any changes you have made.

Cancel   Closes the dialog box and discards any changes you have made.

Related commands:

Respecify binary file ... on page 57

Respecify binary file ...

Menu: **File|Respecify Binary File ...**

Respecify Binary File

This menu choice is enabled only if there is a check mark next to the **Binary Data File** menu choice on the **File** menu.

Choosing **Respecify Binary File** from the **File** menu displays the **Specify source of data** dialog box.

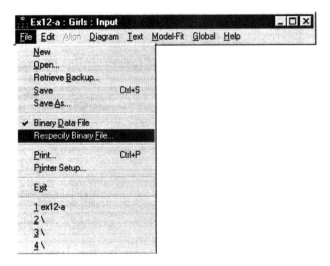

Related commands:

       Binary data file ... on page 50

🖨 Print a path diagram

Menu: **File|Print...**
Hot key: **Ctrl-P**

Pressing this button produces a dialog box for printing path diagrams.

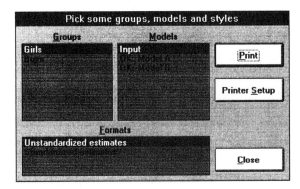

Groups   Allows you to pick the group (or groups) for which you want path
diagrams printed.

Models   Allows you to pick the model (or models) for which you want path
diagrams printed. Before carrying out an Amos analysis, this list box will
contain only the item "Input". After a successful Amos analysis, the list
box will contain "Input" along with one additional item for each model
specified by a **$model** command.

Estimates can be displayed for all models listed in the form
    "OK: ...".
A third type of entry in the **Models** list box has the form
    "XX: ...".
This line identifies models for which parameter estimation was attempted,
but was not successful. It usually means that an error occurred during the
most recent analysis. Of course, no usable parameter estimates or fit
statistics are available for models marked "XX: ...".

If the **Models** list box contains only the item "Input", this means that
parameter estimates aren't available. This could be because you have not
yet carried out an analysis by pressing ▓. Alternatively, it could mean
that you have changed the path diagram so that the results of the most
recent analysis are now obsolete. You have to re-fit your model (by

pressing ) whenever you change it, in order to bring the parameter estimates up to date.

Formats   Allows you to pick a format for displaying parameter values. The two items, "Unstandardized estimates" and "Standardized estimates" will always appear in this list box. In addition, any formats that you have created using 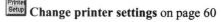 will also appear.

Print   Prints the path diagrams that you have selected in the **Groups**, **Models** and **Formats** list boxes. It is possible that a large number of path diagrams will be printed. If you have picked, say, three items from the "Groups" list box and four items from the "Models" list box, then twelve path diagrams will be printed. Furthermore, if you have picked more than one format, separate path diagrams will be printed using each format in turn.

Printer Setup Allows you to select printers, change printer orientation (portrait or landscape), number of copies, and so on.

Close   Closes the dialog box without printing any path diagrams.

Related commands:

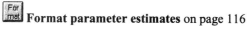 **Calculate estimates** on page 122

Change printer settings on page 60

Format parameter estimates on page 116

Change printer settings

Menu: **File|Printer Setup...**

This button lets you select a printer, choose printer orientation (portrait or landscape), number of copies, and so on.

Related commands:

Print a path diagram on page 58

 # Exit from Amos

Menu: **File|Exit**
Hot key: **Alt-F4**

Press this button to exit from Amos.

⬆ Undo the previous change

Menu: **Edit|Undo**
Hot key: **Alt-Backspace**

Press this button to take back mistakes during creation or editing of a path diagram. By pressing ⬆ repeatedly, you can undo up to four of the most recent changes.

Note: The "undo" function is not available immediately after performing any of the following operations (which clear the history of recent changes):

Calculate estimates on page 122

Change printer settings on page 60

Exit from Amos on page 61

Pick a group and a model on page 124

Print a path diagram on page 58

Read an old path diagram from disk on page 46

Retrieve a previous backup on page 47

Save a path diagram on page 48

Save a path diagram with a new name on page 49

Start a new path diagram on page 45

Related commands:

Undo the previous undo on page 63

⊞ Undo the previous undo

Menu: **Edit|Redo**

You can cancel the effect of the ⊡ button by immediately pressing ⊞.

Related commands:

⊡ **Undo the previous change** on page 62

Copy a diagram to the clipboard

Menu: **Edit|Copy (to clipboard)**
Hot key: **Ctrl-C**

This button copies the path diagram from the Amos window to the Windows clipboard. You can then paste a presentation quality copy of the path diagram into other applications, such as Microsoft Windows compliant word processors, graphics file utilities, spreadsheets and general-purpose drawing programs.

Note: Amos can be configured to automatically activate a particular application after copying the path diagram to the clipboard. Furthermore, a sequence of key strokes can be passed to that application for pasting the path diagram from the clipboard and performing subsequent operations. These functions can be configured with the button.

Related commands:

Choose miscellaneous options on page 159

⌨ Select one object at a time

Menu: **Edit|Select**
Hot key: **F2**

When the ⌨ is in the pressed position, you can select a group of objects by clicking on one object at a time. Every time you click on an object it changes color and becomes part of the "selected" group. (By default, the object turns blue, but you can pick another color by choosing **Colors** from the **Global** menu.) Another method of selecting objects one at a time is to hold the left mouse button down continuously and use the mouse pointer to touch every object that you want to select.

Clicking on an object that has already been selected has the effect of de-selecting it.

Double-clicking on a latent variable will select it along with all of its indicators and associated error variables. Double-clicking on any indicator of a latent variable will select all of the indicators of that latent variable. Double-clicking on a residual variable associated with a latent variable will select all of the residual variables associated with that latent variable.

Amos provides several methods for manipulating a group of selected objects all at once. For example, you can move all of the selected objects at the same time. You can also change the size or shape of all the selected objects, or make a copy of the selected objects in one step. In order to operate on an entire group of objects, you first have to select the objects. Then carry out the operation.

The following operations can be applied to a group of selected objects.

> ▣ **Change the shape of objects** on page 78

> ▣ **Constrain parameter estimates** on page 137

> ▣ **Duplicate objects** on page 72

> ▣ **Move objects** on page 71

> ▣ **Move parameters** on page 74

> ▣ **Touch up a variable** on page 82

The following operations are only meaningful after selecting a group of objects in advance.

> ▣ **Align curvature of double-headed arrows** on page 94

> ▣ **Align font attributes** on page 92

> ▣ **Align font attributes of parameters** on page 91

Align **Align height** on page 87

Align **Align height and width** on page 89

Align **Align objects horizontally** on page 85

Align **Align objects vertically** on page 86

Align **Align parameter position** on page 90

Align **Align the width of lines** on page 93

Align **Align width** on page 88

Space **Space objects horizontally** on page 79

Space **Space objects vertically** on page 80

Related commands:

Change screen colors on page 152

Deselect all objects on page 68

Select all objects on page 67

⬛ Select all objects

Menu: **Edit|Select All**

Pressing ⬛ selects all objects in the path diagram. Then you can use ⬛ to de-select objects if necessary.

Related commands:

⬛ **Deselect all objects** on page 68

⬛ **Select one object at a time** on page 65

▣ Deselect all objects

Menu: **Edit|Deselect All**
Hot key: **F11**

Pressing ▣ clears all previous group selections.

Related commands:

▣ **Select all objects** on page 67

▣ **Select one object at a time** on page 65

Link objects

Menu: **Edit|Link**

This button allows you to form groups of objects that will be treated as a unit in future operations. For example, moving one object that is "linked" to several other objects will cause the entire collection of linked objects to move as a group. The following operations, when applied to an object that is part of a linked group, will affect all the objects in that group.

> **Change the shape of objects** on page 78

> **Duplicate objects** on page 72

> **Move objects** on page 71

> **Move parameters** on page 74

> **Touch up a variable** on page 82

Linking a group of objects together is a two-step operation:

1. Select the group of objects to be linked using .

2. Press .

To find out which objects are already linked to other objects, press repeatedly. Each press of will highlight a group of linked objects in a distinct color (blue, by default). To "unlink" a group of objects, press repeatedly until the desired group of linked objects is highlighted. Then press and click on the objects that you want to unlink.

As an example of the effective use of , consider the following path diagram

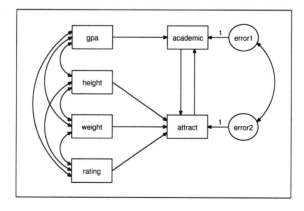

The four variables, **gpa**, **height**, **weight** and **rating** have similar roles in the model, and so they are good candidates for linking. Linking them is a three-step procedure:

1. Press .

2. Select **gpa**, **height**, **weight** and **rating**.

3. Press ⬚.

Afterward, moving **gpa** will also cause **height, weight** and **rating** to move at the same time. Similarly, changing the size of any one of the four boxes will cause the other three to change size also.

In this example, it may also be worthwhile to link **error1** and **error2**.

There is no limit on the number of "link" groups.

Related commands:

⬚ **Preserve symmetries** on page 147

⬚ **Select one object at a time** on page 65

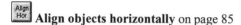 Move objects

Menu: **Edit|Move**
Hot key: **Ctrl-M**

While 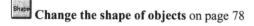 is in the pressed position, you can move objects around the page. Point to an object with the mouse and press the left mouse button. While holding the left mouse button down, move the object to its new position. Then release the mouse button.

To move an arrow, move one end at a time.

If you move a selected variable (see page 65) any other selected variables will move also.

When a group of selected variables is moved, any interconnecting arrows will move too. Any arrows that connect selected variables to unselected variables will be re-drawn.

Note: To move variables vertically or horizontally (but not diagonally), hold the shift key down.

Related commands:

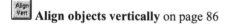 **Align objects horizontally** on page 85

Align objects vertically on page 86

Change the shape of objects on page 78

Duplicate objects on page 72

Space objects horizontally on page 79

Space objects vertically on page 80

 **Duplicate objects**

Menu: **Edit|Duplicate**
Hot key: **Ctrl-O**

This button allows you to copy boxes, ellipses and captions. To make a copy of a single object, point to it with the mouse and press the left mouse button. While holding the left mouse button down, move the mouse pointer to the desired location of the new object. Then release the mouse button.

If you copy a selected variable (see page 65), all selected variables will be copied. Any arrows that connect selected variables will be copied too. Any arrows that connect selected variables to unselected variables will not be copied.

Note: Hold the shift key down while copying, and Amos aligns the copy (or copies) horizontally or vertically with the original(s).

Related commands:

 Change the shape of objects on page 78

 Move objects on page 71

Erase objects

While this button is in the pressed position, you can erase objects by clicking on them one at a time.

Note: You can erase only one object at a time, even if you erase an object that is part of a selected group or a linked group.

Related commands:

Link objects on page 69

Select one object at a time on page 65

Undo the previous change on page 62

 **Move parameters**

Menu: **Edit|Move Parameters**

To move parameters around, first press this button. Then point to an object that has a parameter that you want to move. For example, point to a single-headed arrow if you want to move the regression weight that is associated with it. Press the left mouse button and move the mouse.

If you move a parameter associated with a selected object, parameters associated with other selected objects *of the same kind* will move too. For example, if you move a selected regression weight, any other selected regression weights will also move.

Related commands:

 Align parameter position on page 90

 Constrain parameter estimates on page 137

Reflect the indicators of a latent variable

Menu: **Edit|Reflect**

After has been pressed, the first click on a latent variable reflects its indicators and unique variables through a vertical axis that passes through the center of the latent variable. The second click on the same latent variable reflects its indicators and unique variables through a horizontal axis that passes through the center of the latent variable. The third click reflects through a vertical axis. The fourth click reflects through a horizontal axis. Four clicks in succession restore the latent variable, its indicators and its unique variables to their original state.

For example, clicking on the variable **G** in the following path diagram,

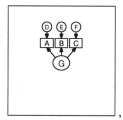,

yields this result:

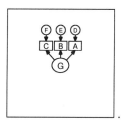.

A second click yields

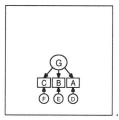.

Related commands:

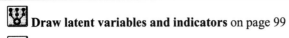

Draw latent variables and indicators on page 99

Preserve symmetries on page 147

Rotate the indicators of a latent variable on page 77

Rotate the indicators of a latent variable

Menu: **Edit|Rotate**

When is in the pressed position, clicking on a latent variable rotates its indicators and unique variables around the center of the latent variable. The rotation is 90 degrees clockwise. For example, clicking on the variable G in the following path diagram,

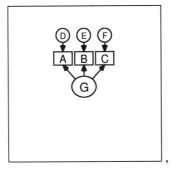

,

yields the following result:

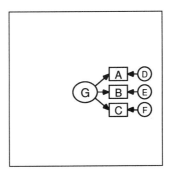

Four consecutive rotations return the indicators and unique variables to their original positions.

Related commands:

 Draw latent variables and indicators on page 99

 Preserve symmetries on page 147

 Reflect the indicators of a latent variable on page 75

Change the shape of objects

Menu: **Edit|Shape of Object**
Hot key: **Ctrl-A**

To change the size and shape of a variable (rectangle or ellipse), press . Then point to the variable, press the left mouse button and move the mouse. If you change the size and shape of a selected variable, the size and shape of other selected variables will also change.

To change the shape (curvature) of a double-headed arrow, press . Then point to the double-headed arrow, press the left mouse button and move the mouse. If you change the curvature of a selected double-headed arrow, the curvature of other selected double-headed arrows will change too.

Related commands:

Duplicate objects on page 72

Move objects on page 71

To arrange objects so they are equally spaced horizontally, first select them and then press . The objects don't have to be lined up in the same horizontal row to begin with. For example, you can make the following path diagram

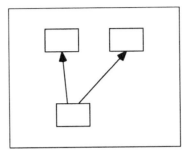

look like this

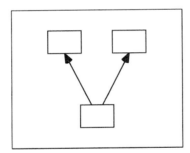

by selecting all three rectangles and pressing .

Related commands:

 Move objects on page 71

 Space objects vertically on page 80

Space objects vertically

To arrange objects so they are equally spaced vertically, first select them and then press . The objects don't have to be lined up in a vertical column to begin with. For example, you can make the following path diagram

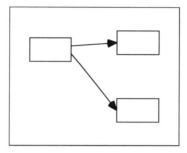

look like this

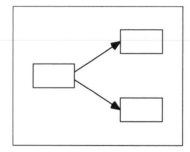

by selecting all three rectangles and pressing .

Related commands:

Move objects on page 71

Space objects horizontally on page 79

Resize the diagram to fit on a page

Menu: **Edit|Fit to Page**
Hot key: **Ctrl-F**

Pressing this button resizes the path diagram so that it just fits on a page.

Note: By default the page size is obtained from the printer settings specified with . You can choose a different size for the path diagram by pressing .

Related commands:

 Change printer settings on page 60

 Change the page layout on page 146

Touch up a variable

Menu: **Edit|Touch Up**
Hot key: **Ctrl-H**

Use the ⬛ button to rearrange the arrows in a path diagram in a way intended to be aesthetically pleasing.

After pressing ⬛, click on a variable to reposition the arrows connected to it. For example, clicking on the variable, **A**, in the path diagram,

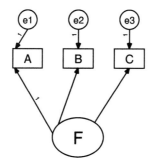

will produce the following result:

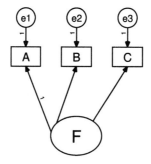

Then clicking on the variable, **F**, will produce the following path diagram.

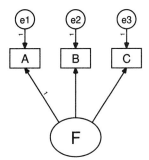

Note: You can use 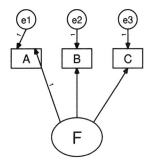 to specify whether arrows that touch a rectangle will be allowed to move to another side of the rectangle. For example, suppose you have the following path diagram.

If you press 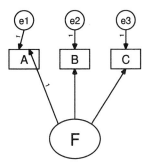 and then click on variable A, there are two possible outcomes. If you have not checked the option "Allow arrows to change sides during touchup" in the 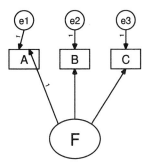 dialog box, the arrows will remain connected to the upper border of variable A. The "touched up" path diagram will look like this.

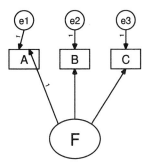

On the other hand, if you *have* checked the option "Allow arrows to change sides during touchup" in the 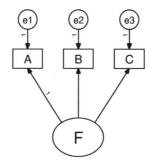 dialog box, the "touched up" path diagram will look like this.

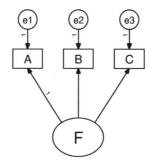

If your path diagram contains two unobserved variables connected by arrows, it may be necessary to touch them both up two or three times, going back and forth between the two variables.

If you touch up a variable that has been selected using , all selected variables will be touched up. If you touch up a variable that has been "linked" to other variables using , all of the linked variables will be touched up.

To touch up an entire path diagram, first use to select the entire path diagram. Then touch up any of its variables.

The button attempts to make a path diagram look good by following simple rules. Whether it succeeds is a matter of personal taste. You will need to experiment with this button to see if it produces results that are satisfactory to you.

Related commands:

 Choose miscellaneous options on page 159

 Link objects on page 69

 Select one object at a time on page 65

Align objects horizontally

Menu: **Align|Horizontal**

To horizontally align several objects (*i.e.*, to line them up in a horizontal row), follow this four-step procedure:

1. If necessary, use to move a "target" variable to the desired position.

2. Select the variables that you want to be lined up in a horizontal row with the target variable.

3. Press .

4. Click on the target variable.

Amos will line up the selected objects in a horizontal row to the left and right of the target variable. Any connecting arrows will be redrawn.

Related commands:

 Align objects vertically on page 86

Move objects on page 71

Select one object at a time on page 65

Align objects vertically

Menu: **Align|Vertical**

To vertically align several objects (*i.e.*, to line them up in a vertical column), follow this four-step procedure:

1. If necessary, use to move a "target" variable to the desired position.
2. Select the variables that you want to be lined up in a vertical column with the target variable.
3. Press .
4. Click on the target variable.

Amos will line up the selected objects in a vertical column above and below the target variable. Any connecting arrows will be redrawn.

Related commands:

Align objects horizontally on page 85

Move objects on page 71

 **Align height**

This button allows you to cause several rectangles and ellipses to have a common height. Aligning height is a four-step procedure:

1. If necessary, use to give a "target" variable (rectangle or ellipse) the desired height.

2. Select the variables that you want to have the same height as the target variable.

3. Press .

4. Click on the target variable.

Amos will adjust the height of each selected variable to match the height of the target variable.

Related commands:

 Align height and width on page 89

 Align width on page 88

 Change the shape of objects on page 78

 Select one object at a time on page 65

 **Align width**

Menu: **Align|Width**

This button allows you to align the width of several rectangles and ellipses. Aligning width is a four-step procedure:

1. If necessary, use to give a "target" variable (rectangle or ellipse) the desired width.

2. Select the variables that you want to have the same width as the target variable.

3. Press .

4. Click on the target variable.

Amos will adjust the width of each selected variable to match the width of the target variable.

Related commands:

 Align height on page 87

 Align height and width on page 89

 Change the shape of objects on page 78

 Select one object at a time on page 65

Align height and width

Menu: **Align|Size**

This button can be used to align several rectangles and ellipses at a common height and width. Aligning height and width is a four-step procedure:

1. If necessary, use to set a "target" variable (rectangle or ellipse) to the desired height and width.

2. Select the variables that you want to have the same height and width as the target variable.

3. Press .

4. Click on the target variable.

Related commands:

 Align height on page 87

 Align width on page 88

 Change the shape of objects on page 78

 Select one object at a time on page 65

Align parameter position

Menu: **Align|Parameter Position**

This button allows you to line up the positions of several parameters. Alignment of parameters is a four-step procedure:

1. If necessary, use to move a "target" parameter to the desired position.
2. Select the objects whose parameters you want to line up with the target parameter.
3. Press .
4. Click on the target parameter.

Related commands:

Move parameters on page 74

Select one object at a time on page 65

Align font attributes of parameters

Menu: **Align|Parameter Font Attributes**

This button allows you to assign the same font attributes to several parameters. Alignment of font attributes is a four-step procedure:

1. If necessary, use 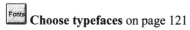 to assign the desired font attributes to one "target" parameter.

2. Select the objects whose parameters shall have the same font attributes.

3. Press 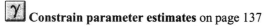.

4. Click on the target parameter.

Related commands:

Choose typefaces on page 121

Constrain parameter estimates on page 137

Select one object at a time on page 65

Align font attributes

Menu: **Align|Font Attributes**

This button allows you to cause several variable names and figure captions to be displayed with the same font attributes. Alignment of font attributes is a four-step procedure:

1. If necessary, use to assign the desired font attributes to a "target" object.

2. Select the objects that shall have the same font attributes.

3. Press .

4. Click on the target object.

Related commands:

 Add captions, names and constraints on page 115

 Add figure captions on page 111

 Choose typefaces on page 121

 Name variables on page 109

 Select one object at a time on page 65

Align the width of lines

Menu: **Align|Pen Width**

This button sets the pen (or line) width with which a group of objects is drawn. Aligning the width of lines is a four-step procedure:

1. If necessary, use to choose a line width, and then draw a "target" object.
2. Select the objects that you want to have drawn with the same line width as the target object.
3. Press .
4. Click on the target object.

Related commands:

 Choose the width of lines on page 157

Select one object at a time on page 65

Align curvature of double-headed arrows

Menu: **Align|Curvature**

This button gives several double-headed arrows the same curvature. Aligning the curvature of double-headed arrows is a four-step procedure:

1. If necessary, use to give one double-headed arrow (the target) the desired curvature.

2. Select the double-headed arrows that you want to have drawn with the same curvature as the target.

3. Press .

4. Click on the target.

Related commands:

 Change the shape of objects on page 78

 Select one object at a time on page 65

⊟ Draw observed variables

Menu: **Diagram|Draw Observed**
Hot key: **F3**

This button allows you to draw rectangles to represent *observed* variables. Place the mouse pointer at the center of the desired rectangle. Press the left mouse button and hold it down while moving the mouse pointer to adjust the size of the new rectangle. Release the button when you are satisfied with the appearance of the rectangle. After you have drawn a rectangle, you can move it using 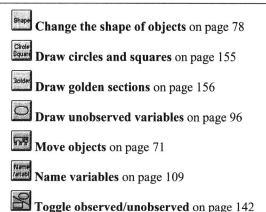 or change its size and shape using ▨.

Related commands:

▨ **Change the shape of objects** on page 78

▨ **Draw circles and squares** on page 155

▨ **Draw golden sections** on page 156

▨ **Draw unobserved variables** on page 96

▨ **Move objects** on page 71

▨ **Name variables** on page 109

▨ **Toggle observed/unobserved** on page 142

◯ Draw unobserved variables

Menu: **Diagram|Draw Unobserved**
Hot key: **F4**

This choice allows you to draw ellipses to represent *unobserved* variables. Place the mouse pointer at the center of the desired ellipse. Press the left mouse button and hold it down while moving the mouse pointer to adjust the size of the new ellipse. Release the button when you are satisfied with the appearance of the ellipse. After you have drawn an ellipse, you can move it using ▦ or change its size and shape using ▦.

Related commands:

▦ **Change the shape of objects** on page 78

▦ **Draw circles and squares** on page 155

▦ **Draw golden sections** on page 156

▦ **Draw latent variables and indicators** on page 99

▦ **Draw observed variables** on page 95

▦ **Draw unique variables** on page 101

▦ **Move objects** on page 71

▦ **Name variables** on page 109

▦ **Toggle observed/unobserved** on page 142

 # Draw paths

Menu: **Diagram|Draw Path**
Hot key: **F5**

Press this button to draw single-headed arrows from one variable to another. Point to one variable and press the left mouse button. While continuing to hold the mouse button down, point to a second variable. Then release the button. This will cause an arrow to be drawn from the first variable to the second.

After you have drawn a single-headed arrow, you can move one end at a time with .

Related commands:

Draw covariances on page 98

Move objects on page 71.

⬌ Draw covariances

Menu: **Diagram|Draw Covariance**
Hot key: **F6**

This button draws double-headed arrows. Point to one variable and press the left mouse button. While continuing to hold the mouse button down, point to a second variable. Then release the button. This will cause the two variables to be connected by a double-headed arrow. The arrow will be curved, in clockwise direction, depending on which variable was pointed to first.

After you have drawn a double-headed arrow, you can change its shape with 🔲. You can move either end of the arrow with 🔲.

Related commands:

🔲 **Change the shape of objects** on page 78.

🔲 **Draw paths** on page 97

🔲 **Move objects** on page 71.

Page 98   **Amos Graphics Reference Guide**   **Amos Users' Guide**

☷ Draw latent variables and indicators

Menu: **Diagram|Draw Indicator Variable**

When this button is in the pressed position you can perform either of two operations.

1. You can draw ellipses in the same way that ▦ allows you to draw ellipses.

2. By clicking on an already-existing ellipse, you can add an indicator together with a unique variable. Scale constraints, necessary for model identification, will be put in place automatically. For example, clicking on the variable, G, in the following path diagram

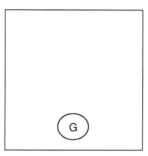

yields

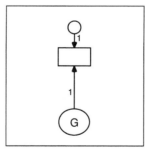

Two more clicks on **G** give

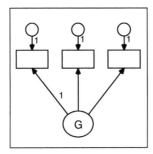

Related commands:

γ **Constrain parameter estimates** on page 137

Draw paths on page 97

Draw unique variables on page 101

Draw unobserved variables on page 96

Reflect the indicators of a latent variable on page 75

Rotate the indicators of a latent variable on page 77

Draw unique variables

Menu: **Diagram|Draw Unique Variable**

Pressing this button will allow you to add a unique variable to an existing variable. For example, clicking on the variable, A, in the following path diagram

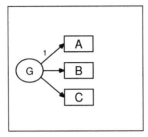

yields

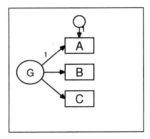

Each additional click on A will rotate its unique variable in the clockwise direction. For example, one more click on A gives

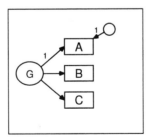

And another click gives

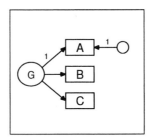

Related commands:

γ Constrain parameter estimates on page 137

Draw latent variables and indicators on page 99

Draw paths on page 97

Draw unobserved variables on page 96

◘ Zoom in on a selected area

Menu: **Diagram|Zoom**
Hot key: **Ctrl-Z**

This choice allows you to fill the Amos window with a selected portion of a path diagram. Move the mouse pointer to the center of the area that you want to focus on. Then press the left mouse button. Move the mouse (while continuing to hold the left button down) to select a rectangular region of the path diagram. When you release the mouse button, the selected region will be enlarged to fill the window.

Related commands:

Scroll on page 107

Zoom in on page 104

Zoom out on page 105

Zoom to view a full page on page 106

 Zoom in

Menu: **Diagram|Zoom In**
Hot key: **F7**

This button magnifies the screen image of the path diagram. It does not affect the printed size of the path diagram.

Related commands:

Scroll on page 107

Zoom in on a selected area on page 103

Zoom out on page 105

Zoom to view a full page on page 106

 Zoom out

Menu: **Diagram|Zoom Out**
Hot key: **F8**

This button reduces the size of the path diagram in the Amos window. It does not affect the printed size of the path diagram.

Related commands:

Scroll on page 107

Zoom in on page 104

Zoom in on a selected area on page 103

Zoom to view a full page on page 106

Zoom to view a full page

Menu: **Diagram|Zoom Page**
Hot key: **F9**

This button resizes the path diagram so that one printed page just fits the Amos window.

Related commands:

Scroll on page 107

Zoom in on page 104

Zoom in on a selected area on page 103

Zoom out on page 105

Scroll

Menu: **Diagram|Scroll**

If you have enlarged the path diagram by pressing 🔳 or 🔍 you may not be able to see the whole path diagram at once. To see a different portion of the path diagram, press 🔳. Then press the mouse button and move the mouse.

Related commands:

🔳 **Zoom in** on page 104

🔍 **Zoom in on a selected area** on page 103

🔳 **Zoom out** on page 105

🔳 **Zoom to view a full page** on page 106

Redraw the path diagram

Menu: **Diagram|Redraw Diagram**

This button erases the path diagram and redraws it.

 # Name variables

This choice allows you to assign names to variables in the path diagram. To name a variable, click on its rectangle or ellipse. A dialog box will prompt you for the variable name.

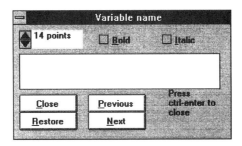

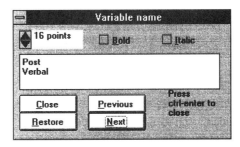	Click here to change the font size of the variable name.
Bold	Display the variable name in bold type.
Italic	Display the variable name in italic type.
Close	Close the dialog box. You can also press **Ctrl-Enter** on the keyboard to close the dialog box.
Previous	Move from the current path diagram object to the one that was created just before it.
Restore	Restore the variable name to the way it was when it was first displayed in the dialog box.
Next	Move from the current path diagram object to the one that was created just after it.

Multi-line names are allowed. In Amos's text input and output, where multiline names are not allowed, the underscore character is used in place of a line separator. For instance, if you give a variable the two-line name then the name will appear in Amos's text output in the form **Post_Verbal**. If the variable is observed, you would also have to refer to it by the name **Post_Verbal** when you list it following Amos's **$inputvariables** command.

Related commands:

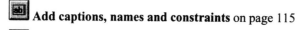 **Add captions, names and constraints** on page 115

Choose typefaces on page 121

Draw observed variables on page 95

Draw unobserved variables on page 96

Add figure captions

Menu: **Text|Figure Caption**

This button lets you create a figure caption or edit an existing caption. To create a caption, click on the spot where you want the caption to appear. (This location will be called the "insertion point" from now on.) The following dialog box will appear:

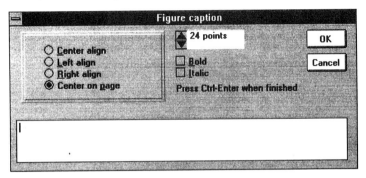

Center align	Center the caption at the insertion point.
Left align	Put the left edge of the caption at the insertion point.
Right align	Put the right edge of the caption at the insertion point.
Center on page	Center the caption on the page.
	Click here to change the font size.
OK	Accept the entries in the dialog box and close it.
Bold	Display the caption in bold face.
Italic	Display the caption in italics.
Cancel	Ignore the entries in the dialog box and close it.

Different captions can have different font characteristics, but they all use the same typeface.

To edit an existing caption, press and click on the caption.

Related commands:

 Add captions, names and constraints on page 115

Fonts **Choose typefaces** on page 121

Text macros

Suppose you type in a figure caption as follows.

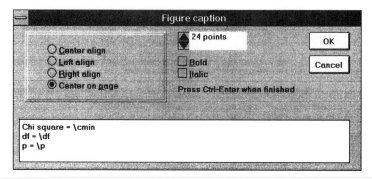

When you view the input path diagram, the caption will look like this:

$$\text{Chi square} = \text{\textbackslash cmin}$$
$$\text{df} = \text{\textbackslash df}$$
$$\text{p} = \text{\textbackslash p}$$

However, once you have fitted your model (using ▦), the path diagram that contains the results of the analysis will have a caption that looks something like this

$$\text{Chi square} = 7.853$$
$$\text{df} = 8$$
$$\text{p} = .448$$

\cmin is a "text macro", a code that Amos fills in with the minimum value of the discrepancy function, C (see Appendix B), once the minimum value is known. Similarly, **\df** is a text macro that Amos fills in with the number of degrees of freedom for testing the model and **\p** is a text macro that Amos fills in with the "p value" for testing the null hypothesis that the model is correct. Here is a list of text macros.

\agfi   Adjusted goodness of fit index (**AGFI**)

\aic   Akaike information criterion (**AIC**)

\bcc	Browne-Cudeck criterion (**BCC**)
\bic	Bayes information criterion (**BIC**)
\caic	Consistent **AIC** (**CAIC**)
\cfi	Comparative fit index (**CFI**)
\cmin	Minimum value of the discrepancy function C in Appendix B
\cmindf	Minimum value of the discrepancy function divided by degrees of freedom
\df	Degrees of freedom
\ecvi	Expected cross-validation index (**ECVI**)
\ecvihi	Upper bound of 90% confidence interval on **ECVI**
\ecvilo	Lower bound of 90% confidence interval on **ECVI**
\f0	Estimated population discrepancy (**F0**)
\f0hi	Upper bound of 90% confidence interval on **F0**
\f0lo	Lower bound of 90% confidence interval on **F0**
\fmin	Minimum value of discrepancy function F in Appendix B
\format	Format name (See 🔲 **Format parameter estimates** on page 116.)
\gfi	Goodness of fit index (**GFI**)
\group	Group name (See 🔲 **Pick a group and a model** on page 124.)
\hfive	Hoelter's critical N for α=.05
\hone	Hoelter's critical N for α=.01
\ifi	Incremental fit index (**IFI**)
\mecvi	Modified **ECVI** (**MECVI**)
\model	Model name (See 🔲 **Pick a group and a model** on page 124.)
\ncp	Estimate of non-centrality parameter (**NCP**)
\ncphi	Upper bound of 90% confidence interval on **NCP**
\ncplo	Lower bound of 90% confidence interval on **NCP**
\nfi	Normed fit index (**NFI**)
\npar	Number of distinct parameters
\p	"p value" associated with discrepancy function (test of perfect fit)
\pcfi	Parsimonious comparative fit index (**PCFI**)
\pclose	"p value" for testing the null hypothesis of close fit (**RMSEA** < .05)

\pgfi	Parsimonious goodness of fit index (**PGFI**)
\pnfi	Parsimonious normed fit index (**PNFI**)
\pratio	Parsimony ratio
\rfi	Relative fit index
\rmr	Root mean square residual
\rmsea	Root mean square error of approximation (**RMSEA**)
\rmseahi	Upper bound of 90% confidence interval on **RMSEA**
\rmsealo	Lower bound of 90% confidence interval on **RMSEA**
\tli	Tucker-Lewis index (**TLI**)

Related commands:

Specify decimal places on page 158

Add captions, names and constraints

Menu: **Text|Text(Enter/Edit)**
Hot key: **Ctrl-T**

This button provides a general-purpose tool for entering text in a path diagram. It combines the function of the following three buttons:

 Add figure captions on page 111

 Constrain parameter estimates on page 137

 Name variables on page 109

After pressing ,

- Clicking on the interior of a rectangle or ellipse allows you to enter a variable name
- Clicking on a point just outside a rectangle or ellipse allows you to constrain a variance, mean and/or intercept
- Clicking on a single-headed arrow allows you to constrain a regression weight
- Clicking on a double-headed arrow allows you to constrain a covariance
- Clicking on an existing figure caption allows you to modify it
- Clicking anywhere else on the path diagram allows you to create a new figure caption.

Related commands:

Choose typefaces on page 121

Format parameter estimates

Menu: **Text|Parameter Format...**

This button lets you specify how parameter estimates are to be displayed on the path diagram. Pressing opens a window that looks something like this:

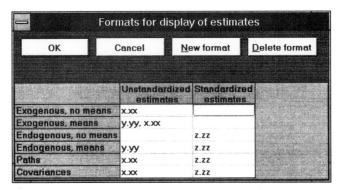

This example shows that there are two formats, named "Unstandardized estimates" and "Standardized estimates". Each "format" is a set of templates that govern how parameters are displayed on a path diagram. There can be one template for exogenous variables when means are estimated, another template for exogenous variables when means aren't estimated, a template for regression weights, and so on.

Amos Graphics understands three parameter symbols that can be used to make up a template:

x.xx	for (unstandardized) variances, covariances, and/or regression weights,
y.yy	for mean and/or intercept terms,
z.zz	for r²-values, correlations and/or standardized path coefficients.

Creating a new format

You can create a new format of your own by pressing **New format.** A dialog box will ask you to make up a name for the new format. Say you call it "My New Format":

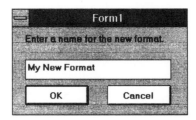

After you press OK the ▣ window will have a new column labeled "My New Format":

	Unstandardized estimates	Standardized estimates	My New Format
Exogenous, no means	x.xx		
Exogenous, means	y.yy, x.xx		
Endogenous, no means		z.zz	
Endogenous, means	y.yy	z.zz	
Paths	x.xx	z.zz	
Covariances	x.xx	z.zz	

Formats for display of estimates — OK   Cancel   New format   Delete format

Now you can define the new format by typing templates into the empty spaces in the "My New Format" column. Using the templates is best explained by example. It is necessary to define several templates—one for each type of path diagram object that can have model parameters associated with it.

Exogenous, no means

When means are not estimated, an exogenous variable only has one parameter associated with it, namely its variance. Here is how various templates would cause a variance of 12.3456789 to be displayed:

Template	Result	Comment
x.xx	12.35	two places to the right of the decimal point
x.xxxxx	12.34568	five places to the right of the decimal point
[x.xx]	[12.35]	characters other than "x", "y", "z" and "." are copied from the template
x.xx*	12.35*	

Exogenous, means

When means are estimated, an exogenous variable has two parameters associated with it: its mean and variance. Here is how various templates would cause a mean of 1.11111111 and a variance of 22.22222222 to be displayed:

Template	Result	Comment
x.xx, y.yyy	1.11, 22.222	
y.yyy, x.xx	22.222, 1.11	
x.xx	1.11	the variance is not displayed
y.yyy	2.222	the mean is not displayed

Endogenous, no means

"No means" is shorthand for "no means and no intercepts". When means and intercepts are not estimated, an endogenous variable has no parameters associated with it. However, Amos can display a squared multiple correlation for an endogenous variable if you have entered an **$smc** command using **$** or **Config**. Here is how various templates would cause a squared multiple correlation of .123456789 to be displayed:

Template	Result
z.zz	.12
z.zzz	.123

Endogenous, means

"Means" is shorthand for "means and intercepts". If means and intercepts are estimated, each endogenous variable is associated with a single intercept, which Amos can display on a path diagram. In addition, Amos can display a squared multiple correlation for an endogenous variable if you have entered an **$smc** command using **$** or **Config**. Here is how various templates would cause an intercept of 11.11111111 and a squared multiple correlation of .22222222 to be displayed:

Template	Result
y.yy, z.zz	11.11, .22
z.zz, y.yy	.22, 11.11
y.yy	11.11
z.zz	.22

Paths

Each path (single-headed arrow) is associated with a regression weight, and possibly a standardized regression weight if you have entered a **$standardized** command using or . Here is how various templates would cause a regression weight of 11.1111111 to be displayed, supposing that the same regression weight is .22222222 after standardizing all variables:

Template	Result
x.xxx, z.zz	11.111, .22
z.zzz, x.xx	.222, 11.11
x.xxx (z.zz)	11.111 (.22)
.zzz**	.222**

Covariances

Each covariance object (double-headed arrow) is associated with a covariance, and possibly a correlation (if you have entered a **$standardized** command using or). Here is how various templates would cause a covariance of 11.1111111 to be displayed, supposing that the corresponding correlation is .22222222:

Template	Result
x.xxx, z.zz	11.111, .22
z.zzz, x.xx	.222, 11.11
x.xxx (z.zz)	11.111 (.22)
.zzz**	.222**

Deleting a format

To delete a format, click on its name and then press the **Delete** button. You can't delete the two default formats named "Unstandardized estimates" and "Standardized estimates".

Leaving a template blank

No values will be displayed for a path diagram object that has a blank template. The "Standardized estimates" format, for example, has two blank templates.

Overriding a format

The formats defined with 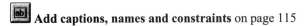 are global -- they affect all parameters. You can use 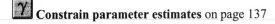 to override the global formats for an individual parameter.

Related commands:

 **Add captions, names and constraints** on page 115

γ **Constrain parameter estimates** on page 137

Edit configuration file on page 129

$** **Enter '$' commands on page 126

Choose typefaces

Menu: **Text|Text Fonts...**

This button allows you to choose typefaces and also to specify font attributes. You can choose one typeface for variable names, another typeface for parameter values, and a third for figure captions.

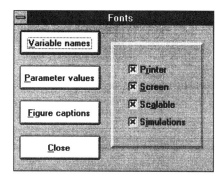

To change the font attributes of an individual object press 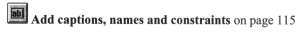.

Related commands:

 **Add captions, names and constraints** on page 115

Add figure captions on page 111

Constrain parameter estimates on page 137

Name variables on page 109

▦ Calculate estimates

Menu: **Model-Fit|Calculate Estimates**
Hot key: **Ctrl-F9**

This button fits the model specified by your path diagram(s) to the data supplied using ▦ . A
window resembling the following will keep you advised of the progress of calculations.

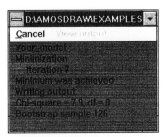

To stop the calculations before a solution has been found, choose **Cancel** from the menu.

The **Cancel** submenu gives two choices that affect what happens when bootstrapping is
interrupted:

Cancel one bootstrap sample: Cancel the current bootstrap sample and continue with the
next bootstrap sample.

Stop the analysis: Cancel the current bootstrap sample, and skip any
remaining bootstrap samples. The bootstrap results will be
based on the bootstrap samples already analyzed.

When the analysis is complete, Amos's text output will appear in a window that looks something like this:

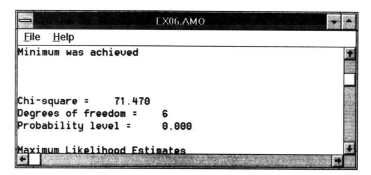

The menu choices in this window are

File|Print   Prints the text output

File|Exit   Closes the text output window.

Help   Displays the section of the Users' Guide that explains the text output. In the above example, selecting **Help** displays the portion of the Users' Guide that explains the **Minimum was achieved** message. (You can also get help by pressing the <F1> key.)

After a successful analysis, you can

1. view the graphics output by pressing ▨.
2. print the graphics output by pressing ▨.

Related commands:

▨ **Choose miscellaneous options** on page 159

▨ **Pick a group and a model** on page 124

▨ **Print a path diagram** ▨ Print a path diagram ▨ Print a path diagram on page 58

Pick a group and a model

Menu: **M̲odel-Fit|G̲roups/Models...**
Hot key: **Ctrl-G**

If you are fitting a model to data from more than one group, this button allows you to add groups one at a time, and to switch back and forth between groups. Also, after you have pressed to fit your model, pressing will let you view the output from the analysis. When you press you will see a dialog box something like the following:

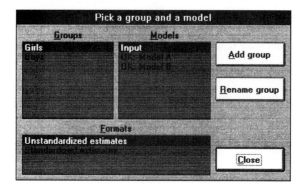

Groups	This list box allows you to pick the group whose path diagram you want to view. When you first start Amos, and after pressing the ⬜ button, there will be only one group, called "Group number 1", on this list. If you are fitting a model to data from more than one group, press **Add group** to add additional groups to the list.
Models	This list box allows you to choose whether to view the path diagram that specifies the model, or a path diagram that displays the results of fitting the model. In the example above, the model has already been fitted to two models called "Model A" and "Model B". If you pick "Input" you will be able to view and modify the model specification. Picking "OK: Model A" will display the results of fitting Model A. Picking "OK: Model B" will display the results of fitting Model B.

If the **Models** list box contains only the item "Input", this means that parameter estimates aren't available. This could be because you have not yet carried out an analysis by pressing ▦. It could also be that an error occurred during the most recent analysis. Finally, it could mean that you have changed the path diagram so that the results of the most recent analysis are now obsolete. You have to re-fit your model (by pressing) after any changes in order to bring the parameter estimates up to date.

If the **Models** list box looks something like this:

Input
OK: Model A
XX: Model B

it means that Model A was fitted successfully, but that an error occurred while attempting to fit Model B.

Formats Allows you to pick a format for displaying parameter estimates. The two items, "Unstandardized estimates" and "Standardized estimates" will always appear in this list box. In addition, any formats that you have previously created using will also appear.

Add group If you are fitting a model to data from more than one group, press this button once for each group beyond the first. You will be asked to give a name for each new group that you add.

Rename group Allows you to rename a group. First click on the name of the group that you want to rename. Then press **Rename group**.

Close Closes the dialog box.

Related commands:

Calculate estimates on page 122

Format parameter estimates on page 116

Start a new path diagram on page 45

$ Enter '$' commands

Menu: **Model-Fit|Enter "$" commands...**
Hot key: **Ctrl-D**

This button creates a text window in which you can type any of the "dollar sign" commands described in the Amos Users' Guide. For instance, if you want Amos to provide standardized estimates, you would enter a line consisting of the command **$standardized**:

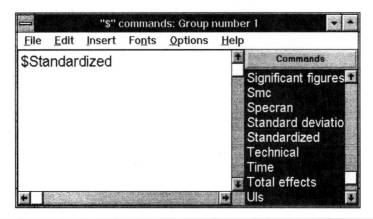

The menu choices are:

File|Print	Print the contents of the window.
File|Diagram	Close the window and reactivate the path diagram window.
Edit|Undo	Undo your most recent change. You can only undo changes that you made by typing at the keyboard. Text that you entered by double-clicking in the **Commands**, **Variables** and **Parameters** list boxes cannot be removed with **Edit|Undo**.
Edit|Cut	Delete the selected text and place it in the Windows clipboard.
Edit|Copy	Place the selected text in the Windows clipboard (but do not delete the text).
Edit|Paste	Paste the contents of the Windows clipboard at the current cursor location.
Edit|Select All	Select all of the text in the window.

Insert|File	Insert a file at the current cursor location.
Fonts|Screen font	Change the window text font.
Fonts|Printer font	Change the font used to print the window contents.
Fonts|List boxes font	Change the font used for the list boxes.
Options|Short list of commands	When this menu item is checked, only the most commonly used commands are shown in the **Commands** list box.
Options|Text colors|foreground	Change the foreground color in the text box.
Options|Text colors|background	Change the background color in the text box.
Options|List colors|foreground	Change the foreground color in the list boxes.
Options|List colors|background	Change the background color in the list boxes.
Help	Displays the section of the Users' Guide that explains the command that is selected in the **Commands** list box. (To select a command in the list box, click on it once.) You can also use the <F1> key to get help.

There are three list boxes, although not all of them are visible at the same time.

Commands	This list box contains Amos's **$** commands. Double click on a command to insert it in the text box. If the command requires an "=" sign followed by a string or a number, you will be prompted for the needed information.

Parameters This list box contains a list of parameters that are named in the path diagram. The list box is visible only when the text box cursor is located just below a **$model** command. Double clicking on a parameter name will insert it in the text box.

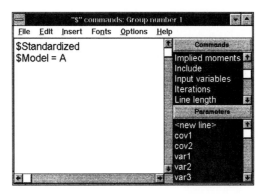

Variables This list box contains a list of observed variables named in the path diagram. The list box is visible only when the text box cursor is located just below an **$inputvariables** command. Double clicking on a variable name will insert it in the text box.

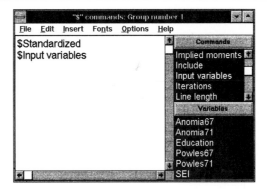

Some **$** commands are not required in the graphics version of Amos. They are not listed in the **Commands** list box. Commands that are not required in the graphics version of Amos are marked with the symbol 🖿 in the section of the Users' Guide that documents the **$** commands.

Edit configuration file

Menu: **Model-Fit|Edit Configuration File...**

This button opens the following window, which allows you to edit the file `config.amd`. For an explanation of the `config.amd` file, see the documentation of the **$include** command.

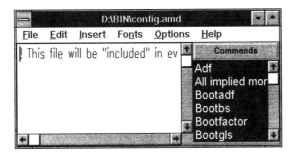

For an explanation of the menu items, **File**, **Edit**, etc., see [$]</span> **Enter '$' commands** on page 126.

Edit an included text file

Menu: **Model-Fit|Edit Include File...**

This button allows you to create or edit a text file. The default extension for files created or edited using ▦ is **.amd**.

▣ View text output

This button allows you to view the text output from previous Amos analyses. Every time you do an Amos analysis (by pressing ▣) the Amos text output is placed in a file with the extension **.amo**. Pressing ▣ displays a list of **.amo** files.

Provide a description for an analysis

Menu: **Model-Fit|Analysis Description...**

This button allows you to enter text to be placed on the title page of Amos's text output.

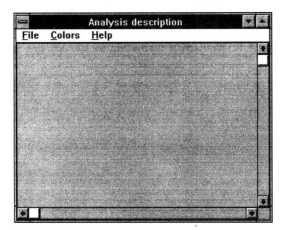

Allow different path diagrams for different groups

Menu: **Model-Fit|Heterogeneous Structures...**

In an analysis of multiple groups, Amos assumes that you want to use the same path diagram for every group, possibly with different parameter constraints for each group. If you want each group to have a different path diagram, press ⬜.

Hint: If the path diagrams for different groups differ only in small ways, first draw the features that all path diagrams have in common, then press ⬜ and proceed to add the features that distinguish one path diagram from another.

Estimate means and intercepts

Menu: **Model-Fit|Means**

If you leave ▣ in the unpressed position, means and intercepts will not be estimated. When ▣ is in the pressed position, Amos automatically adds a default mean/intercept structure to the existing path model. Means and intercepts are estimated, and you can constrain them with ▣.

When the **Means** button is down, the displayed path diagram changes accordingly: on the input and unstandardized output diagrams, *exogenous* variables have a "*mean, variance*" pair of parameters attached to them, while *endogenous* variables are displayed with a single intercept term. In addition, simple identification constraints are added to ensure that the means-level portion of the model is just-identified.

Amos Graphics changes in several ways when the **Means** button is pressed:

- Mean and intercept fields are shown during input, in addition to variances, covariances and/or regression weights.

- By default, **Amos Graphics** sets the means and intercept terms of the latent variables (and residual variables) to zero, while means exogenous observed variables and the intercepts of endogenous observed variables are free parameters to be estimated. The default means-level portion of the model is saturated, since it has as many free parameters as there are observed variables.

- Constraints may be applied to all intercepts, means, regression weights, variances, and covariances in all groups.

- Pressing the **Calculate estimates** button (while the **Means** button is still pressed) estimates means and intercepts — subject to constraints, if any.

- The chi-square statistic reflects the model fit to sample mean *and* covariance structures.

If the **Means** button is *not* down:

- Only fields for variances, covariances and regression weights are displayed during input. Constraints can be placed *only* on these parameters.

- When the **Calculate estimates** button is pressed, Amos estimates covariance structures, but *not* means or intercepts. Only constraints imposed on variances, covariances and regression weights are used in the estimation; any (portions of) constraints involving means and/or intercepts remain inactive.

- The chi-square statistic reflects the model fit to sample covariance structures only.

Related commands:

▣ **Constrain parameter estimates** on page 137

Run the Amos modeling laboratory

Menu: **Model-Fit|Modeling Lab...**

The modeling laboratory allows you to enter parameter values and observe the effect on the implied moments and on the value of the discrepancy function. When you press , a window resembling this one will appear:

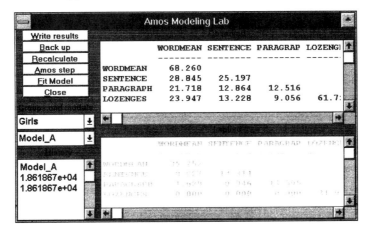

To enter a parameter value, click on a path diagram object that has a parameter associated with it. If you click, say, on an exogenous variable, a window that looks something like the following will appear:

If the window is in the way, you can drag it with the mouse. In this example, the variable's mean is currently equal to zero, and its variance is currently equal to 24.24657. You can type in a new value for either parameter, or for both. To refit the model after entering new parameter values, press the <Enter> key or press **Recalculate**.

Write results	Write the current parameter values and the current discrepancy function value to the text output file (a file with the extension .amo). Then reset the parameter values to Amos's default start values.
Back up	Take back the most recent change to the parameter values.
Recalculate	Recalculate the implied moments and the discrepancy function.

Amos step	Let Amos attempt to improve the parameter estimates by carrying out one iteration of its minimization algorithm.
Fit Model	Let Amos attempt to minimize the discrepancy function.
Observed	This text box shows the observed moments.
Close	Close the Amos modeling lab window.
Groups and models	There are two drop-down list boxes that let you pick a group (if there is more than one group) and a model (if there is more than one model).
	Note: Every time you select a model, Amos sets the parameter values to its own default initial values.
Implied	This text box shows the implied moments.
History	This text box shows the history of discrepancy function values. Each time Amos recalculates the discrepancy function, its value is entered in the "History" text box.

Constrain parameter estimates

Menu: **Model-Fit|Parameter Constraints...**

This button allows you to label each parameter with a character string. In a path diagram, Amos displays each parameter label next to the object it is associated with. Labels for means, variances and intercepts are displayed next to rectangles and ellipses. Regression weights are displayed next to single-headed arrows. Covariances are displayed next to double-headed arrows.

Setting a parameter equal to a constant

Labeling a parameter with a number has the effect of setting the parameter equal to that number. The parameter then does not have to be estimated. In the following path diagram, the regression weight for predicting **C** from **D** is fixed at unity.

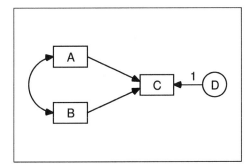

Setting parameters equal to each other

Labeling a parameter with a non-numeric name has no effect on the parameter unless another parameter is given the same name . Parameters that have the same name are constrained to have the same estimate. In the following path diagram, the name 'x' is assigned to two regression weights in order to require them to be equal. Also, one other regression weight is fixed at a constant value of 1. The variances of the three exogenous variables, **A**, **B** and **D** are unlabeled and therefore unconstrained. The covariance between **A** and **B** is also unconstrained.

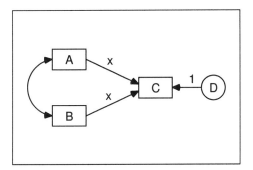

Providing initial values

To provide an initial value for a parameter without constraining it, assign it a numerical label followed by a question mark (*e.g.*, "3.14159?"). To give a parameter both a non-numeric name and an initial value, assign a label that consists of the name followed by a colon and the initial value (*e.g.*, "alpha:3.14159").

How to assign labels to parameters

To label a parameter, or to change a label that has been previously assigned, press 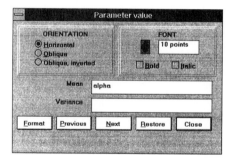. Then click on the object with which the parameter is associated. For example, clicking on an exogenous variable when means and intercepts are being estimated displays the following dialog box:

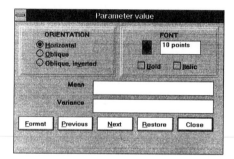

To assign the label "alpha" to the variable's mean, type "alpha" in the "Mean" input area:

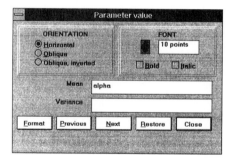

To fix the variable's variance at a constant "1", type a "1" in the "Variance" input area:

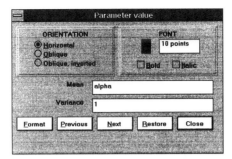

The remaining elements of the "Parameter value" dialog box are:

ORIENTATION

Horizontal   Display the parameter's estimate (and its label) horizontally. For example:

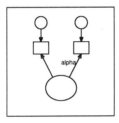

Oblique   Display the parameter's estimate (and its label) at an angle so as to conform to the path diagram object that the parameter is associated with. For example:

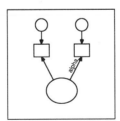

Oblique, inverted   Just like **Oblique**, except that the parameter's estimate (and its label) are displayed upside down. For example:

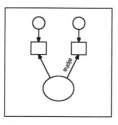

FONT   Click here to change the font size.

Bold   Display the parameter's estimate (and its label) in bold type.

Italic   Display the parameter's estimate (and its label) in italic type.

Format   Override the global formats (see **For mat** **Format parameter estimates** on page 116). Clicking on **Format** will open a dialog box that lets you substitute special formats for the global formats. For example, if you are entering a parameter label for a regression weight, the dialog box will look like this:

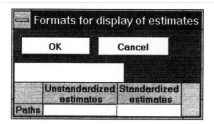

In this example, only the supplied formats, called "Unstandardized estimates" and "Standardized estimates", are listed. If you have created additional global formats of your own, they will also be listed, and you will be able to override them as well. For every existing format, you can change the template that is used for displaying regression weights by typing in a new template. (See **For mat** **Format parameter estimates** on page 116 for an explanation of templates.) In the above example, if you want the regression weight to be displayed with 5 decimal places when unstandardized, and 4 decimal places when standardized, you would fill in the dialog box in the following way:

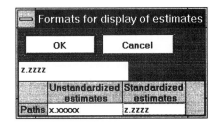

Formats for display of estimates

| OK | Cancel |

z.zzzz

	Unstandardized estimates	Standardized estimates
Paths	x.xxxxx	z.zzzz

Previous	Constrain/view the parameters of the previous object in the path diagram.
Next	Constrain/view the parameters of the next object in the path diagram.
Restore	Restore the parameter label (s) to the way they were when they were first displayed in the dialog box.
Close	Close the dialog box.

Different parameter labels can have different font characteristics, but they are all displayed with the same typeface.

Related commands:

 **Choose typefaces** on page 121

Format parameter estimates on page 116

▓ Toggle observed/unobserved

Menu: **Model-Fit|Toggle Observed/Unobserved**

When this button is in the pressed position, clicking on a rectangle will turn it into an ellipse. Clicking on an ellipse will turn it into a rectangle.

Display degrees of freedom

Menu: **Model-Fit|Degrees of Freedom...**
Hot key: **F12**

This button calculates degrees of freedom. In the following example, the 21 "parameters" include those parameters that are fixed equal to a constant as well as those parameters that are constrained to be equal to some other parameter. The 13 "free parameters" do not include parameters that are fixed equal to a constant. Furthermore, several parameters that are constrained to be equal to each other count as a single free parameter.

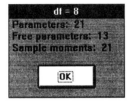

Note: The figures displayed with do not take into account any parameter constraints imposed by **$Model** commands.

▦ View spreadsheet

Menu: **Model-Fit|View Spreadsheet...**
Hot key: **Ctrl-R**

This button displays a model in the form of a rectangular table. For example, if you have drawn the following path diagram,

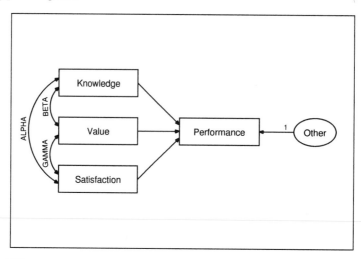

then pressing ▦ will display the table:

	Knowledge	Satisfaction	Value	Other
Performance	*	*	*	1
Knowledge		ALPHA	BETA	
Satisfaction	ALPHA		GAMMA	
Value	BETA	GAMMA		
Other				

All the variables in the model are listed along the left side of the table, endogenous variables first. Those variables that affect other variables are listed along the top of the table, endogenous variables first. Each non-blank entry in the body of the table represents a single- or double-headed arrow in the path diagram. For example, the number "1" in the upper right corner of the table indicates that **Performance** depends on **Other**, with a regression weight that is fixed at one. The entry "*" in the upper left corner of the table indicates that **Performance** depends on **Knowledge**. The corresponding regression weight is unconstrained. The word "ALPHA" indicates that the covariance between **Satisfaction** and **Knowledge** is a parameter of the model.

If there are *m* endogenous variables and *n* exogenous variables in the model, the entries in the first *m* rows of the table will represent regression weights. The lower right corner of the table, consisting of the rightmost *n* columns and the bottommost *n* rows, will represent covariances.

Pressing 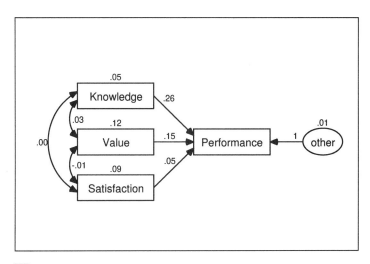 when parameter estimates are displayed on the path diagram will display a table of parameter estimates. For example, suppose you have the following path diagram in the Amos window.

Then pressing ▦ will display the table:

	Knowledge	Satisfaction	Value	Other
Performance	.26	.05	.15	1
Knowledge		.00	.03	
Satisfaction	.00		-.01	
Value	.03	-.01		
Other				

Change the page layout

Menu: **Global|Page Layout...**

This button allows you to specify page size and margins for the printed path diagram. You can also specify whether a frame (*i.e.*, a border) should be placed around the path diagram.

If you specify a page height of zero the printer page height will be used. If you specify a page width of zero, the printer page width will be used.

Related commands:

 Resize the diagram to fit on a page on page 81

Preserve symmetries

Menu: **Global|Smart**
Hot key: **Ctrl-E**

When this button is pressed, Amos attempts to preserve certain symmetries in a path diagram. When you move objects or change their size and shape, Amos makes compensating changes in other parts of the path diagram so as to maintain any pre-existing symmetries.

Amos attempts to preserve symmetries associated with latent variables together with their indicators and residual variables. As an example, consider the following path diagram with a single latent variable and three indicators:

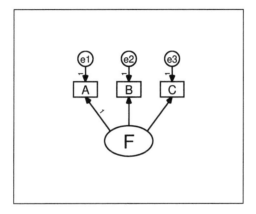

If 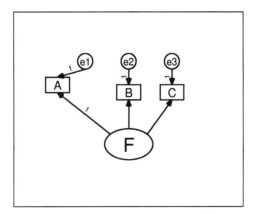 is used to move the variable **A** to the left and a little bit upward, the resulting path diagram will look something like:

However, if you press 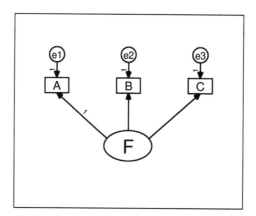 before moving the variable, **A**, you will get the following result instead:

In this case, Amos moved **B**, **C**, **e1**, **e2** and **e3**, so as to preserve the symmetries that were present before the move. In general, whenever you move or resize any indicator or residual variable associated with a latent variable, the other indicators and residual variables associated with that latent variable will be adjusted so as to preserve any symmetries that were originally present. Furthermore, if you move a latent variable, its indicators and their residual variables will move along with it.

When [Smart] is pressed, Amos preserves the spatial relationship between residual variables and the variables that they affect. For example, in the following path diagram, if you move **academic**, **error1** will move along with it. Similarly, if you move **attract**, **error2** will move also.

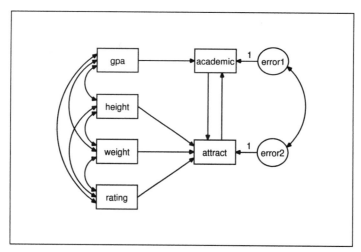

When [Smart] is pressed, Amos attempts to preserve symmetries involving an endogenous variable and its predictors whenever the predictors are selected or if they have been linked. As an example, suppose that the variables **gpa**, **height**, **weight** and **rating** in the previous path diagram have been selected using or linked using . Then moving, say, **rating** upward and to the right will produce the following result when is in the unpressed position,

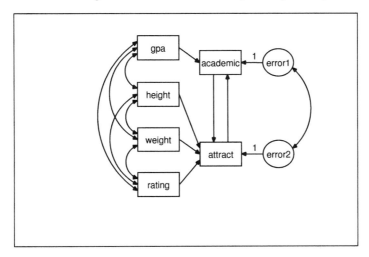

but will produce the following result when is in the pressed position.

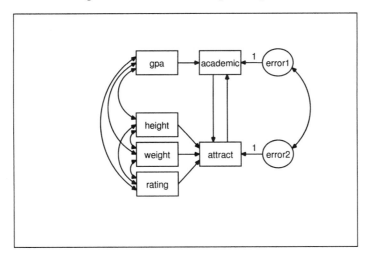

The effect of may not always be what you want. You can use it selectively, pressing before performing some operations, and then releasing it before performing others.

Related commands:

 Draw latent variables and indicators on page 99

 Link objects on page 69

 Select one object at a time on page 65

Snap to a grid

Menu: **Global|Snap...**

This button helps to line things up visually by superimposing a grid on the path diagram. Rectangles and ellipses are then centered on grid points. Their left and right boundaries are at grid points, and so are their top and bottom boundaries. When objects are moved and resized, their appearance and position change in fixed increments.

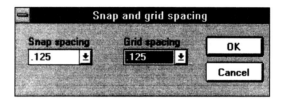

You can choose the spacing of the grid, and whether the grid is visible. It is possible to use one spacing for the visible grid, and another spacing for the grid that is actually used for positioning objects. For example, you could use a grid that has points spaced every eighth of an inch, but display a grid that has points spaced every quarter of an inch.

By setting **Snap spacing** to "Off", you can make the grid visible without employing the snap capability.

Related commands:

 Align height on page 87

 Align height and width on page 89

 Align objects horizontally on page 85

 Align objects vertically on page 86

 Align width on page 88

▥ Change screen colors

This button allows you to change the colors used in the Amos window. It does not affect the appearance of the printed path diagram. Screen colors are selected using the following dialog box.

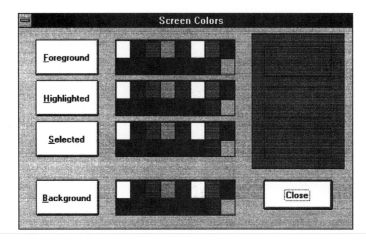

Foreground	The foreground color is used to draw objects on the path diagram. Click on the array of 16 colors to the right of **Foreground** to choose one of those 16 colors as the foreground color. Click on **Foreground** to pick from a larger selection of foreground colors.
Highlighted	The **Highlighted** color is used to highlight objects when you point to them with the mouse pointer. Click on the array of 16 colors to the right of **Highlighted** to choose one of those 16 colors. Click on **Highlighted** to pick from a larger selection of colors.
Selected	The **Selected** color is used for objects that have been selected with ▣ or ▣. Click on the array of 16 colors to the right of **Selected** to choose one of those 16 colors. Click on **Selected** to pick from a larger selection of colors.
Background	Click on the array of 16 colors to the right of **Background** to choose one of those 16 colors as the background color. Click on **Background** to pick from a larger selection of background colors.
Close	Close the dialog box.

Related commands:

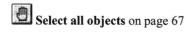 **Select all objects** on page 67

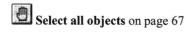 **Select one object at a time** on page 65

![Outline] Display an outline of the path diagram

Menu: **Global|Outline**
Hot key: **Ctrl-B**

When this button is in the pressed position, Amos will not display the following elements of a path diagram:

1. Variable names

2. Parameter constraints

3. Arrow heads

Suppressing these elements speeds up the redrawing of objects that occurs when you modify the path diagram.

Draw circles and squares

Menu: **Global|Shapes|Square**

When this button is in the pressed position, any rectangles you draw will be square. Any ellipses will be circular.

Related commands:

Draw golden sections on page 156

Draw observed variables on page 95

Draw unobserved variables on page 96

 **Draw golden sections**

Menu: **Global|Shapes|Golden**

When this button is in the pressed position, any rectangles you draw will be golden sections. The bounding rectangles of any ellipses will also be golden sections.

Related commands:

Draw circles and squares on page 155

Draw observed variables on page 95

Draw unobserved variables on page 96

Choose the width of lines

Menu: **Global|Pen Width...**

This button lets you choose the width of lines used to draw objects, and the size of arrow heads. You can use as many as four different line widths in a single path diagram. You do not have any control over how the four widths appear on the screen. The thinnest line will be one pixel (one dot) wide on the screen and the thickest line will be four pixels wide. However, you can control how the four line thicknesses will appear when they are printed. You can specify for example, that the thinnest line shall be three pixels wide when printed, that the next thicker line shall be 7 pixels wide, and so on. Pressing displays the following dialog box:

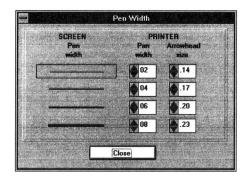

SCREEN Pen width   Four sample lines are displayed. Click on the line whose width you want to use for drawing new objects.

PRINTER Pen width   For each sample line under SCREEN Pen width, choose the line width (in pixels) that you want to use when printing the path diagram.

PRINTER Arrowhead size   For each sample line under SCREEN Pen width, choose the arrowhead length (in inches).

Note: The size of a pixel depends on the printer. For example, a pixel is 1/300 of an inch wide on a 300 dpi printer, and 1/1200 of an inch wide on a 1200 dpi printer.

Related commands:

 Align the width of lines on page 93

Specify decimal places

Press this button to specify the number of decimal places to be used when substituting numeric values for text macros.

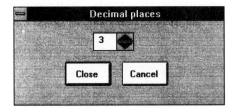

See also:

> **Text macros** on page 112

Choose miscellaneous options

Menu: **Global|Miscellaneous...**

This button opens the following dialog box, which makes available several options.

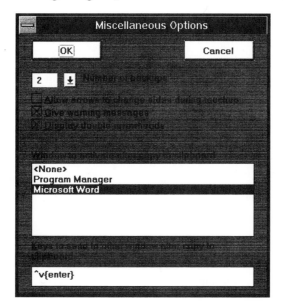

OK	Closes the dialog box and saves any changes that you have made.
Cancel	Closes the dialog box and cancels any changes that you have made.
Number of backups	Specifies how many backup copies of each path diagram Amos should keep. When you use 🔲 to save a file called, say, `charlie.amw`, Amos changes the name of any existing `charlie.amw` to `charlie.bk1`. If a `charlie.bk1` already exists, it is renamed `charlie.bk2`. Any existing `charlie.bk2` is renamed `charlie.bk3`. And so on, up to the limit specified in the 🔲 dialog box. For example, if you specify two backups, only `charlie.bk1` and `charlie.bk2` will be kept. If you specify "zero" backups, no backups will be kept. You can specify as many as nine backups.
	To retrieve a backup, see 🔲 **Retrieve a previous backup** on page 47
Allow arrows to change sides during touchup	Checking this box allows arrows to move from one side of a rectangle to another when you touch up the rectangle with 🔲. The

ability of arrows to change sides can be a mixed blessing. Only if arrows are allowed to change sides can you change

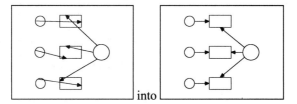 into

by selecting all the objects in the path diagram with 🔲 and touching up one of the objects with 🖱. On the other hand, touching up all the objects in

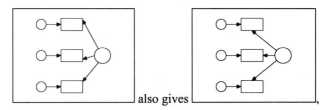 also gives ,

which in my opinion is not as good a result as the following, which is obtained by unchecking "Allow arrows to change sides during touchup".

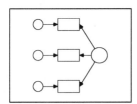

Give warning messages   If you check this box, Amos will warn you about possible errors in a path diagram whenever you attempt an analysis. For example, if your path diagram looks like this when you press 🔳,

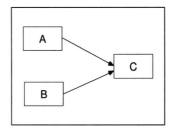

you will see the following dialog box.

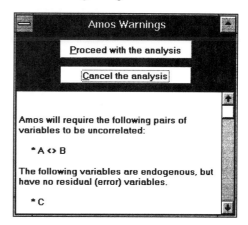

Amos will assume that A and B are uncorrelated because they are not connected by a double-headed arrow. Failing to connect exogenous variables with double-headed arrows is a common mistake. The fact that the endogenous variable, C, has no residual variable associated with it is almost certainly an oversight. If you want to attempt the analysis anyway, press "**Proceed with the analysis**". If not, press "**Cancel the analysis**".

Display double arrowheads

Checking this box causes double-headed arrows to be drawn with arrowheads (the usual convention). Leaving this box unchecked causes arrowheads to be omitted from double-headed arrows. This style for path diagrams was employed by Steiger (1989).

Window to activate after copy to clipboard

This box lists the titles of your open windows. The example below shows that there are two open applications titled "Program Manager" and "Microsoft Word". "Microsoft Word" has been selected. Consequently, whenever the path diagram in the Amos window is copied to the clipboard using ▤, "Microsoft Word" will be activated and the keystrokes described in the following section will be sent to that application.

Keys to send to other window after copy to clipboard

Whenever the path diagram in the Amos window is copied to the clipboard, the contents of this text box will be sent to the application selected in the list box labeled "Window to activate after copy to clipboard". For example, if the "Miscellaneous options" dialog box contains

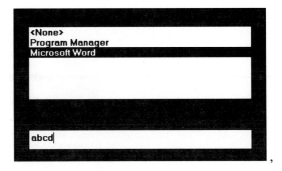
,

then, whenever you copy a path diagram to the clipboard, the characters "abcd" will be sent to "Microsoft Word" just as though you had typed "abcd" into the "Microsoft Word" window yourself.

There is not much reason to send the characters "abcd". The following series of keystrokes is more useful.

It may look as though the nine characters in "^v{enter}" will be sent to "Microsoft Word". However, "^v" is a special code for the character that you type by holding down "Ctrl" and pressing "v", while "{enter}" is a special code for the "enter" key. The upshot is that, whenever you copy a path diagram from the Amos window to the clipboard, the path diagram gets pasted into Microsoft Word, after which a new paragraph is started in Microsoft Word.

"^v" and "{enter}" are just two special codes. There are many others. To specify keys combined with any combination of the Shift, Ctrl, and Alt keys, precede the regular key code with one or more of the following codes:

Key	Code
Shift	+
Control	^
Alt	%

To specify that Shift, Ctrl, and/or Alt should be held down while several other keys are pressed, enclose the keys' code in parentheses. For example, to have the Shift key held down while E and C are pressed, use "+(EC)". To have Shift held down while E is pressed, followed by C being pressed without Shift, use "+EC".

To specify repeating keys, use the form *{key number}*; you must put a space between *key* and *number*. For example, {LEFT 42} means press the Left Arrow key 42 times; {h 10} means press "h" 10 times.

To specify characters that aren't displayed when you press a key (such as Enter or Tab) and keys that represent actions rather than characters, use the codes:

Key	Code
Backspace	{BACKSPACE} or {BS} or {BKSP}
Caps Lock	{CAPSLOCK}
Del	{DELETE} or {DEL}
End	{END}
Esc	{ESCAPE} or {ESC}
Home	{HOME}
Left Arrow	{LEFT}
Page Down	{PGDN}
Print Screen	{PRTSC}
Scroll Lock	{SCROLLLOCK}
Up Arrow	{UP}
Break	{BREAK}
Clear	{CLEAR}
Down Arrow	{DOWN}
Enter	{ENTER} or ~
Help	{HELP}
Ins	{INSERT}
Num Lock	{NUMLOCK}
Page Up	{PGUP}
Right Arrow	{RIGHT}
Tab	{TAB}
F1	{F1}
F2	{F2}
F3	{F3}
F4	{F4}
F5	{F5}
F6	{F6}
F7	{F7}
F8	{F8}
F9	{F9}
F10	{F10}
F11	{F11}
F12	{F12}
F13	{F13}
F14	{F14}
F15	{F15}
F16	{F16}
+	{+}
^	{^}
%	{%}
~	{~}
[	{[}
]	{]}
{	{{}
}	{}}

Example key sequences

Microsoft Word 6.0 for Windows: The key sequence "^v%oBx{enter}{down}" pastes the path diagram from the Windows clipboard to the cursor location in the active Word document ("^v"), puts a box around the pasted figure ("%oBx{enter}") and advances to the next paragraph ("{down}").

Tip: In the Word document, paste the path diagram inside a *Frame*. A frame makes it easier to resize the diagram and position it exactly on the printed page.

HiJaak Pro 2.0 for Windows: The key sequence "+{insert}^a%te%nmyfile.eps{enter}" pastes the path diagram from the Windows clipboard into a new document ("+{insert}"), and saves it as ("^a") an encapsulated Postscript file ("%te") with filename **myfile.eps** ("%nmyfile.eps{enter}").

Note: HiJaak Pro 2.0 prompts for an alternate filename if the file **myfile.eps** already exists.

See also:

 Calculate estimates on page 122

 Retrieve a previous backup on page 47

 Touch up a variable on page 82

 **Move tools**

Menu: **Global|Toolboxes/Menus|Move tools**

This button allows you to reorganize the toolbox that is on the screen. You can make the toolbox bigger (with more buttons) or smaller. Here is how toolbox number 1 looks when Amos is first installed.

After pressing , the toolbox looks like this:

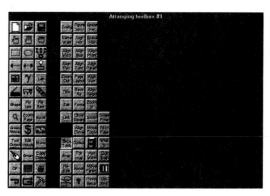

All the toolbox buttons are visible. You can use the mouse to drag the buttons around the toolbox. When you have rearranged the buttons to your satisfaction, click on any part of the path diagram. The toolbox will shrink so that the button is in the lower right corner. (By deciding where to put , you determine the height and width of the toolbox.

Related commands:

    Show or hide the tools on page 167

    Use another toolbox on page 166

 Use another toolbox

Menu: **Global|Toolboxes/Menus|Next Toolbox**
Hot key: Ctrl-N

Amos provides two toolboxes, but you can use only one of them at a time. Pressing toggles the toolboxes.

Related commands:

 Move tools on page 165

Show or hide the tools on page 167

 Show or hide the tools

Menu: **Global|Toolboxes/Menus|Show Tools**

Pressing (or choosing **Global|Toolboxes/Menus|Show Tools** from the menu) will remove the toolbox from the screen.

If the toolbox is not visible, choosing **Global|Toolboxes/Menus|Show Tools** from the Amos menu will cause it to reappear.

If neither the toolbox nor the menu is visible, double clicking anywhere on the path diagram will cause the menu to reappear.

Related commands:

 Move tools on page 165

 Show or hide the menu on page 168

 Use another toolbox on page 166

Show or hide the menu

Menu: **Global|Toolboxes/Menus|Show Menu**

When is in the unpressed position, pressing it will cause the menu to appear. When is in the depressed position, pressing it will make the menu disappear.

Double-clicking anywhere on the path diagram will cause the menu to appear.

Related commands:

 **Show or hide the tools** on page 167

 Get help

Menu: **Help|Contents**

This button opens a help window and displays a table of contents of Amos's help system.

Related commands:

 Get help for a single button or menu item on page 170

Get help for a single button or menu item

Menu: **Help|What Is...**
Hot key: **Shift-F1**

To find out what a particular button or menu item does, press . Then press the button, or select the menu item, for which you want an explanation.

Related commands:

Get help on page 169

 Get version information

Menu: **Help|About Amos...**

This button will display the version number of your copy of Amos.

Amos Text Reference Guide

Text input

Here is an example of an input file for the text based version of Amos. It consists of some (optional) title lines, followed by a series of "commands" shown in bold type.

Title lines.	`SAT, income (thousands of`
	`dollars) and education`
	`Data from Hamilton (1990)`

*In Amos Graphics, the title lines go in the **Analysis Description** window.*	
*Some commands, like **$samplesize**, are followed by a value on the same line*	`#Samplesize = 21`

Some commands stand by themselves	`#Samplemoments`
	`#Smc`
	`#Standardized`

*Some commands must be followed by additional lines. Here, the 21 lines between **$rawdata** and the next $ command belong with the **$rawdata** command*	`#Rawdata`
	`  899   14.345   12.7`
	`  896   16.370   12.6`
	`  897   13.537   12.5`
	`  889   12.552   12.5`
	`  823   11.441   12.2`
	`  857   12.757   12.7`
	`  860   11.799   12.4`
	`  890   10.683   12.5`
	`  889   14.112   12.5`
	`  888   14.573   12.6`
	`  925   13.144   12.6`
	`  869   15.281   12.5`
	`  896   14.121   12.5`
	`  827   10.758   12.2`
	`  908   11.583   12.7`
	`  885   12.343   12.4`
	`  887   12.729   12.3`
	`  790   10.075   12.1`
	`  868   12.636   12.4`
	`  904   10.689   12.6`
	`  888   13.065   12.4`

*The three lines after **$inputvariables** belong with the **$inputvariables** command*	`#Inputvariables`
	`  SAT`
	`  Income`
	`  Education`

*The four lines after **$structure** belong with the **$structure** command. These lines are not used in Amos Graphics.*	`#Structure`
	`  SAT <--- Education`
	`  SAT <--- Income`
	`  SAT <--- Other (1)`
	`  Education <--> Income`

In Amos Graphics, you would type these lines in the window, except for the title lines (which go in the window) and the **$structure** command (which is not allowed in Amos Graphics).

Input line length

The lines in an input file can be up to 256 characters long.

Title lines

The title may consist of any number of lines or may be omitted entirely.

 In Amos Text, you type the title lines at the beginning of the input file (before any **$** commands).

 In Amos Graphics, you type the title lines in the **Analysis Description** window after pressing 🖻.

The first line of the title will be displayed at the top of each page of text output. The entire title, up to a maximum of ten lines, will appear on the first page of text output. Any excess over ten lines will be discarded.

Commands

Amos Text commands begin with the character **$**. A number of commands are available for describing your model and data. **Amos Text** commands do not have to appear in any special order.

Special characters

Dollar signs

Amos Text commands begin with dollar signs (**$**). Dollar signs may not be used for anything else.

Blank spaces and blank lines

Blank spaces and blank lines may be inserted anywhere in order to improve readability. For example, the following lines

```
$input variables

    SAT
    Income
    Education
```

are equivalent to the lines:

```
$inputvariables
SAT
Income
Education
```

Tab characters

Tab characters may be inserted anywhere in order to improve readability.

Semicolons

A semicolon (;) is treated as the end of one line and the beginning of a new one. For example:

```
$input variables;alpha;beta;gamma
```

has the same effect as

```
$input variables
alpha
beta
gamma
```

Exclamation points

An exclamation point (!) starts an inline comment. That is, if an exclamation point appears in the input file, Amos will ignore it and any characters that follow it on the same line (semicolons and all). Ordinarily, the exclamation point is used to insert comments in the input file. It may also be used to disable temporarily a portion of the input file that you do not wish to delete permanently.

Symbolic names

Names for variables, groups and models

Names for variables, groups and models may contain the following characters: letters, numerals, underscore characters (_), and periods (.). Names may not be longer than 29 characters. Because of space limitations, it may turn out that fewer than 29 characters of a variable name are displayed in the output file. Sometimes as few as seven characters of a variable name may be displayed. For this reason, you should choose variable names that are recognizable within the first seven characters.

Here are some examples of acceptable names:

```
abc.xyz
untreated_first_time_offender
123abc
```

And here are some examples of unacceptable names:

```
untreated_first_time_offenders  (too long)
$charlie ('$' not allowed)
```

Parameter names (parameter labels)

Parameter names must start with a letter of the alphabet. In other respects, the rules for parameter names are the same as for variable, group and model names. **Alpha5** would be an acceptable parameter name, but **5alpha** would not.

Upper case and lower case letters

You can use a mixture of upper and lower case letters. Amos is *not* case-sensitive. Any two symbolic names that differ only in case are considered to be identical. For example, a variable called **alpha** in one portion of the input file could be referred to elsewhere as **Alpha** or as **ALPHA**. You can't call one variable **alpha** and then call a different variable **ALPHA.**

Format specifications

You have the option of supplying a format specification with the following commands:

$correlations on page 204

$covariances on page 205

$means on page 224

$rawdata on page 249

$standarddeviations on page 258

Amos has a limited ability to accept standard FORTRAN format specifications. A line that contains a FORTRAN format specification must begin with a left parenthesis and end with a right parenthesis. Only **F** and **X** field specifiers are recognized. The following format specifications, for example, are not acceptable:

```
(10I8)
(10E8.4)
(10D8.4)
(10F5.0//)
```

The following format specifications are acceptable:

```
(10F5.0)
(10F5.0, 5F3.1)
(1X, 10F5.0)
```

Format specifications are optional and may be omitted if a) adjacent numbers are separated by spaces, and b) any decimal points appear explicitly.

Catalog of text-mode commands

$adf

Description	**$adf** requests estimation by Browne's (1982) asymptotically distribution-free criterion, minimizing (D1) together with (D4) in Appendix B.
Syntax	**$adf**
Example	`$adf`
Default	The maximum likelihood criterion (**$ml**) is used.
Related commands	**$bootadf** on page 182 **$gls** on page 215 **$ml** on page 227 **$sls** on page 255 **$uls** on page 269

$allimpliedmoments

Description

$allimpliedmoments reports, for each group, the implied covariance matrix for all variables. When means are constrained or estimated, implied means are also reported.

Syntax

$all implied moments

Example

```
$all implied moments
```

Default

The implied moments for all variables are not reported.

Remarks

The 'implied' variances, covariances and means are estimates of the corresponding population values under the assumption that the specified model is correct.

If you use both **$standardized** and **$allimpliedmoments**, the implied correlation matrix will be reported, in addition to the implied covariance matrix.

$allimpliedmoments is identical to **$impliedmoments**, except that **$allimpliedmoments** displays implied variances, covariances and means for all variables in the model, not just for the observed variables.

Related commands

$impliedmoments on page 217
$noallimpliedmoments on page 236
$residualmoments on page 250
$samplemoments on page 251

$bootadf

Description

$bootadf requests a histogram of the discrepancies,

$$C_{ADF}(\hat{\alpha}_1, \mathbf{a}), \ C_{ADF}(\hat{\alpha}_2, \mathbf{a}),..., \ C_{ADF}(\hat{\alpha}_B, \mathbf{a}),$$

where $\mathbf{a}$ is the vector of sample moments, B is the number of bootstrap samples and $\hat{\alpha}_b$ is the vector of implied moments obtained by fitting the model to the b-th bootstrap sample. The mean and standard deviation of the distribution are also reported.

Syntax

$bootadf

Example

```
$bootadf
```

Default

The distribution of $C_{ADF}(\hat{\alpha}_1, \mathbf{a}), \ C_{ADF}(\hat{\alpha}_2, \mathbf{a}),..., \ C_{ADF}(\hat{\alpha}_B, \mathbf{a})$ is reported only when you use **$adf** and **$bootstrap**.

Remarks

When **$bootstrap** is not used to request bootstrapping, **$bootadf** is ignored. See Example 21 for a demonstration of the **$bootadf** command.

Related commands

$adf on page 180
$bootgls on page 187
$bootml on page 188
$bootsls on page 190
$bootstrap on page 191
$bootuls on page 194
$bootverify on page 195
$nobootadf on page 236
$seed on page 253

$bootbs

Description	**$bootbs** carries out the bootstrap procedure of Bollen and Stine (1992) for testing the hypothesis that the model is correct.
Syntax	**$bootbs**
Example	`$bootbs`
Default	The Bollen-Stine test is not performed.
Remarks	If you use **$bootbs**, you must also use **$bootstrap** to specify the number of bootstrap samples. However, when **$bootbs** is used, bootstrapped standard errors are not reported.
Related commands	**$bootstrap** on page 191 **$bootverify** on page 195 **$seed** on page 253

A demonstration of Bollen-Stine bootstrapping

The Bollen-Stine procedure provides a test of the hypothesis that the model is correct. This is the same null hypothesis that is tested by the conventional chi-square test of fit in maximum likelihood, generalized least squares and asymptotically distribution-free estimation. The objective of the procedure is to ascertain the probability that the discrepancy function would be as large as it actually turned out to be in the current sample, under the hypothesis that your model is correct.

In the Bollen-Stine approach, a transformation of the sample data is carried out so as to make your model fit the transformed data exactly. Bootstrap samples are drawn from the transformed sample data. The distribution of the discrepancy function across bootstrap samples is then taken as an estimate of its distribution under the hypothesis that the model is correct.

To illustrate the method, the analysis of Example 8 was repeated using the following additional commands.

```
$bootbs
$bootstrap = 2000
```

$bootbs requests Bollen-Stine bootstrapping. **$bootstrap=2000** requests 2000 bootstrap samples.

Using maximum likelihood estimation (Amos's default), the likelihood ratio chi-square statistic is 7.853 with 8 degrees of freedom (p = .448). The following output indicates that 46.2% of the 2000 bootstrap samples had a likelihood ratio chi-square statistic greater than 7.853.

```
Testing the null hypothesis that the specified model is correct:
         Bollen-Stine bootstrapped p = 0.462
```

Thus, the departure of the data from the model is significant at the .462 level. In other words, the data do not depart significantly from the model at any conventional significance level. The distribution of 2000 likelihood ratio chi-square statistics obtained from the 2000 bootstrap samples is shown here.

```
                                --------+--------------------
                          0.532|**
                          2.750|************
                          4.968|********************
   Likelihood ratio       7.186|*********************
     chi-square           9.404|****************
                         11.622|*********
                         13.840|*******
         N = 2000        16.058|****
      Mean = 8.327       18.277|**
      S. e. = 0.102      20.495|**
                         22.713|*
                         24.931|*
                         27.149|*
                         29.367|*
                         31.585|*
                                --------+--------------------
```

This distribution resembles the chi-square distribution with eight degrees of freedom insofar as it is positively skewed and has a mean of about eight (actually 8.327). Unfortunately, Amos does not provide the information needed to do a precise comparison with the chi-square distribution.

$bootfactor

Description

$bootfactor provides a means of speeding up the bootstrap algorithm (see **$bootstrap** on page 191) under the assumption that standard errors are inversely proportional to the square root of sample size.

Let m be the value specified after the '=' sign in the **$bootfactor** command. m must be a positive integer. In the example below, $m=5$. Suppose that your data consist of G independent samples (groups) with sample sizes $N_1, N_2, \ldots, N_G$. Each bootstrap sample will be obtained from the original sample by drawing mN_1 observations at random (with replacement) from the first original sample, mN_2 observations from the second original sample, and so on. As an example, suppose you have two independent groups with 20 cases in the first group and 25 cases in the second group, and that you use the command, **$bootfactor=5**. Then each bootstrap sample will consist of 100 cases drawn from the first group and 125 cases drawn from the second group. The bootstrapped standard errors displayed by Amos for any parameter estimate will be the standard deviation of that estimate across bootstrap replications, multiplied by $\sqrt{m}$.

Syntax

$bootfactor = <*positive integer*>

Example

```
$bootfactor = 5
```

Default

$m = 1$

Remarks

Using a value for m other than 1 requires the assumption that the standard error of each estimate is inversely proportional to the square root of sample size.

The use of $m > 1$ can substantially reduce computation time, and will reduce the probability of encountering a bootstrap sample for which parameter estimation is impossible. The larger m is, the larger the bootstrap samples will be, the more closely their sample moments will resemble the moments of the original sample, and the more closely the parameter estimates for the bootstrap samples will resemble the parameter estimates from the original sample. Since the parameter estimates from the original sample are used as initial values in the analysis of each bootstrap sample, a large value for *m* will reduce the amount of computation required to estimate parameters for a bootstrap sample. Of course, if *m* is set to a very large value, generating the bootstrap samples will become the dominant cost factor. A very large *m* may also create numerical problems.

The use of *m > 1* solves a problem described in a special case by Dolker, Halperin and Divgi (1982). With small samples and *m=1*, the sample covariance matrix in a bootstrap sample may be singular even though the covariance matrix in the original sample is nonsingular. The occurrence of a singular covariance matrix in a bootstrap sample will prohibit estimation by **$gls** or **$adf**. The larger *m* is, the smaller the chances of finding a singular sample covariance matrix in a bootstrap sample.

Related commands

$bootstrap on page 191
$bootverify on page 195
$seed on page 253

$bootgls

$bootgls requests a histogram of the discrepancies,

$$C_{GLS}(\hat{\alpha}_1, \mathbf{a}), \ C_{GLS}(\hat{\alpha}_2, \mathbf{a}),\dots, \ C_{GLS}(\hat{\alpha}_B, \mathbf{a}),$$

where $\mathbf{a}$ is the vector of sample moments, B is the number of bootstrap samples and $\hat{\alpha}_b$ is the vector of implied moments obtained by fitting the model to the b-th bootstrap sample. The mean and standard deviation of the distribution are also reported.

Syntax

$bootgls

Example

`$bootgls`

Default

The distribution of $C_{GLS}(\hat{\alpha}_1, \mathbf{a}), \ C_{GLS}(\hat{\alpha}_2, \mathbf{a}),\dots, \ C_{GLS}(\hat{\alpha}_B, \mathbf{a})$ is reported only when you use **$gls** and **$bootstrap**.

Remarks

When **$bootstrap** is not used to request bootstrapping, **$bootgls** is ignored. See Example 21 for a demonstration of the **$bootgls** command.

Related commands

$bootadf on page 182
$bootml on page 188
$bootsls on page 190
$bootstrap on page 191
$bootuls on page 194
$bootverify on page 195
$gls on page 215
$nobootgls on page 236
$seed on page 253

$bootml

Description

$bootml requests a histogram of the discrepancies,

$$C_{KL}(\hat{\alpha}_b, \mathbf{a}_b) - C_{KL}(\mathbf{a}, \mathbf{a}), \ b = 1, \dots, B,$$

where $\mathbf{a}$ is the vector of sample moments, B is the number of bootstrap samples and $\hat{\alpha}_b$ is the vector of implied moments obtained by fitting the model to the b-th bootstrap sample. The mean and standard deviation of the distribution are also reported.

Syntax

$bootml

Example

```
$bootml
```

Default

The distribution of $C_{KL}(\hat{\alpha}_b, \mathbf{a}_b) - C_{KL}(\mathbf{a}, \mathbf{a}), \ b = 1, \dots, B,$ is reported only when you use **$ml** and **$bootstrap**.

Remarks

When **$bootstrap** is not used to request bootstrapping, **$bootml** is ignored. See Example 21 for a demonstration of the **$bootml** command.

Related commands

$bootadf on page 182
$bootgls on page 187
$bootsls on page 190
$bootstrap on page 191
$bootuls on page 194
$bootverify on page 195
$ml on page 227
$nobootml on page 236
$seed on page 253

$bootnormal

Description

When the **$bootnormal** command is used, bootstrap samples are drawn from a multivariate normal population whose means, variances and covariances are the same as the sample means, variances and covariances.

Syntax

$bootnormal

Example

```
$bootnormal
```

Default

Bootstrap samples are drawn with replacement from the original sample.

Remarks

If you do not use the **$bootstrap** command, **$bootnormal** has no effect. **$bootnormal** allows bootstrapping to be carried out (with the assumption of normality) when raw data are not available.

The bootstrap obtained with **$bootnormal** is known as a *parametric bootstrap* (Efron and Tibshirani, 1993). The **$bootnormal** command can be used to carry out Monte Carlo simulations under the assumption of multivariate normality.

Related commands

$bootstrap on page 191
$nobootnormal on page 236
$seed on page 253

$bootsls

Description

$bootsls requests a histogram of the discrepancies,

$$C_{SLS}(\hat{\alpha}_1, \mathbf{a}), \ C_{SLS}(\hat{\alpha}_2, \mathbf{a}),..., \ C_{SLS}(\hat{\alpha}_B, \mathbf{a}),$$

where $\mathbf{a}$ is the vector of sample moments, B is the number of bootstrap samples and $\hat{\alpha}_b$ is the vector of implied moments obtained by fitting the model to the b-th bootstrap sample. The mean and standard deviation of the distribution are also reported.

Syntax

$bootsls

Example

```
$bootsls
```

Default

The distribution of $C_{SLS}(\hat{\alpha}_1, \mathbf{a}), \ C_{SLS}(\hat{\alpha}_2, \mathbf{a}),..., \ C_{SLS}(\hat{\alpha}_B, \mathbf{a})$ is reported only when you use **$sls** and **$bootstrap**.

Remarks

When **$bootstrap** is not used to request bootstrapping, **$bootsls** is ignored.

Related commands

$bootadf on page 182
$bootgls on page 187
$bootml on page 188
$bootstrap on page 191
$bootuls on page 194
$bootverify on page 195
$nobootsls on page 236
$sls on page 255
$seed on page 253

$bootstrap

Description

$bootstrap tells Amos to estimate *standard errors* for parameter estimates using the bootstrap algorithm of Efron (1982). In addition, Amos displays bootstrapped standard errors for the estimates displayed by the commands: **$standardized, $smc, $factorscores, $totaleffects, $samplemoments, $impliedmoments** and **$allimpliedmoments**.

Syntax

$bootstrap = <*number of bootstrap replications*>

Example

The following line requests 200 bootstrap replications.

```
$bootstrap = 200
```

Default

Bootstrapped standard errors are not reported.

Remarks

Bootstrapped standard errors are reported only for those quantities that are estimated. For example, to obtain bootstrapped standard errors for squared multiple correlations, you must use **$smc**. Similarly, to obtain bootstrapped standard errors for sample correlations, you must use **$samplemoments** and **$standardized**.

$bootstrap requires raw data (see **$rawdata** on page 249) unless you use **$bootnormal**.

Related commands

$bootfactor on page 185
$bootnormal on page 189
$bootstrap on page 191
$bootverify on page 195
$confidencebc on page 199
$confidencepc on page 201
$seed on page 253

Accuracy of the bootstrap

The accuracy of bootstrap estimates of standard error increases with sample size and with the number of bootstrap replications. Unfortunately, there are no guidelines regarding adequate sample size for the broad range of models allowed by Amos. As for the required number of bootstrap replications, Efron (1982) gives some suggestions.

Advantages of the bootstrap

Subject to the limitations in the preceding paragraph, bootstrapping offers the following advantages within Amos: Bootstrapping does not require distributional assumptions (although it does require independent observations). Bootstrapped standard errors are available for most of the statistics produced by Amos (not just for model parameters). Bootstrapping works for any estimation criterion, including **$uls** and **$sls**. Bootstrapping works even if the specified model is wrong.

Initial values for the bootstrap

Amos uses the parameter estimates from the original sample as initial estimates in the iterative estimation procedure for each bootstrap sample. An alternative procedure, not implemented in Amos, would be to repeat for each bootstrap sample the same procedure for choosing initial values that was used in the analysis of the original sample. In principle, this approach would provide the most faithful replication of the analysis of the original sample.

The correctness of Amos's strategy for choosing initial values depends on whether the initial values affect the final values, and there are two issues here. One issue concerns the possible existence of multiple local minima of the discrepancy function. If there are multiple local minima, the choice of initial values will determine which local minimum appears as the final solution. For this reason, it may be that using the same initial values for every bootstrap replication would tend to produce unusually small estimated standard errors. Amos's choice of initial values in bootstrap replications is thus problematical in the presence of multiple local minima. On the other hand, it is not clear that computing fresh initial estimates for each bootstrap replication would be worth the trouble. If multiple local minima are suspected, the dependability of the entire estimation procedure is open to question, so that it would be cold comfort in any case to have estimates of standard errors even if they could be had.

A second issue in the choice of initial values for bootstrap replications concerns the numerical accuracy of Amos estimates. Neglecting the possibility of multiple local minima, it remains true that the choice of initial values will have at least a marginal effect on the final parameter estimates in each bootstrap replication. This is partly due to round-off error and partly due to the fact that Amos uses an iterative procedure that terminates at a more or less arbitrary point (see the documentation of the **$crit1** and **$crit2** commands). There is thus the possibility that using the same initial estimates for each bootstrap replication will systematically influence the parameter estimates in each replication in such a way as to affect the bootstrapped standard errors. Numerical experiments have shown, however, that variability in parameter estimates resulting from the manipulation of initial values is negligible compared to variability from one bootstrap sample to another. Of course, for a statistic with a very small standard error, numerical inaccuracies may be the primary source of variability from one bootstrap sample to another. The behavior of Amos in such extreme cases has not been investigated.

Identifiability constraints and the bootstrap

In fitting a structural equation model, you have to impose constraints on the model so as to fix the unit of measurement of each unobserved variable (by using the **$structure** command in **Amos**

Text or the ▣ dialog in **Amos Graphics**). If you are planning to use the **$bootstrap** command, you should fix the scales of the unobserved variables by placing appropriate constraints on the *regression weights*, and not by constraining the variances of the unobserved variables. This method for fixing units of measurement is necessary for the following reason: If the scales of measurement of the unobserved variables are fixed by constraining their variances, the criterion of minimizing the discrepancy function will determine some of the regression weights only up to a sign change. That is, given one set of parameter estimates, it will be possible to change the signs of some of the regression weights without affecting the fit of the model. This is actually an example of nonidentifiability and also an example of multiple local minima, but it is a benign example unless you are bootstrapping. In bootstrapping, if the signs of some regression weights are arbitrary, their estimates will tend to 'jump around' from one bootstrap replication to another, and the reported bootstrap standard errors will be artificially inflated as a result.

Bootstrap error messages

Amos discards a bootstrap sample if it cannot estimate parameters for that sample. (The chances of this happening increase with the number of bootstrap replications and decrease with sample size.) The number of discarded bootstrap samples is reported. Inadmissible solutions and unstable systems encountered during bootstrap replications are not reported.

Computational cost of the bootstrap

The amount of computation required for bootstrapping is highly variable. In general, computational cost increases with the number of bootstrap replications, the number of variables and the number of parameters, and decreases with sample size. For a large problem, it may be advisable to request two or three bootstrap replications (**$bootstrap=2** or **$bootstrap=3**) to get a time estimate.

$bootuls

Description

$bootuls requests a histogram of the discrepancies,

$$C_{ULS}(\hat{\alpha}_1, \mathbf{a}), \ C_{ULS}(\hat{\alpha}_2, \mathbf{a}),..., \ C_{ULS}(\hat{\alpha}_B, \mathbf{a}),$$

where $\mathbf{a}$ is the vector of sample moments, B is the number of bootstrap samples and $\hat{\alpha}_b$ is the vector of implied moments obtained by fitting the model to the b-th bootstrap sample. The mean and standard deviation of the distribution are also reported.

Syntax

$bootuls

Example

```
$bootuls
```

Default

The distribution of $C_{ULS}(\hat{\alpha}_1, \mathbf{a}), \ C_{ULS}(\hat{\alpha}_2, \mathbf{a}),..., \ C_{ULS}(\hat{\alpha}_B, \mathbf{a})$ is reported only when you use **$uls** and **$bootstrap**.

Remarks

When **$bootstrap** is not used to request bootstrapping, **$bootuls** is ignored. See Example 21 for a demonstration of the **$bootuls** command.

Related commands

$bootadf on page 182
$bootgls on page 187
$bootml on page 188
$bootsls on page 190
$bootstrap on page 191
$bootverify on page 195
$nobootuls on page 236
$uls on page 269
$seed on page 253

$bootverify

<table>
<tr><td>Description</td><td>$bootverify reports, for each bootstrap replication, the frequency with which each observation in the original sample appears in the bootstrap sample.</td></tr>
<tr><td>Syntax</td><td>$bootverify</td></tr>
<tr><td>Example</td><td><code>$bootverify</code></td></tr>
<tr><td>Default</td><td>The $bootverify output is not provided.</td></tr>
<tr><td>Related commands</td><td>$bootstrap on page 191
$nobootverify on page 236
$seed on page 253</td></tr>
</table>

$brief

Description	Amos commands tend to have long names. You do not have to spell them out in full if you use the **$brief** command. Following the **$brief** command, you need only give enough of the initial letters of a command name to identify it uniquely.
Syntax	**$brief**
Example	The following lines

```
$brief
$si=4
$l=130
$cova
```

have the same effect as the lines:

```
$significant figures = 4
$line length = 130
$covariances
```

Default	Commands must be spelled out in full.
Related commands	**$extended** on page 212

$chicorrect

Description	**$chicorrect** specifies the value of the constant r in Appendix A.
Syntax	**$chicorrect = <nonnegative integer>**
Example	`$chicorrect = 0`
Default	**$chicorrect = <the number of groups>**
Remarks	The choice of r affects only the discrepancy function and standard errors. It does not affect parameter estimates.

There are few guidelines for departing from Amos's default value for r. Browne (1982, p. 98), mentions favorably a formula due to Swain (1975):

$$r = \frac{p(2p^2 + 3p - 1) - y(2y^2 + 3y - 1)}{12d}$$

where $y = \frac{1}{2}\left[(1 + 8q)^{\frac{1}{2}} - 1\right]$,

using the notation in Appendix A.

The Swain formula is intended for the case of a single group with unconstrained means and intercepts, where the model is invariant under a constant scaling factor. A one-group model in which means and intercepts are unconstrained was called "invariant under a constant scaling factor" by Browne (1982, p. 77) if, given any parameter vector, γ, and a positive number, c, there exists γ^* such that $\Sigma^{(1)}(\gamma^*) = d\,\Sigma^{(1)}(\gamma)$.

When means and intercepts are highly constrained model parameters, some consideration should be given to using **$chicorrect** to set $r = 0$.

 In Amos Text, means and intercepts are explicit parameters if an intercept appears in an equation following the **$structure** command, or if the **$mstructure** command is used.

 In Amos Graphics, means and intercepts are explicit parameters when the "Means" button is in the pressed position, or (equivalently) when "Means" is checked on the "Model-Fit" menu.

$compress

$compress suppresses page ejects and limits the number of consecutive blank lines that may appear in the output file. Page headings are also suppressed. **$compress** affects the entire output file. It is not possible to selectively **$compress** portions of the output listing.

Syntax

$compress

Example

```
$compress
```

Default

Output is compressed.

Related commands

$nocompress on page 236

$confidencebc

Description   **$confidencebc** requests bootstrapped confidence intervals using the bias corrected method (Efron, 1987).

Syntax   **$confidencebc = *<confidence level>***

Example   This example requests 90% confidence intervals.
```
$confidencebc = 90
```

Default   Bias corrected confidence intervals are not reported.

Remarks   Amos can produce bootstrapped confidence intervals for all parameter estimates, as well as for standardized estimates, squared multiple correlations, "factor score" weights and total effects.

Bootstrapped confidence intervals are reported only for those quantities that are reported. For example, to obtain bootstrapped confidence intervals for squared multiple correlations, you must use **$smc** along with **$confidencebc**.

When you use **$confidencebc**, you must also use **$bootstrap** to specify the number of bootstrap replications.

$confidencebc requires raw data (see **$rawdata** on page 249) unless you use **$bootnormal**.

Related commands   **$bootnormal** on page 189
$bootstrap on page 191
$confidencepc on page 201
$noconfidencebc on page 236

Demonstration of bias corrected confidence intervals

To illustrate the use of bootstrap confidence intervals, the analysis of Example 8 is repeated with the commands

```
$bootstrap=2000
$standardized
$confidencebc=90
```

The resulting confidence intervals for standardized estimates appear as follows:

```
90.0% confidence intervals (bias corrected percentile method)

                                  Lower      Upper
Standardized (Beta) Weights:      Bound      Bound        p
. . . . . . . . . . . . . . . .   . . . . .  . . . . .    . . . . .

   VISPERC <-------- SPATIAL       0.493      0.876     0.002
   CUBES <---------- SPATIAL       0.470      0.801     0.001
   LOZENGES <------- SPATIAL       0.559      0.930     0.001
   PARAGRAPH <------ VERBAL        0.793      0.946     0.001
   SENTENCE <------- VERBAL        0.738      0.884     0.002
   WORDMEAN <------- VERBAL        0.748      0.916     0.001


                                  Lower      Upper
Correlations:                     Bound      Bound        p
. . . . . . . . . . . .           . . . . .  . . . . .    . . . . .

   SPATIAL <--------> VERBAL       0.259      0.681     0.002
```

The confidence interval for the correlation between **spatial** and **verbal**, for example, is [.259, .681]. Since the confidence interval does not include zero, you would reject the hypothesis that the correlation is zero in the population, using a two-sided test with a significance level of .10. To carry out a similar two-sided test with a significance level of .05, you would need to request a 95% confidence interval (**$confidencebc=95**). You can also refer to the value in the "p" column. Each "p" value reveals indirectly how small the confidence level would have to be to yield a confidence interval that includes the value zero. A value of p in the "p" column indicates that a $100(1-p)$% confidence interval would have one of its end points at zero. In this sense, a p value can be used to test the hypothesis that an estimate has a population value of zero. For example, the correlation between **spatial** and **verbal** has a p value of .002, which implies that a 99.8% confidence interval would have its lower boundary at zero. In other words, a confidence interval at any conventional confidence level, such as .95 or .99, would not include zero, and you would reject at any conventional significance level the hypothesis that the correlation is zero in the population.

$confidencepc

Description

$confidencepc requests bootstrapped confidence intervals using the percentile method (Efron, 1987).

Syntax

$confidencepc = <confidence level>

Example

This example requests 90% confidence intervals.

```
$confidencepc = 90
```

Default

Percentile confidence intervals are not reported.

Remarks

Amos can produce bootstrapped confidence intervals for all parameter estimates, as well as for standardized estimates, squared multiple correlations, "factor score" weights and total effects.

Bootstrapped confidence intervals are reported only for those quantities that are reported. For example, to obtain bootstrapped confidence intervals for squared multiple correlations, you must use **$smc** along with **$confidencepc**.

If you use **$confidencepc**, you must also use **$bootstrap** to specify the number of bootstrap replications.

$confidencepc requires raw data (see **$rawdata** on page 249) unless you use **$bootnormal**.

Related commands

$bootnormal on page 189
$bootstrap on page 191
$confidencebc on page 199
$noconfidencepc on page 236

Demonstration of percentile confidence intervals

To illustrate the use of bootstrap confidence intervals, the analysis of Example 8 is repeated with the commands

```
$bootstrap=2000
$standardized
$confidencepc=90
```

The resulting confidence intervals for standardized estimates appear as follows:

```
90.0% confidence intervals (percentile method)

                              Lower    Upper
Standardized (Beta) Weights:  Bound    Bound     p
- - - - - - - - - - - - - - - -   - - - - -  - - - - -   - - - - -

   VISPERC <-------- SPATIAL    0.504    0.890   0.001
   CUBES <---------- SPATIAL    0.466    0.798   0.001
   LOZENGES <------- SPATIAL    0.543    0.909   0.001
   PARAGRAPH <------ VERBAL     0.794    0.946   0.001
   SENTENCE <------- VERBAL     0.750    0.891   0.001
   WORDMEAN <------- VERBAL     0.749    0.917   0.001


                              Lower    Upper
Correlations:                 Bound    Bound     p
- - - - - - - - - - - -          - - - - -  - - - - -   - - - - -

   SPATIAL <--------> VERBAL    0.280    0.698   0.001
```

The confidence interval for the correlation between **spatial** and **verbal**, for example, is [.280, .698]. Since the confidence interval does not include zero, you would reject the hypothesis that the correlation is zero in the population, using a two-sided test with a significance level of .10. To carry out a similar two-sided test with a significance level of .05, you would need to request a 95% confidence interval (**$confidencebc=95**). You can also refer to the value in the "p" column. Each "p" value reveals indirectly how small the confidence level would have to be to yield a confidence interval that includes the value zero. A value of p in the "p" column indicates that a $100(1-p)\%$ confidence interval would have one of its end points at zero. In this sense, a p value can be used to test the hypothesis that an estimate has a population value of zero. For example, the correlation between **spatial** and **verbal** has a p value of .001, which implies that a 99.9% confidence interval would have its lower boundary at zero. In other words, a confidence interval at any conventional confidence level, such as .95 or .99, would not include zero, and you would reject at any conventional significance level the hypothesis that the correlation is zero in the population.

$corest

Description

In the case of maximum likelihood (**$ml**), generalized least squares (**$gls**), or asymptotically distribution-free (**$adf**) estimation, **$corest** displays an estimate of the correlation matrix of the parameter estimates produced by Amos. For other estimation criteria, **$corest** has no effect

Syntax

$corest

Example

```
$corest
```

Default

The correlation matrix of parameter estimates is not reported

Related commands

$covest on page 206
$crdiff on page 207
$nocorest on page 236

$correlations

Description

This command is the same as the **$covariances** command, except that it is used to read a sample correlation matrix.

Syntax

$correlations
<*optional format*>   (See page 178)
<*correlation matrix*>

Example

```
$correlations
(2F5.2)
 1.00
  .60 1.00
```

Default

There is no default. Exactly one of the following commands is required: **$correlations**, **$covariances**, **$rawdata**.

Remarks

If correlations are supplied with the **$correlations** command, then standard deviations must also be supplied with the **$standarddeviations** command.

If no format is supplied, Amos reads the correlations in free format, separated by spaces, tab characters and/or line feed characters.

Related commands

$covariances on page 205
$means on page 224
$rawdata on page 249
$standarddeviations on page 258

$covariances

(See page 178)

Description

This command indicates that succeeding lines contain an optional format specification, and then sample covariances. The sample covariances appear as the lower triangular portion of a covariance matrix. That is, the first line contains just one number: the variance of the first observed variable mentioned on the **$inputvariables** list. The line after that contains two numbers: 1) the covariance between the first two variables mentioned on the **$inputvariables** list, 2) the variance of the second variable on the **$inputvariables** list. The line after that contains three numbers, and so on.

Syntax

$covariances
<optional format>
<covariance matrix>

Example

This example shows the use of **$covariances** to read a 2 by 2 covariance matrix.

```
$covariances
(2F3.0)
 16
  6 25
```

Default

There is no default. Exactly one of the following commands is required: **$correlations, $covariances, $rawdata**.

Remarks

By default, Amos assumes that the sample covariances supplied with **$covariances** are maximum likelihood estimates of the population covariances:

$$\frac{1}{N^{(g)}} \sum_{i=1}^{N^{(g)}} \left(\mathbf{x}_i^{(g)} - \overline{\mathbf{x}}^{(g)}\right)\left(\mathbf{x}_i^{(g)} - \overline{\mathbf{x}}^{(g)}\right)' .$$

If the sample covariances supplied with **$covariances** were computed using the formula,

$$\frac{1}{N^{(g)} - 1} \sum_{i=1}^{N^{(g)}} \left(\mathbf{x}_i^{(g)} - \overline{\mathbf{x}}^{(g)}\right)\left(\mathbf{x}_i^{(g)} - \overline{\mathbf{x}}^{(g)}\right)' ,$$

make sure that you use the command **$unbiased.**

If no format statement is supplied, Amos reads the covariance matrix in free format, with numbers delimited by spaces, tab characters and/or line feed characters.

Related commands

$correlations on page 204
$means on page 224
$rawdata on page 249
$standarddeviations on page 258

$covest

Description	In the case of maximum likelihood (**$ml**), generalized least squares (**$gls**), or asymptotically distribution-free (**$adf**) estimation, **$covest** displays an estimate of the covariance matrix of the parameter estimates produced by Amos. For other estimation criteria, **$covest** has no effect.
Syntax	**$covest**
Example	`$covest`
Default	The covariances of the parameter estimates are not reported.
Related commands	**$corest** on page 203 **$crdiff** on page 207 **$nocovest** on page 236

$crdiff

Description

In the case of maximum likelihood (**$ml**), generalized least squares (**$gls**), or asymptotically distribution-free (**$adf**) estimation, **$crdiff** displays a 'critical ratio' for each pair of parameter estimates. The critical ratio for a pair of parameter estimates provides a test of the hypothesis that the two parameters are equal.

Syntax

$crdiff

Example

```
$crdiff
```

Default

Critical ratios for differences between parameters are not reported.

Related commands

$corest on page 203
$covest on page 206
$nocrdiff on page 236

$crit1

Description

This command affects one of the convergence criteria used in deciding whether a local minimum has been reached. Amos requires the absolute value of each first order derivative to be less than the value specified by **$crit1** at the end of the final iteration.

Syntax

$crit1 = <number>

Example

$crit1 = .001

Default

$crit1 = .00001

Related commands

$crit2 on page 209
$fisher on page 214
$iterations on page 221
$technical on page 266
$time on page 267

$crit2

Description	This command affects one of the convergence criteria used in deciding whether a local minimum has been reached. Amos requires that, on the final iteration, the distance traveled in the parameter space (the square root of the sum of squared changes in the parameter values) be less than the value specified by **$crit2**.
Syntax	**$crit2 = <number>**
Example	`$crit2 = .01`
Default	**$crit2 = .001**
Related commands	**$crit1** on page 208 **$fisher** on page 214 **$iterations** on page 221 **$technical** on page 266 **$time** on page 267

$echo

Description

Beginning with the input line immediately after the **$echo** command, and continuing through the next **$noecho** command, all text input lines will be copied to the text output file.

Syntax

$echo

Example

```
$echo
```

Default

Text input lines are not copied to the text output file.

Remarks

If the **$echo** command is not followed by a **$noecho** command, all input lines after the **$echo** command will be copied to the text output file.

$echo has no effect when echoing has previously been enabled. **$noecho** has no effect when echoing has previously been disabled. Neither **$echo** nor **$noecho** affect the analysis of your data.

Several **$echo** and **$noecho** pairs may be used to display selected portions of the input file.

Related commands

$noecho on page 236

$emulisrel6

Description	**$emulisrel6** substitutes (D1a) for (D1) in Appendix B.
Syntax	**$emulisrel6**
Example	`$emulisrel6`
Default	(D1) in Appendix B is minimized.
Remarks	The effect of using **$emulisrel6** is generally small enough to be unimportant. It has no effect at all in single group analyses. (D1a) appears to be the function minimized by the Lisrel program.
Related commands	**$chicorrect** on page 197 **$noemulisrel6** on page 236

$extended

Description	"$" commands that follow the **$extended** command must be spelled out in full.
Syntax	**$extended**
Example	`$extended`
Default	Commands must be spelled out in full.
Remarks	The intended use of **$extended** is to cancel the effect of a preceding **$brief** command.
Related commands	**$brief** on page 196

$factorscores

Description

$factorscores displays regression weights for the regression of the unobserved variables on the observed variables. The regression weights are computed by the formula $\mathbf{W} = \mathbf{BS}^{-1}$ where

W is the matrix of regression weights

S is the matrix of covariances among the observed variables

B is the matrix of covariances between the unobserved and observed variables.

Syntax

$factor scores

Example

`$factor scores`

Default

"Factor score" weights are not reported.

Remarks

This command is called **$factorscores** in conformance with usage in common factor analysis, where scores on the unobserved variables are called 'factor scores'. The use of **$factorscores** is not limited to common factor analysis models, however.

Related commands

$nofactorscores on page 236

$fisher

Description	**$fisher** instructs Amos to use Fisher's scoring method in the case of maximum likelihood estimation (**$ml**), or the Gauss-Newton method in the case of least squares estimation (**$uls**, **$sls**, **$gls** or **$adf**).
	The number after the '**=**' sign in the **$fisher** command places an upper limit on the number of iterations that will be performed by Fisher's scoring method or the Gauss-Newton method. If Amos has not obtained a solution by the time this limit is reached, the program will revert to the standard Amos algorithm.
Syntax	**$fisher = <positive integer>**
Example	`$fisher = 999`
Default	Fisher's scoring method or the Gauss-Newton method is used.
Remarks	For some combinations of a model with an estimation method, the **$fisher** method is highly effective, and may even converge in a single iteration (Kendall and Stuart, 1973, Section 18.21). However, **$fisher** usually makes Amos slower and less reliable.
Related commands	**$crit1** on page 208 **$crit2** on page 209 **$iterations** on page 221 **$technical** on page 266 **$time** on page 267

$gls

Description

$gls requests a generalized least squares solution, obtained by minimizing (D1) together with (D3) in Appendix B.

Syntax

$gls

Example

`$gls`

Default

The maximum likelihood criterion (**$ml**) is used.

Related commands

$adf on page 180
$bootgls on page 187
$ml on page 227
$sls on page 255
$uls on page 269

$groupname ▦ (**Amos Text** only)

Description   This command is used to assign a name to a group.

Syntax   **$groupname = *<group name>***

Example   `$groupname = experimental`

Default   Amos assigns the names 'group number 1', 'group number 2', and so on.

Related commands **$nextgroup** on page 235

$impliedmoments

Description

$impliedmoments displays the implied covariance matrix for the observed variables in each group. If means are constrained or estimated in any group, the implied means in that group will also be displayed. The 'implied' variances, covariances and means are estimates of the corresponding population values under the assumption that the specified model is correct.

Syntax

$impliedmoments

Example

```
$impliedmoments
```

Default

Implied moments are not reported.

Remarks

If you use both **$standardized** and **$impliedmoments**, the implied correlation matrix will be reported, in addition to the implied covariance matrix.

Related commands

$allimpliedmoments on page 181
$noimpliedmoments on page 236
$residualmoments on page 250
$samplemoments on page 251

$include

Description	The **$include** command is used to name a text file that Amos will read as though it is part of the Amos text input file.
Syntax	**$include = <*file name*>**
Example	Suppose that the file **charlie.amd** contains the following lines:

```
$input variables
    alpha
    beta
```

Then the effect of the following three lines,

```
$standardized
$include=charlie.amd
$smc
```

will be the same as the effect of the following 5 lines

```
$standardized
$input variables
    alpha
    beta
$smc
```

Default	**$include** is optional. If it is not present, only the file **config.amd** (discussed below) is "included".
Remarks	The file **config.amd** (discussed below) is always "included".
	A file that is "included" may also contain **$include** commands. That is, the file **charlie.amd** in the above example could have contained additional **$include** commands.

The config.amd file

The file, **config.amd**, is a text file that you can create and modify using any text editor.

config.amd, is included automatically in every input file. It is as though every input file contains the line "**$include=config.amd**". As an example of the use of **config.amd**, suppose that **config.amd** contains the two lines,

```
$standardized
$smc
```

Then Amos will always report standardized parameter estimates and squared multiple correlations. These will be, in effect, new defaults that you can override with the commands **$nostandardized** and **$nosmc**.

Amos searches for **config.amd** in the following way. First, Amos searches for a file called **config.amd** in the directory that contains the Amos input file. If that search fails, Amos checks to see if there is an environment string called "amos" that specifies the directory that contains **config.amd**. If **config.amd** still has not been found, Amos searches the directory that contains the Amos program files.

You can create an environment string with the MS-DOS "set" command. For example, the line "set amos=e:\abc", typed at the MS-DOS command line before running Windows, instructs Amos to search for **config.amd** in the \abc directory on drive E.

$inputvariables

Description

Each variable for which you provide data (either raw data, or sample statistics) must be given a name. This is done on the lines following the **$inputvariables** command. Each variable name goes on a separate line.

Syntax

$inputvariables
<variable names>

Example

In the following example, data will be provided for three variables called **alpha**, **beta** and **gamma**:

```
$input variables
     alpha
     beta
     gamma
```

Default

$inputvariables is required exactly once per group.

Remarks

The order of the variable names is significant, and depends on the layout of the data. See the descriptions of the commands:

$correlations on page 204
$covariances on page 205
$means on page 224
$rawdata on page 249
$standarddeviations on page 258

$iterations

Description

This command places a limit on the number of iterations Amos will perform. If this limit is reached, Amos will display its current estimates of the parameters, even if the convergence criteria (see **$crit1 on page 208** and **$crit2 on page 209**) have not been met.

Syntax

$iterations=<*positive integer*>

Example

In this example, Amos quits after 20 iterations whether or not a local minimum has been reached:

```
$iterations=20
```

Default

There is no limit on the number of iterations.

Related commands

$crit1 on page 208
$crit2 on page 209
$fisher on page 214
$technical on page 266
$time on page 267

$linelength

Description   **$linelength** specifies the maximum number of characters per line in the text output file.

Syntax   **$linelength = <*integer between 80 and 256*>**

Example   In this example, the number of characters per line is set to 130.

```
$line length = 130
```

Default   **$line length = 80**

Remarks   **$linelength** affects only the way matrices are displayed. Other text output is always limited to 80 characters per line.

Related commands   **$pagelength** on page 244

$maxdecimalplaces

Description

$maxdecimalplaces specifies the maximum number of decimal places that will be used in displaying matrices.

Syntax

$maxdecimalplaces=<*positive integer*>

Example

In this example, no fewer than five and no more than nine digits will be displayed to the right of the decimal point. Subject to this constraint, results will be displayed with four significant figures.

```
$min decimal places = 5
$max decimal places = 9
$significant figures = 4
```

Default

$max decimal places = 8

Related commands

$mindecimalplaces on page 225
$significant figures on page 254

$means

Description	This command indicates that succeeding lines contain an optional format specification, followed by the sample means.
Syntax	**$means** **\<optional format\>** (See page 178) **\<sample means\>**
| *Example* | ```
$means
(2F6.3)
  4.32   9.01
``` |
Default	There is no default. **$means** is required only if raw data are not supplied (with **$rawdata**) and if means and intercepts are explicit model parameters.
Remarks	The **$means** command is not allowed if raw data are supplied with **$rawdata**. If no format is supplied, the means must be delimited by spaces, tab characters and/or line feed characters.
Related commands	**$correlations** on page 204 **$covariances** on page 205 **$rawdata** on page 249 **$standarddeviations** on page 258
```

$mindecimalplaces

<table>
<tr><td>*Description*</td><td>**$mindecimalplaces** specifies the minimum number of decimal places that will be used in displaying matrices.</td></tr>
</table>

Description

$mindecimalplaces specifies the minimum number of decimal places that will be used in displaying matrices.

Syntax

$mindecimalplaces=<*positive integer*>

Example

In this example, no fewer than five and no more than nine digits will be displayed to the right of the decimal point. Subject to this constraint, results will be displayed with four significant figures.

```
$min decimal places = 5
$max decimal places = 9
$significant figures = 4
```

Default

$mindecimalplaces = 3

Remarks

By default, no more than 8 decimal places will be used in displaying matrices.

Related commands

$maxdecimalplaces on page 223
$significant figures on page 254

$missing

Description

This command specifies a numerical value that will be interpreted as a 'missing data' indicator.

Syntax

$missing = <*number*>

Example

In this example, any data value of −1 will be interpreted as a missing value.

```
$missing = -1
```

Default

The data are assumed to be complete.

Remarks

Amos performs maximum likelihood estimation in the presence of missing data. The method was described by Arbuckle (1994a).

If you use the **$missing** command, you must explicitly estimate means and intercepts.

 In Amos Text, you need to use the **$mstructure** command, or to specify at least one intercept using the **$structure** command.

 In Amos Graphics you need to make sure that the ▨ button is pressed.

$ml

Description	**$ml** requests estimation by the method of maximum likelihood, minimizing (D1) together with (D2) in Appendix B.
Syntax	**$ml**
Example	$ml
Default	The maximum likelihood criterion (**$ml**) is used.
Remarks	Since maximum likelihood is the default estimation method, the only use of **$ml** is to override any earlier use of **$adf**, **$gls**, **$sls** or **$uls**.
Related commands	**$adf** on page 180 **$bootml** on page 188 **$gls** on page 215 **$sls** on page 255 **$uls** on page 269

$model

Description

$model allows you to place equality constraints on model parameters.

Syntax

The line containing the **$model** command may be followed by additional lines that place constraints on the parameters. Each line that follows a **$model** command can constrain any number of parameters to be equal to each other or to be equal to some constant.

$model = <*model name*>
<equality constraints>

Example

This example is based on Jöreskog and Sörbom's Model D shown in Figure R1. Six variations of Model D are specified. The first variation, called Model B, requires the covariances labeled **cov1** and **cov2** (in Figure R1), to be equal to zero. Model C requires only that the covariance labeled **cov2** be equal to zero. Model D is the model as it appears in Figure R1 without additional constraints. Model E requires the variances labeled **var1** and **var3** to be equal. Model F requires the variances labeled **var2** and **var4** to be equal. Model G incorporates the constraints of both Model E and Model F.

```
$model = B
    cov1 = cov2 = 0
$model = C
    cov2 = 0
$model = D
$model = E
    var1 = var3
$model = F
    var2 = var4
$model = G
    E
    F
```

This example is discussed further, later on in the Section entitled **Demonstration of fitting multiple models.**

Default

Only the constraints specified by the **$structure** and **$mstructure** commands (**Amos Text**), or on the path diagram (**Amos Graphics**) are employed.

Remarks

You can use as many **$model** commands as you want.

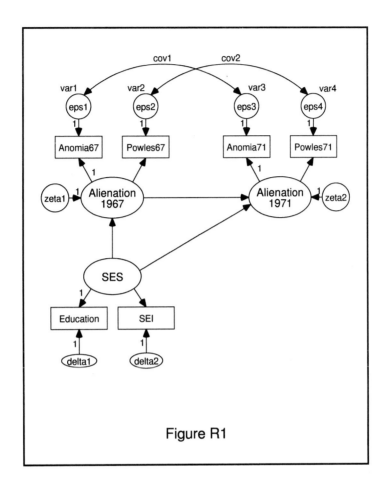

Figure R1

Demonstration of fitting multiple models

Many Amos applications require fitting several alternative models to the same data. You can fit many models at once provided that each model can be obtained by placing equality constraints on the parameters of one special, 'most general', model. An example will help show how to do this. Consider Jöreskog and Sörbom's (1989, p. 205) Model D for the data of Wheaton et al. (1977), shown above in Figure R1. If you are using Amos Text, you can specify the model with the following lines. (The included file, **wheaton.amd**, contains the Wheaton data.)

```
$structure
      anomia67  = (1) alien67  + (1) eps1
      powles67  =     alien67  + (1) eps2
      anomia71  = (1) alien71  + (1) eps3
      powles71  =     alien71  + (1) eps4
      education = (1) ses      + (1) delta1
      sei       =     ses      + (1) delta2

      alien67   =     ses      +         (1) zeta1
      alien71   =     alien67  +  ses + (1) zeta2

      eps1 <> eps3     (cov1)
      eps2 <> eps4     (cov2)
      eps1             (var1)
      eps2             (var2)
      eps3             (var3)
      eps4             (var4)
$include wheaton.amd
```

Six parameters are labeled—**cov1**, **cov2**, **var1**, **var2**, **var3**, **var4**. However, since no two parameters share the same label, the presence of the labels does not place any constraints on the parameters. The purpose of the labels is to allow the use of **$model** to place constraints on the labeled parameters.

Jöreskog and Sörbom proposed other models besides Model D, all but one of which can be obtained by constraining Model D. For instance, their Model C is just like Model D, but with the parameter labeled **cov2** (the covariance between **eps2** and **eps4**) fixed at zero. Their Model B goes even further. It assumes that two parameters (**cov1** and **cov2**) are zero. Amos analyzes Models B and C along with Model D if you add the following lines to the input file.

```
$model = B
     cov1 = cov2 = 0
$model = C
     cov2 = 0
$model = D
```

The first four lines are self-explanatory—they name and describe Models B and C. You may be surprised that the fifth line is necessary. It declares that there is a model called Model D that employs no additional constraints beyond those specified by the **$structure** command. In other words, the fifth line just says to analyze the model specified by the **$structure** command. This line is necessary if you want to analyze Model D. The rule is that, if you use **$model** at all, Amos will only analyze models explicitly named by a **$model** command. This convention allows you to specify an unidentified model, and then to supply enough constraints with each **$model** command to identify the model. If your input file contains no **$model** commands at all, however, Amos will analyze the model specified by the **$structure** and/or **$mstructure** commands (or by the path diagram in Amos Graphics).

Each **$model** command is followed on the same line by an '**=**' sign, and then by a model name. Most models can be specified in several equivalent ways. Model B, for instance, could have been specified in the following way.

```
$model = B
     cov1 = 0
     cov2 = 0
```

Here is another, equivalent, variation.

```
$model = B
    cov1 = cov2
    cov2 = 0
```

There is a shorthand for indicating that one model incorporates all of the constraints of another model. In the present example, Model B includes all of the constraints of Model C, as well as one additional constraint, so Model B could be specified this way:

```
$model = B
    C
    cov1 = 0
```

Three more models for the Wheaton data will now be specified by using **$model**. Notice that **var1** and **var3** are unique variances associated with **anomia** measurements made in 1967 and 1971. It is a plausible hypothesis that the unique variance of **anomia** was the same in both years. This hypothesis can be incorporated into a new model by adding these two lines to the input file.

```
$model = E
    var1 = var3
```

Similarly, since **var2** and **var4** are unique variances associated with **powerlessness** measurements made in 1967 and 1971, it is plausible to set up a model in which those two variances are required to be equal:

```
$model = F
    var2 = var4
```

Finally, both of the models just described could be right. In other words, all of the 1971 parameter values could be the same as the corresponding 1967 values. The following model specification imposes both sets of constraints.

```
$model = G
    E
    F
```

To summarize, six models for the Wheaton data have been described. Each one can be obtained by constraining the most general one of them (Model D). All six can be analyzed simultaneously by including the following lines in the input file.

```
$model = B
    cov1 = cov2 = 0
$model = C
    cov2 = 0
$model = D
$model = E
    var1 = var3
$model = F
    var2 = var4
$model = G
    E
    F
```

$mods

Description

$mods displays the modification indices described by Jöreskog and Sörbom (1984). Only modification indices that exceed the value specified by the **$mods** command will be displayed.

Syntax

$mods = <number>

Example

In this example, modification indices that are greater than 4 will be displayed.

```
$mods=4
```

Default

Modification indices are not reported

Remarks

Amos computes a modification index for each parameter that is fixed at a constant value and for each parameter that is required to equal some other parameter. The modification index for a parameter is an estimate of the amount by which the discrepancy function would decrease if the analysis were repeated with the constraints on that parameter removed. The actual decrease that would occur may be much greater.

Amos computes modification indices, not only for parameters that are explicitly constrained, but also for parameters that are implicitly assumed to be zero. For example, a modification index is computed for every covariance that is fixed at zero by default.

Amos also computes modification indices for paths that do not appear in a model, giving the approximate amount by which the discrepancy function would decrease if such a path were introduced. There are, however, two types of nonexistent paths for which Amos does not compute a modification index. First, Amos does not compute a modification index for a nonexistent path which, if introduced, would convert an exogenous variable into an endogenous variable. Second, Amos does not compute a modification index for a nonexistent path that, if introduced, would create an indirect path from a variable to itself where none already exists. In particular, Amos does not compute a modification index for a nonexistent path that, if introduced, would convert a recursive model to a nonrecursive one.

Each time Amos displays a modification index for a parameter, it also displays an estimate of the amount by which the parameter would change from its current, constrained value if the constraints on it were removed.

Specifying a small number with the **$mods** command can produce a large number of modification indices.

Example of output

Here are the modification indices for Model A of Example 6.

```
Modification Indices
....................


Covariances:                                  M.I.      Par Change
                                           .........   ..........
              eps2 <·············> delta1     5.876      -0.423
              eps2 <·············> eps4      26.496       0.825
              eps2 <·············> eps3      32.027      -0.988
              eps1 <·············> delta1     4.619       0.422
              eps1 <·············> eps4      35.357      -1.070
              eps1 <·············> eps3      40.911       1.255


Variances:                                    M.I.      Par Change
                                           .........   ..........


Regression Weights:                           M.I.      Par Change
                                           .........   ..........
           powles71 <······ powles67          5.445       0.056
           powles71 <······ anomia67          9.010      -0.065
           anomia71 <······ powles67          6.763      -0.069
           anomia71 <······ anomia67         10.359       0.076
           powles67 <······ powles71          5.599       0.053
           powles67 <······ anomia71          7.273      -0.054
           anomia67 <······ powles71          7.700      -0.070
           anomia67 <······ anomia71          9.069       0.068
```

The largest modification index is 40.911, indicating that the chi-square statistic will drop by at least 40.911 if the covariance between **eps1** and **eps3** is allowed to depart from zero (the value at which it is fixed in Model A). The number 1.255 in the `Par Change` column indicates that the covariance will increase by about 1.255 if it is allowed to take on any value. Of course if the covariance (now zero) increases by 1.255 it will then be equal to 1.255. Actually, in Model B, where the covariance between **eps1** and **eps3** is unconstrained, its estimate is 1.887. Kaplan (1989) and Saris, Satorra and Sörbom (1987) discuss the use of estimated parameter changes in exploratory analyses.

$mstructure ⌨   (**Amos Text** only)

Description

$mstructure specifies that means and intercepts are to be treated as explicit model parameters, and allows you to place constraints on means and intercepts.

$mstructure is followed by a list of exogenous variables, with each variable name on a separate line. Variables that are named following the $mstructure command are permitted to have nonzero means, and Amos will estimate their means. Exogenous variables that are not mentioned following the $mstructure command are assumed to have zero means.

Syntax

$mstructure
<variable name> [(<parameter label>)]
<variable name> [(<parameter label>)]
<variable name> [(<parameter label>)]
...

Example

In this example, the mean of **var1** is fixed at 4. The mean of **var2** is not constrained in any way. **var3** and **var4** are required to have the same mean because they are both labeled '**abc**'. Initial values are given for the means of **var5**, **var6**, and **var7** (*see*, **Providing initial values** on page 265). The mean of **var5** is given an initial value of 20. The means of **var6** and **var7** are required to be equal and given an initial value of 10. Any exogenous variables in the model besides **var1**, **var2**, **var3**, **var4**, **var5**, **var6** and **var7** have their means fixed at zero.

```
$mstructure
    var1 (4)
    var2
    var3 (abc)
    var4 (abc)
    var5 (20?)
    var6 (xyz : 10)
    var7 (xyz : 10)
```

Default

If $mstructure is not present, and at the same time no intercepts are specified using $structure, then all means and intercepts are unconstrained. No means or intercepts are estimated.

Remarks

It is possible to name an endogenous variable following the $mstructure command. Doing so has the effect of adding an intercept to the regression equation for that variable. Amos then estimates that intercept. (A better method for specifying an intercept, however, is to include it in a linear equation following the $structure command.)

Related commands

$structure on page 260

$nextgroup ▤ (**Amos Text** only)

Description

When analyzing data from several independent samples, **$nextgroup** is used to separate the portions of the input file that refer to distinct samples. All of the data input commands and model specification commands that occur before the first **$nextgroup** command refer to a single sample. All of the data input commands and model specification commands that occur between two consecutive **$nextgroup** commands refer to a single sample. All of the data input commands and model specification commands that occur after the last **$nextgroup** command refer to a single sample.

Syntax

$nextgroup

Example

```
$next group
```

Default

By default, there is only one group.

Related commands

$groupname on page 216

$noallimpliedmoments - $nouseunbiased

$noallimpliedmoments	$nobootadf
$nobootgls	$nobootml
$nobootnormal	$nobootsls
$nobootuls	$nobootverify
$nocompress	$noconfidencebc
$noconfidencepc	$nocorest
$nocovest	$nocrdiff
$noecho	$noemulisrel6
$nofactorscores	$noimpliedmoments
$nononpositive	$nonormalitycheck
$nooutput	$noresidualmoments
$nosamplemoments	$nosmc
$nospecran	$nostandardized
$notechnical	$nototaleffects
$nounbiased	$nounidentified
$nouseunbiased	

Description

Each of these commands cancels the effect of some other command. For example, **$noallimpliedmoments** cancels any previous **$allimpliedmoments** commands. It also works the other way around: **$allimpliedmoments** cancels any previous **$noallimpliedmoments** commands.

Example

In this example, standardized estimates and sample moments will be reported, but squared multiple correlations will not:

```
$smc
$standardized
$samplemoments
$nosmc
```

$nonpositive

Description	**$nonpositive** command specifies that, for the case of maximum likelihood estimation, Amos should attempt to obtain estimates whether or not the sample covariance matrices are positive definite.
Syntax	**$nonpositive**
Example	`$nonpositive`
Default	Amos reports an error if you attempt a maximum likelihood analysis when a sample covariance matrix fails to be positive definite.
Remarks	If you use **$nonpositive**, Amos will not try to test the hypothesis that your model is correct against the usual alternative that the population moments are unconstrained.
	Wothke (1993) discusses the problem of covariance matrices that are not positive definite.
Related commands	**$nononpositive** on page 236
	$unidentified on page 271

$normalitycheck

Description

$normalitycheck causes Amos to report some statistics on the observed variables to help you judge the extent of any departure from multivariate normality.

Syntax

$normalitycheck

Example

$normalitycheck

Default

No test of normality is performed.

Related commands

$nonormalitycheck on page 236

Demonstration of normality assessment

The Holzinger-Swineford data in the file **grnt_fem.amd** will be used as an example. Using **$normalitycheck** in any input file that includes **grnt_fem.amd** produces the following output.

```
Assessment of normality

                       min      max      skew     c.r.   kurtosis     c.r.
                    -------- -------- -------- -------- --------  --------
          WORDMEAN   2.000   41.000    0.575    2.004   -0.212   -0.370
          SENTENCE   4.000   28.000   -0.836   -2.915    0.537    0.936
         PARAGRAPH   2.000   19.000    0.374    1.305   -0.239   -0.416
          LOZENGES   3.000   36.000    0.833    2.906    0.127    0.221
             CUBES   9.000   37.000   -0.131   -0.457    1.439    2.510
           VISPERC  11.000   45.000   -0.406   -1.418   -0.281   -0.490
        Multivariate                                     3.102    1.353
```

The first row of the table shows that the lowest **wordmean** score was 2 and the highest was 41. **wordmean** had a *sample skewness* of

$$\frac{\sum_{i=1}^{N} (x_i - \bar{x})^3}{N\hat{s}^3} = .575,$$

where $\hat{s}^2$ is the unbiased variance estimate $\hat{s}^2 = \sum (x_i - \bar{x})^2 / (N-1)$. Assuming normality, skewness has a mean of zero and a standard error of $\sqrt{6/N} = .287$. The critical ratio 2.004 in the **c.r.** column is the sample skewness divided by its standard error.

wordmean has a *sample kurtosis* of

$$\frac{\sum_{i=1}^{N}(x_i - \bar{x})^4}{N\hat{s}^4} - 3 = -.212 .$$

Assuming normality, kurtosis has a mean of zero and a standard error of $\sqrt{24/N} = .573$. The critical ratio, $-.370$, is the sample kurtosis divided by its standard error.

The table has a separate row for each observed variable. A final row, labeled 'multivariate', contains Mardia's (1970, 1974) coefficient of *multivariate kurtosis*

$$\frac{1}{N}\sum_{i=1}^{N}\left[(\mathbf{x}_i - \bar{\mathbf{x}})'\hat{\mathbf{S}}^{-1}(\mathbf{x}_i - \bar{\mathbf{x}})\right]^2 - \frac{p(p+2)(N-1)}{N+1} = 3.102 ,$$

where $\mathbf{x}_i$ is the *i*-th observation on the p observed variables, $\bar{\mathbf{x}}$ is the vector of their means and $\hat{\mathbf{S}}^{-1}$ is the unbiased estimate of their population covariance matrix. Assuming normality, this coefficient has a mean of zero and a standard error of $\sqrt{8p(p+2)/N} = 2.294$. The critical ratio obtained by dividing the sample coefficient by its standard error is 1.353, as shown in the **c.r.** column.

Assuming normality in very large samples, each of the critical values shown in the table above is an observation on a standard normally distributed random variable. Even with a very large sample, however, the table is of limited use. All it does is to quantify the departure from normality in the sample and provide a rough test of whether the departure is statistically significant. Unfortunately, this is not enough. In order to make use of this information you also need to know how robust your chosen estimation method is against the departure from normality that you have discovered. A departure from normality that is big enough to be significant could still be small enough to be harmless.

The following table, also produced by **$normalitycheck** from the `grnt_fem.amd` data, provides additional evidence bearing on the question of normality.

```
Observations farthest from the centroid (Mahalanobis distance)

   Observation    Mahalanobis
     number        d-squared          p1              p2
   ------------   -----------    ------------    ------------
      42            18.747          0.005           0.286
      20            17.201          0.009           0.130
       3            13.264          0.039           0.546
      35            12.954          0.044           0.397
      28            12.730          0.048           0.266
```

Only the first five rows of the table are shown here. Specifically, the table focuses on the occurrence of outliers, individual observations that differ markedly from the general run of observations. The table lists the observations that are furthest from the centroid of all observations, using as the distance measure for the *i*-th observation the squared Mahalanobis distance, $d_i^2 = (\mathbf{x}_i - \bar{\mathbf{x}})'\hat{\mathbf{S}}^{-1}(\mathbf{x}_i - \bar{\mathbf{x}})$. Mardia's coefficient of multivariate kurtosis can be written $\sum d_i^4/N - p(p+2)(N-1)/(N+1)$. The first row of the table shows that observation number 42 is furthest from the centroid with $d_{42}^2 = 18.747$. The **p1** column shows that, assuming normality, the probability of d_{42}^2 (or any individual d_i^2) exceeding 18.747 is .005. The **p2** column shows, still assuming normality, that the probability is .268 that the largest d_i^2 would exceed 18.747. The second row of the table shows that: Observation number 20 is the second furthest observation from the centroid with $d_{20}^2 = 17.201$. The probability of any arbitrary d_i^2 exceeding 17.201 is .009. The probability of the second largest d_i^2 exceeding 17.201 is .130. Small numbers in the **p1** column are to be expected. Small numbers in the **p2** column, on the other hand, indicate observations that are improbably far from the centroid under the hypothesis of normality. For the **grnt_fem.amd** data, none of the probabilities in the **p2** column is very small, so there is no evidence that any of the five most unusual observations should be treated as outliers under the assumption of normality. See Bollen (1987) for a discussion of the importance of checking for outliers.

$observed

Description **$observed** is used to list the observed variables in the model.

Syntax
$observed
<variable name 1>
<variable name 2>
<variable name 3>
...

Example In this example it is specified that there are exactly three observed variables, called **var1**, **var2** and **var3**, in the model.

```
$observed
    var1
    var2
    var3
```

Remarks **$observed** is optional. When you use **$observed** to supply a list of observed variable names, Amos uses them for error checking.

Related commands **$ovariablecount** on page 243
$unobserved on page 272
$uvariablecount on page 274
$variablecount on page 275

$output (Amos Text only)

Description

$output causes Amos to write selected output in a text format that is suitable for reading by other programs. The new output file is given the same name as the input file, but with the characters `.amp` appended instead of `.ami`.

Syntax

$output

Example

An input file called `charlie.ami` that contains the following lines will cause factor score weights, total effects and sample moments to be written to a file called `charlie.amp`.

```
$factor scores
$total effects
$samplemom
$output
```

The same results will also appear in the usual text output file (`charlie.amo`) formatted in the usual way.

Default

No `.amp` file is created.

Remarks

Any output that is written to the usual output file in the form of a matrix is also written to the `.amp` file. There is no way to write different portions of the output to different files.

Related commands

$nooutput on page 236

$ovariablecount

Description $ovariablecount specifies the number of observed variables in the model.

Syntax   **$ovariable count = <*positive integer*>**

Example   In this example, Amos will report an error if the number of observed variables in the model fails to be 9.

```
$ovariable count = 9
```

Default   **$ovariablecount** is optional. When it is not used, no error checking is done based on the number of observed variables.

Remarks   If **$ovariablecount** is used, Amos checks the specified value for consistency with the remainder of the input file. If a discrepancy is found, Amos reports the discrepancy and quits. Spelling or typing errors in the input file are frequently detected by this check, since two variant spellings of a variable name will be treated as references to two distinct variables.

In analyzing data from several groups, **$ovariablecount** may be used once per group.

Related commands   **$observed** on page 241
$unobserved on page 272
$uvariablecount on page 274
$variablecount on page 275

$pagelength

Description	**$pagelength** specifies the number of lines per page.
Syntax	**$page length = <*integer greater than 57*>**
Example	In this example, the number of lines per page is set to 88. `$page length = 88`
Default	66 lines per page
Remarks	When **$compress** is used to suppress page ejects, **$pagelength** has no effect.
Related commands	**$compress** on page 198 **$linelength** on page 222

$permute

Description	**$permute** requests a permutation test (Arbuckle, 1994b) of the specified model. Supplying a positive integer with **$permute** results in a randomized permutation test. Supplying a value of zero with **$permute** results in a permutation test based on all permutations of the observed variables.
Syntax	**$permute=<nonnegative integer>**

Example	The following example requests a randomized permutation test based on 100 random permutations of the observed variables.
	`$permute = 100`
	The following example requests a permutation test based on all permutations of the observed variables.
	`$permute = 0`

Default	No permutation test is performed.
Remarks	Bootstrapping cannot be performed simultaneously with the permutation test. That is, you can't use both **$permute** and **$bootstrap**.
Related commands	**$permutedetail** on page 248

Demonstration of the permutation test

To demonstrate the use of **$permute**, Jöreskog and Sörbom's Model D was fitted to the Wheaton data using **$permute=0** together with **$iterations=100**. Here is a portion of the resulting output.

```
Matrix permutations test
-------------------------

Of 719 permutations:

    15 permutations improved the model fit or left it unchanged
    87 permutations resulted in a model that could not be fitted
   617 permutations resulted in a higher discrepancy function

Of the remaining permutations:

     0 resulted in inadmissible estimates and unstable systems
     0 resulted in inadmissible estimates
     0 resulted in unstable systems

p = 16/720 = 0.022
```

With six observed variables, there are 720 possible permutations—719, if you don't count the permutation that leaves each observed variable in its original position. Of the 719 non-identity permutations, 15 made the discrepancy function smaller or left it unchanged. 617 of the permutations made the discrepancy function larger. 87 permutations resulted in a model for which Amos could not find a solution. As noted above, failures are to be expected in fitting a series of generally bad models. The question is, how do you classify the models for which no solution was found? Can it be assumed that each one of those models is worse than the original model? In other words, can you assume that, whenever Amos fails, it's the model's fault rather than Amos's?

Experience shows that Amos's failures to find solutions are *almost* always due to bad models (or samples that are too small). But not always. Therefore, there may be an objection to lumping the 87 permutations that produced an unfittable model together with the 617 permutations that produced a worse fitting model, on the grounds that doing so could result in an overcount of the number of permutations that make the model worse.

With these considerations in mind, Amos follows the convention that unfittable models are "worse than" the model being evaluated. Then out of 720 permutations (including the identity permutation), there are 16 permutations that produce a model that fits as well as or better than the original model. (The original model itself is one of those 16.). In other words, if you picked a model at random out of those generated by permuting the observed variables, there is a probability of 16/720 = .022 of getting a model as good as the one that Jöreskog and Sörbom proposed.

It is possible for an Amos solution to be inadmissible or to consist of an unstable linear system, although neither of these problems arose in the present example. There needs to be a policy on permutations that produce a model with a lower discrepancy function than was obtained for the original model, but for which an inadmissible solution or an unstable system occurs. Amos adheres to the following policy. First of all, if the original model results in an inadmissible solution, Amos disregards the admissibility status of estimates for models that are generated by permutations. Also, if the original model results in an unstable system, Amos ignores any instability that occurs in linear systems that result from permutations. If the original model yields an admissible solution with a stable system of linear equations, Amos reports the number of permutations that lower the discrepancy function while producing an inadmissible solution or an unstable system, and follows the convention that such permutations are harmful (i.e., that they make a model worse).

The frequency of inadmissible solutions and unstable systems is summarized as follows for the present example.

```
Of the remaining permutations:
    0 resulted in inadmissible estimates and unstable systems
    0 resulted in inadmissible estimates
    0 resulted in unstable systems
```

Of the 15 permutations that resulted in a discrepancy function that was reported to be as good as or better than that of the original model, all were in fact exactly as good—none were better. Examination of the **$permutedetail** output reveals that these 15 models are equivalent to the original model in the sense of Stelzl (1986), Lee and Hershberger (1990) and MacCallum, et al. (1993).

In principal, it would be possible to reduce the computational requirements of the permutation test by fitting one representative model from each set of equivalent models. Amos does not do this, however. More importantly, the fact that the "permuted" models come in clusters of equivalent models has a bearing on the interpretation of the permutation test. In the current example, for instance, the proportion of permuted models that fit as well as or better than the original model cannot take on just any of the values 1/720, 2/720, 3/720,.... Instead, the proportion is restricted to the values 16/720, 32/720, 48/720,.... The number of possible p values is still 720/16 = 45, and so it remains an interesting question what the value of p is. However, a serious problem arises when the number of permutations that leave the fit of the model invariant is very large, so that the number of distinct discrepancy function values that can occur is very small. To take an extreme case, consider the common factor model with one common factor, and no parameter constraints other than those required to make the model identified. No permutation of the observed variables will affect the fit of the model, and it will not be possible to apply the permutation test in a meaningful way.

$permutedetail

Description

$permutedetail gives detailed information about the solution obtained for each permutation. First the permutation itself is reported. (That is, the new location of each observed variable in the model is shown after the permutation is carried out.) Then, if a solution is found, the value of the discrepancy function is reported along with a notation of whether the solution was admissible and whether the resulting linear system was stable.

Syntax

$permutedetail

Example

```
$permutedetail
```

Default

Detailed information about each permutation is not reported.

Related commands

$permute on page 245

$rawdata

Description	This command indicates that succeeding lines contain an optional format specification followed by raw data.
Syntax	**$rawdata** **<optional format>** (See page 178) **<raw data>**

Example	The following example illustrates the use of **$rawdata** to read four observations on two variables.
	
	``
	$raw data
	(2F7.2)
	    3.26 20.17
	    3.41 21.15
	    2.94 31.42
	    3.57 24.33
	``

Default	There is no default. Exactly one of the following commands is required: **$correlations**, **$covariances**, **$rawdata**.
Remarks	If no format statement is supplied, Amos reads the raw data in free format, with numbers delimited by spaces, tab characters and/or line feed characters.
Related commands	**$correlations** on page 204 **$covariances** on page 205 **$means** on page 224 **$standarddeviations** on page 258

$residualmoments

Description

$residualmoments reports, for each group, the difference between the sample covariance matrix (displayed by **$samplemoments**) and the implied covariance matrix (displayed by **$impliedmoments**). If means are treated as explicit model parameters, the differences between sample means and implied means will also be reported.

Syntax

$residualmoments

Example

```
$residualmoments
```

Default

Residual moments are not reported

Related commands

$allimpliedmoments on page 181
$impliedmoments on page 217
$noresidualmoments on page 236
$samplemoments on page 251

$samplemoments

Description	**$samplemoments** reports the sample covariance matrix for each group. If means are treated as explicit model parameters, sample means will also be reported.
Syntax	**$samplemoments**
Example	`$samplemoments`
Default	Sample moments are not reported
Remarks	If you use both **$standardized** and **$samplemoments**, the sample correlation matrix will be reported in addition to the sample covariance matrix.
Related commands	**$allimpliedmoments** on page 181 **$impliedmoments** on page 217 **$nosamplemoments** on page 236 **$residualmoments** on page 250 **$unbiased** on page 270 **$useunbiased** on page 273

$samplesize

Description   **$samplesize** is used to specify the number of observations in an individual group.

Syntax   **$sample size = <*positive integer*>**

Example   In this example, the sample size is specified to be 420.

```
$sample size = 420
```

Default   There is no default. **$samplesize** must be used exactly once per group.

Rules of thumb regarding sample size

"Definitive recommendations are not available.... An oversimplified guideline that might serve as a rule of thumb regarding the trustworthiness of solutions and parameter estimates is the following. The ratio of sample size to number of free parameters may be able to go as low as 5:1 under normal and elliptical theory, especially when there are many indicators of latent variables and the associated factor loadings are large. Although there is even less experience on which to base a recommendation, a ratio of at least 10:1 may be more appropriate for arbitrary distributions. These ratios need to be larger to obtain trustworthy z-tests on the significance of parameters, and still larger to yield correct model evaluation chi-square probabilities." (Bentler and Chou, 1987, *pp.* 90–91)

"...we suggest that the estimation of structural equation models by maximum likelihood methods be used only when sample sizes are at least 200. Studies based on samples smaller than 100 may well lead to false inferences, and the models then have a high probability of encountering problems of convergence and improper solutions." (Boomsma, 1987, *p.* 184)

$seed

Description

$seed provides a seed for the random number generator used for bootstrapping and for the permutation test. Using Amos twice with the same seed guarantees getting the same sequence of random numbers both times.

Syntax

$seed = <*integer between 1 and 29999*>

Example

In this example, the seed for the random number generator is initialized to 25.

```
$seed = 25
```

Default

$seed = 1

Related commands

$bootadf on page 182
$bootbs on page 183
$bootgls on page 187
$bootml on page 188
$bootsls on page 190
$bootstrap on page 191
$bootuls on page 194
$bootverify on page 195
$permute on page 245

$significant figures

Description

$significant figures specifies the number of significant figures to be used in displayed matrices. The number of significant figures shown is subject to the limits specified by **$maxdecimalplaces** and **$mindecimalplaces**.

Syntax

$significant figures = *<positive integer>*

Example

In this example, no fewer than five and no more than nine digits will be displayed to the right of the decimal point. Subject to this constraint, results will be displayed with four significant figures.

```
$min decimal places = 5
$max decimal places = 9
$significant figures = 4
```

Default

Matrices are displayed with three significant figures.

Related commands

$maxdecimalplaces on page 223
$mindecimalplaces on page 225

$sls

Description

$sls requests the 'scale free' least squares solution obtained by minimizing (D1) together with (D5) in Appendix B.

Syntax

$sls

Example

```
$sls
```

Default

The maximum likelihood criterion (**$ml**) is used.

Related commands

$adf on page 180
$bootsls on page 190
$gls on page 215
$ml on page 227
$uls on page 269

$smc

Description	**$smc** displays the squared multiple correlation between each endogenous variable and the variables (other than residual variables) that directly affect it.
Syntax	**$smc**
Example	$smc
Default	Squared multiple correlations are not reported.
Related commands	**$nosmc** on page 236

$specran

Description	**$specran** instructs Amos to use a special random number generator that is common to all versions of Amos (since the beginning of time). The random number generator that **$specran** invokes is not very good. It should not be used except for the purpose of replicating an example in which **$specran** was used.
Syntax	**$specran**
Example	`$specran`
Default	The random number generator of Wichman and Hill (1982) is used.
Related commands	**$nospecran** on page 236

$standarddeviations

Description

This command indicates that succeeding lines contain an optional format specification and then the sample standard deviations.

Syntax

$standard deviations
<optional format> (See page 178)
<sample standard deviations>

Example

```
$standard deviations
(2F2.2)
 4 5
```

Default

There is no default. **$standarddeviations** must be used if **$correlations** is used.

Remarks

By default, Amos assumes that the sample standard deviations supplied with **$standarddeviations** were computed using the formula,

$$\sqrt{\frac{\sum_{i=1}^{N}\left(x_i - \bar{x}\right)^2}{N}} \ .$$

If your sample standard deviations were computed using the formula,

$$\sqrt{\frac{\sum_{i=1}^{N}\left(x_i - \bar{x}\right)^2}{N-1}} \ ,$$

make sure that you use the command **$unbiased**.

Related commands

$correlations on page 204
$covariances on page 205
$means on page 224
$rawdata on page 249
$unbiased on page 270

$standardized

$standardized requests the display of correlations among exogenous variables, and of standardized regression weights (beta weights). When used with **$samplemoments**, it results in the display of sample correlations in addition to sample covariances. When used with **$impliedmoments** or **$allimpliedmoments**, it results in the display of implied correlations in addition to implied covariances.

Syntax   **$standardized**

Example $standardized

Default   Correlations and standardized estimates are not reported.

Related commands   **$nostandardized** on page 236

$structure  (**Amos Text** only)

Description

$structure is used to specify a model. The **$structure** command is followed by one or more lines that

- Name the variables in the model.
- Specify the linear dependencies among the variables.
- Place equality constraints on the parameters of the model (i.e., the variances and covariances of the exogenous variables, and the regression weights).

You may, optionally, include intercept terms in the linear dependencies among the variables, and place constraints on the intercepts.

Syntax

$structure

<one or more lines>

Example

This example shows how to specify a model in which one variable (**variable1**) is a linear combination of two other variables (**variable2** and **error**). Amos estimates the weight applied to **variable2**. The weight applied to **error** is fixed at 1.

```
$structure
    variable1 = variable2 + (1) error
```

Here is an alternative way to specify the same model:

```
$structure
    variable1 <--- variable2
    variable1 <--- error (1)
```

Default

At least one of the commands, **$structure** and **$mstructure**, is required by Amos Text. If **$structure** is not present, the variables named following the **$mstructure** command are exogenous with no constraints on their variances or covariances.

Remarks

Use **$mstructure** to constrain the means of the exogenous variables.

Related commands

$mstructure on page 234

Extended explanation of $structure

Each line that occurs between the **$structure** command and the next Amos command refers to one or more of the following:

- a regression (path) weight
- a regression equation
- the covariance between two exogenous variables
- the variance of a single exogenous variable

The **$structure** command may be used only once for each group. However, it may be followed by multiple lines defining any number of regression weights, regression equations, covariances and variances.

Regression (path) weights:

The **$structure** command provides two methods for specifying linear relationships among variables. The first method to be described is intended for persons who find it helpful to visualize linear relationships in terms of path diagrams. This method requires a separate line for each single-headed arrow in a path diagram.

A single-headed arrow in the path diagram may be indicated by the symbol '**<**' or the symbol '**>**', as illustrated in the following two lines:

```
variable1 < variable2
variable2 > variable1
```

These two lines have the same effect. Either line alone declares that **variable1** depends directly on **variable2**. That is, in the path diagram there is an arrow pointing from **variable2** to **variable1**. Amos estimates the corresponding regression weight.

Amos ignores dashes in **$structure** lines, so that the previous example could have been written in any of the following equivalent ways:

```
variable1<variable2
variable1 <--- variable2
variable1  <---------  variable2
variable2  --------->  variable1
```

By default, Amos assumes that the regression weights are unconstrained. However, you can set the value of any regression weight to a constant, and you can require any number of regression weights to be equal to each other. The following example shows how to impose such constraints:

```
$structure
    . . .
    variable1 <--- variable2 (red)
    variable1 <--- variable3 (red)
    variable1 <--- variable4 (1)
    variable1 <--- variable5
    variable1 <--- variable6 (blue)
    variable1 <--- variable7 (blue)
    variable1 <--- variable8 (blue)
    . . .
```

In this example, the first two regression weights are required to be equal because they are both labeled **red**. Similarly, the last three regression weights are required to be equal because they are both labeled **blue**. The regression weight for the regression of **variable1** on **variable4** is fixed at 1. (Amos will not attempt to estimate this regression weight.) The regression weight for predicting **variable1** from **variable5** is not constrained.

Regression equations

Linear relationships may also be described in the form of linear equations as in the following line, which would appear after the **$structure** command.

```
variable1 = () variable2 + () variable3 + () variable4
```

Here, **variable1** is specified to be a linear function of **variable2**, **variable3** and **variable4**. The empty parentheses represent unknown regression weights that Amos will estimate. Actually, the empty parentheses can be left out, as in the following line, which is equivalent to the previous one.

```
variable1 = variable2 + variable3 + variable4
```

Amos takes it for granted that it is supposed to estimate a regression weight for each variable on the right hand side of this equation. The parentheses sometimes contribute to readability, and, as will be shown below, provide the means for placing constraints on regression weights.

In using this method for specifying linear relationships, it is possible to specify one or more intercepts in a regression equation. For example:

```
$structure
    . . .
    var1 = () var2 + ()
    var3 = () var4 + () + ()
    . . .
```

Here, **var1** is specified to be a multiple of **var2**, except for an intercept term. **var3** is specified to be a multiple of **var4**, except for two intercept terms. The five sets of empty parentheses represent five parameters that Amos is supposed to estimate—two regression weights and three intercepts. Again, the empty parentheses can be left out if desired.

Actually the two intercepts in the second line of the previous example will not be identified unless some constraints are placed on them. Constraints may be placed on regression weights and intercepts as in the following example:

```
$structure
    . . .
    var1 = (alpha) var2 + (charlie)
    var3 = (alpha) var4 + (charlie) + (50)
    . . .
```

Here, Amos is required to estimate two parameters. The two regression weights labeled **alpha** are required to be equal. Their common value constitutes one parameter. The two intercepts labeled **charlie** are required to be equal. Their common value constitutes the second parameter. The remaining intercept is fixed at 50, so it doesn't have to be estimated.

A long equation can be continued over several lines in the following way:

```
$structure
    . . .
    crit1 = (weight1) var1 + (weight2) var2
    crit1 = (weight3) var3
    . . .
```

which is equivalent to

```
$structure
    . . .
    crit1 = (weight1) var1 + (weight2) var2 + (weight3) var3
    . . .
```

Covariances

With one exception, Amos Text assumes that the *exogenous variables in a model are correlated*, and it estimates the covariance between every pair of exogenous variables. The exception to this default assumption concerns unique variables—exogenous variables that are unobserved and have a direct effect on only one variable. Amos assumes that *unique variables are uncorrelated* with each other, and with every other exogenous variable in the model.

You may explicitly permit two variables to be correlated by using the string, **<>**, as illustrated in the following example:

```
    variable2 <> variable3
```

where Amos is told that **variable2** and **variable3** may be correlated, and is asked to estimate their covariance.

Amos ignores dashes in **$structure** lines, so that the previous example could have been written in any of the following equivalent ways:

```
variable2<>variable3
variable2 <---> variable3
variable2  <----------->  variable3
```

You can place constraints on the covariances of exogenous variables as in the following example:

```
$structure
    . . .
    variable1 <---> variable2 (alpha)
    variable2 <---> variable3 (alpha)
    variable3 <---> variable4 (alpha)
    variable1 <---> variable3 (beta)
    variable2 <---> variable4 (beta)
    variable1 <---> variable2 (0)
    . . .
```

In this example, the first three covariances listed are required to be equal because they are all labeled `alpha`. Similarly, the two covariances labeled `beta` are required to be equal to each other. **variable1** and **variable2** are declared to be uncorrelated, so that Amos will not attempt to estimate their covariance. (It is also possible to fix a covariance to a nonzero value, although reasons for doing so are rare.)

Variances

By default, Amos assumes that there are no constraints on the variances of the exogenous variables in the model. However, you can constrain the variances, as in the following example:

```
$structure
    . . .
    variable1 (gamma)
    variable2 (gamma)
    variable3 (gamma)
    variable4 (1)
    variable5 (2)
    variable6 (delta)
    variable7 (delta)
    . . .
```

In this example, the variance of **variable4** is fixed at 1, and the variance of **variable5** is fixed at 2. Amos does not attempt to estimate these fixed parameters. **variable1**, **variable2** and **variable3** are required to have the same variance because they are all labeled `gamma`. Similarly, **variable6** and **variable7** are required to have the same variance because they are both labeled `delta`.

Providing initial values

To provide an initial value for a parameter, type the initial value followed by question mark. In the following example the variances of **variable4** and **variable5** are given initial values of 15 and 16:

```
$structure
    . . .
    variable1 (gamma)
    variable2 (gamma)
    variable3 (gamma)
    variable4 (15?)
    variable5 (16?)
    variable6 (delta)
    variable7 (delta)
    . . .
```

To give a parameter a non-numeric label as well as an initial value, type the non-numeric label, followed by a colon, followed by the initial value. In the following example the variances of **variable1**, **variable2** and **variable3** are constrained to be equal and given an initial value of 8, while the variances of **variable6** and **variable7** are constrained to be equal and given an initial value of 9:

```
$structure
    . . .
    variable1 (gamma : 8)
    variable2 (gamma : 8)
    variable3 (gamma : 8)
    variable4 (1)
    variable5 (2)
    variable6 (delta : 9)
    variable7 (delta : 9)
    . . .
```

$technical

Description	The **$technical** command displays information about the progress of minimization of the discrepancy function.
Syntax	**$technical**
Example	`$technical`
Default	Technical output is reported. (The intended use of **$technical** is to override the effect of any prior use of **$notechnical**.
Related commands	**$crit1** on page 208 **$crit2** on page 209 **$fisher** on page 214 **$iterations** on page 221 **$notechnical** on page 236 **$time** on page 267

$time

Description	This command places a time limit (in seconds) on Amos. If the time limit is reached, Amos will display its current estimates of the parameters, even if the convergence criteria (see **$crit1** and **$crit2**) have not been met.
Syntax	**$time=<*positive number*>**
Example	In this example, Amos will quit after 150 seconds whether it has reached a local minimum or not.
	`$time=150`
Default	There is no time limit.
Remarks	It takes some time to display a solution, and you should allow for this by specifying a value with the **$time** command that is smaller than any time limit placed on your job by the operating system.
	Permitted values for the time limit range from one to 2,147,483 seconds.
Related commands	**$crit1** on page 208
	$crit2 on page 209
	$fisher on page 214
	$iterations on page 221
	$technical on page 266

$totaleffects

Description	**$totaleffects** displays total effects. See Fox (1980) for a discussion of total effects.
Syntax	**$total effects**
Example	`$total effects`
Default	Total effects are not reported.
Remarks	Amos does not report indirect effects.
Related commands	**$nototaleffects** on page 236

$uls

Description

$uls requests an unweighted least squares solution, obtained by minimizing (D1) together with (D6) in Appendix B.

Syntax

$uls

Example

```
$uls
```

Default

The maximum likelihood criterion (**$ml**) is used.

Related commands

$adf on page 180
$bootuls on page 194
$gls on page 215
$ml on page 227
$sls on page 255

$unbiased

Description

When the **$unbiased** command appears in your input file, Amos assumes that the sample covariances are unbiased estimates of the corresponding population covariances, and that the squares of the sample standard deviations are unbiased estimates of the corresponding population variances.

Syntax

$unbiased

Example

```
$unbiased
```

Default

Covariances supplied with the **$covariances** command are assumed to be biased estimates of the corresponding population covariances. Similarly, the squares of standard deviations supplied with the **$standarddeviations** command are assumed to be biased estimates of the corresponding population variances.

Remarks

The **$unbiased** and **$useunbiased** commands have different effects. **$unbiased** describes the sample covariances supplied with **$covariances** and the sample standard deviations supplied with **$standarddeviations**. **$useunbiased** tells Amos to *fit the model* to the unbiased form of the sample covariance matrix ($S^{(g)}$ in Appendices A, B).

In an analysis of data from more than one group, **$unbiased** affects all groups.

In an analysis of raw data (supplied with **$rawdata**) **$unbiased** has no effect.

Amos recognizes the alternate spelling, **$unbiassed**.

Related commands

$nounbiased on page 236
$nouseunbiased on page 236
$useunbiased on page 273

$unidentified

Description	**$unidentified** tells Amos to try to estimate the parameters of a model even if the model is not identified.
Syntax	**$unidentified**
Example	`$unidentified`
Default	When Amos finds evidence that a model is not identified, it displays an error message, and quits.
Remarks	Attempting to fit an unidentified model is generally a bad idea for the following reasons: It uses more memory, and usually takes more time. It prevents Amos from using one of its most important tests for a correct solution, namely, that the matrix of second derivatives be positive definite. For hypothesis testing purposes, it requires Amos to make a correction to degrees of freedom based on the number of additional parameter constraints needed to achieve identifiability. The difficulty of numerically recognizing and diagnosing nonidentifiability is discussed in Appendix D.
Related commands	**$nounidentified** on page 236

$unobserved (Amos Text only)

Description $unobserved is used to list the unobserved variables in the model.

Syntax   **$unobserved**
<variable name 1>
<variable name 2>
<variable name 3>
...

Example   In this example there are three unobserved variables, called **uvar1**, **uvar2** and **uvar3**, in the model.

```
$unobserved
    uvar1
    uvar2
    uvar3
```

Default   **$unobserved** is optional. When you use **$unobserved** to supply a list of unobserved variable names, Amos uses them for error checking. If **$unobserved** is not used, this error checking does not take place.

Related commands   **$observed** on page 241
$ovariablecount on page 243
$uvariablecount on page 274
$variablecount on page 275

$useunbiased

Description   **$useunbiased** instructs Amos to fit unbiased covariance matrices.

Syntax   **$useunbiased**

Example $useunbiased

Default   Amos fits the (biased) maximum likelihood estimate of the population covariance matrix.

Remarks   **$useunbiased** and **$unbiased** have different effects. **$unbiased** describes the sample covariances supplied with **$covariances** and the sample standard deviations supplied with **$standarddeviations**. **$useunbiased** tells Amos to *fit the model* to the unbiased form of the sample covariance matrix ($S^{(g)}$ in Appendices A, B).

Amos recognizes the alternate spelling, **$useunbiassed**.

Related commands   **$covariances** on page 205
$nouseunbiased on page 236
$standarddeviations on page 259
$unbiased on page 270

$uvariablecount

Description

$uvariablecount specifies the number of unobserved variables in the model.

Syntax

$uvariable count = <*positive integer*>

Example

In this example, Amos reports an error if the number of unobserved variables in the model fails to be 8.

```
$uvariable count = 8
```

Default

$uvariablecount is optional. When it is not used, no error checking is done based on the number of unobserved variables.

Remarks

If **$uvariablecount** is used, Amos checks the specified number of variables for consistency with the remainder of the input file. If a discrepancy is found, Amos reports the discrepancy and quits. Spelling or typing errors in the input file are frequently detected by this check, since two variant spellings of a variable name will be treated as references to two distinct variables.

In analyzing data from several groups, **$uvariablecount** may be used once per group.

Related commands

$observed on page 241
$ovariablecount on page 243
$unobserved on page 272
$variablecount on page 275

$variablecount

Description	**$variablecount** specifies the number of variables in the model.
Syntax	**$variable count = <*positive integer*>**
Example	In this example, Amos reports an error if the number of variables in the model fails to be 17. `$variable count = 17`
Default	**$variablecount** is optional. When it is not used, no error checking is done based on the number of variables.
Remarks	If **$variablecount** is used, Amos checks the specified number of variables for consistency with the remainder of the input file. If a discrepancy is found, Amos reports the discrepancy and quits. Spelling or typing errors in the input file are frequently detected by this check, since two variant spellings of a variable name will be treated as references to two distinct variables. In analyzing data from several groups, **$variablecount** may be used once per group.
Related commands	**$observed** on page 241 **$ovariablecount** on page 243 **$unobserved** on page 272 **$uvariablecount** on page 274

Text output

Amos's text output contains all of the information present in its graphical output, and more. The text output is written to a file with the extension .amo.

 In Amos Text, if you have created an input file called **alpha.ami**, the text output will be written to the file **alpha.amo**.

 In Amos Graphics, the path diagram will be saved in a file with the extension **.amw**. For example, if you choose the name **alpha** when asked for a file name, the path diagram will be saved with the file name **alpha.amw** and Amos's text output, produced when you press [icon], will be written to the file **alpha.amo**. You can view the text output file by pressing [icon].

On-line help for text output

When viewing Amos's text output under Microsoft Windows, you can get context-sensitive help by pressing the <F1> key or by selecting **Help** from the menu. The help system displays the part of the Users' Guide that describes the portion of the text output file that is currently visible.

Normal output messages

This section explains the major headings in Amos's output file. Wherever the string, **xxxxx**, appears, it represents a portion of an output message that changes from one analysis to another.

Assessment of normality

See **$normalitycheck** on page 238.

Asymptotically distribution-free estimates

This message is followed by parameter estimates. In the analysis of data from more than one group, the message appears once for each group. For each parameter, four numbers are displayed, arranged in columns labeled:

Estimate   The parameter estimate.

S.E.   Approximate standard error.

C.R.   *Critical ratio*. The critical ratio is the parameter estimate divided by an estimate of its standard error. If the appropriate distributional assumptions are met, this statistic has a standard normal distribution under the null hypothesis that the parameter has a population value of zero. For example, if an estimate has a critical ratio greater than two (in absolute value), the estimate is significantly different from zero at the .05 level. Even without distributional assumptions, the critical ratios have the following interpretation: For any unconstrained parameter, the *square* of its critical ratio is, approximately, the amount by which the chi-square statistic would *increase* if the analysis were repeated with that parameter fixed at zero.

Label   If you have assigned a symbolic name to a parameter (see the **$structure** and **$mstructure** commands, or), the name will appear in this column. You will need symbolic names for the parameters in order to interpret output generated by the **$covest**, **$corest** and **$crdiff** commands. If necessary, Amos will make up names for any parameters that you have not named. Amos's made-up names will appear in the `Label` column along with the ones you supply.

Bollen-Stine bootstrapped p = xxxxx

See **$bootbs** on page 183.

Bootstrap distributions

This section of the output displays several histograms along with means and standard deviations. Each histogram shows the distribution of B quantities calculated separately from each of B bootstrap samples. The following notation will be needed to explain this portion of the output. Let $\mathbf{a}_b$ contain the sample moments from the b-th bootstrap sample, let $\hat{\gamma}_b$ be the value of γ that minimizes $C(\alpha(\gamma), \mathbf{a}_b)$, and let $\hat{\alpha}_b = \alpha(\hat{\gamma}_b)$. Most of the histograms show the distribution (across bootstrap samples) of a discrepancy function—either $C(\hat{\alpha}_b, \mathbf{a})$ or $C(\hat{\alpha}_b, \mathbf{a}_b)$.

The histograms are labeled:

ADF discrepancy (implied vs pop)
Shows the distribution of the B quantities,
$$C_{ADF}(\hat{\alpha}_b, \mathbf{a}), \quad b = 1, \ldots, B.$$
You can obtain this distribution even if you do not use **$adf** to minimize C_{ADF}. The distribution is displayed when **$bootstrap** is used with either **$adf** or **$bootadf**.

ADF discrepancy (implied vs sample)
Shows the distribution of the B quantities,
$$C_{ADF}(\hat{\alpha}_b, \mathbf{a}_b), \quad b = 1, \ldots, B.$$
This distribution is displayed only when you use **$adf** (to minimize C_{ADF}) along with **$bootstrap**.

GLS discrepancy (implied vs pop)
Shows the distribution of the B quantities,
$$C_{GLS}(\hat{\alpha}_b, \mathbf{a}), \quad b = 1, \ldots, B.$$
You can obtain this distribution even if you do not use **$gls** to minimize C_{GLS}. The distribution is displayed when **$bootstrap** is used with either **$gls** or **$bootgls**.

GLS discrepancy (implied vs sample)
Shows the distribution of the B quantities,
$$C_{GLS}(\hat{\alpha}_b, \mathbf{a}_b), \quad b = 1, \ldots, B.$$
This distribution is displayed only when you use **$gls** (to minimize C_{GLS}) along with **$bootstrap**.

| ML discrepancy | Shows the distribution of the B quantities, |
| **(implied vs pop)** | $$C_{ML}(\hat{\alpha}_b, \mathbf{a}) = C_{KL}(\hat{\alpha}_b, \mathbf{a}) - C_{KL}(\mathbf{a}, \mathbf{a}), \quad b = 1, \dots, B.$$ |

You can obtain this distribution even if you do not use **$ml** to minimize C_{ML}. The distribution is displayed when **$bootstrap** is used with either **$ml** or **$bootml**.

| ML discrepancy | Shows the distribution of the B quantities, |
| **(implied vs sample)** | $$C_{ML}(\hat{\alpha}_b, \mathbf{a}_b), \quad b = 1, \dots, B.$$ |

This distribution is displayed only when you use maximum likelihood estimation (**$ml**) together with **$bootstrap**.

By way of illustration, here is the distribution of $C_{ML}(\hat{\alpha}_b, \mathbf{a}_b)$ for Model 2R of Example 20, where the minimum of the discrepancy function in fitting the model to the original sample was $C_{ML}(\hat{\alpha}, \mathbf{a}) = 3.638$.

```
                                  --------+-------------------
                           1.566 | *
                           3.935 | ********
                           6.305 | *********************
ML discrepancy             8.674 | *****************
(implied vs sample)       11.044 | ******************
                          13.413 | *************
                          15.783 | *********
       N = 1000           18.152 | *******
   Mean = 11.485          20.522 | *****
   S. e. = 0.177          22.891 | ***
                          25.261 | **
                          27.630 | *
                          30.000 | *
                          32.369 | *
                          34.739 | *
                                  --------+-------------------
```

The difference between $C_{ML}(\hat{\alpha}, \mathbf{a}) = 3.638$ and

$$\overline{C_{ML}(\hat{\alpha}_b, \mathbf{a}_b)} = \frac{1}{B} \sum_{b=1}^{B} C_{ML}(\hat{\alpha}_b, \mathbf{a}_b) = 11.485 \text{ is } 7.847,$$

which is in close agreement with a result of Steiger, Shapiro and Browne (1985) and McDonald (1989), according to which the difference should be $d = 8$.

SLS discrepancy **(implied vs pop)**	Shows the distribution of the B quantities, $$C_{SLS}(\hat{\alpha}_b, \mathbf{a}), \quad b = 1, \ldots, B.$$ You can obtain this distribution even if you do not use **$sls** to minimize C_{SLS}. The distribution is displayed when **$bootstrap** is used with either **$sls** or **$bootsls**.
SLS discrepancy **(implied vs sample)**	Shows the distribution of the B quantities, $$C_{SLS}(\hat{\alpha}_b, \mathbf{a}_b), \quad b = 1, \ldots, B.$$ This distribution is displayed only when you use **$sls** (to minimize C_{SLS}) along with **$bootstrap**.
ULS discrepancy **(implied vs pop)**	Shows the distribution of the B quantities, $$C_{ULS}(\hat{\alpha}_b, \mathbf{a}), \quad b = 1, \ldots, B.$$ You can obtain this distribution even if you do not use **$uls** to minimize C_{ULS}. The distribution is displayed when **$bootstrap** is used with either **$uls** or **$bootuls**.
ULS discrepancy **(implied vs sample)**	Shows the distribution of the B quantities, $$C_{ULS}(\hat{\alpha}_b, \mathbf{a}_b), \quad b = 1, \ldots, B.$$ This distribution is displayed only when you use **$uls** (to minimize C_{ULS}) along with **$bootstrap**.
K-L overoptimism **(unstabilized)**	Shows the distribution of the B quantities, $$R_b = C_{KL}(\hat{\alpha}_b, \mathbf{a}) - C_{KL}(\hat{\alpha}_b, \mathbf{a}_b), \quad b = 1, \ldots, B.$$

K-L overoptimism

(stabilized)

Shows the distribution of the B quantities,

$$R_b{}^* = R_b + \sum_{g=1}^{G} k^{(g)} \left[\mathrm{tr}\left(S_b^{(g)} S^{(g)^{-1}}\right) - p^{(g)}\left(\frac{N^{(g)}-1}{N^{(g)}}\right) \right]$$

$$+ \sum_{g=1}^{G} k^{(g)} \left[\left(\overline{x}_b^{(g)} - \overline{x}^{(g)}\right)' S^{(g)^{-1}} \left(\overline{x}_b^{(g)} - \overline{x}^{(g)}\right) - \frac{p^{(g)}}{N^{(g)}} \right],$$

$$b = 1, \ldots, B,$$

where $k^{(g)} = N^{(g)} - 1$ if the **\$emulisrel6** command has been used, or $k^{(g)} = n\dfrac{N^{(g)}}{N}$ if it has not.

Each bracketed term has zero expectation, so that $R_b{}^*$ and R_b have the same expectation. Experience has shown that $R_b{}^*$ is substantially less variable across bootstrap samples than is R_b.

Bootstrap standard errors

This message is followed by estimates of standard errors and of bias produced by the **\$bootstrap** command. For example, the following output shows bootstrap standard errors for the six squared multiple correlations in Model 2R of Example 20 . There were B=1000 bootstrap samples.

Squared Multiple Correlations:	S.E.	S.E. S.E.	Mean	Bias	S.E. Bias
WORDMEAN	0.064	0.001	0.685	-0.001	0.002
SENTENCE	0.057	0.001	0.680	0.000	0.002
PARAGRAPH	0.061	0.001	0.753	0.000	0.002
LOZENGES	0.131	0.003	0.528	-0.008	0.004
CUBES	0.077	0.002	0.289	0.005	0.002
VISPERC	0.133	0.003	0.416	0.017	0.004

The columns of the table are labeled:

S.E.   Bootstrap estimates of standard error. In the example above, the squared multiple correlation for **WORDMEAN** has a standard deviation of .064 across 1000 bootstrap samples.

S.E./S.E.   An approximate standard error for the standard error in the preceding column, given by $s/\sqrt{2B}$ where s is the standard error from the preceding column and B is the number of bootstrap samples. In the example above, the squared multiple correlation for **WORDMEAN** has a standard error that is estimated to be .064 with a standard error of approximately $.064/\sqrt{2000} = .001$.

Mean	The mean across bootstrap samples of the quantity being estimated. In the example the squared multiple correlation for **WORDMEAN** has a mean of .685 across bootstrap samples.
Bias	The difference between the average of B estimates obtained from B bootstrap samples, and the single estimate obtained from the original sample. In the example above, the squared multiple correlation for **WORDMEAN** has a mean of .685 across bootstrap samples, while the estimate (not shown above) obtained from the original sample is .686. The difference, $.685 - .686 = -.001$, is an estimate of the bias in estimating the squared multiple correlation.
S.E./Bias	An approximate standard error for the bias estimate in the preceding column. The formula used is $s/\sqrt{B}$, where s is the approximate standard error in the S.E. column and B is the number of bootstrap samples. In the example above, the squared multiple correlation for **WORDMEAN** has an estimated bias of $-.001$ with a standard error of approximately $.064/\sqrt{1000} = .002$. Since the estimated bias is smaller in magnitude than its standard error, there is little evidence that the squared multiple correlation is biased.

Bootstrap sample xxxxx

Produced by the **$bootverify** command. This message appears once for each bootstrap sample. It is followed by a list of integers that should be read from left to right, beginning with the first row if there is more than one row. The first integer gives the frequency with which the first observation in the original sample appeared in bootstrap sample number **xxxxx**. The second integer gives the frequency with which the second observation appeared, and so on.

Chi-square = xxxxx

xxxxx is the minimum value of the discrepancy, C (see Appendix B).

Computation of degrees of freedom

This portion of the output shows how Amos arrives at degrees of freedom as the difference between the number of distinct sample moments and the number of distinct parameters that have to be estimated. The number of distinct sample moments always includes the number of variances and covariances. It also includes the number of sample means when means and intercepts are explicit model parameters.

In counting up the number of distinct parameters to be estimated, several parameters that are constrained to be equal to each other count as a single parameter. Parameters that are fixed at a constant value do not count at all. This is why the 'number of distinct parameters to be estimated' may be less than the total number of regression weights, variances, covariances, means and intercepts in the model.

In the analysis of data from several groups, the number of distinct sample moments and the number of distinct parameters to be estimated are grand totals over all groups.

Condition number of sample correlations= xxxxx

This message is produced by **$samplemoments** together with **$standardized** whenever the sample covariance matrix is positive definite. The condition number is the largest eigenvalue of the sample correlation matrix divided by its smallest eigenvalue. Some programs report the condition number of a data matrix, $\mathbf{X}$, whose columns are scaled so that $\mathbf{X'X}$ is the sample correlation matrix. That condition number is the square root of the condition number reported by Amos.

Condition number of sample covariances= xxxxx

This message is produced by **$samplemoments** whenever the sample covariance matrix is positive definite. The condition number is the largest eigenvalue of the sample covariance matrix, $\mathbf{S}^{(g)}$, divided by its smallest eigenvalue. Some programs report the condition number of a data matrix, $\mathbf{X}$, whose columns are scaled so that $\mathbf{S}^{(g)} = \mathbf{X'X}$. That condition number is the square root of the condition number reported by Amos.

xxxxx% confidence intervals (percentile method)

See **$confidencepc** on page 201.

xxxxx% confidence intervals (bias corrected percentile method)

See **$confidencebc** on page 199.

Correlations of estimates

Produced by **$corest**. This matrix has a row and column for each parameter of the model. Each off-diagonal entry in the matrix gives an estimate of the correlation between two parameter estimates. If you have assigned names to the parameters, those names are used to label the rows and columns of this matrix. If not, Amos makes up its own names.

You can find the parameter names next to the parameter estimates, in the `Label` column of one of the following sections of the output file:

Asymptotically distribution-free estimates on page 279

Generalized least squares estimates on page 289

Maximum likelihood estimates on page 291

Critical ratios for differences between parameters

Produced by **$crdiff**. This matrix has a row and column for each parameter of the model. Each off-diagonal entry in the matrix gives a statistic for testing the hypothesis that some two model parameters are equal in the population. If you have assigned names to the parameters, those names are used to label the rows and columns of this matrix. If not, Amos makes up its own names.

You can find the parameter names next to the parameter estimates, in the `Label` column of one of the following sections of the output file:

> **Asymptotically distribution-free estimates** on page 279

> **Generalized least squares estimates** on page 289

> **Maximum likelihood estimates** on page 291

Degrees of freedom = xxxxx

The value **xxxxx** gives the degrees of freedom (d) for testing the model. It is the same number shown elsewhere in the output file under the heading, **Computation of degrees of freedom** (see page 284).

Degrees of freedom (corrected for nonidentifiability) = xxxxx

This message appears if you have used the **$unidentified** command, and if the model is actually unidentified. Amos guesses at the correct degrees of freedom by subtracting the number of constraints that (probably) need to be imposed in order to achieve identifiability, from the degrees of freedom shown earlier under the heading **Computation of degrees of freedom**. The correctness of the resulting figure depends upon Amos's ability to diagnose nonidentifiability, which is discussed in Appendix D.

Determinant of sample covariance matrix = xxxxx

This message is produced by **$samplemoments** whenever the sample covariance matrix is positive definite. In an analysis of data from more than one group, this message appears once for each group in which the sample covariance matrix is positive definite.

In the case of positive definite covariance matrices, a determinant near zero indicates that at least one observed variable is nearly linearly dependent on the others. The consequences of this depend on the specified model and on the discrepancy function. From a numerical point of view, a determinant near zero may make it difficult to estimate the parameters of the model. From a statistical point of view, a determinant near zero may imply poor estimates of some parameters (which will show up as large estimated standard errors).

Discrepancy function = xxxxx

If you have requested unweighted least squares estimation (**$uls**) or 'scale free' least squares estimation (**$sls**), **xxxxx** is the minimum value of the discrepancy function, C, in Appendix B.

Eigenvalues of sample correlations

This message is produced by **$samplemoments** together with **$standardized**.

Eigenvalues of sample covariances

This message is produced by **$samplemoments**.

End of your input lines

This message is displayed when Amos encounters either a **$noecho** command or the end of the input file.

Execution time summary:

This message is followed by a summary of execution times (in seconds) in the following categories:

Minimization:	Time required for Amos's minimization algorithm
Miscellaneous:	Anything not falling into another category, but consisting mostly of input parsing and output formatting.
Bootstrap:	self explanatory
Total:	self explanatory

Factor score weights

Produced by the **$factorscores** command. The table displayed here gives regression weights for predicting the unobserved variables from the observed variables. The table is organized with a separate row for each unobserved variable and a separate column for each observed variable.

Factor score weights - lower bound

This message is produced by **$factorscores** together with either **$confidencebc** or **$confidencepc**. The table displayed here gives, for each factor score weight (see **Factor score weights** on page

287), the lower boundary of a two-sided confidence interval. The confidence level is specified by the **$confidencebc** or **$confidencepc** command.

Related commands: **$confidencebc** on page 199
$confidencepc on page 201
$factorscores on page 213

Factor score weights - standard errors

This message is produced by **$bootstrap** together with **$factorscores**. It is followed by bootstrapped standard errors for the estimates labeled **Factor score weights** (see page 287).

Related commands: **$bootstrap** on page 191
$factorscores on page 213

Factor score weights - two tailed significance

This message is produced by **$factorscores** together with either **$confidencebc** or **$confidencepc**. The table displayed here gives, for each factor score weight (see **Factor score weights** on page 287), a value, p, such that a two-sided $100(1-p)\%$ confidence interval for the factor score weight has one of its boundaries at zero.

Related commands: **$confidencebc** on page 199
$confidencepc on page 201
$factorscores on page 213

Factor score weights - upper bound

This message is produced by **$factorscores** together with either **$confidencebc** or **$confidencepc**. The table displayed here gives, for each factor score weight (see **Factor score weights** on page 287), the upper boundary of a two-sided confidence interval. The confidence level is specified by the **$confidencebc** or **$confidencepc** command.

Related commands: **$confidencebc** on page 199
$confidencepc on page 201
$factorscores on page 213

Function of log likelihood = xxxxx

xxxxx is $-2\log L + K$, where L is the likelihood function and K is a constant that depends only on the sample size of each group and the number of observed variables in each group. This statistic is used for model comparisons in the presence of missing data. (See Example 17.)

Generalized least squares estimates

This message is followed by parameter estimates. In the analysis of data from more than one group, the message appears once for each group. For each parameter, four numbers are displayed, arranged in columns labeled:

Estimate The parameter estimate.

S.E. Approximate standard error.

C.R. *Critical ratio.* The critical ratio is the parameter estimate divided by an estimate of its standard error. If the appropriate distributional assumptions are met, this statistic has a standard normal distribution under the null hypothesis that the parameter has a population value of zero. For example, if an estimate has a critical ratio greater than two (in absolute value), the estimate is significantly different from zero at the .05 level. Even without distributional assumptions, the critical ratios have the following interpretation: For any unconstrained parameter, the *square* of its critical ratio is, approximately, the amount by which the chi-square statistic would *increase* if the analysis were repeated with that parameter fixed at zero.

Label If you have assigned a symbolic name to a parameter (see the **$structure** and **$mstructure** commands, or ⟦γ⟧), the name appears in this column. You need symbolic names for the parameters in order to interpret output generated by the **$covest**, **$corest** and **$crdiff** commands. If necessary, Amos makes up names for any parameters that you have not named. Amos's made-up names will appear in the `Label` column along with the ones you supply.

Related commands: **$gls** on page 215

Implied (for all variables) correlations

This message is produced by **$allimpliedmoments** together with **$standardized**. The correlation matrix displayed is an estimate of the population correlation matrix of all the variables in the model (observed and unobserved) under the hypothesis that the model is correct.

Implied (for all variables) correlations - standard errors

This message is produced by **$bootstrap** together with **$allimpliedmoments** and **$standardized**. It is followed by bootstrapped standard errors for the implied correlations among all variables.

Related commands: **$allimpliedmoments** on page 181
$bootstrap on page 191
$standardized on page 259

Implied (for all variables) covariances

This message is produced by **$allimpliedmoments**. The covariance matrix displayed is an estimate of the population covariance matrix of all the variables in the model (observed and unobserved) under the hypothesis that the model is correct.

Implied (for all variables) covariances - standard errors

This message is produced by **$bootstrap** together with **$allimpliedmoments**. It is followed by bootstrapped standard errors for the implied covariances among all variables.

Related commands: **$allimpliedmoments** on page 181
$bootstrap on page 191

Implied (for all variables) means

This message is produced by **$allimpliedmoments**. The means displayed are estimates of the population means of all the variables in the model (observed and unobserved) under the hypothesis that the model is correct.

Implied (for all variables) means - standard errors

This message is produced by **$bootstrap** together with **$allimpliedmoments**. It is followed by bootstrapped standard errors for the implied means of all variables.

Related commands: **$allimpliedmoments** on page 181
$bootstrap on page 191

Implied correlations

This message is produced by **$impliedmoments** together with **$standardized**. The correlation matrix displayed is an estimate of the population correlation matrix of the observed variables under the hypothesis that the model is correct.

Related commands: **$impliedmoments** on page 217
$standardized on page 259

Implied correlations - standard errors

This message is produced by **$bootstrap** together with **$impliedmoments** and **$standardized**. It is followed by bootstrapped standard errors for the implied correlations among the observed variables.

Related commands: **$bootstrap** on page 191

$impliedmoments on page 217

$standardized on page 259

Implied covariances

This message is produced by **$impliedmoments**. The covariance matrix displayed is an estimate of the population covariance matrix of the observed variables under the hypothesis that the model is correct.

Implied covariances - standard errors

This message is produced by **$bootstrap** together with **$impliedmoments**. It is followed by bootstrapped standard errors for the implied covariances among the observed variables.

Related commands: **$bootstrap** on page 191

$impliedmoments on page 217

Implied means

This message is produced by **$impliedmoments**. The means displayed are estimates of the population means of the observed variables under the hypothesis that the model is correct.

Implied means - standard errors

This message is produced by **$bootstrap** together with **$impliedmoments**. It is followed by bootstrapped standard errors for the implied means of the observed variables.

Related commands: **$bootstrap** on page 191

$impliedmoments on page 217

Matrix permutations test

See **$permute** on page 245.

Maximum likelihood estimates

This message is followed by parameter estimates. In the analysis of data from more than one group, the message appears once for each group. For each parameter, four numbers are displayed, arranged in columns labeled:

Estimate   The parameter estimate.

S.E.   Approximate standard error.

C.R.	*Critical ratio.* The critical ratio is the parameter estimate divided by an estimate of its standard error. If the appropriate distributional assumptions are met, this statistic has a standard normal distribution under the null hypothesis that the parameter has a population value of zero. For example, if an estimate has a critical ratio greater than two (in absolute value), the estimate is significantly different from zero at the .05 level. Even without distributional assumptions, the critical ratios have the following interpretation: For any unconstrained parameter, the *square* of its critical ratio is, approximately, the amount by which the chi-square statistic would *increase* if the analysis were repeated with that parameter fixed at zero.
Label	If you have assigned a symbolic name to a parameter (see the **$structure** and **$mstructure** commands, or ▣), the name appears in this column. You need symbolic names for the parameters in order to interpret output generated by the **$covest**, **$corest** and **$crdiff** commands. If necessary, Amos makes up names for any parameters that you have not named. Amos's made-up names appear in the **Label** column along with the ones you supply.

Minimization history

Produced by the **$technical** command.

Minimum was achieved

Amos reached a local minimum.

Model comparisons

Amos examines every pair of models in which one model can be obtained by placing restrictions on the other. For every such pair of models, Amos reports several statistics intended to be useful in comparing the two models. Let the more constrained of the two models have a discrepancy of $\hat{C}_r$ with degrees of freedom d_r, and let the less constrained model have a discrepancy of $\hat{C}_m$ with degrees of freedom d_m. Then Amos computes the statistic $\hat{C}_r - \hat{C}_m$, which, if the more constrained model is correct, has a chi-square distribution with degrees of freedom equal to $d_r - d_m$. It can be used to test the null hypothesis that the more constrained model is correct under the assumption that the less constrained model is correct. Amos also reports the changes in the fit measures, **NFI**, **TLI**, **RFI** and **IFI**, described in Appendix C.

Here is an example of a model comparison, where Model B is the less constrained model and Model A is the more constrained model:

```
Assuming B to be correct:

                                    NFI       IFI      RFI      TLI
                DF     CMIN     P  Delta-1  Delta-2   rho-1    rho-2
                --    ----   ----- -------- --------  -----    -----
            A    1  65.139   0.000   0.031    0.031    0.075    0.075
```

The output shows that Model A can be obtained by constraining Model B. Under the hypothesis that Model B is correct, a test of the additional constraints of Model A can be based on the chi-square statistic 65.139, which has 1 degree of freedom. The probability of a chi-square statistic with 1 degree of freedom exceeding 65.139 is indistinguishable from zero at three decimal places. Therefore Model A would be rejected at any conventional significance level. In adding one constraint to Model B to obtain Model A, **NFI** and **IFI** both increase by .031 while **RFI** and **TLI** both increase by .075.

Modification indices

Produced by the **$mods** command. Each parameter that has a modification index greater than the value specified with the **$mods** command will appear here, together with two numbers in columns labeled:

> **M.I.**   modification index

> **Par Change**   estimated parameter change

If no modification indices are displayed, this means that none exceeded the threshold specified with the **$mods** command.

For more information and an example, see **$mods** on page 232.

Number of parameters = xxxxx

The value **xxxxx** is the number of *distinct* parameters to be estimated. Several parameters that are constrained to be equal to each other count as a single parameter. Parameters fixed at a constant value are not counted. That is why **xxxxx** will usually be less than the total number of regression weights, variances, covariances, means and intercepts in the model.

Observations farthest from the centroid (Mahalanobis distance)

See **$normalitycheck** on page 238.

Permutations test detail

See **$permutedetail** on page 248

Probability level = xxxxx

If the appropriate distributional assumptions are met and if the specified model is correct, then the value **xxxxx** is the approximate probability of getting a chi-square statistic as large as the chi-square statistic obtained from the current set of data. For example, if **xxxxx** is .05 or less, the departure of the data from the model is significant at the .05 level.

The appropriateness of hypothesis testing in model fitting, even when the necessary distributional assumptions are met, is questionable (*e.g.*, Bollen and Long, 1993).

Probability level cannot be computed

The model has zero degrees of freedom. The model should fit the data perfectly, and the chi-square statistic should be zero. Consequently, no probability level can be assigned to the chi-square statistic. The model is untestable.

Residual covariances

Produced by **$residualmoments**. The symmetric matrix displayed here contains the differences between the sample covariances (see **Sample covariances** on page 295) and the implied covariances (see **Implied covariances** on page 291). If the model is correct, these differences should be small.

Residual means

Produced by **$residualmoments**. The values displayed are the differences between the sample means (see **Sample means** on page 295) and the implied means (see **Implied means** on page 291). If the model is correct, these differences should be small.

Sample correlations

This message is produced by **$samplemoments** together with **$standardized**.

Related commands: **$samplemoments** on page 251
                   $standardized on page 259

Sample correlations - standard errors

This message is produced by **$bootstrap** together with **$samplemoments** and **$standardized**. It is followed by bootstrapped standard errors for the sample correlations.

Related commands: **$bootstrap** on page 191
                   $samplemoments on page 251
                   $standardized on page 259

Sample covariances

This message is produced by **$samplemoments**. If you have used **$useunbiased**, the unbiased covariance matrix,

$$\mathbf{S}_g = \frac{1}{N_g - 1} \sum_{i=1}^{N_g} \left(\mathbf{x}_i^{(g)} - \overline{\mathbf{x}}^{(g)} \right) \left(\mathbf{x}_i^{(g)} - \overline{\mathbf{x}}^{(g)} \right)' \ ,$$

is displayed. Otherwise, the biased covariance matrix,

$$\mathbf{S}_g = \frac{1}{N_g} \sum_{i=1}^{N_g} \left(\mathbf{x}_i^{(g)} - \overline{\mathbf{x}}^{(g)} \right) \left(\mathbf{x}_i^{(g)} - \overline{\mathbf{x}}^{(g)} \right)' \ ,$$

is displayed.

Related commands: **$samplemoments** on page 251
$unbiased on page 270
$useunbiased on page 273

Sample covariances - standard errors

This message is produced by **$bootstrap** together with **$samplemoments**. It is followed by bootstrapped standard errors for the sample covariances.

Related commands: **$bootstrap** on page 191
$samplemoments on page 251

Sample means

This message is produced by **$samplemoments** whenever means are explicit model parameters.

Related commands: **$samplemoments** on page 251.

Sample means - standard errors

This message is produced by **$bootstrap** together with **$samplemoments**. It is followed by bootstrapped standard errors for the sample means.

Related commands: **$bootstrap** on page 191
$samplemoments on page 251

Sample size: xxxxx

The number of observations in a single group. In an analysis of data from more than one group, this message appears once for each group.

Scale-free least squares estimates

This message is followed by parameter estimates. In the analysis of data from more than one group, this message appears once for each group. For each parameter, two numbers are displayed, arranged in columns labeled:

Estimate   The parameter estimate.

Label   If you have assigned a symbolic name to a parameter (see the **$structure** and **$mstructure** commands, or), the name appears in this column.

Related commands: **$sls** on page 255

Squared multiple correlations:

See **$smc** on page 173

Stability index for the following variables is xxxxx

The following list of variables constitutes a 'nonrecursive subset' of the variables in the model. That is, in the path diagram of the model, it is possible to start at any one of the variables in the subset, and, by following a path of single-headed arrows, return to the original variable while never leaving the subset. Suppose there are k variables in the nonrecursive subset and consider the k by k matrix that gives the direct effects of these k variables on each other. Then **xxxxx** is the modulus of the largest eigenvalue of that matrix.

If there is only one nonrecursive subset in the model, the stability index displayed here is identical to the stability index described by Fox (1980) and Bentler and Freeman (1983). If there are several nonrecursive subsets in the model, a stability index will be displayed for each one. In this case, the largest stability index displayed is equal to Fox's stability index. If all stability indices are less than one, the system of linear equations associated with the model is called 'stable'. If any stability index is one or greater, the system is called 'unstable'. A recursive model contains no nonrecursive subsets, and the associated linear system is stable. (Fox's stability index is zero for recursive models.)

Unstable systems present problems of interpretation. Parameter estimates that yield unstable systems are 'impossible' in the same way that inadmissible solutions are impossible. An unstable system of linear equations suggests that your model is wrong or that the sample size is too small.

Standardized residual covariances

Produced by **$residualmoments**. In the symmetric matrix displayed here, each residual covariance (see **Residual covariances** on page 294), has been divided by an estimate of its standard deviation (see Jöreskog and Sörbom, 1984). In sufficiently large samples, these *standardized residual covariances* will have a standard normal distribution if the model is correct. Thus, if the model is correct, most of them should be less than two (in absolute value).

Standardized residual means

Produced by **$residualmoments**. Each figure displayed here is a residual mean (see **Residual means** on page 294), divided by an estimate of its standard deviation. In sufficiently large samples, these *standardized residual means* will have a standard normal distribution if the model is correct. Thus, if the model is correct, most of them should be less than two (in absolute value).

Summary of bootstrap iterations

This message is produced by the **$technical** command together with the **$bootstrap** command. Here is an example of output where 1000 bootstrap samples were requested (**$bootstrap = 1000**).

```
Summary of Bootstrap Iterations

 Iters   m1    m2    m3

     1    0     0     0
     2    0     0     0
     3    0     0     0
     4    0     0     0
     5    0     0     0
     6    0     0     0
     7    0     8     0
     8    0    31     0
     9    0    85     0
    10    0   141     1
    11    0   144     0
    12    0   118     0
    13    0   103     0
    14    0    88     0
    15    0    55     0
    16    0    31     0
    17    0    37     0
    18    0    32     0
    19    0   121     5

 Total    0   994     6

     0 bootstrap samples were unused because of a singular covariance matrix.
    19 bootstrap samples were unused because a solution was not found.
  1000 usable bootstrap samples were obtained.
```

The columns of the table are labeled

Iters	Number of iterations
m1	Minimization method 1—a minimization algorithm that is slow and unreliable for difficult minimization problems, but fast for easy ones. This method is not used in the current release of Amos, and this column will always contain zeros.
m2	Minimization method 2—a pretty reliable and pretty fast minimization algorithm. This is the first minimization method that Amos tries on each bootstrap sample.
m3	Minimization method 3—Amos's most reliable minimization algorithm. During bootstrapping, Amos tries method 3 if method 2 fails.

In the example above, the "8" in the seventh row of the "m2" column indicates that, for eight bootstrap samples, method 2 reached a minimum in seven iterations. The "121" in the 19-th row of the "m2" column indicates that, for 121 bootstrap samples, method 2 reached a minimum in

19 *or more* iterations. The "5" in the 19-th row of the "m3" column indicates that, for five bootstrap samples, method 3 reached a minimum in 19 or more iterations. The "total" row shows that method 2 succeeded 994 times, and that method 3 succeeded 6 times.

The final three lines in the example above show that, in addition to the 1000 bootstrap samples for which a local minimum was reached, there were 19 bootstrap samples for which no local minimum could be found.

Related commands: **$bootstrap** on page 191
$technical on page 266

Summary of models

This section of the output displays numerous measures of fit for each model, including the saturated model and the independence model. The fit measures are described in Appendix C.

Related commands: **$model** on page 228

Summary of parameters

This message is followed by a table that shows the number of model parameters that fall into various categories. The columns of the table are:

Weights:	regression weights
Covariances:	self explanatory
Variances:	self explanatory
Means:	self explanatory
Intercepts:	self explanatory

The rows of the table are:

Fixed:	parameters whose values are fixed at a constant value.
Labeled:	parameters that are labeled.
Unlabeled:	parameters that are neither fixed nor labeled. Such parameters are free to take on any value. (Of course, a parameter that has been associated with a unique label is also free to take on any value.)

In an analysis of data from more than one group, this message appears once per group.

Testing the null hypothesis that the specified model is correct:

See **$bootbs** on page 183.

The model is nonrecursive

A nonrecursive model is one in which some variable has an (indirect) effect on itself. That is, in the path diagram of the model, it is possible to start at some variable and, by following a path of single-headed arrows, return to the original variable.

The model is recursive

A recursive model is one in which no variable in the model has an effect on itself. That is, in the path diagram of the model, it is *not* possible to start at any variable and, by following a path of single-headed arrows, return to the same variable.

The time limit was reached during bootstrapping

The time limit specified with **$time** was exceeded during bootstrapping.

Total effects

Produced by the **$totaleffects** command. The table displayed here gives the total effect (combined direct and indirect effects) of each variable named along the top of the table on each variable named along the side of the table. See Fox (1980) for a discussion of direct, indirect and total effects.

Total effects - lower bound

This message is produced by **$totaleffects** together with either **$confidencebc** or **$confidencepc.** The table displayed gives, for each effect, the lower boundary of a two-sided confidence interval (see **Total effects** on page 299). The confidence level is specified by the **$confidencebc** or **$confidencepc** command.

Related commands: **$confidencebc** on page 199
                        $confidencepc on page 201
                        $totaleffects on page 268

Total effects - standard errors

This message is produced by **$bootstrap** together with **$totaleffects.** It is followed by bootstrapped standard errors for the estimates labeled **Total effects** (see page 299).

Total effects - two tailed significance

This message is produced by **$totaleffects** together with either **$confidencebc** or **$confidencepc.** The table displayed here gives, for each effect (see **Total effects** on page 299), a value, p, such that a two-sided $100(1-p)\%$ confidence interval for the effect has one of its boundaries at zero.

Related commands: **$confidencebc** on page 199
$confidencepc on page 201
$totaleffects on page 268

Total effects - upper bound

This message is produced by **$totaleffects** together with either **$confidencebc** or **$confidencepc.** The table displayed gives, for each effect, the upper boundary of a two-sided confidence interval (see **Total effects** on page 299). The confidence level is specified by the **$confidencebc** or **$confidencepc** command.

Related commands: **$confidencebc** on page 199
$confidencepc on page 201
$totaleffects on page 268

Unweighted least squares estimates

This message is followed by parameter estimates. In the analysis of data from more than one group, this message will appear once for each group. For each parameter, two numbers are displayed, arranged in columns labeled:

Estimate   The parameter estimate.

Label   If you have assigned a symbolic name to a parameter (see the **$structure** and **$mstructure** commands, or ![icon]), the name appears in this column.

Related commands: **$mstructure** on page 234
$structure on page 260

Variance-covariance matrix of estimates

Produced by **$covest**. This matrix has a row and a column for each parameter of the model. Each off-diagonal entry in the matrix gives an estimate of the covariance between two parameter estimates. Each diagonal entry gives the variance of a single parameter estimate. If you have assigned names to the parameters, those names are used to label the rows and columns of this matrix. If not, Amos makes up its own names.

You can find the parameter names next to the parameter estimates, in the `Label` column of one of the following sections of the output file:

Asymptotically distribution-free estimates on page 279

Generalized least squares estimates on page 289

Maximum likelihood estimates on page 291

Your input lines, preceded by line numbers:

This message is displayed when Amos encounters an **$echo** command. After this message appears, lines from the input file are displayed as Amos reads them.

Related commands: $echo on page 210

Your model contains the following variables

This message is followed by a list of all variables in the model, classifying each variable as either observed or unobserved, and as either endogenous or exogenous. A summary table shows the number of variables in each category, as well as the total number of variables in the model.

Spelling or typing errors in the input file can usually be detected by inspecting this portion of the output file, since variant spellings of a variable name will be interpreted as names for distinct variables.

In an analysis of data from several groups, this message will appear once per group.

Error and warning messages

Because $bootbs was used, $confidencebc will be ignored

You can't do Bollen-Stine bootstrapping (**$bootbs**) while also obtaining bootstrapped confidence intervals (**$confidencebc** or **$confidencepc**).

Related commands: **$bootbs** on page 183
                                 $confidencebc on page 199

Because $bootbs was used, $confidencepc will be ignored

You can't do Bollen-Stine bootstrapping (**$bootbs**) while also obtaining bootstrapped confidence intervals (**$confidencebc** or **$confidencepc**).

Related commands: **$bootbs** on page 183
                                 $confidencepc on page 201

It will probably be necessary to impose xxxxx additional constraint(s)

The model is probably unidentified. The number (**xxxxx**) given in this message is not guaranteed to be right, although it almost always is. (See Appendix D.)

Iteration limit exceeded

The number of iterations reached the value specified with the **$iterations** command before a local minimum was found.

Related commands: **$iterations** on page 221

Minimization was unsuccessful

Amos was unable to estimate the parameters of your model. When this message occurs it is usually a sign that the specified model fits the data very poorly, either because the model is wrong or because the sample size is too small. On the other hand, there is no guarantee that Amos will succeed with a well-fitting model.

The analysis will not continue because

Self explanatory. This message will be followed by an extended description of the condition that made it impossible to complete the analysis.

The following covariance matrix is not positive definite

Amos can produce estimates of variances and covariances that yield covariance matrices that are not positive definite (Wothke, 1993). Such a solution is said to be inadmissible. (See the discussion of the message: **This solution is not admissible** on page 305.) Amos does not attempt to distinguish between a solution that is outside the admissible region and one that is on or near its boundary.

The following error occurred

Self explanatory. This message will be followed by an extended description of the error.

The following variances are negative

Although variances cannot be negative, Amos can produce variance *estimates* that are negative. Such a solution is said to be inadmissible. (See the discussion of the message: **This solution is not admissible** on page 305.)

The (probably) unidentified parameters are marked

This message is followed by a list of the parameters of the model. Those that appear to be unidentified are marked with the word **unidentified**. Parameters that are not marked as unidentified are probably identified. Although this classification of parameters as identified and unidentified is usually right, it is fallible (see Appendix D). This portion of the output may be useful in deciding how to impose additional parameter constraints in order to achieve identifiability.

The sample covariance matrix is not positive definite

This message is produced by **$samplemoments** when a sample covariance matrix is not positive definite. The message refers to the sample covariance matrix displayed just above it. Wothke (1993) discusses the problem of covariance matrices that fail to be positive definite.

The specified model is probably unidentified

Self explanatory. The method that Amos uses for determining that a model is unidentified is fallible (see Appendix D).

This solution is not admissible

This message indicates that some variance estimates are negative, or that some exogenous variables have an estimated covariance matrix that is not positive definite. It suggests either that your model is wrong or that the sample is too small (Jöreskog and Sörbom, 1984).

It is possible to prevent the occurrence of negative variance estimates, and it may even be possible to prevent the occurrence of inadmissible solutions in general, by restricting the search for a solution to admissible parameter values. However, Amos does not do this.

Time limit exceeded

The program execution time reached the value specified with the **$time** command before a solution was reached.

Related commands: **$time** on page 267

Warning: Parameter constraints are implausible

This message appears when you require two or more parameters to be equal where it wouldn't usually make sense to do so. For example, this message will appear if you require the variance of some variable to be equal to a regression weight that occurs elsewhere in the model. Usually, it only makes sense to require a variance to be equal to another variance, a covariance to be equal to another covariance, and so on.

Examples

Example 1: Estimating variances and covariance

Purpose

Show how Amos can be used to estimate population variances and covariances. Illustrate the general format of Amos input and output.

The data

Attig (1983) showed forty subjects a booklet containing several pages of advertisements. Then each subject was given three tests of memory performance:

recall: The subject was asked to recall as many of the advertisements as possible. The subject's score on this test was the number of advertisements recalled correctly.

cued: The subject was given some cues and asked again to recall as many of the advertisements as possible. The subject's score was the number of advertisements recalled correctly.

place: The subject was given a list of the advertisements that appeared in the booklet, and asked to recall the page location of each one. The subject's score on this test was the number of advertisements whose location was recalled correctly.

The study was repeated with the same forty subjects after a training exercise intended to improve memory performance. There were thus three performance measures before training and three performance measures after training. In addition, scores on a vocabulary test were recorded, as well as age, sex and level of education. The raw data from the Attig study are provided in the file **attg_yng.amd**. A partial listing of the data file follows on the next page.

```
! Attig (1983) Space data.
! 40 young subjects.
! A data value of  -1  indicates missing data.

$Input variables
      subject_number
      age
      vocab.short     ! Raw score on WAIS subset
      vocabulary      ! Raw score on WAIS
      education       ! Years of schooling
      sex             ! 0=female, 1=male
      recall1         ! Recall pretest
      recall2         ! Recall posttest
      cued1           ! Cued recall pretest
      cued2           ! Cued recall posttest
      place1          ! Place recall pretest
      place2          ! Place recall posttest

$Sample size = 40
$Raw data
  1 20 13 63 14 1 14  9 14 11 36 41
  2 34 12 64 14 0 12  9 14 13 28 34
  3 19 10 59 13 1 12 12 15 14 31 37

         . . .

         (34 similar lines omitted here)

         . . .

 38 26  9 57 15 0 10  8 10  8 40 34
 39 18 12 62 12 1 10 11 10 12 41 35
 40 20  5 48 14 0  8  9 10 13 29 33
```

The file **attg_yng.amd** is arranged in a format suitable for input to Amos. However, there is nothing within **attg_yng.amd** to indicate what kind of analysis is to be done with the Attig data. Additional instructions are still needed to specify the analysis type. Therefore, the data file is discussed in some detail here because it will be reused in several subsequent analyses. Now would be a good time to read through **attg_yng.amd**. The first three lines are comments. They begin with exclamation points. Amos treats all text strings that start with an exclamation point as comments. You can write anything you want after an exclamation point, and Amos will not even be aware of it. The remark on the third line about missing data is intended for human eyes. There is nothing in **attg_yng.amd** to indicate *to Amos* that the Attig data contain missing observations (*Note*: Missing data analysis with Amos is discussed in Examples 17 and 18).

Since the first three lines of **attg_yng.amd** begin with exclamation points, they are treated the same as blank lines. Line four actually *is* blank, and so are a couple of later lines. Amos skips over blank lines as though they weren't there. It also treats consecutive blank spaces within a line the same as a single space, so that all *white space*, including the spaces between words and the indentation of some lines, is there for decorative purposes.

The first line that Amos pays attention to is

```
$Input variables
```

Words that begin with a dollar sign, like **$Input variables**, are special. Amos recognizes several dozen dollar signwords, although you will probably use only a few of them. Each dollar sign word is a special *keyword* or *command* that gives Amos information or tells it to do something.

The **$Input variables** command describes which variables there are in the input file, and in which order. It also tells Amos *how many* variables to read. The command is followed by the names of twelve variables for which data are provided. That number, twelve, does not appear explicitly in **attg_yng.amd**, but the end of the list of twelve names is recognized by the appearance of another dollar sign command (it happens to be **$Samplesize**.) The **$Samplesize** command is used to indicate that the sample size is forty. Amos *must* find the **$Inputvariables** and **$Samplesize** commands in your problem before performing any analysis, and the file which contains your data is a good place in which to keep them.

The **$Rawdata** command is followed by forty lines of data—one line for each subject. Each line holds twelve numbers, which Amos matches up with the twelve variable names that came after the **$Inputvariables** command. Taking the first line after **$Rawdata**, for example, the numbers in this line come from subject number 1, who was 20 years old, had a score of 13 on the WAIS subset, and so on. The spaces in between the numbers on this line are significant. They let Amos know that the line contains twelve separate numbers rather than one long 21 digit number.

It may seem odd that the subject numbers are treated as if they were observations on an ordinary variable (called **subject_number**). However, when data records are read in free format (*i.e.*, blank-delimited), all data fields in a file must be defined as ordinary variables. Amos will then read all fields, but will process only those variables that are actually modeled. Thus, since a variable name is assigned to the *subject number* (but never subsequently used in a model), Amos essentially skips over this field.

Analyzing the data

Now that the Attig data have been described, there is still the matter of telling Amos what kind of analysis to do. There are two methods for entering model specifications. The first method is using *path diagrams* in *Amos Graphics*. The second method is *equation oriented* modeling, which is used in *Amos Text*. Since either mode can be useful in its own right, both are discussed here.

The intent is to estimate the variances and covariances of the **recall** and **place** variables before and after training. Both *Amos Graphics* and *Amos Text* modeling approaches will be described. (You should read *both* sections on modeling, even if you only plan on using one form of Amos, since statistical information may be included in one section, but not in the other.)

Modeling in Amos Graphics

To specify an analysis graphically (by drawing a path diagram), Amos Graphics is started by double-clicking on its icon. When the program has opened, specify a *new* model. First, place four rectangles on the screen to indicate that the model has *four* observed variables. This can be done by selecting the **Draw observed variables** (rectangle) button and dragging the mouse across the screen four times. Or, create one rectangle first and then press the **Duplicate objects** (copy machine) button. After pressing this button, click on the rectangle to be copied, move it to where the next one should be, and release the mouse button. Doing this three times (the **Duplicate** button only needs to be pressed once) makes three exact-size copies. In either case, the result is a simple picture such as the one below:

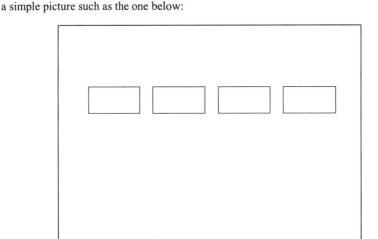

It is important to notice that for every button, there is a *menu option* which performs exactly the same task. For instance, you could have created an observed variable rectangle by clicking on the **Diagram** menu (or pressing **D** while holding down the **Alt** key, called 'Alt-D'), then clicking on the **Draw Observed** command (or pressing **O**). To duplicate an object by using the menu, click on the **Edit** menu, and then on the **Duplicate** command. Also, some buttons can be activated by pressing one or two *hot keys*. The hot key combinations for **Draw Observed** and **Duplicate** are **F3** and **Ctrl-O,** respectively. You know that these commands have been activated if the cursor now has a miniature rectangle or copy machine trailing it. At this point, it doesn't matter how you obtained the command: you would proceed as if you had just pressed the button. For instance, after you have chosen **Draw observed variable**, by button, menu command, or hot key, you can now draw the rectangle.

> From now on, the menu commands and hot keys for each command will not be listed. The important thing is that you familiarize yourself with whatever option you find easiest to use for invoking the commands.

 The next step is to associate the rectangles with the names of the variables. This is done by selecting the **Text (enter/edit)** button (or the option **Text (enter/edit)** from the **Text** menu), moving the arrow to any of the objects, and clicking on the left mouse button (from now on 'click' will automatically mean 'click with the left mouse button'). Then type the variable names at the appropriate prompts. Afterwards, the diagram should look like the display below:

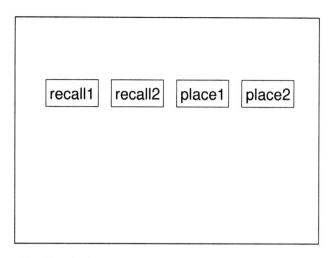

This diagram identifies the four variables. Note that the remaining eight variables in the data file are not mentioned. Amos automatically disregards any variable that has not been included in the path diagram.

If the path diagram were left as is, Amos would estimate the variances of the four variables, but not the covariances between them. Amos' rule is to assume a correlation or covariance of zero whenever two variables are not connected by arrows. To estimate the covariances between the observed variables, we must first connect all pairs with two-way arrows. This is done by selecting the **Draw covariances (double-headed arrows)** button, and dragging connecting arrows from one variable to the next. Altogether, six two-way arrows need to be drawn. The input **path diagram** will look somewhat like this picture:

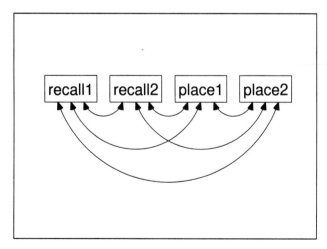

Only one additional step is needed now: We must tell Amos where to find the data for this problem. For this purpose (and for specifying various other modeling options listed in the reference guide), each path diagram is associated with a *text command* file, activated via the **$ command** (dollar sign) button. For the present example, this file should contain the line

```
$Include = attg_yng.amd
```

as shown in this window:

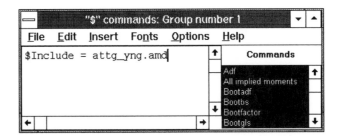

If the data file is located outside the Amos working directory, then its path (disk and/or directory) must also be specified, for instance:

```
$Include = c:\data\attg_yng.amd
```

When the text command file is complete, press **<ctrl>-D,** or select the **Diagram** option in the **File** menu, to close the **$** command window.

To estimate the model parameters with Amos, we simply click on the **Calculate estimates** (abacus) button. To save your new path diagram, select the **File** menu, and then select the **Save As** option. You will then be prompted for a file name. We have already set up this example (and all of the others), and saved it under the name **ex01.amw**.

Modeling in Amos Text

In the text mode version of Amos, models are specified as sets of equations, rather than via the 'boxes and arrows' notation introduced in the previous section. The equation interface is a little more old-fashioned and possibly somewhat less attractive at first sight, but can be unbeatable as a workhorse for larger models and batch-oriented model estimation. Whenever you are more interested in the parameter values than in the paths themselves, equation mode can be the more efficient interface.

To activate the text version of Amos, double-click on the **Amos Text** icon (in the Amos program group). Doing so displays the option box below:

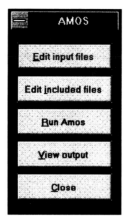

To set up an input file for analysis from scratch, press the **Edit input files** button. Enter the filename for the new **Amos Text** command file. The program will require an additional confirmation that you want to create a new file. For specifying a model in equation mode, two dollar sign commands are available. The one that we will use in this example is **$Structure**. The other one, **$Mstructure**, will be explained in future examples. Consider adding the following five lines to the file `attg_yng.amd`.

```
$Structure
    recall1
    recall2
    place1
    place2
```

The **$Structure** command is followed by a list of the four variable names. While the list does not look like much of a model yet, it still informs Amos Text that the four variables are the object of analysis, and that any other variables will be ignored. In the absence of additional instructions, Amos Text will, by default, estimate the variances of the four named variables, and the covariances among them. So, if the five lines shown above are added to `attg_yng.amd`, you get estimates of the variances and covariances for **recall1**, **recall2**, **place1** and **place2**.

Where should the five new lines be put? The end of the file is an acceptable place. Or the beginning. The order of the dollar sign commands does not matter. You could even rearrange the dollar sign commands that are already in `attg_yng.amd` if you wanted to. There is a restriction, however, concerning the lines that lie in between the dollar sign commands. The four lines that come after the **$Structure** command must come *immediately* after it. Similarly, the twelve lines that come after **$Inputvariables** must come immediately after it. The same goes for the forty lines that come after **$Rawdata**. In other words, the five new lines must *not* become separated and, for instance, plopped down in the middle of the list of input variable names.

One more thing before looking at the results of the analysis just described: You can modify `attg_yng.amd` by adding the five-line **$Structure** command section, or make a copy of `attg_yng.amd` and modify the copy. This may be convenient if you plan to perform only one analysis of the Attig data. But if many different analyses of the same set of data are planned, you will end up with several relatively large files that are almost, but not quite, identical. This is an undesirable state of affairs for several reasons, but there is a way to avoid it. Suppose **attg_yng.amd** is left alone, and a brand new file is created, called, say, **ex01.ami**, containing the following six lines:

```
$Structure
        recall1
        recall2
        place1
        place2
$Include = attg_yng.amd
```

If you use **ex01.ami** as an input file to Amos Text, the program will read the first five lines in the normal way, but when it encounters the line

```
$Include = attg_yng.amd
```

Amos Text will replace that line with the entire contents of **attg_yng.amd**. In other words, the six-line file, **ex01.ami**, will have the same effect as a 66-line file (five lines from **ex01.ami** and 61 lines from **attg_yng.amd**).

Run Amos

Once you have set up and saved the input file, click on the **Amos** window, then press the **Run Amos** button.

Output from the analysis

Amos Text output

Both the text and the path diagram versions of Amos produce a text output file, which in this example is called **ex01.amo**. Later in this section, we will discuss graphical output available with the path diagram version.

Amos will produce some output that has no use in the present simple analysis. Only selected, relevant portions of the output will be discussed here. The message

```
Minimum was achieved
```

indicates that Amos has successfully estimated the variances and covariances.

The occurrence of a message indicating success suggests the disturbing possibility of other messages that report failure. It is possible for Amos to fail. If Amos does fail, you will get a quite prominent message in place of the scarcely noticeable one you get with a successful analysis. Usually, when Amos fails, it is because you have posed a problem that has no solution, or no unique solution. For example, if you attempt an analysis of a set of observed variables that are linearly dependent, Amos will fail because such an analysis cannot be done (unless you use the **$Uls** or **$Gls** command). Problems that have no unique solution are discussed later under the subject of identifiability. Less commonly,

Amos can fail because you have posed a very difficult problem. The possibility of such failures is generic to programs for analysis of moment structures. Although the computational method used by Amos is highly effective, no computer program that does the kind of analysis that Amos does can promise success in every case.

Here are the estimates of variances and covariances that we asked for:

```
Maximum Likelihood Estimates
- - - - - - - - - - - - - - - - - - - - - - - - - -


Covariances:                                Estimate    S.E.     C.R.    Label
- - - - - - - - - - - -                     - - - - - - - -  - - - - - - -  - - - - - - -  - - - - - - -
           recall1 <---> recall2            2.556       1.160    2.203
           recall1 <----> place1            4.337       2.338    1.855
           recall2 <----> place1            2.014       2.635    0.764
           recall1 <----> place2            3.575       1.902    1.880
           recall2 <----> place2            0.427       2.126    0.201
           place1 <-----> place2            17.905      5.225    3.427


Variances:                                  Estimate    S.E.     C.R.    Label
- - - - - - - - - -                         - - - - - - - -  - - - - - - -  - - - - - - -  - - - - - - -
                       recall1              5.787       1.311    4.416
                       recall2              7.944       1.799    4.416
                       place1               33.577      7.604    4.416
                       place2               22.160      5.018    4.416
```

The heading, Maximum Likelihood Estimates, refers to the criterion according to which these estimates were chosen. The criterion is called *maximum likelihood*. It is beyond the scope of this document to say much about the maximum likelihood criterion, except that it produces estimates with very desirable properties. Even if you do not know what these properties are, you can take considerable comfort in the fact that unless stated otherwise by the user, Amos estimates are maximum likelihood estimates.

The claim that Amos' estimates are maximum likelihood estimates depends on certain statistical distribution assumptions that are discussed in the technical note at the end of Example 1 (*p.* 322). Let's make these assumptions and proceed.

The first estimate appearing above is of the covariance between **recall1** and **recall2**. The covariance is estimated to be 2.556. Right next to that estimate, in the S.E. column, is an estimate of the standard error of the covariance, 1.160. If the assumptions of Appendix A are met, the estimate 2.556 is an observation on an approximately normally distributed random variable centered around the population covariance with a standard deviation of about 1.160. You can use these figures to construct, say, a 95% confidence interval on the population covariance by computing $2.556 \pm 1.96 \times 1.160 = 2.556 \pm 2.274$. Later on you will see that you can use Amos to estimate many kinds of population parameters besides covariances, and you will be able to follow the same procedure to set a confidence interval on any one of them.

Right next to the standard error, in the C.R. column, is the *critical ratio* obtained by dividing the covariance estimate by its standard error ($2.203 = 2.556/1.160$). This ratio is relevant to the null hypothesis that, in the population from which Attig's forty subjects came, the covariance between **recall1** and **recall2** is zero. If this hypothesis is true, and still under the assumptions of page 322, the critical ratio is an observation on a random variable that has an approximate standard normal distribution. Thus, using a significance level of .05, any critical ratio that exceeds 1.96 in magnitude would be called significant. In this example, since 2.203 is greater than 1.96, you would say that the covariance between **recall1** and **recall2** is significantly different from zero at the .05 level.

The assertion that the parameter estimates are normally distributed is only an approximation. Moreover, the standard errors reported in the S.E. column are only approximations, and may not be the best available. Consequently, the confidence interval and the hypothesis test just discussed are also only approximate. This is because the theory on which these results are based is *asymptotic*, which means that it can be made to apply with any desired degree of accuracy, but only by using a sufficiently large sample. Whether the approximation is satisfactory with the present sample size will not be discussed because there would be no way to generalize the conclusions to the many other kinds of analyses that you can do with Amos. However, it may be instructive to re-examine the null hypothesis that **recall1** and **recall2** are uncorrelated, just to see what is meant by an *approximate* test. We previously concluded that the covariance is significantly different from zero on the grounds that 2.203 exceeds 1.96. The *p* value associated with a standard normal deviate of 2.203 is .028 (two tailed), which of course is less than .05. By contrast, the conventional *t* statistic (*e.g.*, Runyon and Haber, 1980, *p*. 226) is 2.509 with 38 degrees of freedom ($p = .016$). In this example, both *p* values are less than .05, so both tests agree in rejecting the null hypothesis at the .05 level. In some other situation the two *p* values might lie on opposite sides of .05, which you might or might not regard as especially serious. At any rate, the two tests can give different results. There should be no doubt about which test is better. The *t* test is exact under the assumptions of normality and independence of observations, no matter what the sample size. The test based on Amos' critical ratio depends on the same assumptions, but with a finite sample the test is only approximate. For many interesting applications of Amos, there is no exact test or exact standard error or exact confidence interval available for statistical comparisons.

On the bright side, when fitting a model for which conventional estimates exist, maximum likelihood point estimates (*i.e.*, the numbers in Amos' Estimate column) are generally identical to the conventional estimates.

The following little table plays an important role in every Amos analysis:

```
Computation of Degrees of Freedom

             Number of distinct sample moments:   10
  Number of distinct parameters to be estimated:   10
             ------------------------
                         Degrees of freedom:    0
```

The sample moments that Amos can deal with are sample means, variances and covariances. In most analyses, like the present one, Amos ignores means, so that the relevant sample moments are the sample variances of the four variables, **recall1**, **recall2**, **place1** and **place2**, and their sample covariances. There are four sample variances and six sample covariances, for a total of ten sample moments. As for the parameters to be estimated, they are the corresponding population variances and covariances. There are of course four population variances and six population covariances, which makes ten parameters to be estimated. The degrees of freedom is the amount by which the number of sample moments exceeds the number of parameters to be estimated. In this example, there is a one-to-one correspondence between the sample moments and the parameters to be estimated, so it is no accident that there are zero degrees of freedom.

As we will see beginning with Example 2, any nontrivial null hypothesis about the parameters will effectively reduce the number of parameters that have to be estimated. The result will be positive degrees of freedom. For now, there is no null hypothesis being tested. Without a null hypothesis to test, the following table is not very interesting.

```
Chi-square =      .000
Degrees of freedom =     0
Probability level cannot be computed
```

If there *had* been an hypothesis under test in this example, the chi-square value would have been a measure of the extent to which the data were incompatible with the hypothesis. A chi-square value of zero would ordinarily indicate no departure from the null hypothesis. But in the present example, the zero value for degrees of freedom and the zero chi-square value merely reflect the fact that there was no null hypothesis in the first place.

Amos Graphics output

Amos Graphics is somewhat different from text mode output. After finishing the iterative procedure, the program first displays a message as to whether the solution has converged or not. This message is given in a separate window as part of a larger text-mode output file. You can scroll up and down in this window to examine the other sections of the output file. They are essentially the same as the text-mode list output already discussed.

 Graphical path diagram output can be obtained by pressing the **Groups and Models** button. Clicking on it produces the **Pick a group and a model** dialog box, Amos' general selection device for all its graphics input and output screens:

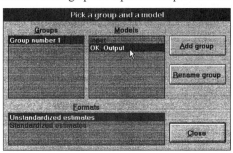

When we select the **OK:Output** item from the **Models** menu (upper right) and close the dialog box, Amos displays the output path diagram with parameter estimates inserted:

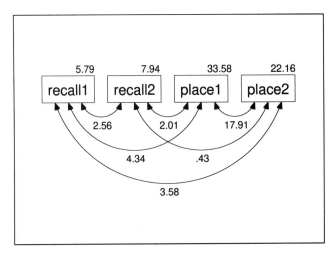

In the output path diagram, the numbers displayed near the upper left or right corner of each box are the variance estimates, and the numbers displayed next to the two-way arrows are the estimated covariances. For instance, the variance of **recall1** is estimated at 5.79, and that of **place1** at 33.58. The estimated covariance between these two variables is 4.34.

Optional output

So far, we have only been discussing the Amos default output that would be obtained without any special requests. To see more, there are additional dollar sign commands that can be placed in the file, **ex01.ami**, or in the input file that opens when the **Edit input file** button in Amos Graphics is pressed.

You may be surprised to find estimates of covariances rather than correlations, which are more familiar in the social sciences. When the scale of measurement is arbitrary or of no substantive interest, correlations have more descriptive meaning than covariances. Nevertheless, Amos and similar programs insist on estimating covariances. Also, as will soon be seen, Amos provides a simple method for testing hypotheses about covariances, but not about correlations. This is mainly because it is easier to write programs that way. On the other hand, it isn't hard to derive correlation estimates once the relevant variances and covariances have been estimated. Amos displays estimates of the correlations if the **$Standardized** command is used. It can be added to the file **ex01.ami** anywhere before the **$Structure** command or after the list of variable names. The resulting output would be:

```
Correlations:                                    Estimate
..............                                   ........

                recall1 <---> recall2            0.377
                recall1 <----> place1            0.311
                recall2 <----> place1            0.123
                recall1 <----> place2            0.316
                recall2 <----> place2            0.032
                place1 <-----> place2            0.656
```

These correlation estimates are obtained in the usual way from the estimated covariances and variances shown previously. Being functions of maximum likelihood estimates, they are also maximum likelihood estimates. Similarly, standardized path diagram output may be obtained by selecting the "Standardized estimates" item from the **Formats** menu of the **Groups/Models** dialog box (this also requires that a **$Standardized** command be added to the Amos text command file associated with the path diagram.

To see all of the estimated variances and covariances collected into one matrix, use the **$Implied moments** command. **$Implied moments** displays the estimated variances and covariances after the maximum likelihood estimates.

```
Implied Covariances

            place2    place1    recall2   recall1
            ........  ........  ........  ........
place2      22.160
place1      17.905    33.577
recall2      0.427     2.014     7.944
recall1      3.575     4.337     2.556     5.787
```

If you want to see the *sample* variances and covariances, use **$Samplemoments**. The **$Sample moments** command displays the sample moments in a similar fashion, before the Computation of degrees of freedom section.

```
Sample Covariances

            place2    place1    recall2   recall1
            ........  ........  ........  ........
place2      22.160
place1      17.905    33.578
recall2      0.427     2.014     7.944
recall1      3.575     4.338     2.556     5.788
```

Now you can see what may have been suspected all along: Amos' estimates are identical to the sample variances and covariances that could have been computed by hand. Seeing Amos perform such an analysis is like watching an elephant pick up a pea. On the other hand, it is a reassuring performance, inasmuch as the sample values *are* maximum likelihood estimates of the corresponding population values, and Amos found them.

Technical Note: Distribution Assumptions for Amos Models.

Hypothesis testing procedures, confidence intervals and claims for efficiency in maximum likelihood or generalized least squares estimation by Amos depend on certain statistical distribution assumptions. First, observations must be independent. For instance, the forty young people in the Attig study have to be picked independently from the population of young people. Second, the exogenous variables must meet certain distributional requirements. For instance, if the exogenous variables have a multivariate normal distribution, that will suffice. Multivariate normality of all exogenous variables is a standard distribution assumption in many structural equation modeling and factor analysis applications.

There is another, more general situation under which maximum likelihood estimation can be applied. If some exogenous variables are *fixed*, *i.e.*, they are either known beforehand or measured without error, their distribution may have any shape, provided that

1. For any value pattern of the *fixed* variables, the remaining (random) variables have a (conditional) normal distribution.

2. The (conditional) variance-covariance matrix of the random variables is the same for every pattern of the *fixed* variables.

3. The (conditional) expected values of the random variables depend linearly on the values of the *fixed* variables.

A typical example of a fixed variable would be an experimental *treatment*, classifying respondents into a study and a control group, respectively. This is all right as long as the other exogenous variables are normally distributed for study and control cases alike, and with the same conditional variance-covariance matrix. Note that an experimental grouping variable must be regarded as fixed, because the group assignment is completely determined by the experimenter.

Predictor variables in regression analysis (*cf.*, Example 4) are usually regarded as fixed, exogenous variables. A test of this type of assumption will be demonstrated in Example 5.

Many people are accustomed to the requirements for normality and independent observations, since these are the usual requirements for many conventional procedures. However, with Amos, you have to remember that meeting these requirements leads only to asymptotic conclusions (*i.e.*, conclusions that are approximately true for *large* samples).

Example 2: Testing hypotheses

Purpose

The purpose of this example is to show how Amos can be used to test simple hypotheses about variances and covariances. The chi-square test for goodness of fit is introduced, and the concept of degrees of freedom is elaborated.

Data

Attig's (1983) spatial memory data will again be used for this example. The data were described in Example 1.

Placing constraints on parameters

Modeling using Amos Graphics

Here is the path diagram that was used in Example 1. We can think of the variable objects as having small boxes nearby, which represent the variances, that are filled in once Amos has computed the parameter estimates.

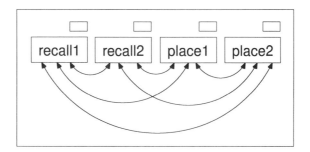

 Actually, you can fill these boxes in yourself. To do so, press the **Parameter constraints (gamma)** button (it should become highlighted). Now you can constrain the variance of any variable to a fixed value. Suppose you wanted to set the variance of **recall1** to 6. Just click on the **recall1** object. The **Parameter value** dialog box appears:

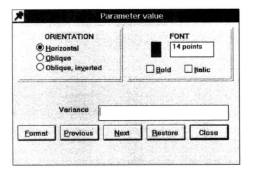

Enter 6 in the **Variance** field of the **Parameter value** dialog box. In a similar manner, or by using the **Next** button in the dialog box, you can set the variance of **recall2** to 8. After leaving the **Parameter Value** dialog box, **Amos Graphics** displays the newly fixed parameter values in the path diagram:

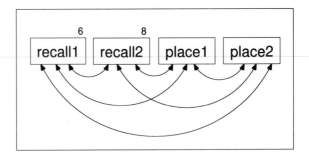

Of course, this was probably not a very realistic example because the numbers, 6 and 8, were just picked out of the air. Realistic value constraints must be based on good theory, previous analyses of similar data, or derived from study design or model identification rules. However, there are other things besides numbers that you can enter in the **Parameter value** dialog.

Frequently, you will be interested in the plausibility of the variances being equal in the population, particularly in related variables such as **recall1** and **recall2**. You might very well believe this, or at least want to investigate the possibility, without having a particular value for the variances in mind. In such a scenario the **Parameter constraints** button may be used again. Yet, instead of equating the two variance parameters to different numeric values, you should simply equate them to a common symbolic name, such as the label v_recall (*note*: parameter labels may be up to 29 characters long and must begin with a letter). If the variances of both **recall1** and **recall2** are set to the same label v_recall, then any subsequent analysis will set these variances equal.

We are going to tamper with the input file a little more before looking at any results, but maybe we should pause and ask why you would want to specify that two parameters, like the variances of **recall1** and **recall2**, are equal. Here are two benefits:

- If you specify that two parameters are equal in the population, and if you are correct in this specification, then you will get more accurate estimates, not only of the parameters that are equal, but usually of the others as well. This is the only benefit if you happen to know for a fact that the parameters are equal.

- If the equality of two parameters is a mere hypothesis, requiring their estimates to be equal will result in a test of that hypothesis.

You may also want to consider the possibility that **place1** has the same variance as **place2**. In this example we are using the label v_place to constrain the variances of **place1** and **place2** to the same, estimated value.

Your model may also include restrictions on parameters other than variances. For example, you may hypothesize that the covariance between **recall1** and **place1** is equal to the covariance between **recall2** and **place2**. To do so, make sure the **Parameter constraints** button is pressed (highlighted) and click on the double-headed covariance path between **recall1** and **place1**. In the **Parameter value** dialog box, set the value of this path to a symbolic constant, such as cov_rp. Then, set the covariance path between **recall2** and **place 2** to cov_rp as well.

Finally, remember to again place the line

```
$Include = attg_yng.amd
```

in your input command file. *Every* Amos command file must reference an external data file in this manner (or contain the actual data records). While the **$Include** command will no longer be discussed explicitly in most of the following examples, you should understand that it has to be there, or the data themselves have appear inside the command file. Otherwise, Amos would terminate with an error message.

Moving variable objects

Up to now, and throughout the first example, we have displayed the four variable objects all in a line. While this is fine for small examples such as these, it is not practical for more complex analyses. Suppose we want to display the objects in a boxlike fashion. Simply press the **Move objects (moving truck)** button, click on the object you want moved, and with the mouse button still pressed, move the object (a shadow of the object will help you) to its desired location. Below is the final path diagram, which can be found in **ex02.amw**:

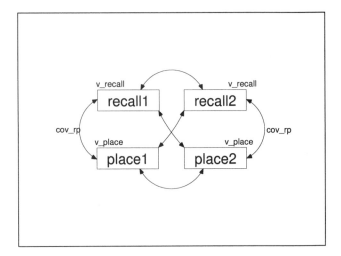

There are some additional buttons that can be helpful in making your path diagram look just like the one above, in addition to the **Moving objects** button. These buttons correspond to commands found in the **Align** menu. Some of these will be described in later examples, but you should study the Reference section of this manual for a complete description. Learning them can greatly reduce the time it takes to produce a publication-quality path diagram.

Modeling in Amos Text

Specifying the constrained model in **Amos Text** requires a modification similar to that of adding the small boxes near each variable. Here, the boxes take the form of parentheses:

```
$Structure
    recall1 ( )
    recall2 ( )
    place1 ( )
    place2 ( )
```

The space in between the parentheses can now be filled in with any value or variance label. Again, using the same label in more than one set of parentheses will force Amos to set the corresponding variance estimates equal to each other.

Covariance constraints require two more lines to be added, one for each covariance term:

```
    recall1 <> place1 ( )
    recall2 <> place2 ( )
```

The two-character symbol "<>" is implemented in **Amos Text** to resemble the bi-directional arrows of covariances in the path diagram. It is permissible to insert one or more hyphens between the two angle brackets, such as in "<-->". Finally, the two covariances are constrained to be equal by simply typing the same parameter label in the two pairs of parentheses. Here is the structure command with the three constraints in place (from the file **ex02.ami**):

```
$Structure
    recall1 (v_recall)
    recall2 (v_recall)
    place1 (v_place)
    place2 (v_place)
    recall1 <> place1 (cov_rp)
    recall2 <> place2 (cov_rp)
```

Text output from the analysis

Moment estimates

Below are the maximum likelihood estimates resulting from putting all three constraints in place:

Covariances:		Estimate	S.E.	C.R.	Label
recall1 <----> place1		2.712	1.821	1.489	cov_rp
recall2 <----> place2		2.712	1.821	1.489	cov_rp
recall1 <---> recall2		2.872	1.208	2.377	
recall2 <----> place1		2.220	2.216	1.002	
recall1 <----> place2		4.608	2.166	2.127	
place1 <-----> place2		17.149	5.155	3.327	

Variances:		Estimate	S.E.	C.R.	Label
recall1		7.055	1.217	5.798	v_recal
recall2		7.055	1.217	5.798	v_recal
place1		27.525	5.177	5.317	v_place
place2		27.525	5.177	5.317	v_place

You can see that the parameters that were specified to be equal do have equal estimates. The standard errors here are generally smaller than the standard errors obtained in Example 1. For instance, the standard errors of the four variances, in the order they are listed here, were 1.311, 1.799, 7.604, and 5.018 in Example 1.

Note that Amos shortened the name v_recall, for space reasons. You should be aware that variable names can be shortened to as few as seven characters in the output, so that names that start with the same seven letters should be avoided.

Because of the constraints on the parameters, there are now positive degrees of freedom:

```
Computation of Degrees of Freedom

                    Number of distinct sample moments:    10
        Number of distinct parameters to be estimated:     7
                    ------------------------------
                               Degrees of freedom:     3
```

While there are still ten sample variances and covariances, the number of parameters to be estimated is only seven. Here is how the number seven is arrived at: The variances of **recall1** and **recall2**, labeled v_recall, are constrained to be equal, and thus count as a single parameter. The variances of **place1** and **place2** (labeled v_place) count as another single parameter. A third parameter corresponds to the equal covariances recall1 <> place1 and recall2 <> place2 (labeled cov_rp). These three parameters, plus the four unlabeled, unrestricted covariances, add up to *seven* parameters that have to be estimated.

The degrees of freedom $(10 - 7 = 3)$ may also be viewed as the number of constraints placed on the original ten variances and covariances. One degree of freedom is gained from each of the three equality constraints, so there are three degrees of freedom in this example.

With the three equality constraints in place, the fitted variances and covariances are no longer equal to the sample moments. By including the lines **$Implied moments** and **$Sample moments** in the command file, the respective estimated and sample variances and covariances will be displayed in separate matrices.

```
Implied Covariances

             place2   place1   recall2  recall1
             -------- -------- -------- --------
place2       27.525
place1       17.149   27.525
recall2       2.712    2.220    7.055
recall1       4.608    2.712    2.872    7.055
```

```
Sample Covariances

             place2   place1   recall2  recall1
             -------- -------- -------- --------
place2       22.160
place1       17.905   33.578
recall2       0.427    2.014    7.944
recall1       3.575    4.338    2.556    5.788
```

Hypothesis testing

The *implied* covariances are the best estimates of the population variances and covariances under the null hypothesis that the parameters required to have equal estimates are truly equal in the population, whereas the *sample* covariances are the best estimates obtained without making any equality assumptions. If the null hypothesis is correct, both the implied and sample covariances are maximum likelihood estimates of the corresponding population values, but the implied covariances are better estimates, as the standard errors are reduced. If however, the null hypothesis is incorrect, the sample covariances are preferred, and the implied covariances should not be used. Thus it is of interest to test the veracity of the null hypothesis. The chi-square statistic is an overall measure of how much the implied and sample covariances differ, and is at least 0 (and that occurs only with a perfect fit). The more the implied and sample covariances differ, the bigger the chi-square statistic, and the stronger the evidence against the null hypothesis.

Here is the chi-square test against the null hypothesis that includes the two variance and one covariance constraint:

```
Chi-square =        6.276
Degrees of freedom =    3
Probability level =     0.099
```

If the null hypothesis is true, the chi-square statistic will follow an approximate chi-square distribution with three degrees of freedom, and will have a value in the neighborhood of the degrees of freedom. The probability that such a chi-square statistic equals or exceeds a value of 6.276 is about 0.099. In this situation, the evidence against the null hypothesis is not significant at the 5% level.

Amos Graphics output

Moment estimates

As in Example 1, you can enter the **Groups/Models** dialog box to request that the covariance and variance estimates be inserted in the output path diagram. Simply highlight both "Unstandardized estimates" in the **Formats** list box and "OK:Output" in the **Models** list box, and press the **Close** button. Alternatively, you can request *correlation* estimates in the path diagram by highlighting the "Standardized estimates" item.

Here is the path diagram for the correlations:

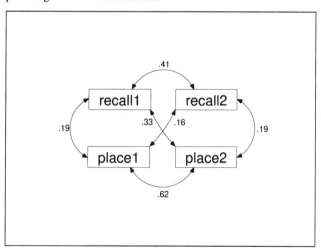

Particularly in larger models, it may be difficult to remember whether the displayed output are covariances or correlations. Amos provides for labeling the output so this is not a problem. Note that the file **ex02.amw** contains a description at the bottom of the screen. Clicking on this description while the **Text (enter/edit)** button is highlighted displays the actual contents of the text caption:

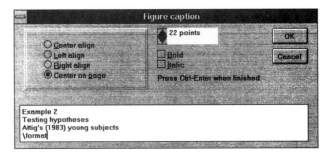

The line of interest is the word **\format** (you will need to press the down arrow key a few times to see it). **\format** and other words which begin with a backward slash are called *text macros*, which are replaced with information about the currently-displayed model. The text macro **\format** will be replaced by the heading "Model Specification", "Unstandardized estimates", or "Standardized estimates", or by a custom format defined by you, depending on which version of the path diagram is in view.

Hypothesis testing

In a similar manner, you can get the chi-square goodness of fit information to appear on the screen along with the path diagram, by typing **\cmin** and **\df** in a text field. These text macros are replaced by the chi-square statistic and the degrees of freedom, respectively, when Amos output is displayed. The text macro **\p** can be used to display the corresponding right tail probability under the chi-square distribution. The following figure shows the completely labeled unstandardized output of **ex02.amw**:

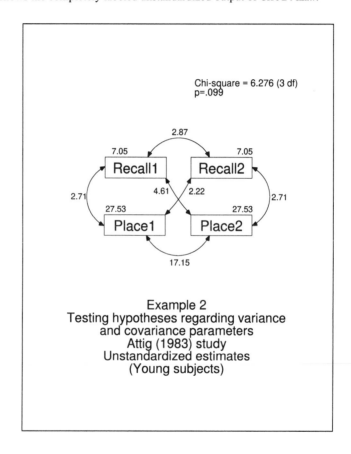

Chi-square = 6.276 (3 df)
p=.099

Example 2
Testing hypotheses regarding variance
and covariance parameters
Attig (1983) study
Unstandardized estimates
(Young subjects)

Example 3: More hypothesis testing

Purpose

This example shows how to test the null hypothesis that two variables are uncorrelated. The example also reinforces the concept of degrees of freedom, and a note at the end of the example shows in a concrete way what is meant by an *asymptotically correct* test.

The data

Attig's (1983) spatial memory data will be used for this example. This is the same data set used in the first two examples, but the two variables **age** and **vocabulary** will be used.

Testing a hypothesis that two variables are uncorrelated

Among Attig's (1983) forty young subjects, the sample correlation between **age** and **vocabulary** was .25, indicating a slight tendency for older people to have larger vocabularies than younger ones. Let us now ask if this correlation is significant. In other words, we will test the null hypothesis that, in the population from which these forty subjects came, the correlation between age and vocabulary is zero. We will do this by estimating the variance-covariance matrix under the constraint that **age** and **vocabulary** are uncorrelated.

Modeling in Amos Graphics

Once the two observed variables, **age** and **vocabulary**, are created in the path diagram, Amos graphics provides two methods by which their covariance parameter can be constrained to zero.

One obvious way of setting the implied covariance of **age** and **vocabulary** to zero is by simply *not drawing* a covariance path between the two observed variables. In the Amos Graphics path diagram, the lack of a two-headed arrow corresponds to an implied covariance of zero, as long as the two variables are not connected indirectly via additional predictors. So the model estimated from the simple diagram below constrains the covariance (and thus the correlation) between **age** and **vocabulary** to zero:

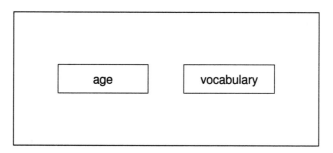

The second method of constraining a covariance parameter in Amos Graphics is the more general procedure introduced in Example 2. This method requires three steps: first, a covariance path is drawn between the two observed variables. Then, with the **Constrain parameter estimates (gamma)** button selected, click on the covariance path with the left mouse button. This action produces the **parameter value dialog box**, by which the covariance parameter may be constrained to *any* desired value or variable. To specify a zero covariance between age and vocabulary, enter 0 in the *covariance* field. The resulting path diagram is shown below, and can also be found in **ex03.amw**:

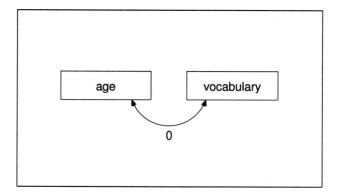

Modeling in Amos Text

An **Amos Text** input file that will accomplish the same covariance constraint is:

```
$Structure
    age
    vocabulary
    age <--> vocabulary (0)

$Include = attg_ymd.amd
```

The three lines after the **$Structure** command request variance estimates of **age** and **vocabulary** while fixing the covariance (and hence the correlation) of these two variables to zero. You might be interested in knowing that the following, shorter input file will work just as well:

```
$Structure
     age <> vocabulary (0)

$Include = attg_yng.amd
```

As long as a variable is mentioned after the **$Structure** command, **Amos Text** will estimate its variance. Since **age** and **vocabulary** are both mentioned in the covariance specification, it is unnecessary to specifically request estimates of their variances.

Results of the analysis

The parameter estimates are not of primary interest in this analysis, but here they are:

```
Covariances:                        Estimate   S.E.     C.R.      Label
.............

      age <----------> vocabulary     0.000


Correlations:                       Estimate
.............

      age <----------> vocabulary     0.000


Variances:                          Estimate   S.E.     C.R.      Label
...........

                            Age        22.510   5.098    4.416
                     Vocabulary        73.240  16.586    4.416
```

In this analysis, there is one degree of freedom, corresponding to the single constraint that **age** and **vocabulary** be uncorrelated. The degrees of freedom can also be arrived at by the computation shown in the Amos output listing:

```
Computation of Degrees of Freedom

                 Number of distinct sample moments:      3
     Number of distinct parameters to be estimated:      2
                                                   -------------------------
                                Degrees of freedom:      1
```

Amos Graphics Output

Amos Graphics provides a similar account of the parameters and degrees of freedom for the model when you press the **Display degrees of freedom (**word '**DF**') button. This produces the following display:

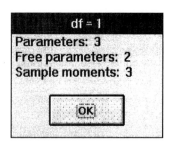

The three sample moments are the variances of **age** and **vocabulary**, and their covariance. The two parameters to be estimated are the two population variances. The model covariance term is fixed at zero, not estimated from the sample information.

Here is the path diagram output of the unstandardized estimates, along with the test of the null hypothesis that **age** and **vocabulary** are uncorrelated:

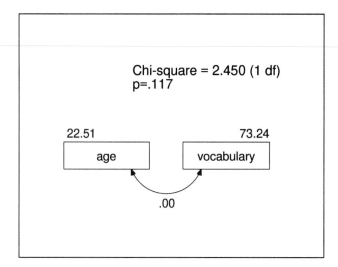

The probability of accidentally getting this, or even a larger departure from the null hypothesis is .117. The null hypothesis would not be rejected at any conventional significance level.

The usual *t* statistic for testing this null hypothesis is 1.57 (*df* = 38, *p* = .125). The probability level associated with the *chi-square* statistic is *off*, as usual, owing to the fact that the statistic is only *asymptotically* distributed chi-square. However, even with a small sample size of 40, the results are not that far apart in this example.

Here is an interesting question: Suppose you use the probability level displayed by Amos to test the null hypothesis at either the .05 or .01 level. Then what is the *actual* probability of rejecting a true null hypothesis? In the case of the present null hypothesis, this question has an answer, although the answer depends on the sample size. The second column of Table 3.1 (below) shows, for several sample sizes, the real probability of a Type I error when using Amos to test the null hypothesis of *zero correlation* at the .05 level. The third column shows the real probability of a Type I error if you use a significance level of .01. The table shows that, the bigger the sample size, the closer the true significance level is to what it is supposed to be. Unfortunately, such a table cannot be easily constructed for every hypothesis that Amos can be used to test. However, this much can be said about any such table: moving from top to bottom, the numbers in the .05 column would approach .05, and the numbers in the .01 column would approach .01. This very property is what is meant by an *asymptotically correct* hypothesis tests.

Sample Size	Nominal Significance Level	
	.05	**.01**
3	.250	.122
4	.150	.056
5	.115	.038
10	.073	.018
20	.060	.013
30	.056	.012
40	.055	.012
50	.054	.011
100	.052	.011
150	.051	.010
200	.051	.010
≥500	.050	.010

Table 3.1: Realized Type I rejection rates when using Amos to test the hypothesis that two variables are uncorrelated.

Example 4: Conventional linear regression

Purpose

This example will demonstrate a conventional regression analysis, predicting a single observed variable as a linear combination of three other observed variables. The example also introduces the concept of identifiability.

The data

Warren, White and Fuller (1974) studied 98 managers of farm cooperatives. Four of the measurements made on each manager were

performance: A 24-item test of performance related to "planning, organization, controlling, coordinating and directing."

knowledge: A 26-item test of knowledge of "economic phases of management directed toward profit-making ... and product knowledge."

value: A 30-item test of "tendency to rationally evaluate means to an economic end."

satisfaction: An 11-item test of "gratification obtained ... from performing the managerial role."

A fifth measure, *past training*, was reported, but will not be employed in this example. The sample variances and covariances are:

	performance	knowledge	value	satisfaction
performance	.0209			
knowledge	.0177	.0520		
value	.0245	.0280	.1212	
satisfaction	.0046	.0044	-.0063	.0901

The variance-covariance matrix, and the sample means, are contained in the file `warren5v.amd`. Raw data are not available, but they are not needed in Amos for most

---

analyses as long as the sample moments (*i.e.*, means, variances and covariances) are provided. In fact, only sample variances and covariances are required in this example. The sample means in **warren5v.amd** will not be needed for the time being, and Amos will ignore them.

Analysis of the data

Suppose you would like to use scores on **knowledge, value** and **satisfaction** to predict **performance**. More specifically, suppose you think that **performance** scores can be approximated by a *linear combination* of **knowledge, value** and **satisfaction**. The prediction will not be perfect however, and the model should thus include an *error term*. Here is the initial path diagram for this relationship:

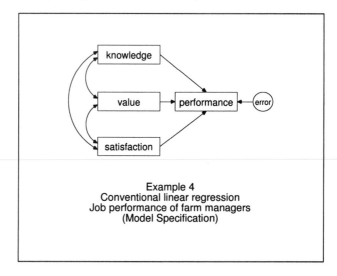

Example 4
Conventional linear regression
Job performance of farm managers
(Model Specification)

The single-headed arrows represent linear dependencies. For example, the arrow leading from **knowledge** to **performance** indicates that **performance** scores depend, in part, on **knowledge**. The variable **error** is enclosed in a circle because it is not directly observed. **Error** represents not only random fluctuations in **performance** scores due to measurement error but also a composite of age, socioeconomic status, verbal ability, and anything else on which **performance** may depend, but which was not measured in this study. This variable is essential because the path diagram is supposed to show *all* variables that affect **performance** scores. Without the circle, the path diagram would make the implausible claim that **performance** is an *exact* linear combination of **knowledge, value** and **satisfaction**.

The double-headed arrows in the path diagram connect variables that may be correlated with each other. They include the predictor variables **knowledge, value** and **satisfaction.** The absence of a double-headed arrow connecting **error** with any other variable indicates that **error** is assumed to be uncorrelated with every other predictor variable—a fundamental assumption in linear regression. **Performance** is also not connected to any other variable by a double-headed arrow, but this is for a different reason. Since

performance *depends* on the other variables, it goes without saying that it might be correlated with them.

Modeling in Amos Graphics

Two new buttons or commands are needed to draw the path diagram for this example. The first is the **Draw unobserved variable (ellipse)** button, or the equivalent command from the **Diagram** menu. Use this command to draw a circle or ellipse for the **error** variable. The tasks of naming and moving unobserved variables are performed in the same manner as they are for observed variables.

The next button is the **Draw paths** (single-headed arrow) button. Simply click on it, so that it becomes highlighted. Then click on an *exogenous* or predictor variable (**knowledge**, **value**, **satisfaction**, or **error**) and, with the left mouse button still pressed, drag out a path with the mouse to the *endogenous* or response variable (**performance**) and release the mouse button. A shadow of the path will help you as you draw. The arrow points to the object you drew *to*. Repeat this step for the other three exogenous variables. If you have done this part correctly, all of the arrows should point towards **performance**.

> This is one way to think about exogenous and endogenous variables. Endogenous variables have at least one single-headed path pointing towards them. Exogenous variables, in contrast, only *send out* single-headed paths, but do not *receive* any.

To finish the path diagram, draw in three **covariance paths** between the observed predictor variables. The diagram now looks complete, so it will come as quite a shock that, when you ask for parameter estimates, Amos will produce this error message, instead:

```
**********************************************************************
The analysis will not continue because

The specified model has negative degrees of freedom.
That is, the number of parameters to be estimated exceeds
the number of distinct sample moments.
Such a model cannot be identified.
**********************************************************************
```

Identification

The error message indicates a modeling problem known as *nonidentifiability*. Identifiability, or the lack of it, is a difficult subject, but it is too important to be set in small type to be skipped on a first reading. The problem in this example is that it is impossible to estimate the regression weight for the regression of **performance** on **error**, and the variance of **error** at the same time. It is akin to being told "I bought $5 worth of widgets," and then asked to determine both the price of each widget and the number purchased. There is just not enough information.

This problem can be solved by *fixing* either the path coefficient from **error** to **performance**, or the variance of the **error** variable itself, at an arbitrary, non-zero value. We will discuss trade-offs between the two options later with the Amos output for this example. For the time being, we choose to fix the path coefficient at unity. This will yield the same estimates as conventional linear regression. To implement the identification constraint, select the **Parameter constraints (gamma)** button, and click on the path from **error** to **performance**. Enter the value '1' in the dialog box.

Remembering to constrain every path between an error and another parameter can become tedious. Fortunately, **Amos Graphics** provides a default solution which works well in most cases. You can simply select the **Add a unique variable** button. Then, when you click on an endogenous variable, Amos Graphics will automatically attach a latent exogenous variable to it, complete with a fixed path coefficient of '1'. Clicking on the observed variable repeatedly will change the position of the error variable.

A few minor adjustments are still needed (or may be desirable) before Amos can calculate the estimates. First, a name is needed for the unique variable. Select the **Text (enter/edit)** button, click on the circle and type the label **error** in the dialog box. Also, if you wish to change the shape or size of the **error** object, select the **Change the shape of objects** (word '**shape**') button, and then drag the object into its desired shape.

Finally, **Amos Graphics** requires that you connect the observed exogenous variables (**knowledge**, **satisfaction**, and **value**) with three two-headed covariance arrows, to allow them to be freely correlated. Forgetting to do so would generate the warning message:

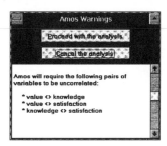

When all modeling components, including the identification constraint, are in place, then the input path diagram will look similar to:

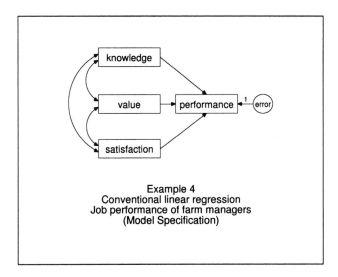

Example 4
Conventional linear regression
Job performance of farm managers
(Model Specification)

Modeling in Amos Text

This example represents a single linear regression equation, as there is only one endogenous variable. Each single-headed arrow corresponds to a regression weight, and it is these regression weights that need to be estimated. Here is an **Amos Text** input file that will do the job:

```
$Structure
    performance <--- knowledge
    performance <--- value
    performance <--- satisfaction
    performance <--- error (1)

$Include = warren5v.amd
```

The four lines that come after the **$Structure** command represent the single-headed arrows in the **Amos Graphics** path diagram (the dashes in '**<- - -**' are optional; you can use them to approximate path symbols somewhat from within **Amos Text** input mode). The *identification* constraint appears as the '(1)' symbol in line five, fixing the path coefficient from **error** to **performance** at unity.

Defaults for correlations among the exogenous variables

The **Amos Text** program uses certain default correlation (or covariance) structures of the exogenous variables in the model that are not incorporated in **Amos Graphics**. These defaults simplify the specifications for many types of models with **Amos Text** commands, especially with models containing many parameters. The differences between **Amos Graphics** and **Amos Text** are as follows:

1. **Amos Graphics** has no defaults whatsoever for correlation or covariance structures. The program is entirely WYSIWYG. If a two-headed path is drawn (but not constrained) between two variables (latent or observed), **Amos Graphics** will attempt to estimate the associated correlation or covariance term. Alternatively, if the path is missing, then the associated terms will not be estimated.

2. The **Amos Text** default rules for correlation/covariance structures are:

   a. *Unique latent* variables (*e.g.*, error terms or structural residuals) are uncorrelated with each other and with all other exogenous variables.

   b. All *Observed* exogenous and *non-unique* latent exogenous variables are correlated with each other. Non-unique latent variables (factors) are introduced in Example 5.

The **Amos Text** defaults reflect the standard assumptions of conventional linear regression analysis. That is, the predictor variables **knowledge**, **value**, and **satisfaction** are assumed to be correlated, and the unique latent variable **error** is treated as being independent of the other exogenous variables.

Alternative equation input

As a further option, **Amos Text** permits model specification in equation format rather than by the pseudo-paths shown above. For instance, the following **$Structure** command describes the path model as a single linear regression equation in which **performance** depends on the three other observed variables and an error term:

```
$Structure
    performance = () knowledge + () value + () satisfaction + (1) error

$Include = warren5.amd
```

The empty parentheses stand for the path coefficients (or regression weights) that are to be estimated, but are actually redundant (**Amos Text** assumes free path coefficients by default). Thus, even when the empty parentheses are left out, Amos will estimate a regression weight for each predictor. In that case the input file will look like this:

```
$Structure
    performance = knowledge + value + satisfaction + (1) error

$Include = warren5v.amd
```

The four versions of the input file (one Amos Graphics and three Amos Text versions) all produce the same text output. The choice among them is a matter of personal preference.

Results of the Analysis

Text output

Amos Text displays the maximum likelihood estimates:

```
Regression Weights:                      Estimate    S.E.     C.R.    Label
-------------------                      --------   -------  -------  -------

    performance <-------- knowledge        0.258     0.054    4.822
    performance <----------- value         0.145     0.035    4.136
    performance <----- satisfaction        0.049     0.038    1.274


Covariances:                             Estimate    S.E.     C.R.    Label
------------                             --------   -------  -------  -------

    knowledge <------------> value         0.028     0.009    3.276
    knowledge <------> satisfaction        0.004     0.007    0.632
    value <----------> satisfaction       -0.006     0.011   -0.593


Variances:                               Estimate    S.E.     C.R.    Label
----------                               --------   -------  -------  -------

                       knowledge          0.052     0.007    6.964
                           value          0.121     0.017    6.964
                    satisfaction          0.090     0.013    6.964
                           error          0.013     0.002    6.964
```

The path **performance <- - - error** is not displayed because its value is fixed at the default '1'. You may wonder how much the other estimates would be affected if a different identification constant had been chosen. It turns out that only the variance estimate for **error** is subject to any changes. All other estimates would remain constant.

Table 4.1 gives the resulting variance estimates for various choices of fixing the path coefficient **performance <- - - error.**

Path Constraint	Variance of **error**
0.5	0.050
0.707	0.025
1.0	0.0125
1.414	0.00625
2.0	0.00313

Table 4.1: Variance Estimate as a Function of the Identification Constraint

Suppose you fixed the path coefficient at 2 instead of 1. Then the variance estimate would essentially have to be divided by a factor of 4. You can extrapolate the rule that multiplying the path coefficient by a fixed factor goes along with dividing the error variance by the square of the same factor. Extending this, the product of the *squared* regression weight and the error variance is always a constant. This is what is meant by saying that the regression weight (together with the error variance) is unidentified. If you assign a value to one of them, the other can be estimated, but they cannot both be estimated at the same time.

The identifiability problem just discussed arises from the fact that the variance of a variable, and any regression weights associated with it, depend on the units in which the variable is measured. Since **error** is an unobserved variable, there is no natural way to specify a measurement unit for it. Assigning an arbitrary value to a regression weight associated with **error** can be thought of as a way of indirectly choosing a unit of measurement for **error**. Every unobserved variable presents this identifiability problem, which must be resolved by imposing some constraint that will determine its unit of measurement.

Changing the scale unit of the unobserved **error** variable does not change the overall model fit. In all five analyses you get:

```
Chi-square =      0.000
Degrees of freedom =    0
Probability level cannot be computed
```

There are four sample variances and six sample covariances, for a total of ten sample moments. There are three regression paths, four model variances, and three model covariances, for a total of ten parameters that must be estimated. Hence the model has zero degrees of freedom. Such a model is often called *saturated* or *just-identified*.

The *standardized* coefficient estimates are:

```
Standardized Regression Weights:          Estimate
--------------------------------          --------

    performance <-------- knowledge        0.407
    performance <----------- value         0.349
    performance <----- satisfaction        0.101


Correlations:                             Estimate
-------------                             --------

    knowledge <------------> value         0.353
    knowledge <------> satisfaction        0.064
    value <----------> satisfaction       -0.060
```

These estimates are also displayed in the path diagram output at the end of this example. The standardized regression weights and the correlations are independent of the units in which all variables are measured. Therefore, they will not be affected by the choice of identification constraints.

The optional **$Smc** command displays the squared multiple correlation, a useful statistic that is also independent of all units of measurement:

```
Squared Multiple Correlations:          Estimate
- - - - - - - - - - - - - - - - - - - - - - -   - - - - - - - - -
                       performance        0.399
```

Amos will display a squared multiple correlation for each endogenous variable. A variable's squared multiple correlation is the proportion of its variance that is accounted for by its predictors. In the present example, **knowledge**, **value** and **satisfaction** account for 39.9 percent of the variance of **performance**.

Graphics output

The path diagram output, for both unstandardized and standardized model solutions, follows below. Here is the diagram with unstandardized values:

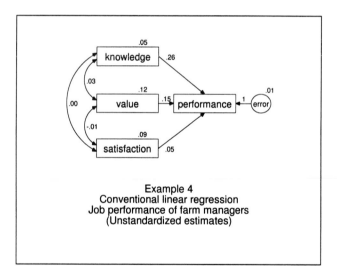

Example 4
Conventional linear regression
Job performance of farm managers
(Unstandardized estimates)

The standardized solution is:

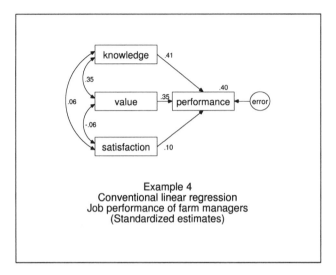

Example 4
Conventional linear regression
Job performance of farm managers
(Standardized estimates)

Note that the estimates are displayed in relatively fixed locations in the path diagrams. Their positions are assigned according to the rules in Table 4.2.

Location	Unstandardized Estimates	Standardized Estimates
Near Single-Headed Arrows	Regression weights	Standardized regression weights
Near Double-Headed Arrows	Covariances	Correlations
Near Endogenous Variables	Intercepts[1]	Squared multiple correlations
Near Exogenous Variables	Means[1] and variances	_____

Table 4.2: Location of Parameter Estimates in the Path Diagram Output

---

[1] Only when mean structures are analyzed, see Examples 13 through 16.

Additional output

Diagnostic information about the model appears at the beginning of the Amos text output. For instance, the following portion of the output file shows each variable in the model and its status:

```
Your model contains the following variables

          performance               observed    endogenous

          knowledge                 observed    exogenous
          value                     observed    exogenous
          satisfaction              observed    exogenous

          error                     unobserved  exogenous


              Number of variables in your model:    5
              Number of observed variables:         4
              Number of unobserved variables:       1
              Number of exogenous variables:        4
              Number of endogenous variables:       1
```

Again, *endogenous* variables are those that have single-headed arrows pointing to them in the path diagram, and depend on other variables. *Exogenous* variables are those that do not have arrows pointing at them; they do not depend on other variables in a regression setting.

Inspecting the list above will help you catch the most common (and insidious) errors in an input file: typing errors. If you try to type `performance` twice, but unintentionally misspell it as `performence` one of those times, both versions will appear on the list.

The following message indicates that there are no *loops* in the path diagram:

```
The model is recursive.
```

Later on you will see path diagrams in which you can pick a variable and, by tracing along the single-headed arrows, follow a path that leads again to the same variable. Path diagrams that have such feedback loops are called *nonrecursive*. Those that do not are called *recursive* (from the Latin *recurso*, meaning "I return"). When we step backwards through the paths of a recursive model, we are forced to return to the exogenous variables in a finite number of steps.

Because the model is saturated, there are zero degrees of freedom (as explained previously), and the estimated variances and covariances obtained with the **$Implied moments** command are identical to the sample values:

```
Implied Covariances

            satisfact value     knowledge performan
            --------- --------- --------- ---------
satisfacti   0.09010
value       -0.00630   0.12120
knowledge    0.00440   0.02800   0.05200
performanc   0.00460   0.02450   0.01770   0.02090
```

Example 5: Unobserved variables

Purpose

This example demonstrates a regression analysis with unobserved variables, as a means of taking the unreliability of the observed variables into consideration.

The data

When we use variables, such as **performance** and **satisfaction** in the previous example, we expect the values these variables take to be *reliable* measures of 'true' manager performance and satisfaction. However, the variables used in Example 4 were based on psychological tests. They were thus surely unreliable to some degree, if for no other reason than that replacement of some test items, or test administration on a different day, would have resulted in numerically different measurements.

The fact that the reliability of **performance** is unknown presents a minor problem when it comes to interpreting the fact that the predictors only account for 39.9 percent of the variance of **performance**. If the test were extremely unreliable, that fact in itself would explain why the **performance** score would not be predicted accurately. Unreliability of the *predictors*, on the other hand, presents a more serious problem because it frequently leads to biased regression estimates. Lack of predictive power of the regression model may thus have several reasons:

- **performance** is an unreliable measure of 'true' performance. Measurement error in the dependent variable deflates the squared multiple correlation and increases the standard error of the estimated regression weights.

- **knowledge**, **value**, and/or **satisfaction** may also be unreliable measures. Error in predictor variables tends to bias both the estimates of the regression weights and the squared multiple correlation (Bollen, 1989, *pp.* 151-176; Rigdon, 1994).

- Omitted variables: All measures may be reliable, but one or more important exogenous variables for predicting job performance of farm managers are left out of the model. In this instance, both regression estimates and squared multiple correlation are often biased (Draper and Smith, 1981, *pp.* 117-121).

None of these situations can be compensated for by an increase in sample size, however large.

The present example, based on Rock, *et al.* (1977), will assess the reliabilities of the four tests included in the previous analysis, and will obtain estimates of regression weights for perfectly reliable, hypothetical versions of the four tests. Rock, *et al.* re-examined the data of Warren, White and Fuller (1974) that were discussed in the previous example. This time, each test was randomly split into two halves, and each half was scored separately. The sample variances and covariances of these subtests are contained in the file **warren9v.amd**. The sample means that appear in the file will not be used in this example. Statistics on formal education (**past_training**) are present in the file, but they also will not enter into the present analysis.

Here are the contents of **warren9v.amd**:

```
! Managerial Role Performance of Farm Managers

! Sample means from
!      Warren, White, and Fuller (1974).
! Sample covariance matrix from
!      Joreskog and Sorbom (1984).

$Sample size = 98

$Input variables

    1performance   ! 12-item subtest of Role Performance
    2performance   ! 12-item subtest of Role Performance
    1knowledge     ! 13-item subtest of Knowledge
    2knowledge     ! 13-item subtest of Knowledge
    1value         ! 15-item subtest of Value Orientation
    2value         ! 15-item subtest of Value Orientation
    1satisfaction  !  5-item subtest of Role Satisfaction
    2satisfaction  !  6-item subtest of Role Satisfaction
    past_training  ! Degree of formal education

$Covariances
 .0271
 .0172  .0222
 .0219  .0193  .0876
 .0164  .0130  .0317  .0568
 .0284  .0294  .0383  .0151  .1826
 .0217  .0185  .0356  .0230  .0774  .1473
 .0083  .0011 -.0001  .0055 -.0087 -.0069  .1137
 .0074  .0015  .0035  .0089 -.0007 -.0088  .0722
 .1024
 .0180  .0194  .0203  .0182  .0563  .0142 -.0056
-.0077  .0946

$Means
0.0646 0.0542 1.4333 1.3259 2.8404 2.9143
2.4514 2.4711 2.1174
```

Names of the split-half subtests are composed of the name of the respective measured attribute (**performance**, **knowledge**, **value**, and **satisfaction**), preceded by a number (**1** or **2**) to identify the subscale.

Model A

The path diagram below presents a model for the eight subtests:

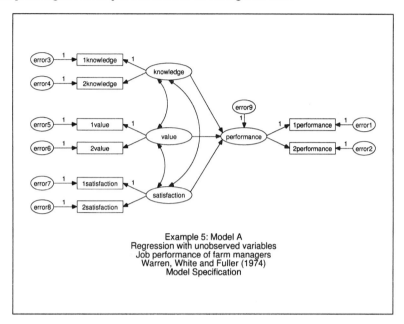

Example 5: Model A
Regression with unobserved variables
Job performance of farm managers
Warren, White and Fuller (1974)
Model Specification

Four ellipses in the figure are labeled **knowledge**, **value**, **satisfaction**, and **performance**. They represent the unobserved variables that are indirectly measured by the eight split-half tests.

The set of connections between the observed and unobserved variables is often called the measurement model. The current problem has four distinct measurement submodels:

Measurement Model

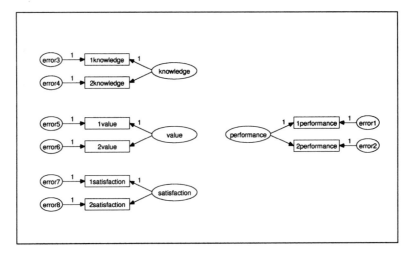

Consider, for instance, the **knowledge** submodel: the scores of the two split-half subtests, **1knowledge** and **2knowledge**, are thought to depend on the single underlying, but not directly observed variable **knowledge**. The two observed scores are not expected to be identical, though, due to the influence of **error3** and **error4**, the respective measurement error components of the two subtests.

The measurement model for **knowledge** forms a pattern which is repeated three more times in the above path diagram:

> Two or more observed variables, each depending on a common unobserved variable, and on a specific error or *unique* variable. The observed variables in such a pattern may be regarded as imperfect observable measures, or *indicators*, of the common unobserved variable. The unobserved common variable in such a measurement model is often referred to as a *factor* or *latent construct*.

The model component connecting the unobserved variables to each other is often called the structural model:

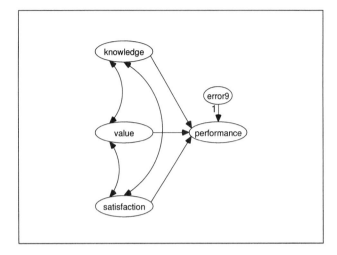

The relationship between these four variables is identical to the regression model used in Example 4, except with *unobserved* variables in place of the observed ones. It is the measurement model in which Examples 4 and 5 differ.

Identification

With thirteen unobserved variables in this model, it is certainly not identified. It will be necessary to fix the unit of measurement of each unobserved variable by suitable constraints on the parameters. This can be done by repeating thirteen times the trick that was used for the single unobserved variable in the previous example: Find a single-headed arrow leading away from each unobserved variable in the path diagram, and fix the corresponding regression weight to unity. If there is more than one single-headed arrow leading away from an observed variable, any one of them will usually do, although in some cases better parameter estimates will be obtained when the most reliable indicator variable is chosen. In this example, all paths from unobserved variables towards the indicator variables whose names start with the numeral '1', such as between **knowledge** and **1knowledge**, will be constrained. All paths connecting the (unique) error components will also be set to unity.

Modeling in Amos Graphics

Before you begin to draw the path diagram for this example, notice the boundaries on the screen. Nothing should be drawn beyond these boundaries, or otherwise that portion of your work will not be printed or copied to the clipboard. **Amos Graphics** uses the page size and orientation of your printer setup by default. Alternatively, the dimensions of the path diagram drawing area can be set explicitly via the

Page Layout command of Amos's **Global** menu. Example 5 is better run if the drawing area is in *landscape* orientation, and diagrams in `ex05-a.amw` and `ex05-b.amw` are formatted at 8.5 inches height and 11 inches width (approximately 21.5 by 28 cm).

If the printer is set up for printing in *portrait* mode (a likely case), the vertical extension of your drawing area will be longer than its horizontal boundary, essentially clipping the right-hand portion of landscape diagrams. To print the entire path diagram, set the printer to landscape mode by selecting the **Printer Setup...** command from the Amos **File** menu.

There is, of course, also an **Amos Graphics** button command to change the printer setup. It is located in the second of the two toolboxes. To toggle to *toolbox #2*, click on the **Use another toolbox (hammer)** button. Clicking on the **Printer Setup** button produces the **Print** dialog box. Then continue from item 2 in the list given above.

Now you are ready to set up the model as specified in the path diagram on page 353. This can be done in a number of ways. Several drawing and editing tools make it more efficient to start with the measurement model first. Here, we demonstrate how to construct the measurement model for one of the variables, **knowledge**, say, and use it as a stencil for the remaining three.

First draw the ellipse for the unobserved variable **knowledge**:

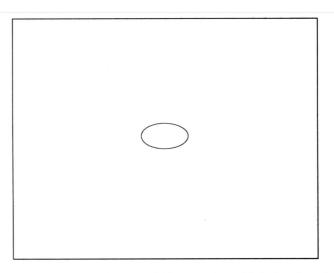

As a shortcut for drawing the indicator variables, complete with their paths and unique error components, **Amos Graphics** provides the **Draw indicator variable (circle/square branch)** button. To add the two indicator branches for the **knowledge** variable, select the **Draw indicator variable** button and then click twice on the ellipse. **Amos Graphics** will instantly create the branches for the two split-half tests:

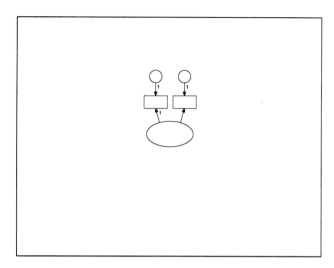

With the **Draw indicator variable** button selected, you can click multiple times on an unobserved variable to create all its indicator branches. **Amos Graphics** maintains suitable spacing among the indicators and inserts the required identification constraints.

Now you have all of the variables you need for the **knowledge** structure, except that the structure points upwards from the large ellipse instead of to its left. One tool to change the orientation of the indicator branches is the **Rotate** command. Simply select the **Rotate** button, then click on the large ellipse. Each time you click on the common latent variable, all its indicator branches will be rotated 90° clockwise. Clicking on the ellipse three times brings the structure to its desired orientation:

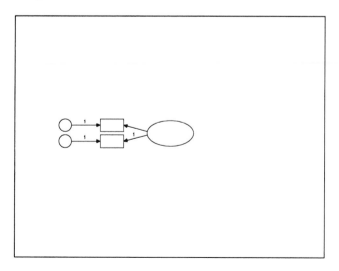

After creating the measurement model for **knowledge**, you might want to adjust the shape of the objects with the **Shape** button (see Example 4). Afterwards, *select the entire measurement model* for **knowledge** and use the **Duplicate** button to create the **value** and **satisfaction** structures. You can make a third copy for **performance**, then use either the **Rotate** or the **Reflect** button to reorient the structure to the right. To complete the measurement model, enter the *variable names* in all objects.

Now, we can turn to the structural model. Just a few things are left to do:

1. Draw in the three covariance paths between **knowledge**, **value**, and **satisfaction**.

2. Draw the single-headed paths from each of the unobserved predictors, **knowledge**, **value**, and **satisfaction**, to the latent dependent variable, **performance**.

3. Add the unobserved variable **error9** to **performance** (use the **Add a unique variable** button).

The path diagram should now look similar to the full specification on page 353. The Amos Graphics input file is `ex05-a.amw`.

Modeling in Amos Text

Here is an **Amos Text** input file that incorporates the model with the same identification constraints:

```
$Standardized
$Smc

$Structure
     1performance <--- performance (1)
     2performance <--- performance
     1knowledge <--- knowledge (1)
     2knowledge <--- knowledge
     1value <--- value (1)
     2value <--- value
     1satisfaction <--- satisfaction (1)
     2satisfaction <--- satisfaction

     1performance <--- error1 (1)
     2performance <--- error2 (1)
     1knowledge <--- error3 (1)
     2knowledge <--- error4 (1)
     1value <--- error5 (1)
     2value <--- error6 (1)
     1satisfaction <--- error7 (1)
     2satisfaction <--- error8 (1)

     performance <--- knowledge
     performance <--- satisfaction
     performance <--- value
     performance <--- error9 (1)

$Include = warren9v.amd
```

Because of the **Amos Text** default assumptions about the correlations among exogenous variables (discussed in Example 4), it is not necessary to indicate that **knowledge**, **value** and **satisfaction** may be correlated, nor is it necessary to specify that **error1**, **error2**, ... **error9** are uncorrelated among themselves and with every other exogenous variable.

Results for Model A

As an exercise, you might want to confirm the following degrees of freedom calculation:

```
Computation of Degrees of Freedom
                    Number of distinct sample moments:    36
        Number of distinct parameters to be estimated:    22
                    ------------------------
                                Degrees of freedom:    14
```

The chi-square test shows that Model A is reasonable:

```
Chi-square =      10.335
Degrees of freedom =    14
Probability level =       0.737
```

The parameter estimates can be difficult to interpret, since they would have been different if different identification constraints had been imposed:

Regression Weights:		Estimate	S.E.	C.R.	Label
performance <----------	knowledge	0.337	0.125	2.697	
performance <-------	satisfaction	0.061	0.054	1.127	
performance <-------------	value	0.176	0.079	2.225	
1performance <-------	performance	1.000			
2performance <-------	performance	0.867	0.116	7.450	
1knowledge <----------	knowledge	1.000			
2knowledge <----------	knowledge	0.683	0.161	4.252	
1value <------------------	value	1.000			
2value <------------------	value	0.763	0.185	4.128	
1satisfaction <-----	satisfaction	1.000			
2satisfaction <-----	satisfaction	0.792	0.438	1.806	

Covariances:		Estimate	S.E.	C.R.	Label
knowledge <-------------->	value	0.037	0.012	3.036	
knowledge <-------->	satisfaction	0.004	0.009	0.462	
value <----------->	satisfaction	-0.008	0.013	-0.610	

Variances:	Estimate	S.E.	C.R.	Label
knowledge	0.046	0.015	3.138	
value	0.101	0.032	3.147	
satisfaction	0.091	0.052	1.745	
error9	0.007	0.003	2.577	
error1	0.007	0.002	3.110	
error2	0.007	0.002	3.871	
error3	0.041	0.011	3.611	
error4	0.035	0.007	5.167	
error5	0.081	0.025	3.249	
error6	0.088	0.018	4.891	
error7	0.022	0.050	0.451	
error8	0.045	0.032	1.420	

Results produced by the **$Standardized** command, on the other hand, are not affected by the identification constraints:

```
Standardized Regression Weights:        Estimate
--------------------------------        --------

    performance <---------- knowledge     0.516
    performance <------- satisfaction     0.130
    performance <------------- value      0.398
    1performance <------- performance     0.856
    2performance <------- performance     0.819
    1knowledge <----------- knowledge     0.728
    2knowledge <----------- knowledge     0.618
    1value <------------------ value      0.745
    2value <------------------ value      0.633
    1satisfaction <----- satisfaction     0.896
    2satisfaction <----- satisfaction     0.747

Correlations:                           Estimate
-------------                           --------

    knowledge <--------------> value      0.542
    knowledge <--------> satisfaction     0.064
    value <-----------> satisfaction     -0.084
```

Amos Graphics Output

The path diagram with standardized parameter estimates inserted is:

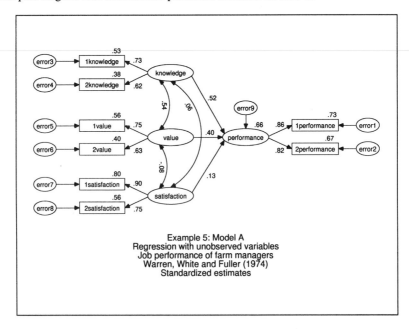

Example 5: Model A
Regression with unobserved variables
Job performance of farm managers
Warren, White and Fuller (1974)
Standardized estimates

The value above the **performance** object indicates that 'pure' **knowledge**, **value** and **satisfaction** account for 66 percent of the variance of the hypothetical 'pure' **performance** construct. The values printed over the observed variables are the reliability estimates for the eight individual subtests. A formula to compute the reliabilityof the original tests (before they were split in half) can be found in Rock *et al.* (1977) or any book on mental test theory.

Model B

Assuming that Model A is correct (there is no evidence to the contrary), consider the additional hypothesis that **1knowledge** and **2knowledge** are parallel tests, *i.e.*, two tests with a same-sized common variance component and equal-sized error variances. Under the parallel test hypothesis, the regression of **1knowledge** on **knowledge** should be the same as the regression of **2knowledge** on **knowledge**. Furthermore, the 'error' variables associated with **1knowledge** and **2knowledge** should have identical variances. Similar consequences flow from the assumptions that **1value** and **2value** are parallel tests, and that **1performance** and **2performance** are parallel tests. It is not altogether reasonable, however, to assume that **1satisfaction** and **2satisfaction** are parallel inasmuch as one of the subtests is slightly longer than the other. (The original test had an odd number of items, so it couldn't be split exactly in half). **2satisfaction** is 20 percent longer than **1satisfaction**. Assuming that the tests differ only in length leads to the following conclusions:

- The weight for regressing **2satisfaction** on the unobserved **satisfaction** variable should be 1.2 times the weight for regressing **1satisfaction** on **satisfaction**.

- Given equal variances for **error7** and **error8**, the (fixed) regression weight for **error8** should be $\sqrt{1.2} = 1.095445$ times as large as the (fixed) regression weight for **error7**.

Whichever method of input you use, you do not need to completely re-enter the input file or redraw the path diagram. You can just open the **Amos Text** or **Amos Graphics** file you created for Model A, modify it, and save the input as a new file.

Below are the model specifications in the **Amos Text** form. The input file supplies all constraints for the regression weight and error variance parameters:

```
$Standardized
$Smc

$Structure
     1performance <--- performance (1)
     2performance <--- performance (1)
     1knowledge <--- knowledge (1)
     2knowledge <--- knowledge (1)
     1value <--- value (1)
     2value <--- value (1)
     1satisfaction <--- satisfaction (1)
     2satisfaction <--- satisfaction (1.2)

     performance <--- knowledge
     performance <--- value
     performance <--- satisfaction
     performance <--- error9 (1)

     1performance <--- error1 (1)
     2performance <--- error2 (1)
     1knowledge <--- error3 (1)
     2knowledge <--- error4 (1)
     1value <--- error5 (1)
     2value <--- error6 (1)
     1satisfaction <--- error7 (1)
     2satisfaction <--- error8 (1.095445)

     error1 (alpha)
     error2 (alpha)
     error8 (delta)
     error7 (delta)
     error6 (gamma)
     error5 (gamma)
     error4 (beta)
     error3 (beta)

$Include = warren9v.amd
```

The corresponding **Amos Graphics** model specification is:

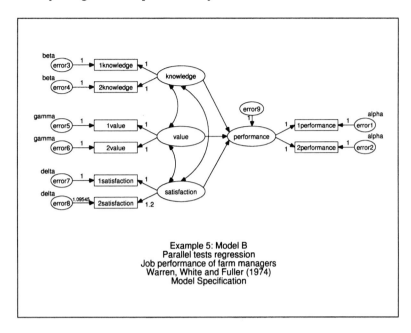

Example 5: Model B
Parallel tests regression
Job performance of farm managers
Warren, White and Fuller (1974)
Model Specification

Analysis of Model B

The additional parameter constraints of Model B have resulted in increased degrees of freedom for the model:

```
Computation of Degrees of Freedom

                Number of distinct sample moments:    36
        Number of distinct parameters to be estimated:  14
        - - - - - - - - - - - - - - - - - - - - - - - -
                        Degrees of freedom:   22
```

The chi-square statistic has also increased, but not by much. There is still no indication that Model B might be particularly bad:

```
Chi-square =     26.967
Degrees of freedom =    22
Probability level =     0.212
```

If Model B is indeed correct, the associated parameter estimates are to be preferred over those obtained under Model A. The raw parameter estimates will not be presented here, since they are too much affected by the choice of identification constraints. However, here are the standardized estimates and squared multiple correlations, both in **Amos Text** and **Amos Graphics** output:

```
Standardized Regression Weights:              Estimate
- - - - - - - - - - - - - - - - - - - - - -   - - - - - - -

    performance <- - - - - - - - - - knowledge       0.529
    performance <- - - - - - - - - - - - - value      0.382
    performance <- - - - - - - satisfaction          0.114
    1performance <- - - - - - - performance          0.835
    2performance <- - - - - - - performance          0.835
    1knowledge <- - - - - - - - - - - knowledge       0.663
    2knowledge <- - - - - - - - - - - knowledge       0.663
    1value <- - - - - - - - - - - - - - - value        0.685
    2value <- - - - - - - - - - - - - - - value        0.685
    1satisfaction <- - - - - satisfaction            0.790
    2satisfaction <- - - - - satisfaction            0.816
    2satisfaction <- - - - - - - - - - - error8       0.578


Correlations:                                 Estimate
- - - - - - - - - - - -                       - - - - - - -

    knowledge <- - - - - - - - - - - - - - -> value    0.565
    knowledge <- - - - - - - - -> satisfaction        0.094
    value <- - - - - - - - - - - -> satisfaction      -0.085

Squared Multiple Correlations:                Estimate
- - - - - - - - - - - - - - - - - - - - - -   - - - - - - -

                      performance             0.671
                     2satisfaction            0.666
                     1satisfaction            0.625
                          2value              0.469
                          1value              0.469
                       2knowledge             0.439
                       1knowledge             0.439
                      2performance            0.698
                      1performance            0.698
```

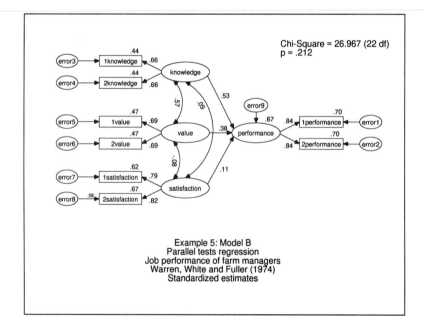

Example 5: Model B
Parallel tests regression
Job performance of farm managers
Warren, White and Fuller (1974)
Standardized estimates

Testing Model B against Model A

Sometimes you may have two alternative models for the same set of data, and you would like to know which model fits the data better. A direct comparison is possible whenever one of the models can be obtained by placing additional constraints on the parameters of the other. We have such a case here. We obtained Model B by imposing *eight* additional constraints on the parameters of Model A. Let us say that Model B is the stronger of the two models, in the sense that it represents the strongest hypothesis about the population parameters (Model A would, consequently, be the weaker model). In a case like this, the stronger model will necessarily have both larger degrees of freedom and a larger chi-square statistic.

A test of the stronger model (Model B here) against the weaker one (Model A) can be obtained by subtracting the smaller chi-square statistic from the larger one. In this example, the new statistic is 16.632 (*i.e.*, 26.967 - 10.335). If the stronger model (Model B) is correctly specified, this statistic will have an approximate chi-square distribution with degrees of freedom equal to the difference between the degrees of freedom of the competing models. In this example, the difference in degrees of freedom is 8 (*i.e.*, 22 - 14). That is, Model B imposes all of the parameter constraints of Model A, plus an additional 8.

To repeat: If Model B is correct, the value 16.632 comes from a chi-square distribution with 8 degrees of freedom. If only the weaker model (Model A) is correct, but the additional constraints of Model B are not supported by the data, then the new statistic will tend to be large. Hence, the stronger model (Model B) is to be rejected in favor of the weaker model (Model A) when the new chi-square statistic is unusually large. With 8 degrees of freedom, chi-square values greater than 15.507 are significant at the .05 level. Based on this test, we reject Model B.

This seems like a paradoxical decision, for how can we now *reject* the more restrictive Model B, if we already accepted it based on its chi-square fit statistic of 26.967 (22 df, p=.212)? The disagreement between the two conclusions can be explained by noting that the two tests differ in their baseline assumptions. The test we just calculated, based on 8 df, evaluates the likelihood of Model B under the assumption that Model A is correct. The initial test based on 22 degrees of freedom makes no such assumptions about Model A. It should be used if Model A was never considered an interesting alternative (and therefore never tested). If you are quite sure that Model A is correct, you should use the test comparing Model B against Model A. On the other hand, if Model A had been found to be unrealistic, then there would have been no reason to consider the more constrained (thus even less realistic) Model B.

Example 6: Exploratory analysis

Purpose

This example introduces structural modeling of time-dependent latent variables. Modification indices and critical ratios are used to explore autocorrelations among error terms. As a technique for efficient model comparisons, the example shows how to specify multiple, related models in a single file. Computation of fitted moments, factor score weights and total effects is also demonstrated.

The data

Wheaton *et al.* (1977) report a longitudinal study of 932 persons over the four-year period from 1966 to 1971. One aim of the study was to determine reliability and stability of alienation, a social psychological variable measured by attitude scales. Jöreskog and Sörbom (1984), and others since, have used the Wheaton data to demonstrate analysis of moment structures. Six of Wheaton's measures will be employed in this example:

anomia67:	1967 score on the *anomia* scale.
anomia71:	1971 *anomia* score.
powles67:	1967 score on the *powerlessness* scale.
powles71:	1971 *powerlessness* score.
education:	Years of schooling recorded in 1966.
SEI:	Duncan's Socioeconomic Index administered in 1966.

The sample means, standard deviations and correlations for these six measures are contained in the file **wheaton.amd**, listed below. Upon reading the data, Amos converts the standard deviations and correlations into variances and covariances, as needed for the analysis. The sample means will not be used in the analysis.

```
! Alienation and socioeconomic status.
! Correlations, standard deviation and means
! from Wheaton et al. (1977).

$Inputvariables
    anomia67        ! Anomia score in 1967
    powles67        ! Powerlessness score in 1967
    anomia71        ! Anomia score in 1971
    powles71        ! Powerlessness score in 1971
    education       ! Years of schooling completed
                    !   in 1966
    sei             ! Duncan's socioeconomic index
                    !   measured in 1966

$Samplesize=932
$Correlations
 1.00
  .66  1.00
  .56   .47  1.00
  .44   .52   .67  1.00
 -.36  -.41  -.35  -.37  1.00
 -.30  -.29  -.29  -.28   .54  1.00
$Standard deviations
 3.44  3.06  3.54  3.16  3.10 21.22
$Means
13.61 14.76 14.13 14.90 10.90 37.49
```

Model A for the Wheaton data

Jöreskog and Sörbom (1984) proposed the model shown on page 369 for the Wheaton data, referring to it as their Model A. The model asserts that all of the observed variables depend on underlying, unobserved variables. For example, **anomia67** and **powles67** both depend on the unobserved variable **67_alienation** (a hypothetical variable that Jöreskog and Sörbom referred to as alienation). The unobserved variables **eps1** and **eps2** appear to play the same role as the variables **error1** and **error2** did in Example 5. However, their interpretation here is different. In Example 5, **error1** and **error2** had a natural interpretation as errors of measurement. In the present example, since the anomia and powerlessness scales were not designed to measure the exact same construct, it seems reasonable to believe that differences between them will be due to more than mere measurement error. So in this case **eps1** and **eps2** should be thought of as representing not only errors of measurement in **anomia67** and **powles67**, but every other variable that might affect scores on the two tests besides **67_alienation** (the one variable that affects them both).

Modeling in Amos Graphics

Here is a path diagram for Model A:

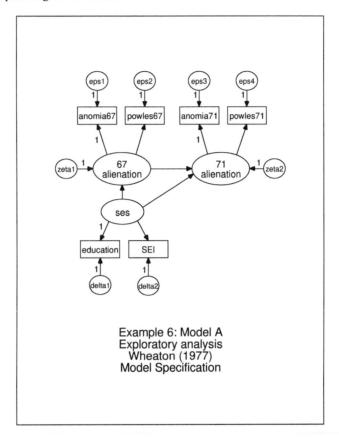

Example 6: Model A
Exploratory analysis
Wheaton (1977)
Model Specification

If you just finished Example 5, remember to return your printer to **Portrait** mode, using the **Print Setup** command under the **File** menu. Your print area should be longer in height than width. To specify Model A in **Amos Graphics**, construct the path model shown above, or use the example file `ex06-a.amw`.

Identification

Model A is identified except for the usual problem that the measurement scale of each unobserved variable is indeterminate. The measurement scale of each unobserved variable may be fixed arbitrarily by setting a coefficient to unity (1) in one of the paths that are pointing away from it. The path diagram shows 11 regression weights fixed at unity (1), *i.e.*, one value constraint for each unobserved variable. These constraints are sufficient to make the model identified for **Amos Graphics** input.

Modeling in Amos Text

The following **Amos Text** input file (from **ex06-a.ami**) specifies Model A with the same identification constraints:

```
Example 6, Model A:
Exploratory analysis

Stability of alienation, mediated by ses.
Correlations, standard deviations and
means from Wheaton et al. (1977).

$Mods=4

$Structure
      anomia67 <--- 67_alienation (1)
      anomia67 <--- eps1 (1)
      powles67 <--- 67_alienation
      powles67 <--- eps2 (1)

      anomia71 <--- 71_alienation (1)
      anomia71 <--- eps3 (1)
      powles71 <--- 71_alienation
      powles71 <--- eps4 (1)

      67_alienation <--- ses
      67_alienation <--- zeta1 (1)

      71_alienation <--- 67_alienation
      71_alienation <--- ses
      71_alienation <--- zeta2 (1)

      education <--- ses (1)
      education <--- delta1 (1)
      SEI <--- ses
      SEI <--- delta2 (1)

$Include = wheaton.amd
```

The eight unique variables **delta1, delta2, zeta1, zeta2,** and **eps1** through **eps4** are uncorrelated among themselves, and with the three common factors **ses, 67_alienation,** and **71_alienation**.

Output from the analysis of Model A

The model has 15 parameters to be estimated (6 regression weights and 9 variances). There are 21 sample moments (6 sample variances and 15 covariances). This leaves 6 degrees of freedom:

```
Computation of Degrees of Freedom

                Number of distinct sample moments:    21
      Number of distinct parameters to be estimated:  15
                ------------------------
                            Degrees of freedom:    6
```

Model A does not fit the Wheaton data particularly well:

```
Chi-square =    71.544
Degrees of freedom =    6
Probability level =    0.000
```

There are several courses open to you when a proposed model has to be rejected on statistical grounds:

- You can point out that statistical hypothesis testing can be a poor tool for choosing a model. Jöreskog (1967) discussed this issue in the context of factor analysis. It is a widely accepted view that a model can be only an approximation at best, and that, fortunately, a model can be useful without being true. This point of view implies that models are never perfectly correct and thus can always be rejected on statistical grounds if tested against a big enough sample. Consequently, rejection of a model on purely statistical grounds, particularly with a large sample, is not necessarily a condemnation.

  While this argument is generally recognized as valid, most published applications of analysis of moment structures do have statistically acceptable fit. While the publication practice of peer-reviewed journals may follow much stricter guidelines, moderately misfitting models can be entertained throughout the research process.

- You can start from scratch to devise another model to replace the rejected one.

- You can try to modify the rejected model in small ways to improve its fit to the data.

It is the last tactic that will be demonstrated in this example. The most natural way of modifying a model to make it fit better is to relax some of its assumptions. For example, Model A assumes that **eps1** and **eps3** are uncorrelated. This is a restriction that could be relaxed by connecting **eps1** and **eps3** with a double-headed arrow. The model also specifies that **anomia67** does not depend directly on **ses**. This assumption could be removed by drawing a single-headed arrow from **ses** to **anomia67**. Model A does not happen to constrain any parameters to be equal to other parameters, but if such constraints were present you might consider removing them in hopes of getting a better fit. Of course you have to be careful when relaxing the assumptions of a model that you do not turn an identified model into an unidentified one.

You can test various modifications of a model by carrying out a separate analysis for each proposed modification, but this approach is unnecessarily time-consuming. Typing the **$Mods** command into your **Amos Text** input file, or your **Amos Graphics** command file, allows you to examine all potential modifications in a single analysis. The **$Mods** command produces suggestions for modifications that will likely result in lower chi-square values. Here is the output produced by the command **$Mods=4**:

```
Covariances:                                    M.I.      Par Change
                                              ----------  ----------
        eps2 <------------------> delta1        5.905       -0.424
        eps2 <------------------> eps4         26.545        0.825
        eps2 <------------------> eps3         32.071       -0.989
        eps1 <------------------> delta1        4.609        0.421
        eps1 <------------------> eps4         35.367       -1.070
        eps1 <------------------> eps3         40.911        1.254

Variances:                                      M.I.      Par Change
                                              ----------  ----------


Regression Weights:                             M.I.      Par Change
                                              ----------  ----------
     powles71 <-------------- powles67          5.457        0.057
     powles71 <-------------- anomia67          9.006       -0.065
     anomia71 <-------------- powles67          6.775       -0.069
     anomia71 <-------------- anomia67         10.352        0.076
     powles67 <-------------- powles71          5.612        0.054
     powles67 <-------------- anomia71          7.278       -0.054
     anomia67 <-------------- powles71          7.706       -0.070
     anomia67 <-------------- anomia71          9.065        0.068
```

The column heading M.I. in this table is short for **modification index**. The modification indices produced by the **$Mods** command are those described byJöreskog and Sörbom (1984). The first modification index above (5.905) is a conservative estimate of the decrease in chi-square if **eps2** and **delta1** were allowed to correlate. If the additional parameter were indeed added, then the degrees of freedom associated with the new model would be one less. The new chi-square statistic would have 5 (= 6 – 1) degrees of freedom, and would be no greater than 65.639 (*i.e.*, 71.544 –5.905). The actual decrease of the chi-square statistic might be much larger than 5.905. The column labeled Par change gives approximate estimates of how much the parameter would change if it were relaxed. Amos estimates that the covariance between **eps2** and **delta1** would be

–0.424. Based on the small modification index, it does not look as though much would be gained by allowing **eps2** and **delta1** to be correlated. Besides, it would be hard to justify this particular modification on theoretical grounds even if it did produce a numerically acceptable fit.

> *Note*: The numeral 4 in the command **$Mods=4** above specifies that only modification indices greater than 4 shall be displayed. The command **$Mods=0** would have displayed all modification indices greater than zero; yet, many of these would have been small, and thus of little interest.

The largest modification index in Model A is 40.911. It indicates that allowing **eps1** and **eps3** to be correlated will decrease the chi-square statistic by at least 40.911. This is a modification well worth considering, particularly because autocorrelated residuals are frequently encountered in time-structured models. The substantive reasoning would be approximately this:

> The term **eps1** represents variability in **anomia67** that is not due to variation in **67_alienation**. Similarly, **eps3** represents variability in **anomia71** that is not due to variation in **71_alienation**. **Anomia67** and **anomia71** are scale scores on the same instrument (at different times). If

the anomia scale also reflects some other attitude besides alienation, you would expect to find a nonzero correlation between **eps1** and **eps3**. In fact, you would expect the correlation to be positive, which is consistent with the fact that the number in the Par Change column is positive.

The theoretical reasons for suspecting that **eps1** and **eps3** might be correlated apply to **eps2** and **eps4** as well. The modification indices also suggest allowing **eps2** and **eps4** to be correlated. However, we will ignore this potential modification and proceed immediately to look at the results of modifying Model A by allowing **eps1** and **eps3** to be correlated.

Model B for the Wheaton data

If you are using **Amos Text**, you can turn Model A into Jöreskog and Sörbom's Model B by adding the following line in the **$Structure** section of the input file:

```
eps1 <---> eps3
```

With **Amos Graphics**, you simply draw a covariance path between **eps1** and **eps3** in the input path diagram. If the path goes beyond the bounds of the print area, you can use the **Shape** button to adjust the curvature of the covariance curve or make it arc in the other direction. The **Move** button will let you reposition the end points of the covariance path, if needed. The **Amos Graphics** file for this example is **ex06-b.amw**.

Analysis of Model B

Amos Text output

The added covariance between **eps1** and **eps3** decreases the degrees of freedom by one:

```
Computation of Degrees of Freedom

                    Number of distinct sample moments:   21
        Number of distinct parameters to be estimated:   16
                                            ----------------------
                                  Degrees of freedom:    5
```

The chi-square statistic is reduced by substantially more than the promised 40.911:

```
Chi-square =      6.383
Degrees of freedom =    5
Probability level =     0.271
```

Model B cannot be rejected. Since the fit of Model B is reasonable, we will not pursue the possibility, mentioned above, that **eps2** and **eps4** might also be correlated (an argument could be made that a nonzero correlation between **eps2** and **eps4** should be allowed in order to achieve a symmetry that is now lacking in the model).

The raw parameter estimates must be interpreted cautiously since they would have been different if different identification constraints had been imposed. The text output of the parameter estimates is:

```
Regression Weights:                        Estimate   S.E.     C.R.      Label
-------------------                        --------   -------  -------   -------

  67_alienation <------------- ses          -0.550    0.053   -10.294
  71_alienation <---- 67_alienation          0.617    0.050    12.421
  71_alienation <------------- ses          -0.212    0.049    -4.294
  anomia67 <--------- 67_alienation          1.000
  powles67 <--------- 67_alienation          1.027    0.053    19.322
  anomia71 <--------- 71_alienation          1.000
  powles71 <--------- 71_alienation          0.971    0.049    19.650
  education <----------------- ses           1.000
  SEI <---------------------- ses            5.164    0.421    12.255


Covariances:                               Estimate   S.E.     C.R.      Label
------------                               --------   -------  -------   -------

  eps1 <--------------------> eps3           1.888    0.240     7.866


Variances:                                 Estimate   S.E.     C.R.      Label
----------                                 --------   -------  -------   -------

                             ses            6.879    0.658    10.458
                           zeta1            4.705    0.433    10.864
                           zeta2            3.866    0.343    11.257
                            eps1            5.065    0.371    13.650
                            eps2            2.213    0.318     6.968
                            eps3            4.811    0.395    12.173
                            eps4            2.684    0.330     8.137
                          delta1            2.731    0.516     5.292
                          delta2          266.853   18.193    14.668
```

Note the large critical ratio associated with the new covariance path. The covariance parameter between **eps1** and **eps3** is clearly different from zero. This explains the poor fit of Model A, which fixed this covariance at zero.

Amos Graphics output

The following path diagram displays the standardized estimates (near the paths) and squared multiple correlations (near the endogenous variables):

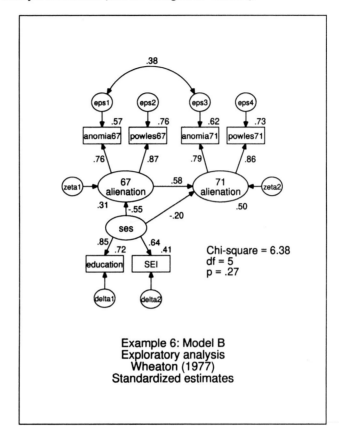

Example 6: Model B
Exploratory analysis
Wheaton (1977)
Standardized estimates

Because the error variables in the model represent more than just measurement error, the squared multiple correlations cannot be interpreted as estimates of reliabilities. Rather, each squared multiple correlation may serve as a lower-bound estimate of the corresponding reliability. Take **education**, for instance. 72 percent of its variance is accounted for by **ses**. Hence, you would estimate that its reliability be at least 0.72. Considering that **education** is measured in years of schooling, the reliability of this variable ought to be closer to 1.

Misuse of Modification indices

In trying to improve upon a model, you should not be guided exclusively by the modification indices. A modification must only be considered if it makes theoretical or common sense. Without such a limitation, slavish reliance on modification indices will amount to sorting through a very large number of potential modifications in search of one that provides a big improvement in fit. Such a strategy is, through capitalization on chance, prone to producing incorrect models in the sense that their low chi-square values will not likely be replicated by cross-validation. There is also the danger that the structure and the parameter estimates of the resulting model could be fairly absurd. These issues are discussed by MacCallum (1986) and by MacCallum, Roznowski and Necowitz (1992).

Improving a model by adding new constraints

Modification indices suggest ways of improving a model by increasing the number of parameters in such a way that the chi-square statistic decreases faster than the degrees of freedom. This device can be misused, but it has a legitimate place in exploratory studies. There is another trick that can be used to produce a model with a more acceptable chi-square value. This technique introduces additional constraints in such a way as to produce a relatively large increase in degrees of freedom coupled with a relatively small increase in the chi-square statistic. Many such modifications can be roughly evaluated by looking at the critical ratios in the C.R. column. We have already seen (in Example 1) how a single critical ratio can be used to test the hypothesis that a single population parameter equals zero.

If two parameter estimates turned out to be nearly equal you might be able to improve the chi-square test of fit by postulating a new model in which those two parameters are assumed to be exactly equal. Amos provides a powerful exploratory tool for separating promising from unlikely candidates for equality constraints. The **$Crdiff** command produces a listing of critical ratios for the pairwise differences among all parameter estimates. **$Crdiff** changes the Amos output listing in two ways: first, unique labels are attached to the parameter estimates. These will be the labels supplied by the model specification, plus simple default labels for all other estimated parameters, such as the par-*nn* labels in this output listing:

```
Regression Weights:                             Estimate    S.E.      C.R.     Label
-------------------                             --------   -------   -------   -------

   67_alienation <-------------- ses             -0.550     0.053   -10.294    par-6
   71_alienation <---- 67_alienation              0.617     0.050    12.421    par-4
   71_alienation <------------- ses              -0.212     0.049    -4.294    par-5
   powles71 <--------- 71_alienation              0.971     0.049    19.650    par-1
   anomia71 <--------- 71_alienation              1.000
   powles67 <--------- 67_alienation              1.027     0.053    19.322    par-2
   anomia67 <--------- 67_alienation              1.000
   education <----------------- ses               1.000
   SEI <---------------------- ses                5.164     0.421    12.255    par-3


Covariances:                                    Estimate    S.E.      C.R.     Label
------------                                     --------   -------   -------   -------

   eps1 <--------------------> eps3               1.888     0.240     7.866    par-7

Variances:                                      Estimate    S.E.      C.R.     Label
----------                                       --------   -------   -------   -------

                               ses               6.879     0.658    10.458    par-8
                             zeta1               4.705     0.433    10.864    par-9
                             zeta2               3.866     0.343    11.257    par-10
                              eps1               5.065     0.371    13.650    par-11
                              eps2               2.213     0.318     6.968    par-12
                              eps3               4.811     0.395    12.173    par-13
                              eps4               2.684     0.330     8.137    par-14
                            delta1               2.731     0.516     5.292    par-15
                            delta2             266.853    18.193    14.668    par-16
```

Secondly, the parameter labels are used to identify the critical ratio statistics in the following table:

```
Critical Ratios for Differences between Parameters

          par-1     par-2     par-3     par-4     par-5     par-6     par-7
         --------  --------  --------  --------  --------  --------  --------
par-1      0.000
par-2      0.877     0.000
par-3      9.883     9.741     0.000
par-4     -4.429    -5.931   -10.579     0.000
par-5    -17.943   -16.634   -12.284   -18.098     0.000
par-6    -22.343   -26.471   -12.661   -17.300    -5.115     0.000
par-7      3.908     3.693    -6.757     5.058     8.490    10.122     0.000
par-8      8.957     8.868     1.713     9.577    10.994    11.795     7.128
par-9      8.367     7.875    -0.706     9.258    11.311    12.045     5.388
par-10     7.785     8.044    -2.353     9.472    11.683    12.628     4.668
par-11    11.109    11.708    -0.177    11.971    14.038    15.429     9.773
par-12     3.829     3.339    -5.592     5.001     7.697     8.252     0.740
par-13    10.427     9.662    -0.611    10.308    12.712    13.574     8.318
par-14     4.700     4.909    -4.635     6.355     8.554     9.601     1.798
par-15     3.395     3.285    -7.265     4.020     5.507     5.974     1.482
par-16    14.615    14.612    14.192    14.637    14.687    14.712    14.563

          par-8     par-9     par-10    par-11    par-12    par-13    par-14
         --------  --------  --------  --------  --------  --------  --------
par-8      0.000
par-9     -2.996     0.000
par-10    -4.112    -1.624     0.000
par-11    -2.402     0.548     2.308     0.000
par-12    -6.387    -5.254    -3.507    -4.728     0.000
par-13    -2.695     0.169     1.554    -0.507     5.042     0.000
par-14    -5.701    -3.909    -2.790    -4.735     0.999    -3.322     0.000
par-15    -3.787    -2.667    -1.799    -3.672     0.855    -3.199     0.077
par-16    14.506    14.439    14.458    14.387    14.544    14.400    14.518

          par-15    par-16
         --------  --------
par-15     0.000
par-16    14.293     0.000
```

Ignoring the zeros down the main diagonal, the table of critical ratios contains 120 entries, one for each pair of parameters. Take the figure 0.877 near the upper left corner of the table. This critical ratio is the difference between the parameters labeled par-1 and par-2 divided by the estimated standard error of this difference. The two parameters in question are the path coefficients for powles67 <-- 67_alienation and powles71 <-- 71_alienation. Under the distribution assumptions stated in the technical note at the end of Example 1, the critical ratio statistic can be compared to a table of the standard normal distribution to test whether the two parameters are equal in the population. Since 0.877 is less in magnitude than 1.96, you would not reject, at the .05 level, the hypothesis that the two regression weights are equal in the population. More importantly, you can justify theoretically why these two paths could be equal: the relationship between alienation and powerlessness might well remain constant over the four-year period.

The *square* of the critical ratio for differences between parameters is approximately the amount by which the chi-square statistic would increase if the two parameters were set equal to each other. Since the square of 0.877 is 0.769, modifying Model B so that the two regression weights are estimated at one equal value would yield a chi-square value of about 6.383 + 0.769 = 7.152. The degrees of freedom for the new model would be 6 instead of 5. This would be an improved fit (p = 0.307 *vs.* 0.275 for Model B), but we can do much better than that.

Let's look for the smallest critical ratio to use as an example. The smallest critical ratio in the table is 0.077, for the parameters labeled par-14 and par-15. These two parameters are the variances of **eps4** and **delta1**. The square of 0.077 is 0.006. A modification of Model B that assumes **eps4** and **delta1** to have equal variances will result in a chi-square value that exceeds 6.383 by about 0.006, but with 6 degrees of freedom instead of 5. The associated probability level would be about 0.381. The only problem with this modification is that there is absolutely no justification for it. That is, we cannot think of any *a priori* reason why **eps4** and **delta1** should have equal variances.

We have just been discussing a misuse of the table of critical ratios for differences. However the table does have legitimate exploratory use in the quick examination of a small number of hypotheses. As an example of the proper use of the table, consider the fact that observations on **anomia67** and **anomia71** were obtained by using the same instrument on two occasions. The same goes for **powles67** and **powles71**. It is plausible that the tests would behave the same way on the two occasions. The critical ratios for differences are consistent with this hypothesis. The variances of **eps1** and **eps3** (par-11 and par-13) differ with a critical ratio of -0.507. The variances of **eps2** and **eps4** (par-12 and par-14) differ with a critical ratio of 0.999. The weights for the regression of powerlessness on alienation (par-1 and par-2) differ with a critical ratio of 0.877. None of these differences, taken individually, is significant at conventional significance levels. This suggests that it may be worthwhile to investigate more carefully a model in which all three differences are constrained to be zero. We will call the new model, Model C, and we are interested in evaluating its fit to the data, above and beyond the fit of the more general Model B.

Model C for the Wheaton data

The **Amos Text** input for Model C, from file **ex06-c.ami**, is:

```
$Structure
    anomia67 <--- 67_alienation (1)
    anomia67 <--- eps1 (1)
    powles67 <--- 67_alienation (path_p)
    powles67 <--- eps2 (1)
    anomia71 <--- 71_alienation (1)
    anomia71 <--- eps3 (1)
    powles71 <--- 71_alienation (path_p)
    powles71 <--- eps4 (1)

    67_alienation <--- ses
    67_alienation <--- zeta1 (1)
    71_alienation <--- 67_alienation
    71_alienation <--- ses
    71_alienation <--- zeta2 (1)

    education <--- ses (1)
    education <--- delta1 (1)
    SEI <--- ses
    SEI <--- delta2 (1)

    eps3 <--> eps1

    eps1 (var_a)
    eps2 (var_p)
    eps3 (var_a)
    eps4 (var_p)

$Include = wheaton.amd
```

The label path_p sets the path coefficients from alienation to powerlessness to the same value at the two measurement occasions. The label var_a is used to specify that **eps1** and **eps3** have the same variance. The label var_p specifies that **eps2** and **eps4** have the same variance. The corresponding **Amos Graphics** model specification, from **ex06c.amw**, is:

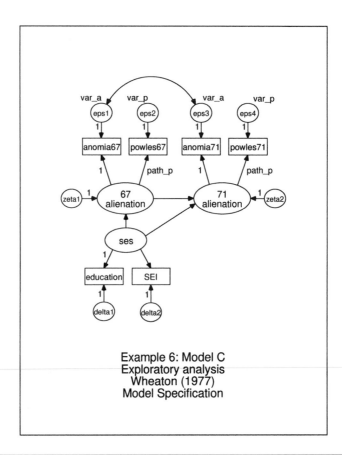

Example 6: Model C
Exploratory analysis
Wheaton (1977)
Model Specification

Output from the analysis of Model C

Model C has 3 more degrees of freedom than Model B:

```
Computation of Degrees of Freedom

             Number of distinct sample moments:    21
    Number of distinct parameters to be estimated:  13
             ---------------------------
                        Degrees of freedom:   8
```

Testing Model C

As expected, Model C has an acceptable fit, with a higher probability level than Model B:

```
Chi-square =      7.501
Degrees of freedom =    8
Probability level =    0.484
```

Model C may be tested against Model B by examining the difference in chi-square values (7.501 − 6.383 = 1.118) and the difference in degrees of freedom (8 - 5 = 3). A chi-square value of 1.118 with 3 degrees of freedom is not significant.

Parameter estimates for Model C

The raw parameter estimates for Model C will not be discussed because they are affected by the identification constraints. The standardized estimates are:

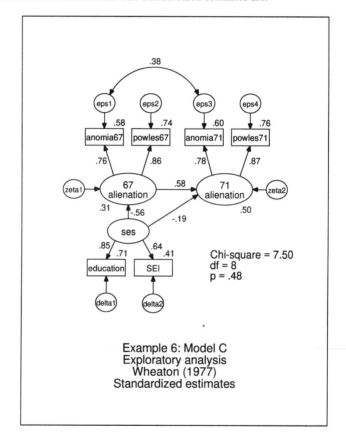

Example 6: Model C
Exploratory analysis
Wheaton (1977)
Standardized estimates

Multiple models in a single file

Both **Amos Graphics** and **Amos Text** allow for the inclusion of multiple models in a single file. There are two reasons for doing so: not only are all of your results maintained under a single heading, but several models can be estimated together. In addition, Amos prints the chi-square difference tests between any two nested models, along with the *p* values for these comparisons. Putting all three models in a single file in this example requires a little foresight, for the individual models must be expressed as restricted versions of the most general model considered.

Modeling in Amos Text

Suppose you took the **Amos Text** command file for Model B and added unique labels to get the file below:

```
$Structure
     anomia67 <--- 67_alienation (1)
     anomia67 <--- eps1 (1)
     powles67 <--- 67_alienation (b_pow67)
     powles67 <--- eps2 (1)

     anomia71 <--- 71_alienation (1)
     anomia71 <--- eps3 (1)
     powles71 <--- 71_alienation (b_pow71)
     powles71 <--- eps4 (1)

     67_alienation <--- ses
     67_alienation <--- zeta1 (1)
     71_alienation <--- 67_alienation
     71_alienation <--- ses
     71_alienation <--- zeta2 (1)

     education <--- ses (1)
     education <--- delta1 (1)
     SEI <--- ses
     SEI <--- delta2 (1)

     eps3 <--> eps1 (cov1)

     eps1 (var_a67)
     eps2 (var_p67)
     eps3 (var_a71)
     eps4 (var_p71)
$Include wheaton.amd
```

All three of the models discussed are manifestations of this new model. Model A did not include a covariance term between **eps1** and **eps3**; this is equivalent to setting cov1=0. Model B is the most general model—it imposes no constraints on the parameters. Model C specifies time-invariance measurement relationships for the alienation construct. This is equivalent to adding the three equality constraints:

```
b_pow67 = b_pow71
var_a67 = var_a71
var_p67 = var_p71
```

For completeness sake, a fourth specification (Model D) might be considered that combines the single constraint of Model A with the three constraints of Model C. The models can easily be specified in the **Amos Text** command file through use of the **$Model** command. This has been done in the example file **ex06-all.ami**. The model definition section of this command file is:

```
$Model = Model_A:_no_autocorrelation
    cov1 = 0
$Model = Model_B:_most_general
$Model = Model_C:_time-invariance
    b_pow67 = b_pow71
    var_a67 = var_a71
    var_p67 = var_p71
$Model = Model_D:_A_and_C_combined
    Model_A:_no_autocorrelation
    Model_C:_time-invariance
```

Each model specification begins with a **$Model** command and a label for the particular model. The label is used in the list output to identify the results. The label can also be used as a reference in subsequent model specifications.

Parameter constraints appear immediately after the **$Model** command, *i.e.*, before any other **$** commands. Note that the line $Model = Model_B:_most_general is followed immediately by another **$Model** command, indicating that Model B does not impose any parameter restrictions.

The last model specification (Model D) demonstrates how earlier model specifications can easily be assembled into a more restricted, combined model. To enter all constraints used by a previous model, the label of that model may be used as a reference. This back-referencing facility makes systematic model comparisons quite easy.

Modeling in Amos Graphics

Entering multiple models into a path diagram input file is done in much the same way as under **Amos Text**. First, add unique parameter labels to the path diagram (using, for instance, the **Text(Enter/Edit)** command button). Then press the **$** commands button and define each individual model by a separate **$Model** command.

Output from multiple models

Amos Graphics output

When multiple models are run, you can use the **Groups/Models** button to display the diagrams from different models. This button produces the following dialog box, from which the desired model output can be selected:

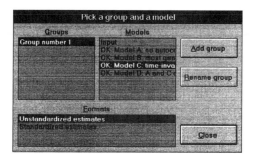

Amos Text output

When multiple models are specified, Amos computes and prints the estimates and related output for each model in turn. In addition, near the end of the list output file, various fit statistics for the models are summarized:

```
Summary of models
- - - - - - - - - - - - - - - - -

            Model  NPAR       CMIN   DF            P     CMIN/DF
- - - - - - - - - - - - - - -   - - - -   - - - - - - - - -   - -   - - - - - - - - -   - - - - - - - - -
Model_A:_no_autocorr    15     71.544    6        0.000      11.924
Model_B:_most_genera    16      6.383    5        0.271       1.277
Model_C:_time-invari    13      7.501    8        0.484       0.938
Model_D:_A_and_C_com    12     73.077    9        0.000       8.120
     Saturated model    21      0.000    0
    Independence model   6   2131.790   15        0.000     142.119
```

With maximum likelihood estimation (default), the column labeled CMIN contains the usual chi-square fit statistics (except when incomplete data are analyzed, in which case the fit chi-square is replaced by the likelihood itself). The column labeled p contains the corresponding upper tail probabilities for testing the null hypothesis. At the very end of the list output file, Amos provides tables of model comparisons, complete with chi-square difference tests and their associated p values:

```
Model Comparisons
- - - - - - - - - - - - - - - - -

Assuming model Model_A:_no_autocorrelation to be correct:

                                      NFI      IFI      RFI      TLI
               DF     CMIN      P   Delta-1  Delta-2   rho-1    rho-2
               - -    - - - -   - - - - -  - - - - - - - -  - - - - - - - -  - - - - -  - - - - -
Model_D:_A_and_C_comb   3    1.533  0.675    0.001    0.001   -0.027   -0.027


Assuming model Model_B:_most_general to be correct:

                                      NFI      IFI      RFI      TLI
               DF     CMIN      P   Delta-1  Delta-2   rho-1    rho-2
               - -    - - - -   - - - - -  - - - - - - - -  - - - - - - - -  - - - - -  - - - - -
Model_A:_no_autocorre   1   65.160  0.000    0.031    0.031    0.075    0.075
Model_C:_time-invaria   3    1.117  0.773    0.001    0.001   -0.002   -0.002
Model_D:_A_and_C_comb   4   66.693  0.000    0.031    0.031    0.048    0.048


Assuming model Model_C:_time-invariance to be correct:

                                      NFI      IFI      RFI      TLI
               DF     CMIN      P   Delta-1  Delta-2   rho-1    rho-2
               - -    - - - -   - - - - -  - - - - - - - -  - - - - - - - -  - - - - -  - - - - -
Model_D:_A_and_C_comb   1   65.576  0.000    0.031    0.031    0.051    0.051
```

Because the four models in this example follow a two-by-two factorial design, the chi-square comparisons for relative model fit can be arranged more compactly in Table 6.1.

| | Measurement of alienation | | Chi-square difference |
	varying	time-invariant	
cov1 estimated	Model B: $\chi^2_5 = 6.38$	Model C: $\chi^2_8 = 7.50$	$\chi^2_3 = 1.12$
cov1 = 0	Model A: $\chi^2_6 = 71.54$	Model D: $\chi^2_9 = 73.08$	$\chi^2_3 = 1.53$
Chi-square difference	$\chi^2_1 = 65.16$	$\chi^2_1 = 65.58$	

Table 6.1 : χ^2 Fit Statistics of Models A through D, and χ^2–Differences.

The chi-square difference statistics in the bottom margin of the table do not support the hypothesis that the autocorrelation parameter cov1 equals zero, no matter which of the two measurement models for alienation is chosen. The chi-square values in the right margin of the table indicate that the time-invariant measurement model performs as well as the more general (varying) model, no matter whether the parameter cov1 is estimated or fixed at zero. According to this table, Model C wins the competition for the simplest model to fit the Wheaton *et al.* (1977) data.

Other optional output

The variances and covariances among the observed variables under Model C can be deduced from the parameter estimates, by using the **$Implied moments** command. The implied variances and covariances of the *unobserved* common variables may be obtained with the **$All implied moments** command. For Model C, this command gives the following output:

```
Implied (for all variables) Covariances

              ses      67_alien 71_alien SEI      educatio powles71 anomia71
           -------- -------- -------- -------- -------- -------- --------
ses           6.866
67_aliena    -3.842    6.922
71_aliena    -3.724    4.982    7.574
SEI          35.522  -19.879  -19.267  450.288
education     6.866   -3.842   -3.724   35.522    9.610
powles71     -3.721    4.978    7.568  -19.252   -3.721   10.000
anomia71     -3.724    4.982    7.574  -19.267   -3.724    7.568   12.529
powles67     -3.839    6.916    4.978  -19.864   -3.839    4.975    4.978
anomia67     -3.842    6.922    4.982  -19.879   -3.842    4.978    6.872

              powles67 anomia67
           -------- --------
powles67      9.349
anomia67      6.916   11.877
```

As you can see, the moments for the observed variables are not the same as the sample variances and covariances. As estimates of the corresponding population values, the variances and covariances displayed by **$(All) implied moments** are more efficient than

the sample variances and covariances (assuming that Model C is correct). When both the
$Standardized and **$All implied moments** commands are specified, the implied
correlation matrix of all variables will also be listed.

The variances and covariances produced by the **$All implied moments** command can be
used to estimate the scores of the unobserved variables, based on the values of the
observed variables. The **$Factor scores** command produces the required regression
weights based on the implied covariance matrix:

```
Factor Score Weights

              SEI    educatio  powles71  anomia71  powles67  anomia67
            --------  --------  --------  --------  --------  --------
ses          0.0289    0.5418   -0.0547   -0.0164   -0.0686   -0.0275
67_aliena   -0.0033   -0.0610    0.1338   -0.0265    0.4715    0.2423
71_aliena   -0.0026   -0.0486    0.4907    0.2534    0.1338   -0.0308
```

The table of factor score weights has a separate row for each unobserved variable, and a
separate column for each observed variable. Here is how you would use the table:
Suppose you wanted to estimate the **ses** score of an individual. You would compute a
weighted sum of the individual's observed scores using the weights found in the **ses** row
of the table.

The coefficients associated with the single-headed arrows in a path diagram are often
called the *direct effects* among the variables. In Model C, for example, **ses** has a direct
effect on **71_alienation**. **71_alienation**, in turn, has a direct effect on **powles71**. **ses** is
then said to have an *indirect* effect (through the intermediary of **71_alienation**) on
powles71. The accumulation of direct and indirect effects is displayed in the table of
'total effects' produced by the **$Total effects** command:

```
Total Effects

              ses    67_alien  71_alien
            --------  --------  --------
67_aliena   -0.560     0.000     0.000
71_aliena   -0.542     0.607     0.000
SEI          5.174     0.000     0.000
education    1.000     0.000     0.000
powles71    -0.542     0.607     0.999
anomia71    -0.542     0.607     1.000
powles67    -0.559     0.999     0.000
anomia67    -0.560     1.000     0.000
```

The first row indicates that **67_alienation** depends, directly or indirectly, on **ses** only. The
total effect of **ses** on **67_alienation** is -0.560. The fact that the effect is negative means
that, all other things being equal, relatively high **ses** scores are associated with relatively
low **67_alienation** scores. Looking in the fifth row of the table, **powles71** depends,
directly or indirectly, on **ses**, **67_alienation**, and **71_alienation**. Low scores on **ses**, high
scores on **67_alienation**, and high scores on **71_alienation** are associated with high
scores on **powles71**. Fox (1980) may be consulted for more help in interpreting direct,
indirect, and total effects.

Example 7: A nonrecursive model

Purpose

Structural equation modeling with a nonrecursive model. The example investigates a model with two structural equations where the dependent variable of each equation appears as a predictor variable in the other equation.

The data

Felson and Bohrnstedt (1979) studied 209 girls from sixth through eighth grade. They recorded the variables shown:

academic:	Perceived academic ability, a sociometric measure based on the item *Name who you think are your three smartest classmates*.
attract:	Perceived attractiveness, a sociometric measure based on the item *Name the three girls in the classroom who you think are the most good-looking (excluding yourself)*.
GPA:	Grade point average.
height:	Deviation of height from the mean height for a subject's grade and sex.
weight:	Weight, adjusted for height.
rating:	Ratings of physical attractiveness obtained by having children from another city rate photographs of the subjects.

Sample correlations, means and standard deviations for these six variables are contained in the file `fels_fem.amd,` listed below. The sample means are not used in this example.

```
Felson and Bohrnstedt (1979)
! study of perceived attractiveness and academic
! ability in teenagers, sixth through eighth grade.

$Input variables
     academic               ! Perception of
                            !     academic ability.
     athletic               ! Perception of
                            !     athletic ability.
     attract                ! Perception of physical
                            !     attractiveness.
     GPA                    ! Grade point average.
                            !
     height                 ! Height minus group
                            !     mean for age and sex.
     weight                 ! Weight with height
                            !     'controlled'.
     rating                 ! Strangers' rating of
                            !     attractiveness.

$Sample size = 209
$Correlations
 1.00
  .43 1.00
  .50  .48 1.00
  .49  .22  .32 1.00
  .10 -.04 -.03  .18 1.00
  .04  .02 -.16 -.10  .34 1.00
  .09  .14  .43  .15 -.16 -.27 1.00
$Standard deviations
 .16 .07 .49 3.49 2.91 19.32 1.01
$Means
 .12 .05 .42 10.34 .00 94.13 2.65
```

Felson and Bohrnstedt's model

Felson and Bohrnstedt proposed the model shown below. Perceived **academic** performance is modeled as a function of **GPA** and perceived attractiveness (**attract**). Perceived attractiveness, in turn, is modeled as a function of perceived **academic** performance, **height**, **weight**, and the **rating** of attractiveness by children from another city. Particularly noteworthy in this model is that perceived academic ability depends on perceived attractiveness, and vice versa. A model with these feedback loops is called *nonrecursive* (the terms *recursive* and *nonrecursive* were defined earlier in Example 4). The current model is *nonrecursive* because we can trace the path from attract to academic and back *infinitely* many times, and never be forced to return to the exogenous variables.

Modeling in Amos Graphics

The Felson and Bohrnstedt model can be specified in **Amos Graphics** as:

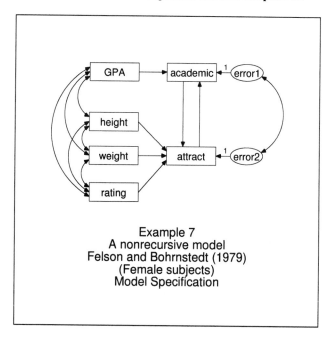

Example 7
A nonrecursive model
Felson and Bohrnstedt (1979)
(Female subjects)
Model Specification

Making a second path in between **academic** and **attract** is no more difficult than making the first, except for remembering that the object you drew *towards* in making the first path is the object you draw *away from* in making the second. The **Amos Graphics** file for this example is **ex07.amw**.

Note: **Amos Graphics** features several drawing functions to make the path diagram look neat. For instance, **GPA**, **height**, **weight**, and **rating** can be *aligned vertically*, using the button of the same name or the **Vertical** command in the **Align** menu. To do so, select three of the variables into one group and activate the vertical alignment command. Then, click on the remaining fourth variable. Similarly, **GPA**, **academic**, and **error1** can be aligned horizontally with the **Align Horizontal** command. Finally, the **Align Size** command may be used to draw the six observed variables in the same size, or align the height and width of the two error variables.

The **Preserve symmetries ('smart')** button helps to maintain proper spacing in selected groups of objects. Suppose that you want to move the **height** object, but simultaneously wish to move the **rating** object so that **height**, **weight** and **rating** remain equidistant. Select the three objects and click on the **Preserve symmetries** button. Then when you move one of the outer two objects up or down, the opposite object will also move, maintaining the same distance from **weight**.

Model identification

For identification purposes it will be necessary to establish measurement units for the two unobserved variables, **error1** and **error2**. The figure above shows two regression weights fixed at unity (1). These two constraints will suffice to make the model identified.

Modeling in Amos Text

The **Amos Text** model specification is:

```
$Structure
      academic <--- GPA
      academic <--- attract
      academic <--- error1 (1)

      attract <--- height
      attract <--- weight
      attract <--- rating
      attract <--- academic
      attract <--- error2 (1)

      error2 <--> error1

$Include = fels_fem.amd
```

It is necessary to include a line asking for an estimate of the covariance of **error1** and **error2**, because Felson and Bohrnstedt's model permits the residual terms to be correlated. Ordinarily, Amos assumes that *error* variables are uncorrelated.

The alternate **Amos Text** specification may be used instead, expressing the model in equation format. The following input file is a straightforward transcription of the path notation shown above, with a separate line for each endogenous variable:

```
$Structure
     academic = GPA + attract + error1 (1)
     attract  = height + weight + rating + academic + error2 (1)

     error2 <--> error1

$Include = fels_fem.amd
```

Output from the analysis

The resulting model has two degrees of freedom, and there is no significant evidence that the model is wrong.

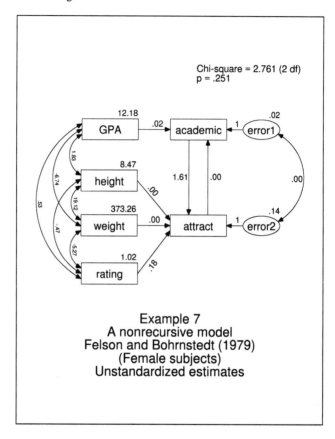

Example 7
A nonrecursive model
Felson and Bohrnstedt (1979)
(Female subjects)
Unstandardized estimates

There is, however, some evidence that the model is unnecessarily complicated, as indicated by the low critical ratios in the list output:

```
Regression Weights:                         Estimate    S.E.      C.R.      Label
-------------------                         --------    ------    ------    -------

          academic <--------- GPA            0.023      0.004     6.241
          attract <------- height            0.000      0.010     0.050
          attract <------- weight           -0.002      0.001    -1.321
          attract <------- rating            0.176      0.027     6.444
          academic <----- attract           -0.002      0.051    -0.039
          attract <----- academic            1.607      0.349     4.599


Covariances:                                Estimate    S.E.      C.R.      Label
------------                                --------    ------    ------    -------

     GPA <---------> height                  1.828      0.716     2.555
     GPA <---------> weight                 -6.743      4.699    -1.435
     height <------> weight                 19.115      4.117     4.643
     GPA <---------> rating                  0.529      0.247     2.139
     height <------> rating                 -0.470      0.206    -2.279
     weight <------> rating                 -5.269      1.401    -3.759
     error1 <------> error2                 -0.004      0.011    -0.382


Variances:                                  Estimate    S.E.      C.R.      Label
----------                                  --------    ------    ------    -------

                     GPA                    12.180      1.194    10.198
                  height                     8.468      0.830    10.198
                  weight                   373.262     36.601    10.198
                  rating                     1.020      0.100    10.198
                  error1                     0.020      0.003     5.747
                  error2                     0.143      0.014     9.974
```

Judging by the critical ratios, each of these three null hypotheses would be accepted at conventional significance levels:

- Perceived attractiveness does not depend on height (critical ratio = 0.050).

- Perceived academic ability does not depend on perceived attractiveness (critical ratio = −.039). However, there is some evidence that girls who are perceived as academically able are perceived as more attractive than others (critical ratio = 4.599).

- The residual terms **error1** and **error2** are uncorrelated (critical ratio = −.382).

Strictly speaking, you cannot use the critical ratios to test all three hypotheses at once. Instead, you would have to construct a model that incorporates all three constraints simultaneously. However, we will not pursue further modifications of this model.

The raw parameter estimates reported above are not affected by the identification constraints (except for the variances of **error1** and **error2**). They are, of course, affected by the units in which the observed variables are measured. The standardized estimates produced by the **$Standardized** command are, as usual, independent of the unit of measurement:

```
Standardized Regression Weights:                Estimate
- - - - - - - - - - - - - - - - - - - - - - -   - - - - - - - -

        academic <- - - - - - - - - GPA          0.492
        attract <- - - - - - - height             0.003
        attract <- - - - - - - weight            -0.078
        attract <- - - - - - - rating             0.363
        academic <- - - - - attract              -0.006
        attract <- - - - - academic               0.525


Correlations:                                   Estimate
- - - - - - - - - - - -                         - - - - - - - -

        GPA <- - - - - - - - - -> height          0.180
        GPA <- - - - - - - - - -> weight         -0.100
        height <- - - - - - -> weight             0.340
        GPA <- - - - - - - - - -> rating          0.150
        height <- - - - - - -> rating            -0.160
        weight <- - - - - - -> rating            -0.270
        error1 <- - - - - - -> error2            -0.076
```

Here it can be seen that the regression weights and the correlation that we judged earlier to be statistically insignificant, are also, speaking descriptively, negligible.

The squared multiple correlations produced by **$Smc** are also independent of the unit of measurement:

```
Squared Multiple Correlations:                  Estimate
- - - - - - - - - - - - - - - - - - - - - - -   - - - - - - - -

                        attract                  0.402
                        academic                 0.236
```

The two endogenous variables in this model are not predicted very accurately by the other variables in the model. This goes to show that the chi-square test of fit is *not* a measure of accuracy of prediction. Here is the path diagram output with standardized estimates and squared multiple correlations as produced by **Amos Graphics**:

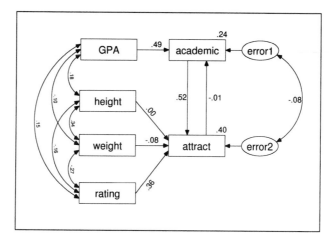

Stability index

The existence of feedback loops in a *nonrecursive* model permits certain problems to arise that cannot occur in recursive models. In the present model, attractiveness depends on perceived academic ability, which in turn depends on attractiveness, which depends on perceived academic ability, and so on. This appears to be an infinite regress, and it is. One wonders whether this infinite sequence of linear dependencies can actually result in well defined relationships among attractiveness, academic ability and the other variables of the model. The answer is that they might—or they might not—depending on the regression weights. For some values of the regression weights, the infinite sequence of linear dependencies will converge to a set of well defined relationships. In this case the system of linear dependencies is called *stable*. Otherwise, it is called *unstable*. You cannot tell whether a linear system is stable by looking at the path diagram. You need to know the regression weights. Amos cannot know what the regression weights are in the population, but it estimates them, and from the estimates it computes a **stability index** (Fox, 1980; Bentler and Freeman, 1983). If the stability index falls between −1 and +1, the system is stable. Otherwise, it is unstable. In the present example, the system is stable:

```
Stability index for the following variables is      0.003

            attract
            academic
```

An unstable system (with a stability index equal to or greater than one) is *impossible*, in the same sense that, say, a negative variance is impossible. If you do obtain a stability index of one (or greater than one), this implies that your model is wrong or that your sample size is too small to provide accurate estimates of the regression weights. If there are several loops in a path diagram, Amos will compute a stability index for each one. If any one of the stability indices equals or exceeds one, the linear system is unstable and should not be modeled in its current form.

Example 8: Factor analysis

Purpose

This is an example of confirmatory common factor analysis.

The data

Holzinger and Swineford (1939) administered twenty-six psychological tests to 301 seventh and eighth grade students in two Chicago schools. In the present example, we use scores obtained by the 73 girls from a single school (the Grant-White school). The file, **grnt_fem.amd**, partially listed below, contains their scores on the following six tests:

- Visual perception (denoted **visperc**)

- **cubes** test of spatial visualization

- **lozenges** test of spatial orientation

- Paragraph comprehension (denoted **paragraph**)

- Sentence completion (denoted **sentence**)

- Word meaning (denoted **wordmean**)

```
! Holzinger and Swineford (1939) Grant-White sample.
! Intelligence factor study. Raw data of 73 female
! students from the Grant-White high school, Chicago.

$Input variables
     visperc        ! Visual perception score
     cubes          ! Test of spatial visualization
     lozenges       ! Test of spatial orientation
     paragraph      ! Paragraph comprehension score
     sentence       ! Sentence completion score
     wordmean       ! Word meaning test score

$Sample size =    73
$Raw data
    33.   22.   17.    8.   17.   10.
    30.   25.   20.   10.   23.   18.
    36.   33.   36.   17.   25.   41.
                ...          (67 similar lines omitted here).
    35.   28.   10.    9.   13.   11.
    18.   24.   13.    7.   16.    7.
    28.   22.   15.   11.   23.   30.
```

A common factor model

Consider the model shown below for the six tests. The model conjectures an unobserved variable called **spatial** upon which the first three tests depend. **Spatial** can be interpreted as an underlying (spatial) ability that is not directly observed. According to the model, performance on the first three tests depends on this ability. In addition, performance on each of these tests may depend on something other than spatial ability as well: in the case of **visperc**, for example, the unique variable **err_v** is also involved. **err_v** represents any and all influences on **visperc** that are not shown elsewhere in the path diagram. **err_v** represents error of measurement in **visperc**, certainly, but also components of knowledge, ability and/or aptitude that might specifically affect the **visperc** scores.

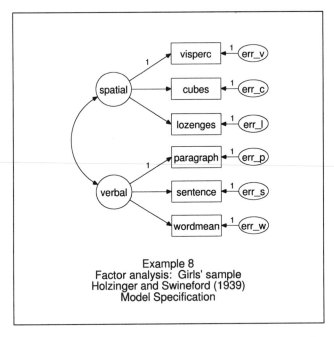

Example 8
Factor analysis: Girls' sample
Holzinger and Swineford (1939)
Model Specification

The model under consideration is a common *factor analysis* model. In the lingo of common factor analysis, the unobserved variable **spatial** is called a *common factor* and the three unobserved variables, **err_v**, **err_c** and **err_l**, are called *unique factors*. This path diagram also shows another common factor, **verbal**, upon which the last three tests depend, and three more unique factors, **err_p**, **err_s** and **err_w**. The two common factors, **spatial** and **verbal**, are allowed to be correlated. However, the unique factors are assumed to be uncorrelated with each other and with the common factors. The path coefficients leading from the common factors to the observed variables are often called *factor weights* or *factor loadings*.

Identification

This model is identified except for the fact that, as usual, the measurement scale of each unobserved variable is indeterminate. The measurement scale of each unobserved variablemay be fixed arbitrarily by setting its regression weight to one (1) in some regression equation. These constraints are sufficient to make the model identified, and have been included in the preceding path diagram.

The proposed model is a particularly simple version of the common factor analysis model, in that each observed variable depends on just one common factor. In other applications of common factor analysis, an observed variable can depend on any number of common factors at the same time. In the general case, it can be very difficult to decide whether a common factor analysis model is identified or not (Davis, 1993; Jöreskog, 1969, 1979). The treatment of identifiability given in this and earlier examples made the issue appear simpler than it actually is, perhaps leaving the impression that lack of a unit of measurement for unobserved variables might be the sole cause of nonidentification. It is true that lack of a unit of measurement for unobserved variables is an ever-present cause of nonidentification which, fortunately, is easy to cure, as we have done repeatedly.

Yet, other kinds of underidentification can also arise for which there is no such corresponding set of remedies. Conditions for identifiability have to be established separately for individual models. Jöreskog and Sörbom (1984) show how to achieve identification of a number of models by imposing equality constraints on their parameters. In the case of the factor analysis model, and many others, figuring out what must be done to make the model identified requires a pretty deep understanding of the model. If you are unable to tell whether a model is identified, you can try using the model in order to see whether Amos reports that it is unidentified. In practice, this empirical approach works quite well, although there are objections to it in principle (McDonald and Krane, 1979), and it is no substitute for an *a priori* awareness of the identification status of a model. Causes and treatments of many types of nonidentification are discussed in the excellent textbook by Bollen (1989).

Model Input

Modeling in Amos Graphics

Amos Graphics analyzes the model directly from the preceding path diagram. Notice that the model can conceptually be separated into **spatial** and **verbal** branches. You can use the structural similarity of the two branches to accelerate drawing the model. After you have drawn the first branch to your liking, simply **select** that entire branch into an object **group**, for instance by double-clicking on the latent variable. Then, **copy** this group to form the second branch (hold down the shift-key while copying, so that the new and old branches line up neatly). Notice that you must connect the **spatial** and **verbal** objects with a two-headed arrow, or else **Amos Graphics** will assume that the two common factors be uncorrelated. The **Amos Graphics** file for this example is ex08.amw.

Modeling in Amos Text

The following input file specifies the factor model for the Holzinger and Swineford data in **Amos Text** equation format:

```
$Standardized
$Smc

$Structure
    visperc   = (1) spatial + (1) err_v
    cubes     =     spatial + (1) err_c
    lozenges  =     spatial + (1) err_l

    paragraph = (1) verbal  + (1) err_p
    sentence  =     verbal  + (1) err_s
    wordmean  =     verbal  + (1) err_w

$Include = grnt_fem.amd
```

Because of the **Amos Text** default correlation assumptions for common factors and unique factor components, it is not necessary to specify explicitly that the common factors, **spatial** and **verbal**, may be correlated. Nor is it necessary to specify that the unique factors are uncorrelated with each other and the two common factors.

Results of the analysis

The unstandardized results of the analysis are displayed below. As shown at the upper right corner of the figure, the model fits the data quite well.

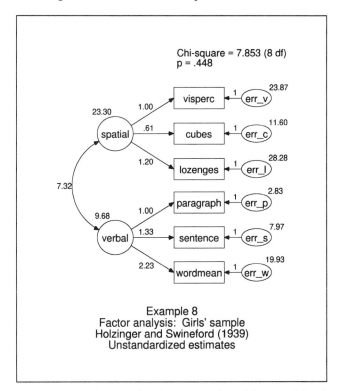

Chi-square = 7.853 (8 df)
p = .448

Example 8
Factor analysis: Girls' sample
Holzinger and Swineford (1939)
Unstandardized estimates

As an exercise, you may wish to confirm the computation of degrees of freedom:

```
Computation of Degrees of Freedom

                Number of distinct sample moments:    21
    Number of distinct parameters to be estimated:    13
                    ------------------------
                            Degrees of freedom:     8
```

The model estimates, both in their original scale and standardized form, are shown below. As you would expect, the weights are positive, as is the correlation between the **spatial** and **verbal** common factors.

```
Regression Weights:                         Estimate    S.E.      C.R.      Label
-------------------                         --------    -------   -------   -------

         visperc <-------- spatial          1.000
         cubes <---------- spatial          0.610       0.143     4.250
         lozenges <------- spatial          1.198       0.272     4.405
         paragraph <------ verbal           1.000
         sentence <------- verbal           1.334       0.160     8.322
         wordmean <------- verbal           2.234       0.263     8.482


Standardized Regression Weights:            Estimate
--------------------------------            --------

         visperc <-------- spatial          0.703
         cubes <---------- spatial          0.654
         lozenges <------- spatial          0.736
         paragraph <------ verbal           0.880
         sentence <------- verbal           0.827
         wordmean <------- verbal           0.841


Covariances:                                Estimate    S.E.      C.R.      Label
------------                                --------    -------   -------   -------

         spatial <--------> verbal          7.315       2.571     2.846


Correlations:                               Estimate
-------------                               --------

         spatial <--------> verbal          0.487


Variances:                                  Estimate    S.E.      C.R.      Label
----------                                  --------    -------   -------   -------

                         spatial           23.302       8.123     2.868
                          verbal            9.682       2.159     4.485
                           err_v           23.873       5.986     3.988
                           err_c           11.602       2.584     4.490
                           err_l           28.275       7.892     3.583
                           err_p            2.834       0.868     3.263
                           err_s            7.967       1.869     4.263
                           err_w           19.925       4.951     4.024
```

Here are the squared multiple correlations displayed by the **$Smc** command.

```
Squared Multiple Correlations:              Estimate
------------------------------              --------

                        wordmean            0.708
                        sentence            0.684
                       paragraph            0.774
                        lozenges            0.542
                           cubes            0.428
                         visperc            0.494
```

The standardized estimates can be displayed in **Amos Graphics** by choosing **Standardized estimates** from the **Groups/Models** dialog box.

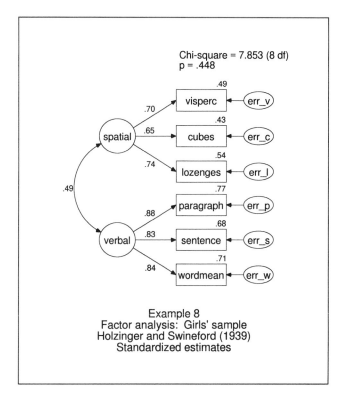

In this example, the squared multiple correlations can be interpreted as follows. For example, 71% of the variance of **wordmean** is accounted for by the variance in verbal ability. The remaining 29% of the variance of **wordmean** cannot be explained by this model, and is thus attributed to the unique factor **err_w**. If **err_w** represented measurement error only, we could say that the estimated *reliability* of **wordmean** would be 0.71. As it is, however, the term **err_w** may comprise systematic unique variance components in addition to random error. Thus, the figure 0.71 has to be regarded as a lower-bound estimate of the reliability.

> *Note*: The Holzinger and Swineford data have been analyzed repeatedly in textbooks and other demonstrations of modern factor analysis. The six tests discussed in this example are taken from a larger subset of nine tests used in a similar example by Jöreskog and Sörbom (1984). The factor analysis model employed here is also adapted from theirs. Because of the long history of exploring the Holzinger and Swineford data by factor analytic methods, it is no accident that our factor model fits the data very well. Even more than usual, the results presented here require confirmation on a fresh set of data.

Example 9: An alternative to analysis of covariance

Purpose

Demonstration of a simple alternative to an analysis of covariance which does not require perfectly reliable covariates. A further, more exact but also more complicated alternative will be discussed in Example 16.

Introduction

Analysis of covariance is a technique that is frequently employed in experimental and quasi-experimental studies to reduce the error variance due to pre-existing differences within treatment groups. When random assignment to treatment groups has eliminated the possibility of systematic pretreatment differences among groups, analysis of covariance can pay off in evaluating treatment effects with higher precision. Alternatively, when random assignment is not employed, analysis of covariance will lead to *conditional* inferences, for treatment and control cases with equal values of the covariate(s).

The usefulness of the analysis of covariance is closely tied to the assumption that each covariate be measured *without error*. The method makes other assumptions as well, but the assumption of perfectly reliable covariates has received particular attention (*e.g.*, Cook and Campbell, 1979). In part, this is because the effects of violating the assumption can be disastrous: using unreliable covariates can lead to the erroneous conclusion that a treatment has an effect when it really doesn't, or *vice versa*. Really unreliable covariates can make a treatment appear to be harmful when it is actually beneficial. At the same time, unfortunately, the assumption of perfectly reliable covariates is almost impossible to meet.

The present example demonstrates an alternative to analysis of covariance which allows measurement error in the covariates. The method to be demonstrated here has been employed by Bentler and Woodward (1979) and others. Another, more general and somewhat more complicated approach, due to Sörbom (1978), will be demonstrated in Example 16. The virtue of the current example is its relative simplicity, and the liabilities of its method (and the assumptions it makes) will be held up to closer scrutiny in Example 16.

The present example employs two treatment groups and a single covariate. It may be generalized to any number of treatment groups and any number of covariates. The data used for this example, and also for Example 16, were used by Sörbom (1978). The analysis closely follows Sörbom's example.

The data

Olsson (1973) administered a battery of eight tests to 213 11-year old students on two occasions. Two of the eight tests, called *Synonyms* and *Opposites*, will be employed in this example. Between the two administrations of the test battery, 108 of the students (the experimental group) received training that was intended to improve performance on the tests. The other 105 students (the control group) did not receive any special training. As a result of taking two tests on two occasions, each of the 213 students obtained four scores:

pre_syn: Pretest scores on the Synonyms test.

pre_opp: Pretest scores on the Opposites test.

post_syn: Post-test scores on the Synonyms test.

post_opp: Post-test scores on the Opposites test.

treatment: A dichotomous variable taking on the value 1 for students who received the special training, and 0 for those who did not. This variable was created especially for the analyses in this example.

Correlations and standard deviations on these five measures for the entire group of 213 students are contained in the file **olss_all.amd**, and shown below:

```
! Olsson's (1973) two-wave, pre- and post-test
! coaching study data. Two measures of verbal
! reasoning are each assessed at the two
! occasions. 108 of the 213 study participants
! received coaching (treatment) between pre- and
! post-test assessments.

$Input variables
     pre_syn    ! Pre-test:  synonyms score
     pre_opp    ! Pre-test:  opposites score
     post_syn   ! Post-test: synonyms score
     post_opp   ! Post-test: opposites score
     treatment  ! Indicator variable:
                !     1=treated, 0=untreated

$Sample size = 213

$Correlations
  1.00000000
  0.78255618  1.00000000
  0.78207295  0.69286541  1.00000000
  0.70438031  0.77390019  0.77567354  1.00000000
  0.16261758  0.07784579  0.37887943  0.32533034
1.00000000
$Standard deviations
  6.68680566  6.49938562  6.95007062  6.95685347
0.49995040
```

There are positive correlations between **treatment** and each of the post-tests, which indicates that the trained students did better on the post-tests than the untrained students. The correlations between **treatment** and each of the pretests are positive but relatively small, indicating that the control and experimental groups did about equally well on the pretests. Since students were randomly assigned to the control and experimental groups, this was to be expected.

Analysis of covariance

A traditional method for evaluating the effect of training on performance is analysis of covariance (ANCOVA). In an analysis of covariance of two-wave data, one of the post-tests is often used as the response variable while the corresponding pretest would be treated as a covariate. In order for this analysis to be appropriate, the selected pretest, either the Synonym test or the Opposites test, would have to be perfectly reliable.

Model A for the Olsson data

Consider the model for the Olsson data shown in the path diagram below. The model asserts that **pre_syn** and **pre_opp** are both imperfect measures of an unobserved ability called **pre_verbal** that might be thought of as verbal ability at the time of the pretest. The *unique* variables **eps1** and **eps2** represent errors of measurement in **pre_syn** and **pre_opp**, as well as any other influences on the two tests that are not represented elsewhere in the path diagram.

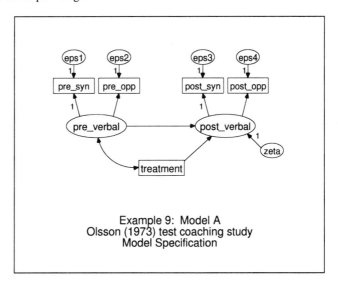

Example 9: Model A
Olsson (1973) test coaching study
Model Specification

Similarly, **post_syn** and **post_opp** are asserted to be imperfect measures of an unobserved ability called **post_verbal** that might be thought of as verbal ability at the time of the post-test. **eps3** and **eps4** represent errors of measurement and other sources of variation not shown elsewhere in the path diagram.

The model shows two variables that may be useful in accounting for verbal ability at the time of the post-test. One such predictor is verbal ability at the time of the pretest. We would expect that verbal ability at the time of the post-test depends on verbal ability at the time of the pretest. Because past performance is often an excellent predictor of future performance, the model uses the latent variable **pre_verbal** as a covariate. However, our primary interest lies in the second predictor, **treatment**. We are mostly interested in the regression weight associated with the arrow pointing from **treatment** to **post_verbal**, and whether it is significantly different from zero. That is, we will eventually want to know whether the model shown above could be accepted as correct under the additional hypothesis that the particular regression weight is zero. But first, we had better ask whether Model A can be accepted as it stands.

Identification

The units of measurement of the seven unobserved variables are indeterminate. This indeterminacy can be remedied by finding one single-headed arrow pointing away from each unobserved variable in the above figure, and fixing the corresponding regression weight to unity. The seven ones (1) shown in the path diagram above indicate a satisfactory choice of identification constraints.

Input file for Model A

Entering a path diagram that emulates the figure above, and including the data file named `olss_all.amd` in the command file, adequately sets up Model A. The name of the **Amos Graphics** input file is `ex09-a.amw`. For **Amos Text**, the specification of Model A is given in the file `ex09-a.ami`, shown below:

```
$Mods=4
$Standardized
$Smc

$Structure
    pre_syn      = (1) pre_verbal  + (1) eps1
    pre_opp      =     pre_verbal  + (1) eps2

    post_syn     = (1) post_verbal + (1) eps3
    post_opp     =     post_verbal + (1) eps4

    post_verbal = pre_verbal + treatment + (1) zeta

$Include = olss_all.amd
```

Testing Model A

There is considerable empirical evidence *against* Model A:

```
Chi-square =     33.215
Degrees of freedom =    3
Probability level =     0.000
```

This is bad news. If we had been able to accept Model A for Olsson's data, examining and testing the path coefficient going from **treatment** to **post_verbal** would have been the logical next step. But there is no point in doing that now. We have to start with a model that we believe is correct before using it as a basis for a stronger version of the model to test the hypothesis of 'no treatment effect'.

Searching for a better model

We can possibly modify Model A to improve its fit to the Olsson data. Some suggestions for suitable modifications can be obtained by using the **$Mods** command. The $Mods = 4 command included in the input file produces the following additional output:

```
Modification Indices
· · · · · · · · · · · · · · · · · · · ·


Covariances:                                 M.I.     Par Change
                                            · · · · · · · · ·   · · · · · · · · ·
           eps2 <· · · · · · · · · · · · · · · · · > eps4     13.161        3.264
           eps2 <· · · · · · · · · · · · · · · · · > eps3     10.813       -2.836
           eps1 <· · · · · · · · · · · · · · · · · > eps4     11.968       -3.243
           eps1 <· · · · · · · · · · · · · · · · · > eps3      9.788        2.812


Variances:                                   M.I.     Par Change
                                            · · · · · · · · ·   · · · · · · · · ·


Regression Weights:                          M.I.     Par Change
                                            · · · · · · · · ·   · · · · · · · · ·
```

According to the first modification index in the M.I. column, the chi-square statistic will decrease by at least 13.161 when the *unique* terms **eps2** and **eps4** are allowed to correlate (the actual decrease may be greater). This fit improvement would cost one degree of freedom for the extra parameter to be estimated. Since 13.161 is the largest modification index, we should consider it first, and ask whether it is reasonable to think that **eps2** and **eps4** might be correlated.

Since **eps2** and **eps4** represent the *unique* terms of the same *Opposites* test at two different measurement occasions—terms not shared with the *Synonyms* reasoning test— it may indeed be reasonable to assume that **eps2** and **eps4** are correlated over time. Furthermore, the expected parameter change (the number in the Par Change column) associated with the covariance between **eps2** and **eps4** is positive, as one would expect when stable systematic components correlate over time.

It might be added that the same reasoning which suggests allowing **eps2** and **eps4** to be correlated applies almost as well to **eps1** and **eps3**, whose covariance also has a fairly large modification index. For now, however, we will add only one parameter to Model A: the covariance between **eps2** and **eps4**. The new specification will be called *Model B*.

Model B for the Olsson data

The path diagram for Model B is shown below. The model can be specified either by adding the line eps2 <- - -> eps4 to the **$Structure** section in the **Amos Text** command file, or by adding a covariance path between the **eps2** and **eps4** objects in the **Amos Graphics** path diagram input. The resulting **Amos Text** input file is **ex09-b.ami**, the path diagram input is located in the file **ex09-b.amw**.

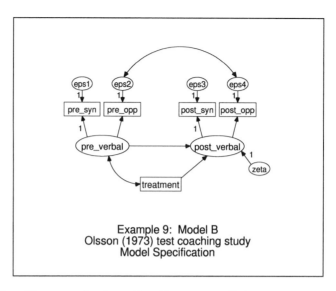

Example 9: Model B
Olsson (1973) test coaching study
Model Specification

Note: If you are using **Amos Graphics**, you may find your error variables already positioned against the top drawing boundary, with nowhere to draw the covariance path. This problem may be alleviated by using **Fit to Page** command (under the **Edit** menu, or in toolbox #2) . Just draw your path out of bounds, then activate this command. Your path diagram will be shrunk down to fit within the boundary of the page, although text elements will not. If you find that your variable names are too long for the objects they now occupy, you can just change the font size of one variable object, then use the **Align Font** command in the same way you would use any other alignment command.

Results for Model B

Allowing **eps2** and **eps4** to be correlated results in a dramatic reduction of the chi-square statistic:

```
Chi-square =      2.684
Degrees of freedom =    2
Probability level =     0.261
```

You may recall from the results of Model A that the modification index for the covariance between **eps1** and **eps3** was 9.788. Clearly, freeing that covariance in addition to the **eps2–eps4** covariance would not have produced an additional drop in the chi-square statistic of 9.788, since this would imply a negative chi-square statistic. Thus, the modification indices represent the minimal drop in the chi-square statistic if the corresponding constraint, and *only* that constraint, is removed.

The raw parameter estimates are difficult to interpret because they are partially a function of the identification constraints:

Regression Weights:	Estimate	S.E.	C.R.	Label
post_verbal <····· pre_verbal	0.889	0.053	16.900	
post_verbal <······ treatment	3.640	0.477	7.625	
pre_syn <········· pre_verbal	1.000			
pre_opp <········· pre_verbal	0.881	0.053	16.606	
post_syn <······· post_verbal	1.000			
post_opp <······· post_verbal	0.906	0.053	16.948	

Covariances:	Estimate	S.E.	C.R.	Label
pre_verbal <······> treatment	0.469	0.227	2.066	
eps2 <················> eps4	6.829	1.350	5.059	

Variances:	Estimate	S.E.	C.R.	Label
pre_verbal	38.672	4.522	8.552	
treatment	0.250	0.024	10.296	
zeta	4.846	1.337	3.625	
eps1	6.041	1.509	4.004	
eps2	12.313	1.610	7.646	
eps3	6.577	1.509	4.360	
eps4	14.754	1.821	8.102	

The covariance between **eps2** and **eps4** is positive, as expected. The most interesting result that appears along with the parameter estimates is the critical ratio for the effect of **treatment** on **post_verbal**. This critical ratio shows that **treatment** has a highly significant effect on **post_verbal**. We will shortly obtain a better test of the significance of this effect by modifying Model B so that this regression weight is fixed at zero. In the meantime, here are the standardized results displayed by **Amos Graphics**, as well as the squared multiple correlations:

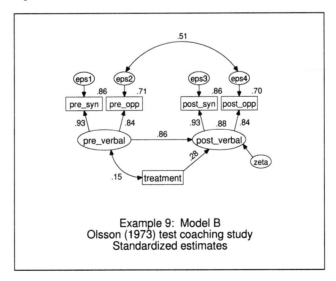

Example 9: Model B
Olsson (1973) test coaching study
Standardized estimates

Note: In this example, we are primarily concerned with testing a particular hypothesis, and not so much with parameter estimation. However, even when the parameter estimates themselves are not of primary interest, it is a good idea to look at them anyway to see if they are *reasonable*. Here, for instance, you may not care exactly what the correlation between **eps2** and **eps4** is, but you would expect it to be positive. Similarly, you would be surprised to find any negative estimates for regression weights in this model. In any model, you know that variables cannot have negative variances, and so a negative variance estimate would always be an unreasonable estimate. If estimates cannot pass a gross sanity check, particularly with a reasonably large sample size, you have to question the correctness of the model, no matter how 'good' the chi-square or any other fit statistic may be.

Model C for the Olsson data

Now that we have a model (Model B) that we can reasonably believe is correct, let's see how it fares if we add to it the constraint that **post_verbal** not depend on **treatment**. That is, we will test a new model, Model C, that is just like Model B, except that the new model will specify that **post_verbal** has a zero regression weight on **treatment**. Here is the **Amos Text** input file (**ex09-c.ami**) that describes this model:

```
Example 9, Model C:
Latent-variable ANCOVA w. autocorrelated errors
                 -- no treatment effect --

Olsson's (1973) two-wave, pre- and post-test
coaching study data. Two measures of verbal
reasoning are each assessed at the two
occasions. 108 of the 213 study participants
received coaching (treatment) between pre- and
post-test assessments.

$Mods=4
$Standardized
$Smc

$Structure
    pre_syn     = (1) pre_verbal  + (1) eps1
    pre_opp     =     pre_verbal  + (1) eps2

    post_syn    = (1) post_verbal + (1) eps3
    post_opp    =     post_verbal + (1) eps4

    post_verbal = pre_verbal + (0) treatment + (1) zeta

    eps2 <---> eps4

$Include = olss_all.amd
```

In **Amos Graphics**, start with Model B, then use the **Parameter constraints** button to constrain the path treatment ---> post_verbal to zero (0). The path diagram specification is located in **ex09-c.amw**.

Multiple model input

The following **Amos Text** input file (**ex09-all.ami**) specifies all three models (A through C) at once:

```
Example 9, Models A through C:
Latent-variable ANCOVA.

Varying assumptions about autocorrelated error
terms and treatment effect.

Olsson's (1973) two-wave, pre- and post-test
coaching study data. Two measures of verbal
reasoning are each assessed at the two
occasions. 108 of the 213 study participants
received coaching (treatment) between pre- and
post-test assessments.

$Mods=4
$Standardized
$Smc

$Structure
      pre_syn     = (1) pre_verbal  + (1) eps1
      pre_opp     =     pre_verbal  + (1) eps2

      post_syn    = (1) post_verbal + (1) eps3
      post_opp    =     post_verbal + (1) eps4

      post_verbal = pre_verbal + (effect) treatment + (1) zeta

      eps2 <---> eps4 (cov2_4)

$Include = olss_all.amd

$Model=Model_A
   cov2_4 = 0
$Model=Model_B
$Model=Model_C
   effect = 0
```

If you are using **Amos Graphics**, make the proper adjustments to your path diagram using the **Parameter constraints** button, and include the last seven lines from the listing above in the **$** command file. The multiple model input for this problem is **ex09-all.amw**:

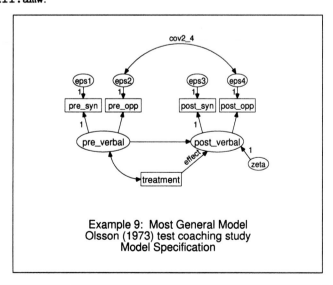

Example 9: Most General Model
Olsson (1973) test coaching study
Model Specification

Results for Model C

Model C has to be rejected at any conventional significance level:

```
Chi-square =      55.396
Degrees of freedom =    3
Probability level =     0.000
```

Assuming Model B is correct, and that only the correctness of Model C is in doubt, a better test of Model C can be obtained as follows: in changing from Model B to Model C, the chi-square statistic increased by 52.712 (= 55.396 − 2.684), while the number of degrees of freedom increased by 1 (= 3 − 2). If Model C is correct, 52.712 is an observation on a random variable that has an approximate chi-square distribution with 1 degree of freedom (with multiple model input, this value is calculated near the end of the text output). The probability of such a random variable exceeding 52.712 is vanishingly small. Thus Model C is rejected in favor of Model B: **treatment** has a significant effect on **post_verbal**.

Example 10: Simultaneous analysis of several groups

Purpose

This demonstration shows how to fit a model to two sets of data at once. Amos is capable of modeling data from multiple groups (or samples) simultaneously. This multi-group facility allows for many additional types of analyses, as will be illustrated in the next several examples.

Introduction

Data from Attig's (1983) young subjects were introduced and analyzed in Examples 1 through 3. You can imagine repeating the same pair of analyses with Attig's old subjects. Then you could compare the results from the two groups to see how similar they were. This is the purpose of the present example—to compare the young subjects and the old subjects. However, the comparison will not be done by performing separate analyses for old people and young people. Instead, a single analysis will estimate parameters and test hypotheses about both groups at once. The method demonstrated here has two advantages over doing separate analyses for the young and old groups. First, it provides a test for the significance of *any* differences found between young and old people. Second, if it can be concluded that there is no difference between young and old people, or if the group differences concern only a few model parameters, multi-group analysis provides *more efficient* parameter estimates than either of the two single-group models.

The data

Attig's data on spatial memory were described in Example 1. Data from both young and old subjects will be used here. A partial listing of the data file for the old subjects, named `attg_old.amd`, is displayed below. This file is identical to the file for the young subjects, `attg_yng.amd`, except for the numbers themselves. In this example, only the measures **recall1** and **cued1** will be used.

Note: With multi-group analyses, Amos requires that the data be separated in different files, one file for each group.

```
! Attig (1983) Space data.
! 40 old subjects.
! A data value of  -1  indicates missing data.

$Input Variables
      subject_number
      age
      vocab.short    ! Raw score on WAIS subset
      vocabulary     ! Raw score on WAIS
      education      ! Years of schooling
      sex            ! 0=female, 1=male
      recall1        ! Recall pretest
      recall2        ! Recall posttest
      cued1          ! Cued recall pretest
      cued2          ! Cued recall posttest
      place1         ! Place recall pretest
      place2         ! Place recall posttest

$Sample size = 40
$Raw data
1 65 12 72 16 1  5 11  5 11 30 32
 2 68 14 77 18 0 12 16 14 16 35 32
 3 64 14 74 17 1 11 11 10 11 33 30
        . . .

        (34 similar lines omitted here)

        . . .

38 70 14 80 14 0  8 13  8 13 32 31
39 64 14 78 13 0 12 13 12 14 26 31
40 63 13 66 12 0  9 10 11 11 29 31
```

Model A

We will begin with a truly trivial model (Model A) for the two variables, **recall1** and **cued1**. The model simply says that, for young subjects as well as old subjects, **recall1** and **cued1** are two variables that have some unspecified variances and some unspecified covariance. The variances and covariance terms can be different for young and old people.

Modeling in Amos Text

Here is an **Amos Text** input file (**ex10-a.ami**) that directs Amos to estimate the variances and the covariance for both populations:

```
Example 10, Model A: Example 10: Model A
Simultaneous analysis of variances
and covariances in several groups.

This model places no restrictions on
any variance or covariance terms.
Attig's (1983) data of old and young
subjects.

$Group name = young_subjects
$Structure
     recall1
     cued1

$Include = attg_yng.amd

$Next group

$Group name = old_subjects
$Structure
     recall1
     cued1

$Include = attg_old.amd
```

The **$Nextgroup** command near the middle of this input file splits the file into two parts. The part of the file that comes before the **$Nextgroup** command contains a model for the young subjects together with a file reference for their data. The model is the trivial one that simply says that **recall1** and **cued1** are two variables with unspecified variances and an unspecified covariance. The remainder of the file contains the same trivial, unrestricted model for the old subjects and a file reference for their data. The **$Groupname** command, while truly optional in single-group analyses, becomes an important part of multi-sample input files, structuring both input and result files with meaningful headings.

Modeling in Amos Graphics

Model specification in **Amos Graphics** is somewhat different from **Amos Text**. In particular, **Amos Graphics** has several specific *default rules* for multi-group analyses:

- All groups in the analysis will have the *identical* path diagram *structure*, unless explicitly declared otherwise. To specify Model A, for instance, the model structure only needs to be drawn for the first group (young subjects). All other groups will have the same model structure by default.

- Unnamed parameters may (and generally will) take on different values in the different groups. Thus, the default multi-group model under **Amos Graphics** uses the *same model structure*, but allows *different parameter values*.

- Parameters in different groups can be constrained to the same value by giving them the same label (this will be demonstrated in Model B, later in this example).

- **Amos Graphics** maintains a separate **$** command section for *each* group. Each **$** command section must contain the group's data, or an **$Include** command referencing its external data file, if any.

- Global **$** commands, such as **$Mods** or **$Standardized**, apply to all groups, even if they are specified in just one of the **$** command sections.

To set up this example, first set up the path diagram for the young subjects. Draw the path diagram of these two correlated variables and insert the line
`$include = attg_yng.amd` in the **$** command section for the young subjects. Or copy the path diagram from Example 1.

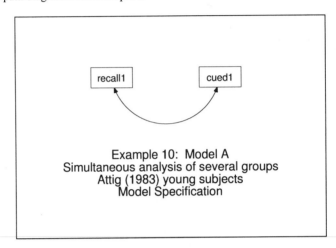

recall1   cued1

Example 10: Model A
Simultaneous analysis of several groups
Attig (1983) young subjects
Model Specification

After drawing the path diagram and referencing the data, click on the **Groups/Models** button to produce the familiar dialog box below:

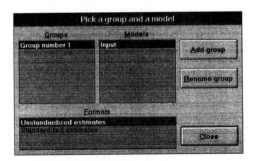

Pick a group and a model

Groups	Models	
Group number 1	Input	Add group
		Rename group

Formats

Unstandardized estimates
Standardized estimates   Close

Press the **Rename group** button to change the name of the current group. You will be prompted for a new name for this group; type in "young subjects":

Click on the "OK" button to return to the **Pick a group and a model** dialog box. The entry in the **Groups** list has changed from the default label "Group number 1" to the new group name "young subjects":

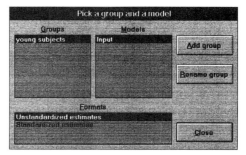

At this point, the model for the second group can be added. Press the **Add group** button. This step is non-reversible and requires explicit confirmation:

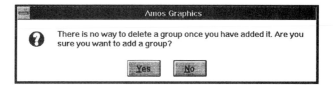

Click on "Yes" to confirm. **Amos Graphics** then displays the dialog box below, prompting for the name of the second group:

Enter "old subjects" and click on the "OK" button to return to the **Pick a group and a Model** dialog box. The **Groups** list box now has two entries from which you can choose:

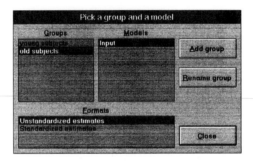

To edit the model specification for the second group, select the entry "old subjects" in the **Groups** list box and click on the **Close** button. **Amos Graphics** now returns to path diagram mode, showing the model specification for the old subjects:

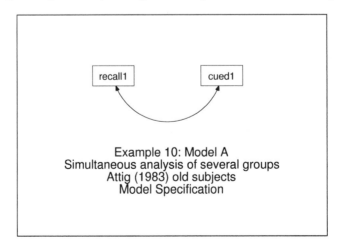

To complete the path diagram version of the model, enter the text command $Include = attg_old.amd in the $ command section for the old subjects.

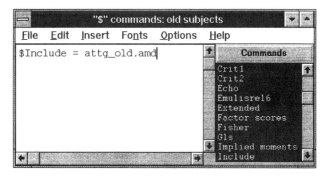

The file **ex10-a.amw** contains the full **Amos Graphics** specification for Model A.

Output from Model A

As should be expected, Model A has zero degrees of freedom:

```
Computation of Degrees of Freedom
                    Number of distinct sample moments:     6
       Number of distinct parameters to be estimated:      6
                    ----------------------------------
                              Degrees of freedom:          0
```

Here is how the number of distinct sample moments was computed: The young subjects have two sample variances and one sample covariance, which makes three sample moments. The old subjects also have three sample moments, which makes a total of six sample moments. The parameters to be estimated are the population moments, and there are six of them too. Since there are zero degrees of freedom, we cannot test this model for goodness of fit:

```
Chi-square =      0.000
Degrees of freedom =    0
Probability level cannot be computed
```

The unstandardized parameter estimates for the young subjects are:

Covariances:		Estimate	S.E.	C.R.	Label
recall1 <-----> cued1		3.225	0.944	3.416	
Variances:		Estimate	S.E.	C.R.	Label
recall1		5.788	1.311	4.416	
cued1		4.210	0.953	4.416	

And for the old subjects:

Covariances:		Estimate	S.E.	C.R.	Label
recall1 <-----> cued1		4.887	1.252	3.902	

Variances:	Estimate	S.E.	C.R.	Label
recall1	5.569	1.261	4.416	
cued1	6.694	1.516	4.416	

Use the **Groups/Models** dialog box to select the output path diagrams for the young or old subject groups, or to toggle between standardized and unstandardized estimates:

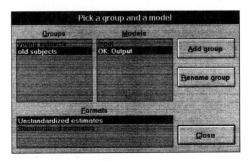

Here is the unstandardized **Amos Graphics** output for the two groups:

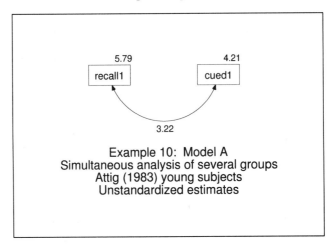

Example 10: Model A
Simultaneous analysis of several groups
Attig (1983) young subjects
Unstandardized estimates

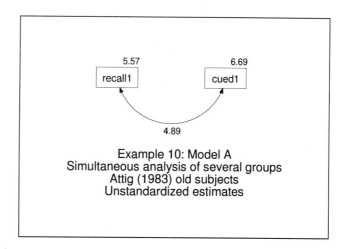

5.57   6.69

recall1   cued1

4.89

Example 10: Model A
Simultaneous analysis of several groups
Attig (1983) old subjects
Unstandardized estimates

Model B

It is easy to see that the parameter estimates are different for the two groups. But are the differences significant or still within the margin of sampling error? One way to find out is to repeat the analysis, but this time requiring that each parameter in the young population be equal to the corresponding parameter in the old population. The resulting model will be called Model B.

Modeling in Amos Text

The **Amos Text** input file for Model B is **ex10-b.ami**. Here is the file listing:

```
Example 10: Model B
Homogenous covariance structures
in two groups.

Attig's (1983) data of old and young
subjects.

$Standardized

$Group name = Young_subjects
$Structure
    recall1             (var_rec)
    cued1               (var_cue)
    recall1 <> cued1    (cov_rc)

$Include = attg_yng.amd

$Next group

$Group name = Old_subjects
$Structure
    recall1             (var_rec)
    cued1               (var_cue)
    recall1 <> cued1    (cov_rc)

$Include = attg_old.amd
```

The names var_rec, var_cue and cov_rc, appearing in parentheses are used to specify that the model parameters are the same for old and young people. The name var_rec is used to specify that **recall1** has the same variance in the two populations. Similarly, the name var_cue is used to specify that **cued1** has the same variance in the two populations. The name cov_rc is used to specify that **recall1** and **cued1** have the same covariance in the two populations.

Modeling in Amos Graphics

To set up Model B with path diagram input, first follow the setup for Model A. Then use the **Parameter constraints** button to add the variable names var_rec, var_cue, and cov_rc into the Young subjects path diagram. Make sure that the "All groups" box is checked, so that the parameters are constrained to be equal across the two groups.

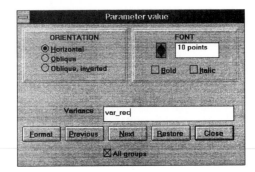

The resulting **Amos Graphics** model specification appears in the file **ex10-b.amw**.

Multiple model input

In **Amos Text**, the multiple models input is not that much different from single models. Here is the **Amos Text** command file (**ex10-all.ami**) which specifies both Models A and B at once:

```
Example 10: Models A and B
Testing homogeneity of covariance
structures in two groups.

Attig's (1983) data of old and young
subjects.

$Standardized

$Group name = young_subjects
$Structure
      recall1              (yng_rec)
      cued1               (yng_cue)
      recall1 <> cued1    (yng_rc)

$Include = attg_yng.amd

$Next group

$Group name = old_subjects
$Structure
      recall1              (old_rec)
      cued1               (old_cue)
      recall1 <> cued1    (old_rc)

$Include = attg_old.amd

$Model = Model_A
$Model = Model_B
      yng_rec = old_rec
      yng_cue = old_cue
      yng_rc  = old_rc
```

It does not matter much where in the **Amos Text** command file the **$Model** command section appears, but after the **$Structure** and file information for the last group is as good a place as any.

Specification of multiple models in the same **Amos Graphics** file is similar to using **Amos Text**. You can insert the parameter names yng_rec, yng_cue, and yng_rc in the path diagram for the young subjects' data, and the names old_rec, old_cue, and old_rc in the diagram for the old subjects' data.

> *Note*: Make sure that the "All Groups" check box remains *empty* when setting up multi-group, multiple model specification, or else the parameter labels typed last will overwrite the corresponding labels in all the other groups.

Afterwards, **Amos Graphics** understands all these parameter names, no matter which of the groups is currently in the foreground. Thus, you can enter the **$Model** section, *i.e.*, the last five lines of the **Amos Text** file, in the **Amos Graphics $** command section for *one* of the two groups, and it doesn't matter which one. Strictly speaking, the various **$Model** commands do not all have to appear in the same group, but it is strongly recommended that they do, in order to keep the specification section both manageable and readable.

After calculating the estimates for multiple model specifications with **Amos Graphics,** click on the **Groups/Models** button to select the group and model for which the estimates (unstandardized or standardized) should be displayed in the output path diagram:

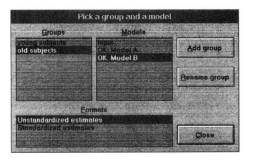

Output from Model B

Text output

Because of the constraints imposed in Model B, only three distinct parameters are estimated instead of six. As a result, the number of degrees of freedom has increased from zero to three.

```
Computation of Degrees of Freedom
                 Number of distinct sample moments:      6
      Number of distinct parameters to be estimated:     3
                                 --------------------------
                                 Degrees of freedom:      3
```

Model B is acceptable at conventional significance levels.

```
Chi-square =      4.588
Degrees of freedom =     3
Probability level =      0.205
```

Here are the parameter estimates obtained under Model B for the young subjects:

Covariances:	Estimate	S.E.	C.R.	Label
recall1 <-----> cued1	4.056	0.780	5.202	cov_rc
Variances:	**Estimate**	**S.E.**	**C.R.**	**Label**
recall1	5.678	0.909	6.245	var_rec
cued1	5.452	0.873	6.245	var_cue

The parameter estimates and standard errors are, of course, the same in both groups. You can see that the standard error estimates obtained under Model B are smaller (for the young subjects, 0.780, 0.909, and 0.873) than the corresponding estimates obtained under Model A (0.944, 1.311, and 0.953). This is exactly what is meant by the term *more efficient*, applied to parameter estimates. The Model B estimates are to be preferred over the ones from Model A as long as you believe that Model B is correct—at a probability level of .205, there is not much evidence to the contrary.

Below is the **Amos Graphics** output with standardized estimates from Model B.

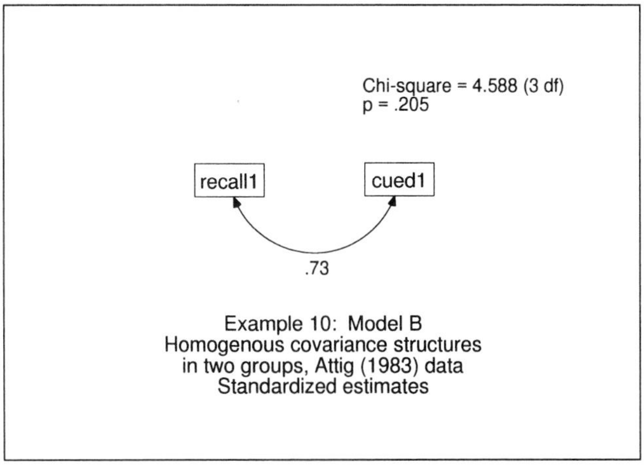
Chi-square = 4.588 (3 df)
p = .205
recall1
cued1
.73
Example 10: Model B
Homogenous covariance structures
in two groups, Attig (1983) data
Standardized estimates

Example 11: Felson and Bohrnstedt's girls and boys

Purpose

Fitting a complex regression model to two sets of data at once.

Introduction

Example 7 tested Felson and Bohrnstedt's (1979) model for perceived attractiveness and perceived academic ability using a sample of 209 girls. The present example reconsiders the Felson and Bohrnstedt model and attempts to apply it simultaneously to the Example 7 data, and to data from another sample of 207 boys. We will examine the question of whether attractiveness and academic ability follow the same dynamics in boys as in girls and, if not, explore the source of difference between the two sexes.

The data

The Felson and Bohrnstedt (1979) data for girls were described in Example 7. A listing of the boys' data follows, from the file `fels_mal.amd`. Note that there are eight variables in the boys' data file, but only seven in the girls'. Amos can accommodate modeling situations where the measured variables differ between groups. However, in the present example the added variable **skill** is not mentioned in any model. Amos therefore skips this variable, like any other variable not entered in a model.

```
! Felson and Bohrnstedt (1979)
! study of perceived attractiveness and academic
! ability in teenagers, sixth through eighth grade.

$Input variables
    academic            ! Perception of
                        !     academic ability.
    athletic            ! Perception of
                        !     athletic ability.
    attract             ! Perception of physical
                        !     attractiveness.
    GPA                 ! Grade point average.
                        !
    skills              ! Athletic skills.
                        !
    height              ! Height minus group
                        !     mean for age and sex.
    weight              ! Weight with height
                        !     'controlled'.
    rating              ! Strangers' rating of
                        !     attractiveness.
$Sample size = 207
$Correlations
 1.00
  .47 1.00
  .49  .72 1.00
  .58  .27  .30 1.00
  .35  .65  .44  .35 1.00
 -.02  .15  .04 -.11  .12 1.00
 -.11 -.01 -.19 -.16 -.05  .51 1.00
  .11  .24  .28  .13  .38  .06 -.18 1.00
$Standard deviations
.16 .21 .49 4.04 .74 3.41 24.32 .97
$Means
.10 .17 .44 8.63 2.93 .00 101.91 2.59
```

Model A for girls and boys

Modeling in Amos Graphics

Consider extending the Felson and Bohrnstedt model of perceived attractiveness and academic ability to boys as well as girls. This is the model that was used for girls alone in Example 7. We can now re-use the **Amos Graphics** model specification from the single group model. If you have already made the path diagram for Example 7, no additional drawing needs to be done for this model. Just *retrieve* your diagram from Example 7, *rename* (using the **Groups/Models** button) Group number 1 as girls, and *add* a new group. The new group should be named boys. Click on the boys item in the **Pick a Group and a Model** dialog box to display the input path diagram for the boys' sample — it should be identical to the that of the girls. An $Include statement must also be added to the $ command section for the boys' group, to reference the boys' data. This statement should read:

```
$Include = fels_mal.amd
```

Remember that, in **Amos Graphics**, all groups *automatically* have the same *structure*, unless you explicitly declare otherwise.

If you did not create Example 7, just make the path diagram below for the girls' data, and enter

```
$Include = fels_fem.amd
```

in the **$** command section. Then follow the instructions in the first paragraph of this section in order to extend the model to the second sample (of boys' data). The input file for this model is **ex11-a.amw**. The path diagram specification for the boys' sample is:

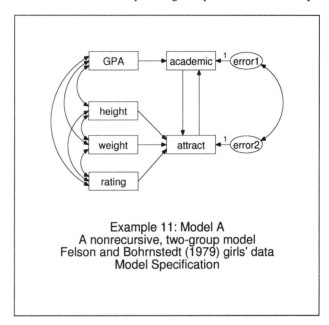

Example 11: Model A
A nonrecursive, two-group model
Felson and Bohrnstedt (1979) girls' data
Model Specification

Modeling in Amos Text

The following **Amos Text** input file gives the equivalent model for the two groups:

```
Example 11: Model A
A nonrecursive, two-group model

$Group name = girls
$Structure
     academic = GPA + attract + error1 (1)
     attract  = height + weight + rating + academic + error2 (1)

     error2 <--> error1

$Include = fels_fem.amd

$Next group

$Group name = boys
$Structure
     academic = GPA + attract + error1 (1)
     attract  = height + weight + rating + academic + error2 (1)

     error2 <--> error1

$Include = fels_mal.amd
```

Notice that, while the same model structure is specified for girls and boys, there is no restriction that the parameters must have the same values in the two groups. This means that the regression weights, covariance paths, and variances may all be different for boys and girls.

Output from Model A

With two groups instead of one (as in Example 7), there are twice as many sample moments and twice as many parameters to be estimated. Hence there are twice as many degrees of freedom as there were in Example 7.

```
Computation of Degrees of Freedom

              Number of distinct sample moments:    42
      Number of distinct parameters to be estimated:   38
              ------------------------
                        Degrees of freedom:    4
```

The model fits the data from both groups quite well:

```
Chi-square =      3.183
Degrees of freedom =    4
Probability level =     0.528
```

We accept the hypothesis that the Felson and Bohrnstedt model is correct for both boys and girls. The next thing to look at is the parameter estimates. We will be interested in how the girls' estimates compare to the boys' estimates.

First, here are the girls' parameter estimates:

Regression Weights:	Estimate	S.E.	C.R.	Label
academic <--------- GPA	0.023	0.004	6.241	
attract <------- height	0.000	0.010	0.050	
attract <------- weight	-0.002	0.001	-1.321	
attract <------- rating	0.176	0.027	6.444	
academic <----- attract	-0.002	0.051	-0.039	
attract <----- academic	1.607	0.350	4.599	

Covariances:	Estimate	S.E.	C.R.	Label
GPA <----------> height	1.828	0.716	2.555	
GPA <----------> weight	-6.743	4.699	-1.435	
height <-------> weight	19.115	4.117	4.642	
GPA <----------> rating	0.529	0.247	2.139	
height <-------> rating	-0.470	0.206	-2.279	
weight <-------> rating	-5.269	1.401	-3.759	
error1 <-------> error2	-0.004	0.011	-0.382	

Variances:	Estimate	S.E.	C.R.	Label
GPA	12.180	1.194	10.198	
height	8.468	0.830	10.198	
weight	373.262	36.602	10.198	
rating	1.020	0.100	10.198	
error1	0.020	0.003	5.747	
error2	0.143	0.014	9.974	

These parameter estimates are exactly the same as those reported in Example 7, as we would expect them to be. The standard errors and critical ratios are also the same in this case.

Next are the unstandardized estimates for the boys' sample:

```
Regression Weights:                         Estimate    S.E.     C.R.     Label
- - - - - - - - - - - - - - - - - - -       - - - - -   - - - -  - - - -  - - - -

           academic <--------- GPA           0.021     0.003    6.927
           attract <------- height           0.019     0.010    1.967
           attract <------- weight          -0.003     0.001   -2.484
           attract <------- rating           0.095     0.030    3.150
           academic <----- attract           0.063     0.059    1.071
           attract <----- academic           1.386     0.315    4.398


Covariances:                                Estimate    S.E.     C.R.     Label
- - - - - - - - - - -                       - - - - -   - - - -  - - - -  - - - -

           GPA <----------> height          -1.515     0.966   -1.569
           GPA <----------> weight         -15.720     6.933   -2.268
           height <-------> weight          42.295     6.486    6.521
           GPA <----------> rating           0.509     0.275    1.850
           height <-------> rating           0.198     0.231    0.860
           weight <-------> rating          -4.246     1.670   -2.543
           error1 <-------> error2          -0.010     0.011   -0.898


Variances:                                  Estimate    S.E.     C.R.     Label
- - - - - - - - - -                         - - - - -   - - - -  - - - -  - - - -

                             GPA            16.322     1.608   10.149
                          height            11.628     1.146   10.149
                          weight           591.462    58.278   10.149
                          rating             0.941     0.093   10.149
                          error1             0.015     0.002    7.571
                          error2             0.165     0.016   10.149
```

The girls' parameter estimates in path diagram format are:

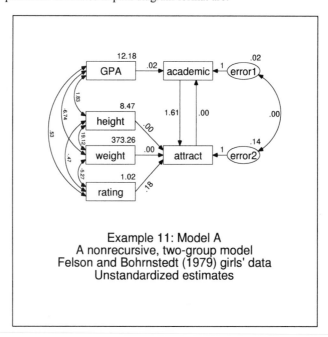

Example 11: Model A
A nonrecursive, two-group model
Felson and Bohrnstedt (1979) girls' data
Unstandardized estimates

And here is the path diagram with the boys' estimates:

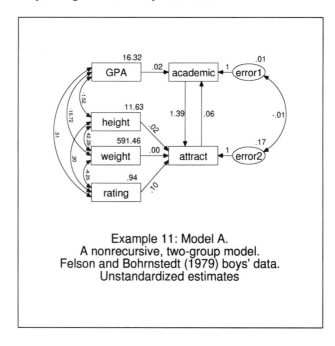

Example 11: Model A.
A nonrecursive, two-group model.
Felson and Bohrnstedt (1979) boys' data.
Unstandardized estimates

You can visually inspect the girls' and boys' estimates in Model A, looking for differences between them. By a rough inspection, the regression paths appear relatively similar, with the exception of `attract <--- rating` (path difference 0.081, pooled s.e. 0.040). To find out if girls and boys differ significantly with respect to any single parameter, you could use the **$Crdiff** command. However, we follow a somewhat more structured approach.

Model B for girls and boys

Suppose our main interest lies with the regression weights, and we entertain the hypothesis (Model B) that the girls and boys have the same regression weights. Under this model, the variances and covariances of the exogenous variables would still be allowed to differ between the groups while the regression weights are group-invariant.

> Models that restrict only the regression weights across groups appear in a number of statistical techniques: in analysis of variance, we would speak of a *main-effects* model; in analysis of covariance, *homogeneity of within-group regressions* is an important model assumption (Huitema, 1980; Winer, 1971). Examples 12 and 15 (below) will demonstrate multi-group factor analysis models with *group-invariant factor patterns*.

The motivation for the group-invariant regression weights proposed in Model B is as follows: It is probably reasonable to assume that perceived height and weight have different variances and covariances among boys and girls. We might also want to permit the other exogenous variables in the model to take on different variances and covariances across groups. Under Model B, however, we evaluate whether a fixed unit change on an exogenous variable will always correspond to the same change of the endogenous variable (s), independent of whether the respondent is male or female. If Model B is confirmed by the data, the same regression weights can be used for all groups, which simplifies the prediction of the endogenous variables. Another advantage of Model B will be that the regression weights themselves will be estimated more efficiently.

Modeling in Amos Text

Here is the **Amos Text** input file for Model B, using parameter labels `p1`–`p6` to impose equality constraints across groups:

```
Example 11: Model B
A nonrecursive, two-group model with
some parameters being group-invariant.

$Group name = girls
$Structure
   academic = (p1) GPA + (p2) attract + (1) error1
   attract  = (p3) height + (p4) weight + (p5) rating + (p6) academic + (1) error2

   error2 <--> error1

$Include = fels_fem.amd

$Next group

$Group name = boys
$Structure
   academic = (p1) GPA + (p2) attract + (1) error1
   attract  = (p3) height + (p4) weight + (p5) rating + (p6) academic + (1) error2

   error2 <--> error1

$Include = fels_mal.amd
```

Modeling in Amos Graphics

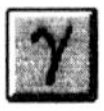

To set up Model B using path diagram input, you need to constrain twelve paths. For the present example, this task can be cut in half by checking the **All groups** option in the **Parameter constraints** dialog box. Simply set the parameter names in one group, and after setting each name, check the **All groups** field to indicate that the parameter name should carry over to the other groups:

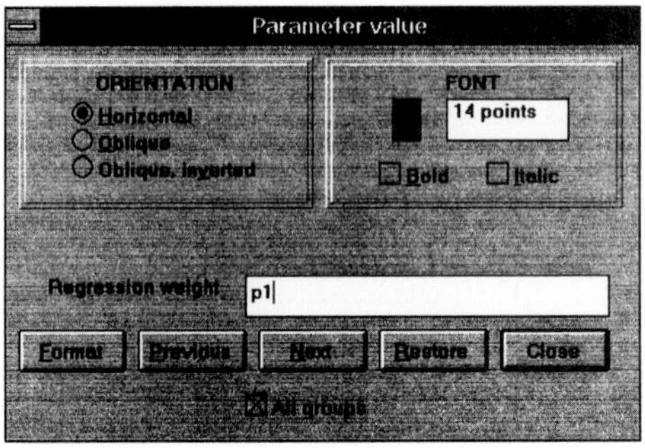

Afterwards, the path diagram for either of the two samples will look about like this:

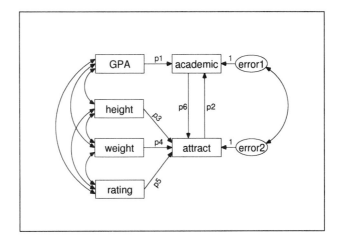

Multiple model input

An **Amos Text** stacked input file for both Models A and B can be written as:

```
Example 11: Models A and B stacked.
Nonrecursive, two-group models.
Felson and Bohrnstedt (1979) data.

$Group name = girls
$Structure
    academic = (g1) GPA + (g2) attract + (1) error1
    attract  = (g3) height + (g4) weight + (g5) rating + (g6) academic + (1) error2

    error2 <--> error1

$Include = fels_fem.amd

$Next group

$Group name = boys
$Structure
    academic = (b1) GPA + (b2) attract + (1) error1
    attract  = (b3) height + (b4) weight + (b5) rating + (b6) academic + (1) error2

    error2 <--> error1

$Include = fels_mal.amd

$Model=Model_A
$Model=Model_B
    g1 = b1
    g2 = b2
    g3 = b3
    g4 = b4
    g5 = b5
    g6 = b6
```

The same, stacked model is easily specified in **Amos Graphics**. You can start from the path diagram for Model A and use the **Parameter constraints** button to assign a total of twelve (12) unique parameter labels to the six (6) path coefficients in the two groups. To be consistent with the Amos Text specification above, you may want to use the labels g1–g6 in the girls' group and b1–b6 in the boys' group (make sure to keep the **All**

groups field *empty* when defining each of these labels). Then, include the last 8 lines from the preceding **Amos Text** specification in one of the **$** command sets. The completed **Amos Graphics** multiple-model specification is given in the file `ex11-ab.amw`.

Some of the path diagram *text macros* may be worth mentioning here. Here are three text macros that occur in the Figure caption of `ex11-ab.amw`:

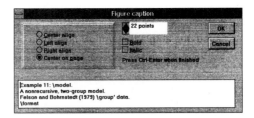

In the path diagram view, the text macro **\model** is replaced by the model name in view, in the present example 'Most General Model' on input, and 'Model A' or 'Model B' on output. The **\group** macro changes to the name of the group that is currently displayed. The **\format** macro is replaced by the display format, 'Model Specification' on input, and 'Unstandardized Estimates' or 'Standardized Estimates' on output.

Output from Model B

Amos Text output

Model B fits the data very well:

```
Chi-square =       9.493
Degrees of freedom =   10
Probability level =     0.486
```

Comparing Model B against Model A gives a nonsignificant chi-square of $9.516 - 3.191 = 6.325$ with $10 - 4 = 6$ degrees of freedom. Assuming that Model B is indeed correct, the Model B estimates are preferable over the Model A estimates.

The unstandardized parameter estimates for the girls' sample are:

```
Regression Weights:                      Estimate    S.E.      C.R.    Label
-------------------                      --------  -------   -------   -------

          academic <--------- GPA          0.022    0.002     9.475    g1
          attract <------- height          0.008    0.007     1.177    g3
          attract <------- weight         -0.003    0.001    -2.453    g4
          attract <------- rating          0.145    0.020     7.186    g5
          academic <----- attract          0.018    0.039     0.469    g2
          attract <----- academic          1.448    0.232     6.234    g6


Covariances:                             Estimate    S.E.      C.R.    Label
------------                             --------  -------   -------   -------

       GPA <----------> height            1.828    0.716     2.555
       GPA <----------> weight           -6.743    4.699    -1.435
       height <-------> weight           19.115    4.117     4.642
       GPA <----------> rating            0.529    0.247     2.139
       height <-------> rating           -0.470    0.206    -2.279
       weight <-------> rating           -5.269    1.401    -3.759
       error1 <-------> error2           -0.004    0.008    -0.464


Variances:                               Estimate    S.E.      C.R.    Label
----------                               --------  -------   -------   -------

                          GPA           12.180    1.194    10.198
                       height            8.468    0.830    10.198
                       weight          373.262   36.602    10.198
                       rating            1.020    0.100    10.198
                       error1            0.019    0.003     7.111
                       error2            0.144    0.014    10.191
```

By virtue of the Model B specification, the estimated regression weights for the boys are the same as those for the girls. The variance and covariance estimates for the boys' sample are:

```
Covariances:                             Estimate    S.E.      C.R.    Label
------------                             --------  -------   -------   -------

       GPA <----------> height           -1.515    0.966    -1.569
       GPA <----------> weight          -15.720    6.933    -2.268
       height <-------> weight           42.295    6.486     6.521
       GPA <----------> rating            0.509    0.275     1.850
       height <-------> rating            0.198    0.231     0.860
       weight <-------> rating           -4.246    1.670    -2.543
       error1 <-------> error2           -0.004    0.008    -0.466


Variances:                               Estimate    S.E.      C.R.    Label
----------                               --------  -------   -------   -------

                          GPA           16.322    1.608    10.149
                       height           11.628    1.146    10.149
                       weight          591.462   58.278    10.149
                       rating            0.941    0.093    10.149
                       error1            0.016    0.002     7.220
                       error2            0.168    0.017    10.146
```

The output path diagram for the girls is:

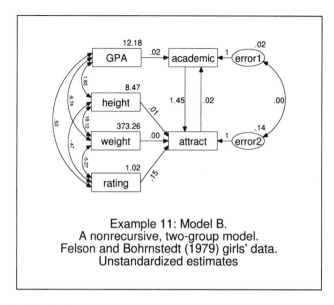

Example 11: Model B.
A nonrecursive, two-group model.
Felson and Bohrnstedt (1979) girls' data.
Unstandardized estimates

And the output for the boys:

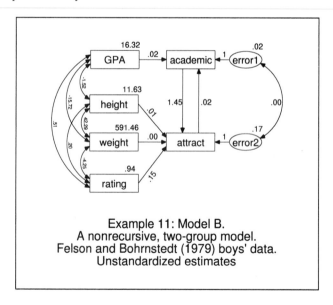

Example 11: Model B.
A nonrecursive, two-group model.
Felson and Bohrnstedt (1979) boys' data.
Unstandardized estimates

Model C for girls and boys

You might consider adding additional constraints to Model B, making *every* parameter
the same for boys as for girls. This, of course, would imply that the entire
variance/covariance matrix of the observed variables must be the same for boys as for
girls, while also requiring that the Felson and Bohrnstedt model be correct for both
groups. Instead of following this course, we will now abandon the Felson and Bohrnstedt
model, and concentrate on the hypothesis that the observed variables have the same
variance/covariance matrix for girls and boys. It is possible to construct a model (Model
C) that embodies this hypothesis.

Modeling in Amos Text

Here an input file that describes Model C:

```
! Felson and Bohrnstedt (1979) study of perceived
! attractiveness and academic ability in teenagers,
! sixth through eighth grade.
! Testing the homogeneity of boys' and girls'
! variance-covariance matrices.

$Group name = Girls
$Structure
     academic    (a)
     attract     (b)
     GPA         (c)
     height      (d)
     weight      (e)
     rating      (f)
     academic <> attract    (g)
     academic <> GPA        (h)
     academic <> height     (i)
     academic <> weight     (j)
     academic <> rating     (k)
     attract  <> GPA        (l)
     attract  <> height     (m)
     attract  <> weight     (n)
     attract  <> rating     (o)
     GPA      <> height     (p)
     GPA      <> weight     (q)
     GPA      <> rating     (r)
     height   <> weight     (s)
     height   <> rating     (t)
     weight   <> rating     (u)
$Include = fels_fem.amd

$Next group

$Group name = Boys
$Structure
     academic    (a)
        ...

          (Structure same as above)

        ...

$Include = fels_mal.amd
```

Modeling in Amos Graphics

Because each group's model specification contains fifteen covariance terms, connecting
each variable to the other five, we will have to take a little care drawing the path diagram
so that it remains readable. In this particular model it is convenient to place the variable
objects in a circular arrangement.

Several Amos Graphics commands will be helpful to create a readable setup. You already know that you can reposition variable objects and the two-headed covariance arrows with the **Move** button. You can also use the **Shape** button to flatten, curve and/or reflect the covariance arrows, so that they remain clear of each other. Finally, the **Move Param** button may be used to migrate the parameter values to a different place alongside the variable or covariance object, away from the cluttered areas.

The file **ex11-c.amw** contains the Amos Graphics specification for Model C. Here is the group-invariant input path diagram:

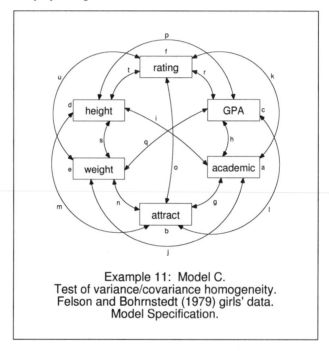

Example 11: Model C.
Test of variance/covariance homogeneity.
Felson and Bohrnstedt (1979) girls' data.
Model Specification.

Results for Model C

Model C would have to be rejected at any conventional significance level.

```
Chi-square =      48.981
Degrees of freedom =    21
Probability level =     0.001
```

The above result means that you should not waste time on any model that allows no differences at all between boys and girls. The variances and/or covariances of the exogenous variables are different in the two samples.

Example 12: Simultaneous factor analysis for several groups

Purpose

This example carries out a factor analysis on data from several populations at once (Jöreskog, 1971). This demonstration includes a test of whether the same factor model holds for each of several populations (possibly with different parameter values for different populations).

The data

The Holzinger and Swineford (1939) data described in Example 8 will be used again for the present example. This time, however, data from the 72 boys in the Grant-White sample will be analyzed along with data from the 73 girls studied in Example 8. The girls' data are contained in the file, **grnt_fem.amd**, and are described in Example 8. The boys' data are contained in the file, **grnt_mal.amd**, shown below.

```
! Holzinger and Swineford (1939) Grant-White sample.
! Intelligence factor study. Raw data of 72 male
! students from the Grant-White high school, Chicago.

$Input variables
      visperc        ! Visual perception score
      cubes          ! Test of spatial visualization
      lozenges       ! Test of spatial orientation
      paragraph      ! Paragraph comprehension score
      sentence       ! Sentence completion score
      wordmean       ! Word meaning test score

$Sample size =    72
$Raw data
   23.   19.    4.  10.  17.   10.
   34.   24.   22.  11.  19.   19.
   29.   23.    9.   9.  19.   11.
                    ...    (66 similar lines omitted here).
   24.   28.   11.   8.  17.    7.
   26.   27.    4.  11.  18.   14.
   26.   24.   27.  11.  23.   22.
```

Model A for the Holzinger and Swineford boys and girls

Consider the hypothesis that the common factor analysis model of Example 8 (shown again below) holds for boys as well as for girls. For **Amos Graphics**, the path diagram associated with Example 8 is again used for this model, and the boys' sample is simply added as a second group. Because **Amos Graphics** automatically assumes that both groups have the same structure, the path diagram need only be created once. The path diagram file for this model is **ex12-a.amw**.

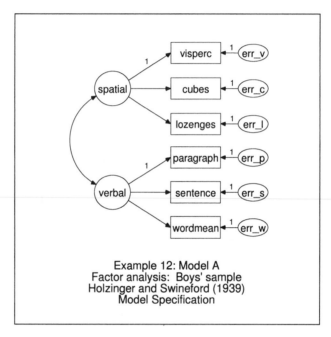

Example 12: Model A
Factor analysis: Boys' sample
Holzinger and Swineford (1939)
Model Specification

Alternatively, the **Amos Text** input file (**ex12-a.ami**) illustrated below fits this model for both boys and girls.

```
Example 12, Model A:
Factor analysis in several groups.

Holzinger and Swineford (1939) Grant-White sample.
Intelligence factor study.  Raw data of 73 female
and
72 male students from the Grant-White high school,
Chicago.

$Standardized
$Smc

$Group name = Girls
$Structure
    visperc   = (1) spatial + (1) err_v
    cubes     =     spatial + (1) err_c
    lozenges  =     spatial + (1) err_l

    paragraph = (1) verbal  + (1) err_p
    sentence  =     verbal  + (1) err_s
    wordmean  =     verbal  + (1) err_w

$Include = grnt_fem.amd

$Next group

$Group name = Boys
$Structure
    visperc   = (1) spatial + (1) err_v
    cubes     =     spatial + (1) err_c
    lozenges  =     spatial + (1) err_l

    paragraph = (1) verbal  + (1) err_p
    sentence  =     verbal  + (1) err_s
    wordmean  =     verbal  + (1) err_w

$Include = grnt_mal.amd
```

Again, notice that while the same model *structure* is specified for boys and girls, the regression weights are allowed to be different for the two groups. The unique variances may be different too, and so may the variances and the covariance of the common factors.

Results for Model A

In the calculation of degrees of freedom for this model, all of the numbers from Example 8 are exactly doubled:

```
Computation of Degrees of Freedom

                Number of distinct sample moments:     42
    Number of distinct parameters to be estimated:    26
                                                    ------------------------
                               Degrees of freedom:    16
```

Model A is acceptable at any conventional significance level. Had Model A been rejected, we would have had to make changes in the path diagram for at least one of the two groups:

```
Chi-square =    16.480
Degrees of freedom =   16
Probability level =     0.420
```

Here are the (unstandardized) parameter estimates for the 73 girls. They are the same estimates that were obtained in Example 8 where the girls alone were studied:

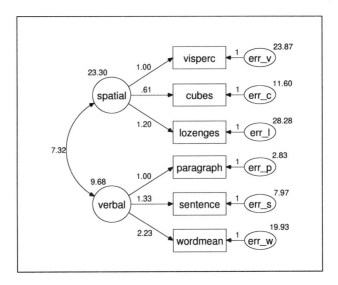

The corresponding output path diagram for the 72 boys is:

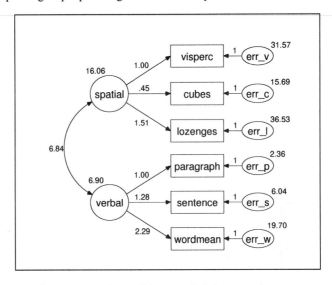

Notice that the estimated regression weights vary little between the two groups. It is quite plausible that the two groups share the same path values—a hypothesis that will be tested in Model B.

Example 12: Multi-group factor analysis   **Amos Users' Guide**

Model B for the Holzinger and Swineford boys and girls

Having accepted the hypothesis that the same factor analysis model holds for both boys and girls, the next step is to ask whether boys and girls share the same parameter values. The model to be considered next (Model B) does not go as far as requiring every parameter for the population of boys to equal the corresponding parameter for the population of girls. What it does require is that the factor pattern (*i.e.*, the regression weights) be the same for both groups. Model B still permits different unique variances for boys and girls. The common factor variances and covariances may also differ in the two groups. The **Amos Text** file for Model B is **ex12-b.ami**, listed below:

```
Example 12, Model B:
Factor analysis in several groups.

$Standardized
$Smc

$Group name = Girls
$Structure
     visperc  =         (1) spatial + (1) err_v
     cubes    = (cube_s) spatial + (1) err_c
     lozenges = (lozn_s) spatial + (1) err_l

     paragraph =        (1) verbal  + (1) err_p
     sentence = (sent_v) verbal  + (1) err_s
     wordmean = (word_v) verbal  + (1) err_w

$Include = grnt_fem.amd

$Next group

$Group name = Boys
$Structure
     visperc  =         (1) spatial + (1) err_v
     cubes    = (cube_s) spatial + (1) err_c
     lozenges = (lozn_s) spatial + (1) err_l

     paragraph =        (1) verbal  + (1) err_p
     sentence = (sent_v) verbal  + (1) err_s
     wordmean = (word_v) verbal  + (1) err_w

$Include = grnt_mal.amd
```

Model B is set up in **Amos Graphics** by entering the parameter names shown above within the corresponding regression paths in the path diagram. Be sure to use the **All groups** option box when you assign these parameter constraints. The input file for Model B is **ex12-b.amw**.

Results for Model B

Because of the additional constraints in Model B, four fewer parameters have to be estimated from the data, increasing the number of degrees of freedom accordingly:

```
Computation of Degrees of Freedom

                    Number of distinct sample moments:   42
         Number of distinct parameters to be estimated:  22
                    ------------------------
                             Degrees of freedom:   20
```

The chi-square fit statistic is acceptable:

```
Chi-square =      18.292
Degrees of freedom =    20
Probability level =      0.568
```

The chi-square difference between the two models, $18.292 - 16.480 = 1.812$, is not significant at any conventional level, either. Thus, Model B, assuming a group-invariant factor pattern, is supported by the Holzinger and Swineford data.

Here are the parameter estimates for the 73 girls:

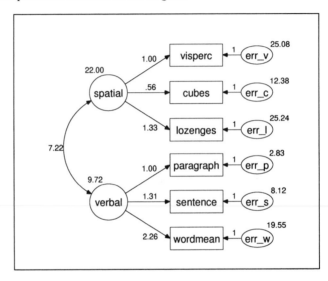

And the parameter estimates for the 72 boys:

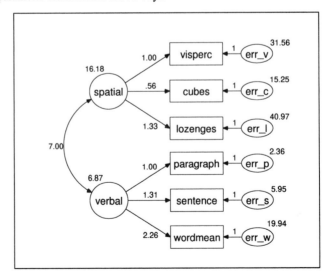

Not surprisingly, the Model B parameter estimates are different from the Model A estimates. The following table shows estimates and standard errors for the two models side by side:

Parameter	Model A		Model B	
Girls' sample	Estimate	Standard Error	Estimate	Standard Error
g: cubes <--- spatial	0.610	0.143	0.557	0.114
g: lozenges <--- spatial	1.198	0.272	1.327	0.248
g: sentence <--- verbal	1.334	0.160	1.305	0.117
g: wordmean <--- verbal	2.234	0.263	2.260	0.200
g: spatial <---> verbal	7.315	2.571	7.225	2.458
g: var(spatial)	23.302	8.124	22.001	7.078
g: var(verbal)	9.682	2.159	9.723	2.025
g: var(err_v)	23.873	5.986	25.082	5.832
g: var(err_c)	11.602	2.584	12.382	2.481
g: var(err_l)	28.275	7.892	25.244	8.040
g: var(err_p)	2.834	0.869	2.835	0.834
g: var(err_s)	7.967	1.869	8.115	1.816
g: var(err_w)	19.925	4.951	19.550	4.837
Boys' sample	Estimate	Standard Error	Estimate	Standard Error
b: cubes <--- spatial	0.450	0.176	*(same as for girls' sample)*	
b: lozenges <--- spatial	1.510	0.461	*(same as for girls' sample)*	
b: sentence <--- verbal	1.275	0.171	*(same as for girls' sample)*	
b: wordmean <--- verbal	2.294	0.308	*(same as for girls' sample)*	
b: spatial <---> verbal	6.840	2.370	6.992	2.090
b: var(spatial)	16.058	7.516	16.183	5.886
b: var(verbal)	6.904	1.622	6.869	1.465
b: var(err_v)	31.571	6.982	31.563	6.681
b: var(err_c)	15.693	2.904	15.245	2.934
b: var(err_l)	36.526	11.532	40.974	9.689
b: var(err_p)	2.364	0.726	2.363	0.681
b: var(err_s)	6.035	1.433	5.954	1.398
b: var(err_w)	19.697	4.658	19.937	4.470

All but two of the estimated standard errors are smaller in Model B, including those for the unconstrained parameters. Hence, the Model B estimates are somewhat more efficient (assuming that the model is correct). Indeed, one of the reasons for imposing constraints while estimating the parameters of a model is to get more efficient parameter estimates for the population. The other reason is, of course, to test the hypothesis that the imposed constraints indeed hold in the population.

Example 13: Estimating and testing hypotheses about means

Purpose

This example shows how to estimate means, and how to test hypotheses about means. The method demonstrated here is, for large samples, equivalent to a multivariate analysis of variance (MANOVA).

Introduction

Amos and similar programs are usually used to estimate models consisting of variances, covariances and regression weights, and to test hypotheses about these parameters. Means are often ignored in such models, and so are intercepts in regression equations. One reason for the relative absence of mean and intercept components in structural equation and factor analysis models has been rooted in the relative difficulty of specifying these kinds of parameters with existing software. Amos, however, was designed to make means and intercept modeling easy. The present example is the first of several showing how to specify hypotheses about mean and intercept terms. (Actually, in the present example, the parameters consist only of variances, covariances, and means, and do not involve any regression paths or intercepts.)

The data

Attig's (1983) spatial memory data were described in Example 1. Data from both young and old subjects are used here. The raw data for the two groups are contained in two data files, `attg_yng.amd` and `attg_old.amd`, and were listed in Examples 1 and 10. In this example, only the measures **recall1** and **cued1** will be used.

Model A for young and old subjects

In the analysis of Model B of Example 10, it was concluded that **recall1** and **cued1** have the same variances and covariance for both old and young people (at least, the evidence against that hypothesis was found to be insignificant). The following input file will repeat the analysis of Example 10's Model B with an added twist. This time, the means of the two variables, **recall1** and **cued1**, will also be estimated.

Mean structure modeling in Amos Graphics

Under **Amos Graphics**, estimating and testing hypotheses involving means is not that much different from analyzing variance and covariance structures. It does, however, require a few additional steps. Suppose you start with the structure of Example 10, Model B, specifying group-invariant variance and covariance terms for the young and old subjects. Restrictions or comparisons of means, however, were not considered in that model. In fact, Example 10 did not use the sample means at all.

 Incorporating means and intercepts in **Amos Graphics** is simple: just click on the **Means** button. When the **Means** button is down, the program automatically adds a default mean/intercept structure to the existing path model.

The displayed path diagram changes accordingly: on the input and unstandardized output diagrams, *exogenous* variables have a "*mean, variance*" pair of parameters attached to them, while *endogenous* variables are displayed with a single intercept term. The input diagram below shows the labels for variance parameters preceded by commas. These commas imply the presence of yet unlabeled mean parameters. The new path specification is given in file **ex13-a.amw**:

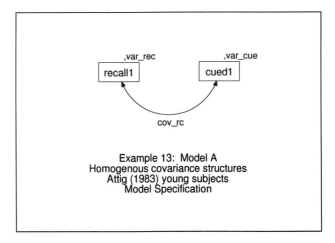

Example 13: Model A
Homogenous covariance structures
Attig (1983) young subjects
Model Specification

Had you constrained the means (to be demonstrated later, in Model B), parameter labels for the means would have been shown to the left of each comma, opposite the variance labels.

Amos Graphics changes in several ways when the **Means** button is pressed:

- Mean and intercept fields are shown during input, in addition to variances, covariances and/or regression weights.

- Constraints may be applied to all intercepts, means, regression weights, variances, and covariances in all groups.

- Pressing the **Calculate estimates** button (while the **Means** button is still pressed) estimates means and intercepts — subject to constraints, if any.

- The chi-square statistic reflects the model fit to sample mean *and* covariance structures.

If the **Means** button is *not* down:

- Only fields for variances, covariances and regression weights are displayed during input. Constraints can be placed *only* on these parameters.

- When the **Calculate estimates** button is pressed, Amos estimates covariance structures, but *not* means or intercepts. Only constraints imposed on variances, covariances and regression weights are used in the estimation; any (portions of) constraints involving means and/or intercepts remain inactive.

- If you turn *off* the **Means** button after the means model has *already* been estimated, the output path diagram will continue to show mean and intercept terms. To display the correct output path diagram without means or intercepts, *recalculate* the model estimates with the **Means** button in the *off* position.

- The chi-square statistic reflects the model fit to sample covariance structures only.

Given these rules, the **Means** button makes estimating and testing means models as easy as traditional path modeling.

Mean structure modeling in Amos Text

The **Amos Text** specification of Model A appears in the file **ex13-a.ami**. It maintains the variance and covariance restrictions used by Example 10, Model B, but adds terms for the variable means in the two groups:

```
Example 13: Model A
Homogenous covariance structures
in two groups, Attig (1983) data.

$Group name = young_subjects
$Structure
     recall1              (var_rec)
     cued1                (var_cue)
     recall1 <> cued1     (cov_rc)
$Mstructure
     recall1
     cued1

$Include = attg_yng.amd

$Next group

$Group name = old_subjects
$Structure
     recall1              (var_rec)
     cued1                (var_cue)
     recall1 <> cued1     (cov_rc)
$Mstructure
     recall1
     cued1

$Include = attg_old.amd
```

It is the **$Mstructure** command (appearing twice) that causes the means of **recall1** and **cued1** to be estimated. Except for the use of the **$Mstructure** command (and changes to the comment section at the top), the input file is identical to that of Example 10, Model B. When you do *not* use the **$Mstructure** command, **Amos Text** makes no assumptions about the means of any of the variables in your model, and it will not estimate any of the means either. On the other hand, when you do use the **$Mstructure** command, **Amos Text** estimates the means of the exogenous variables whose names follow the **$Mstructure** command, and it assumes that all of the other exogenous variables (*i.e.*, those whose names do not follow the **$Mstructure** command) have *zero means*. It is easy to forget that **Amos Text** behaves this way when you use **$Mstructure**, so you have to keep reminding yourself that:

> If you use the **$Mstructure** command anywhere in an **Amos Text** specification, then it must list all exogenous variables that are allowed to have nonzero means. Any exogenous variable that does not appear in an **$Mstructure** command is assumed to have a mean of zero (0).

> This is different from **Amos Graphics**, where pressing the **Means** button estimates the means of *all* exogenous variables (subject to constraints, if any). In **Amos Graphics**, if a variable is supposed to have a zero mean, this must be made explicit by a value constraint.

There is more to be learned about the **$Mstructure** command, but the full story will be told in Example 14, when models with regression intercepts are entertained.

Output for Model A

Amos Text output

The number of degrees of freedom for this model is the same as for Model B of Example 10, but is arrived at in a different way. This time, the *number of distinct sample moments* includes the sample means as well as the sample variances and covariances. In the young sample, there are two variances, one covariance and two means, for a total of five sample moments. Similarly, there are five sample moments in the old sample, so that, taking both samples together, there are ten sample moments. As for the *parameters to be estimated*, there are seven of them, namely var_rec (the common variance of **recall1**), var_cue (the common variance of **cued1**), cov_rc (the common covariance between **recall1** and **cued1**), the means of **recall1** among young and old people (2), and the means of **cued1** among young and old people (2).

The number of degrees of freedom thus works out to be:

```
Computation of Degrees of Freedom

                    Number of distinct sample moments:    10
        Number of distinct parameters to be estimated:     7
                    - - - - - - - - - - - - - - - - - - - - - -
                                  Degrees of freedom:     3
```

The chi-square statistic here is also the same as in Model B of Example 10. The hypothesis that old people and young people share the same variances and covariance would be accepted at any conventional significance level.

```
Chi-square =      4.588
Degrees of freedom =     3
Probability level =      0.205
```

Here are the parameter estimates for the group of 40 young subjects:

Means:	Estimate	S.E.	C.R.	Label
recall1	10.250	0.382	26.862	
cued1	11.700	0.374	31.292	

Covariances:	Estimate	S.E.	C.R.	Label
recall1 <-----> cued1	4.056	0.780	5.202	cov_rc

Variances:	Estimate	S.E.	C.R.	Label
recall1	5.678	0.909	6.245	var_rec
cued1	5.452	0.873	6.245	var_cue

And here are the estimates for the 40 old subjects:

Means:		Estimate	S.E.	C.R.	Label
	recall1	8.675	0.382	22.735	
	cued1	9.575	0.374	25.609	

Covariances:		Estimate	S.E.	C.R.	Label
recall1 <----> cued1		4.056	0.780	5.202	cov_rc

Variances:		Estimate	S.E.	C.R.	Label
	recall1	5.678	0.909	6.245	var_rec
	cued1	5.452	0.873	6.245	var_cue

Except for the means, these estimates are the same as those obtained in Model B of Example 10. The estimated standard errors and critical ratios are the same as well. This goes to show that merely estimating means, without placing any constraints on them, has no effect on the estimates of the remaining parameters or their standard errors.

Amos Graphics Output

The path diagram output for the two groups follows below. Note that the means are displayed to the left of the variance estimates. For instance, among the young subjects, variable **recall1** has an estimated mean of 10.25 and an estimated variance of 5.68. Mean and variance values, separated by commas, are paired up next to their exogenous variable objects.

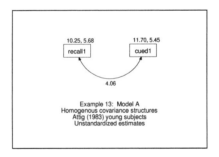

Example 13: Model A
Homogenous covariance structures
Attig (1983) young subjects
Unstandardized estimates

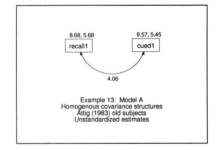

Example 13: Model A
Homogenous covariance structures
Attig (1983) old subjects
Unstandardized estimates

Model B for young and old subjects

We now assume that Model A is correct, and consider the more restrictive hypothesis that the means of the variables **recall1** and **cued1** do not change across the two groups.

Modeling in Amos Graphics

In order to set up Model B in **Amos Graphics**, the means for **recall1** and **cued1** must be constrained in the same way that variances and covariances were constrained in previous examples. To do so, simply press the **Parameter constraints** button while the **Means** button is depressed. Then click on the corresponding variable object. **Amos Graphics** will present a **Parameter value** dialog box with an added **Mean** field:

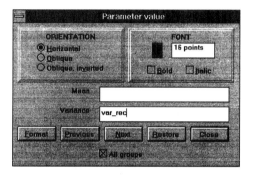

You can now enter a number or variable name to force the mean of **recall1** to be equal to a value, or to another parameter. We can choose the name mn_rec, for instance. If the **All groups** box remains checked, the parameter name for the mean of **recall1** in the young subjects will carry over to the old subjects, forcing the means to be equal in both groups. Correspondingly, the means of **cued1** for young and old subjects can be constrained by a common parameter label such as mn_cue. The path diagram below (from file **ex13-b.amw**) displays the **Amos Graphics** specification of Model B for either of the two groups. Notice that the new mean parameter names appear alongside the variance parameter names for each variable object.

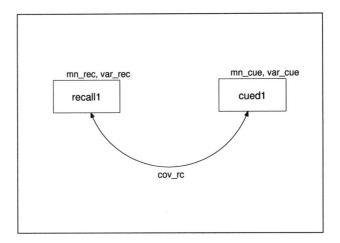

Modeling in Amos Text

The file **ex13-b.ami** specifies the same model for **Amos Text**. In addition to group-invariant variances and covariances, the means are also restricted to be equal across the two groups:

```
Example 13: Model B
Homogenous means and covariance
structures in two groups,
Attig (1983) data.

$Group name = young_subjects
$Structure
      recall1              (var_rec)
      cued1                (var_cue)
      recall1 <> cued1     (cov_rc)
$Mstructure
      recall1              (mn_rec)
      cued1                (mn_cue)

$Include = attg_yng.amd

$Next group

$Group name = old_subjects
$Structure
      recall1              (var_rec)
      cued1                (var_cue)
      recall1 <> cued1     (cov_rc)
$Mstructure
      recall1              (mn_rec)
      cued1                (mn_cue)

$Include = attg_old.amd
```

Multiple model input

Models A and B can, of course, be specified simultaneously in the same **Amos Graphics** or **Amos Text** input file, and a good reason for doing so may be the convenience of having the chi-square differences and *p*-values for model comparisons printed near the end of the list output.

```
Example 13: Models A and B
Testing mean differences in
two groups, Attig (1983) data.

$Group name = young_subjects
$Structure
      recall1              (var_rec)
      cued1               (var_cue)
      recall1 <> cued1    (cov_rc)
$Mstructure
      recall1             (yng_rec)
      cued1               (yng_cue)

$Include = attg_yng.amd

$Next group

$Group name = old_subjects
$Structure
      recall1              (var_rec)
      cued1               (var_cue)
      recall1 <> cued1    (cov_rc)
$Mstructure
      recall1             (old_rec)
      cued1               (old_cue)

$Include = attg_old.amd

$Model = Model_A
$Model = Model_B
      yng_rec = old_rec
      yng_cue = old_cue
```

In **Amos Graphics**, the multiple-model specification is entered in much the same way. Although not reproduced in this document, the corresponding **Amos Graphics** input file for this example is **ex13-all.amw**.

Results for Model B

With the new constraints on the means, Model B has five (5) degrees of freedom:

```
Computation of Degrees of Freedom

                  Number of distinct sample moments:    10
          Number of distinct parameters to be estimated:    5
                  - - - - - - - - - - - - - - - - - - - - - - - -
                            Degrees of freedom:    5
```

Model B has to be rejected at any conventional significance level:

```
Chi-square =      19.267
Degrees of freedom =     5
Probability level =      0.002
```

Comparison of Model B with Model A

If Model A is correct and Model B is wrong (which is at least plausible, since Model A was accepted and Model B was rejected) then the assumption of equal means must be wrong. A better test of the hypothesis of equal means under the assumption of equal variances and covariances can be obtained in the following way. When the multiple-model specification is used (*e.g.*, files **ex13-all.ami** or **ex13-all.amw**), the following model comparison appears near the end of the list output file (**ex13-all.amo**):

```
Model Comparisons
- - - - - - - - - - - - - - - - -

Assuming Model_A to be correct:

                   df    chi-2     p
                   --    -----   -----
          Model_B   2   14.679   0.001
```

In comparing Model B with Model A, the difference between the chi-square fit statistics is 14.679, based on two (2) degrees of freedom. Since Model B is obtained by placing additional constraints on Model A, we can say that, if Model B is correct then 14.679 is an observation on a chi-square variable with 2 degrees of freedom. However, the probability of obtaining this large (or a larger) chi-square value is 0.001—rather unlikely, in other words. Hence we reject Model B in favor of Model A: *the two groups have different means.*

> *Note*: This comparison of nested means-level models, given homogenous covariance structures, is as close as Amos can come to conventional multivariate analysis of variance. In fact, Amos's test is equivalent to a conventional MANOVA except that the chi-square test provided by Amos is only asymptotically correct. However, *F*-tests used by a conventional MANOVA provide an exact test even for small samples.
>
> This example is meant to be a simple demonstration of Amos's mean-level capabilities. In real life, such a problem would be treated by MANOVA, while Amos would be reserved for investigating more complex structural equation models for which the exact small-sample distribution of the test statistic would not always be known. In the latter case, Amos's bootstrapping option (demonstrated in Example 19) could be used to verify the standard errors and confidence intervals obtained by the maximum likelihood method.

Example 14: Regression with an explicit intercept

Purpose

Estimate the regression intercept in an ordinary regression analysis.

Introduction

Ordinarily, when you specify that some variable depends linearly on some others, Amos assumes that the linear equation expressing the dependency contains an additive constant, or intercept. For instance, in Example 4, a variable called **performance** was specified to depend linearly on three other variables called **knowledge**, **value** and **satisfaction**. Amos assumed that the regression equation was of the following form:

```
performance = a + b₁*knowledge + b₂*value + b₃*satisfaction + error
```

where b_1, b_2, and b_3 are the regression weights, and a is the intercept. In Example 4, the regression weights b_1 through b_3 were estimated. The intercept term a, however, was not actually estimated, nor was it mentioned explicitly in the **Amos Graphics** or **Amos Text** input files. Nevertheless, Amos takes for granted that an intercept is present in the regression equation. You will usually be satisfied with this method of handling intercepts in regression equations. Sometimes, however, you will want to see an estimate of an intercept, or to test a hypothesis about an intercept. Then you will need to take the steps demonstrated below.

The data

The data of Warren, White and Fuller (1974) that were used in Example 4 will be used again here. The sample moments (means, variances and covariances) are contained in the file **warren5v.amd**, shown below:

```
! Managerial role performance
! (Warren, White and Fuller, 1974).
! Study of managers of farm co-operatives.

$Sample size = 98

$Input variables

     performance        ! 24 item test of role performance
     knowledge          ! 26 item test of knowledge
     value              ! 30 item test of value orientation
     satisfaction       ! 11 item test of role satisfaction
     past_training      ! Years of formal education

$Covariances
  .0209
  .0177   .0520
  .0245   .0280   .1212
  .0046   .0044  -.0063   .0901
  .0187   .0192   .0353  -.0066   .0946

$Means
0.0589   1.3796   2.8773   2.4613   2.1174
```

Input file for the regression analysis

Modeling in Amos Graphics

You can set up the regression model the same as in Example 4. In fact, if you have
already gone through Example 4, all you may need to do is copy that input file and press
the **Means** button before running the analysis. However, you should check the input
display with the **Means** button pressed. Your diagram (from the **Amos Graphics** input
file **ex14.amw**) will look something like this:

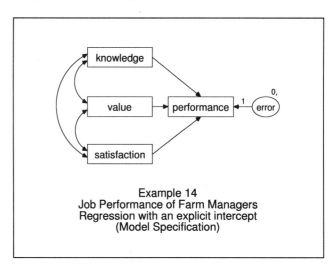

Example 14
Job Performance of Farm Managers
Regression with an explicit intercept
(Model Specification)

An important feature of this path diagram is the string "0," displayed above the **error**
object. It indicates that the mean of the residual values is assumed to be zero — a
standard assumption in linear regression models. By default, **Amos Graphics** sets the

means of regression error terms to zero, so you do not have to worry about using the **Parameter constraints** command.

Conversely, if you specified the mean of the error term as a parameter to be estimated, rather than being fixed at zero, Amos would produce the error message:

```
**********************************************************************
The analysis will not continue because
the specified model has negative degrees of freedom.
That is, the number of parameters to be estimated exceeds
the number of distinct sample moments.
Such a model cannot be identified.
**********************************************************************
```

The error would occur because Amos was trying to simultaneously estimate a mean for **error** and an intercept for the dependent variable **performance**. We know from regression theory that the mean of the residual error term *must* be 0 if there is also an intercept. This is another (and more clear) example of unidentification.

 Recall the discussion in Example 13 of several modeling situations affected by the **Means** command. In the present example, the **Means** button must be pressed in order to estimate or display the regression intercept (s) and means of the predictor variables. The display of variances, covariances and regression weights will not be affected.

Modeling in Amos Text

By way of reminder, here is the **Amos Text** input file used in Example 4 (equation version):

```
Example 4:
Conventional Linear Regression

Multiple regression model predicting the
Job Performance of Farm Managers.
Warren, White and Fuller (1974)

$Standardized
$Smc
$Implied moments
$Sample moments

$Structure
      performance = knowledge + value + satisfaction + error (1)

$Include warren5v.amd
```

The **Amos Text** input (from file **ex14.ami**) will produce all the same results, plus the mean and intercept estimates:

```
Example 14:
Regression with an explicit intercept

Multiple regression model predicting the
Job Performance of Farm Managers.
Warren, White and Fuller (1974)

$Standardized
$Smc
$Implied moments
$Sample moments

$Structure
    performance = () + knowledge + value + satisfaction + error (1)
$Mstructure
    knowledge
    value
    satisfaction

$Include warren5v.amd
```

The important differences in the new input file are an extra pair of empty parentheses and a 'plus' sign in the equation statement following the **$Structure** command. The extra pair of empty parentheses represents the intercept in the regression equation. One result of the analysis will now be an estimate of that intercept.

The **$Mstructure** command requests estimates for the means of **knowledge**, **value** and **satisfaction**. All exogenous variables with means other than zero have to be listed under the **$Mstructure** command. On the other hand, if the **$Mstructure** command were not given, **Amos Text** would use the default for mean-level models, *i.e.*, the means of all exogenous variables would be fixed to zero (*cf.*, Example 13).

Rules for modeling means and intercepts in **Amos Text**, in addition to those already stated in Example 13, are:

> If an *endogenous variable* is listed under the **$Mstructure** command, then an intercept will automatically be added to the regression equation for that variable. This function facilitates mean-level model specifications in **Amos Text** *path* format.

> However, when regression *equations* appear in **$Structure** statements, it is advisable to state the intercept term there, and use the **$Mstructure** command only for the *exogenous* variables. This way, it will be easier to keep track of which command produced the intercept terms.

Results of the regression analysis

Text output

The present analysis is the same as the analysis of Example 4, but with the explicit estimation of three means and an intercept. The number of degrees of freedom is again zero, but the calculation goes a little differently. Sample means are required for this analysis, and so the *number of distinct sample moments* includes the sample means as well as the sample variances and covariances. There are four sample means, four sample variances and six sample covariances, for a total of 14 sample moments. As for the parameters to be estimated, there are three regression weights and an intercept. Also, the three predictors have, among them, three means, three variances and three covariances. Finally, there is one error variance, for a total of 14 parameters to be estimated.

```
Computation of Degrees of Freedom

                  Number of distinct sample moments:    14
         Number of distinct parameters to be estimated:   14
                                       -------------------------
                                       Degrees of freedom:   0
```

With zero degrees of freedom, there is no hypothesis to be tested:

```
Chi-square =      0.000
Degrees of freedom =     0
Probability level cannot be computed
```

The estimates for regression weights, variances and covariances are the same as in Example 4, and so are the associated estimates for standard errors and the critical ratios.

```
Regression Weights:                           Estimate    S.E.      C.R.      Label
-------------------                           --------    ----      ----      -----

    performance <-------- knowledge            0.258     0.054     4.822
    performance <----------- value             0.145     0.035     4.136
    performance <----- satisfaction            0.049     0.038     1.274


Standardized Regression Weights:              Estimate
--------------------------------              --------

    performance <-------- knowledge            0.407
    performance <----------- value             0.349
    performance <----- satisfaction            0.101


Means:                                        Estimate    S.E.      C.R.      Label
------                                         --------    ----      ----      -----

                      knowledge                1.380     0.023    59.585
                          value                2.877     0.035    81.399
                   satisfaction                2.461     0.030    80.758


Intercepts:                                   Estimate    S.E.      C.R.      Label
-----------                                    --------    ----      ----      -----

                    performance               -0.834     0.140    -5.951


Covariances:                                  Estimate    S.E.      C.R.      Label
------------                                    --------    ----      ----      -----

    knowledge <-------------> value            0.028     0.009     3.276
    knowledge <------> satisfaction            0.004     0.007     0.632
    value <----------> satisfaction           -0.006     0.011    -0.593


Correlations:                                 Estimate
-------------                                   --------

    knowledge <-------------> value            0.353
    knowledge <------> satisfaction            0.064
    value <----------> satisfaction           -0.060


Variances:                                    Estimate    S.E.      C.R.      Label
----------                                      --------    ----      ----      -----

                      knowledge                0.052     0.007     6.964
                          value                0.121     0.017     6.964
                   satisfaction                0.090     0.013     6.964
                          error                0.013     0.002     6.964
```

In this case, the estimated means and intercepts do not appear to be especially interesting from a theoretical point of view. However, they would be needed in a prediction equation for the performance scores. This exercise shows how to obtain estimates of all parameters in the equation when needed.

Amos Graphics output

Below is the path diagram which contains the unstandardized estimates for this example. The intercept of −.83 is shown above the endogenous variable **performance**:

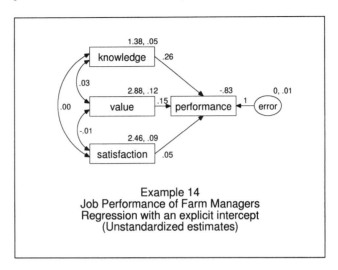

Example 14
Job Performance of Farm Managers
Regression with an explicit intercept
(Unstandardized estimates)

Example 15: Factor analysis with structured means

Purpose

Estimation of factor means in a common factor analysis of data from several populations.

Introduction

Conventionally, the common factor analysis model does not make any assumptions about the means of any variables. In particular, the model makes no assumptions about the means of the common factors. As it happens, in a conventional factor analysis of data from a single sample, it is not even possible to estimate factor means or to test hypotheses about them. At least, it is not possible without making assumptions that would be unrealistic in most cases.

However, in a simultaneous analysis of data from several samples, Sörbom (1974) showed that it *is* possible, under realistic assumptions, to make inferences about factor means. Using Sörbom's approach, one cannot estimate the mean of every factor for every population, but it is still possible to assess any *differences* in factor means among two or more populations. For instance, think about the analysis reported in Example 12, where a common factor analysis model was fit simultaneously to a sample of girls and a sample of boys. For each group, there were two common factors, interpreted as *verbal ability* and *spatial ability*. The method used in Example 12 did not permit an examination of mean verbal ability or mean spatial ability. Sörbom's method, however, while not providing separate mean estimates for both girls and boys, provides an estimate of *mean differences* due to the respondents' sex. In this example, we will fix the boys' mean verbal and spatial abilities, and then estimate the amount by which girls' mean abilities *differ* from the boys'. This method also provides a test of significance for differences of factor means.

> *Note*: The identification status of the factor analysis model can be a difficult subject when factor means are to be estimated. Sörbom's original guidelines for achieving model identification are followed in the present example.

The data

The Holzinger and Swineford (1939) data introduced in Examples 8 and 12 will be used for this example. Data from the 73 girls in the Grant-White sample, described in Example 8, will be analyzed along with data from the 72 boys, introduced in Example 12. The data files for these two groups are **grnt_fem.amd** and **grnt_mal.amd**, respectively.

Model A for boys and girls

Modeling in Amos Graphics

Consider testing this hypothesis: "On average, the boys and girls from which these samples are drawn are equal in their spatial and verbal abilities (defined by three tests for each ability)." It is apparent that in order for this statement to have any real meaning, we must define the **spatial** and **verbal** factors in the same way for both groups. As a result, all regression *parameters* and *intercepts* must be *equal* in the two groups.

Setting up this example follows much the same route as Model B of Example 12, with the exception that the **Means** button is pressed. The **Amos Graphics** input file for Model A is **ex15-a.amw**.

Model A imposes group-invariant factor loading and intercept patterns for the observed variables. In addition, the *means* of the boys' **spatial** and **verbal** factor are fixed at zero (0).

The Amos Graphics input path diagram for the 73 girls is:

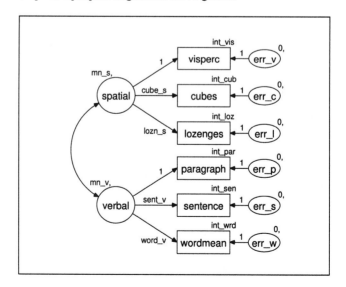

Next is the input path diagram for the 72 boys:

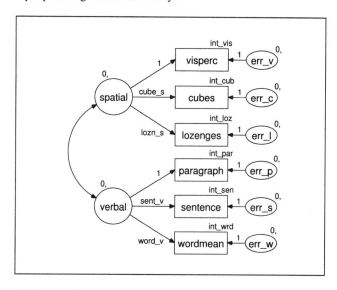

The two path diagrams show explicit intercepts for all observed variables, required to be the same for boys and girls. For example, the label int_vis is used to estimate the same intercept for the indicator variable **visperc** in the two groups. The path coefficients are also constrained to be the same for boys as for girls. For instance, the label cube_s is used in both groups to force the factor loading of the observed variable **cubes** to be group-invariant.

It is an empirical question whether the joint constraints on intercepts and regression weights are appropriate. One result of fitting this model will be a test of whether these constraints hold in the populations of girls and boys. The reason for starting out with these constraints is that (as Sörbom points out) it is necessary to impose *some* constraints on the intercepts and regression weights in order to make the model identified when estimating factor means. The constraints employed here are not the only ones that would make the model identified, but they are plausible ones.

The only difference in the setup for boys and girls is in the two common factor *means*, which are set to zero for the boys' group. In the girls' part of the model, both factor means are estimated, and the unique label mn_s and mn_v are used to identify these parameters in the input path diagram.

The specification of zero means for verbal ability and spatial ability among boys was made in order to make the model identified. Sörbom showed that, even with the constraints already imposed here on the intercepts and regression weights, it is still not possible to estimate factor means for both boys and girls simultaneously. Take verbal ability, for example. If you fix the boys' mean verbal ability at some constant (like zero) then you will be able to estimate the girls' *relative* mean verbal ability. Alternatively, you could fix the girls' mean verbal ability at some constant, and then you would be able to estimate the boys' *relative* mean verbal ability. You just cannot estimate both means at once. The situation is not as bad as it could be, though, because the difference between the boys' mean and the girls' mean will be the same no matter which mean is fixed, and the same no matter at which particular value it is fixed.

Modeling in Amos Text

Defining the group-invariant factor analysis model for boys and girls (Model A) in **Amos Text** is straightforward. The **Amos Text** commands in file `ex15-a.ami` correspond closely to the preceding path diagrams:

```
Example 15: Model A
Factor analysis with structured means

Holzinger and Swineford (1939) Grant-White sample.
Raw data of 73 female and 72 male students.

$Standardized
$Smc

$Group name = Girls
$Structure
    visperc   = (int_vis) +          (1) spatial + (1) err_v
    cubes     = (int_cub) + (cube_s) spatial + (1) err_c
    lozenges  = (int_loz) + (lozn_s) spatial + (1) err_l

    paragraph = (int_par) +          (1) verbal  + (1) err_p
    sentence  = (int_sen) + (sent_v) verbal  + (1) err_s
    wordmean  = (int_wrd) + (word_v) verbal  + (1) err_w
$Mstructure
    spatial  (mn_s)
    verbal   (mn_v)

$Include = grnt_fem.amd

$Next group

$Group name = Boys
$Structure
    visperc   = (int_vis) +          (1) spatial + (1) err_v
    cubes     = (int_cub) + (cube_s) spatial + (1) err_c
    lozenges  = (int_loz) + (lozn_s) spatial + (1) err_l

    paragraph = (int_par) +          (1) verbal  + (1) err_p
    sentence  = (int_sen) + (sent_v) verbal  + (1) err_s
    wordmean  = (int_wrd) + (word_v) verbal  + (1) err_w
$Mstructure
    spatial  (0)
    verbal   (0)

$Include = grnt_mal.amd
```

The **$Structure** sections show the measurement model for each observed variable, including intercept term, in equation format. The **$Mstructure** command in the girls' group specifies that the means of the verbal ability and spatial ability factors are freely estimated, relative to the boys' factor means. The **Amos Text** file uses the **$Mstructure** command once more to specify that verbal ability and spatial ability have zero means in the boys' group (**Amos Text** would have assumed zero means anyway; this second **$Mstructure** command is thus redundant).

Results for Model A

Amos Text output

There is no reason to reject Model A at any conventional significance level:

```
Chi-square =      22.593
Degrees of freedom =   24
Probability level =      0.544
```

Amos Graphics output

We are primarily interested in estimates of mean verbal ability and mean spatial ability, and not so much in estimates of the other parameters. However, as always, all the estimates should be inspected to make sure that they are reasonable. Here are the (unstandardized) parameter estimates for the 73 girls:

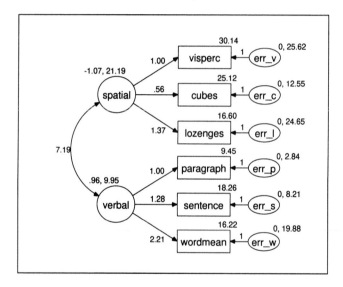

Many of the (unstandardized) parameter estimates for the boys' data are the same, except for the (fixed) means of the spatial and verbal factors, and the variances and covariances (which were not constrained):

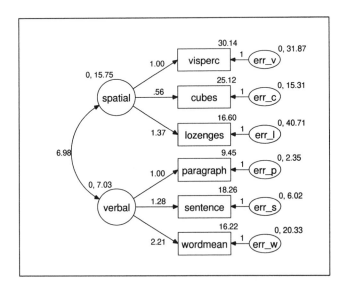

Girls have a mean spatial ability estimated to be –1.066. The mean of boys' spatial ability was fixed at zero. Thus, the girls' spatial ability is estimated to be 1.066 units *below* the boys' spatial ability. This difference is not affected by the initial decision to fix the boys' mean at zero. If we had fixed the boys' mean at 10.000, the girls' mean would have been estimated to be 8.934. If we had fixed the girls' mean at zero, the boys' mean would have been estimated to be 1.066. Of course, there is the question of what units spatial ability is expressed in. A difference of 1.066 verbal ability units may be important or not, depending on how big a unit is. Since the regression weight for regressing **visperc** on spatial ability is equal to one, we can say that spatial ability is expressed in the same units as scores on the **visperc** test. Of course this is useful information only if you happen to be familiar with the **visperc** test. There is another approach to evaluating the mean difference of 1.066, which does not involve **visperc**. Spatial ability has a standard deviation of about 4.0 among boys, and about 4.6 among girls. With standard deviations this large, a difference of 1.066 would not be considered very large for most purposes, certainly not when considering the moderate sample sizes of the Holzinger and Swineford study.

The statistical significance of the 1.066 unit difference between girls and boys is easy to evaluate. Since the boys' mean was fixed at zero, we only need to ask whether the girls' mean differs significantly from zero. Here are the girls' factor mean estimates given by **Amos Text** together with standard error and critical ratio statistics:

Means:	Estimate	S.E.	C.R.	Label
spatial	-1.066	0.881	-1.209	mn_s
verbal	0.956	0.521	1.836	mn_v

The girls' mean spatial ability has a critical ratio of –1.209, so it is not significantly different from zero. In other words, it is not significantly different from the boys' mean.

Turning to verbal ability, the girls' mean is estimated 0.956 units *above* the boys' mean. For comparative purposes, verbal ability has a standard deviation of about 2.7 among boys, and about 3.15 among girls. Thus 0.956 verbal ability units is about one third of a standard deviation in either group. The difference between boys and girls approaches significance at the .05 level (the critical ratio for the girls' mean verbal ability is 1.836, close to the critical value for a standard normally distributed random variable.

Model B for boys and girls

In the discussion of Model A, we used critical ratios to carry out two tests of significance: a test for sex differences in spatial ability and a test for sex differences in verbal ability. We will now carry out a single test of the null hypothesis that all factor means are the same in both sexes. For this purpose, we will repeat the previous analysis with the additional constraint that boys and girls have the same average spatial and verbal abilities. Since the boys' means were fixed at zero in the previous analysis, requiring the girls' means to be the same as the boys' means amounts to setting the girls' means be equal to zero also. Here is the listing of an **Amos Text** input file, **ex15-all.ami,** implementing the new Model B as a two-model comparison:

```
Example 15: Models A and B
Factor analysis with structured means

Holzinger and Swineford (1939) Grant-White sample.
Raw data of 73 female and 72 male students.

$Standardized
$Smc

$Group name = Girls
$Structure
      visperc   = (int_vis) +        (1) spatial + (1) err_v
      cubes     = (int_cub) + (cube_s) spatial + (1) err_c
      lozenges  = (int_loz) + (lozn_s) spatial + (1) err_l

      paragraph = (int_par) +        (1) verbal  + (1) err_p
      sentence  = (int_sen) + (sent_v) verbal  + (1) err_s
      wordmean  = (int_wrd) + (word_v) verbal  + (1) err_w
$Mstructure
      spatial (mn_s)
      verbal  (mn_v)

$Include = grnt_fem.amd

$Next group

$Group name = Boys
$Structure
      visperc   = (int_vis) +        (1) spatial + (1) err_v
      cubes     = (int_cub) + (cube_s) spatial + (1) err_c
      lozenges  = (int_loz) + (lozn_s) spatial + (1) err_l

      paragraph = (int_par) +        (1) verbal  + (1) err_p
      sentence  = (int_sen) + (sent_v) verbal  + (1) err_s
      wordmean  = (int_wrd) + (word_v) verbal  + (1) err_w
$Mstructure
      spatial (0)
      verbal  (0)

$Include = grnt_mal.amd

$Model = Model_A    ! Sex difference in factor means.
$Model = Model_B    ! Equal factor means.
      mn_s = 0
      mn_v = 0
```

With **Amos Graphics** input, the only adjustment that is required from the previous model is to set the means of **spatial** and **verbal** to 0 in the girls' model. This can be accomplished using the **Parameter constraints** command (as shown in the file **ex15-b.amw**). Alternatively, the two models can be estimated simultaneously by placing the last four lines from the above listing (*i.e.*, the **$Model** commands) in a **$** command section. The file **ex15-all.amw** contains this two-model setup.

Results for Model B

Had we not previously considered Model A, then we would now probably accept Model B at some conventional significance level:

```
Chi-square =      30.624
Degrees of freedom =   26
Probability level =     0.243
```

However, a stronger test of Model B is the comparison against Model A. The chi-square difference and its associated *p*-value is shown near the end of the list output in the two-model setup:

```
Model Comparisons
- - - - - - - - - - - - - - - -

Assuming Model_A to be correct:

                        df     chi-2     p
                        --     -----    -----
             Model_B    2      8.030    0.018
```

The test statistic for Model B, given Model A, is 8.030 with two degrees of freedom. The associated tail probability is only 0.018, indicating some evidence against Model B.

Example 16: Sörbom's alternative to analysis of covariance

Purpose

This example demonstrates latent structural equation modeling with longitudinal observations in two or more groups. The models used generalize traditional analysis of covariance techniques by incorporating latent variable terms and autocorrelated residuals (*cf.*, Sörbom, 1978). It is shown how specific assumptions employed by traditional analysis of covariance can be tested with this more general approach.

Introduction

Example 9 demonstrated an alternative to conventional analysis of covariance that works even with unreliable covariates. Unfortunately, analysis of covariance also depends on other assumptions besides the assumption of perfectly reliable covariates, and the method of Example 9 depends on those too. Sörbom (1978) developed a more general approach that allows testing and relaxing many of those assumptions.

The present example uses the same data that Sörbom used to introduce his method, and the modeling strategy in this example follows his exposition.

The data

The Olsson (1973) study introduced in Example 9 will be used again for the present example. The sample means, variances and covariances from the 108 experimental subjects, as contained in the file **olss_exp.amd**, are:

```
! Olsson's (1973)two-wave, pre- and post-test
! coaching study data. Two measures of verbal
! reasoning are each assessed at the two
! occasions.
!
! The following data are from the 108 participants
! of the experimental condition which received
! test coaching (treatment) between pre- and
! post-test assessments.

$Group name = experimental

$Input variables
      pre_syn    ! Pre-test:  synonyms score
      pre_opp    ! Pre-test:  opposites score
      post_syn   ! Post-test: synonyms score
      post_opp   ! Post-test: opposites score

$Sample size = 108
$Unbiased         ! (N-1) used as denominator for
                  ! sample variances and covariances
$Covariances
(4F7.3)
 50.084
 42.373 49.872
 40.760 36.094 51.237
 37.343 40.396 39.890 53.641
$Means
(4F7.3)
 20.556 21.241 25.667 25.870
```

The sample means, variances and covariances from the 105 control subjects are given in the file **olss_cnt.amd**, displayed below:

```
! Olsson's (1973)two-wave, pre- and post-test
! coaching study data. Two measures of verbal
! reasoning are each assessed at the two
! occasions.
!
! The following data are from the 105 participants
! of the control condition which did NOT receive
! any coaching (treatment) between pre- and
! post-test assessments.

$Group name = control

$Input variables
      pre_syn    ! Pre-test:  synonyms score
      pre_opp    ! Pre-test:  opposites score
      post_syn   ! Post-test: synonyms score
      post_opp   ! Post-test: opposites score

$Sample size = 105
$Unbiased         ! (N-1) used as denominator for
                  ! sample variances and covariances
$Covariances
(4F7.3)
 37.626
 24.933 34.680
 26.639 24.236 32.013
 23.649 27.760 23.565 33.443
$Means
(4F7.3)
 18.381 20.229 20.400 21.343
```

Note: Both data files contain the **$Unbiased** command, indicating that the sample variances and covariances are the unbiased—rather than the (default) maximum likelihood—estimates of the population variances and covariances. The computational difference is that the unbiased estimator uses a denominator of $(N - 1)$, while the maximum likelihood estimator uses N, the sample size of each group. At the sample size of the current example, the two estimators yield values that are identical within three significant digits.

Model A

Modeling in Amos Graphics

Consider Sörbom's initial model (Model A) for the Olsson data. The control group specification is:

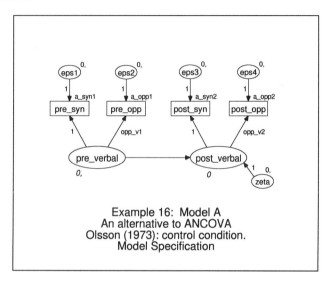

Example 16: Model A
An alternative to ANCOVA
Olsson (1973): control condition.
Model Specification

And for the experimental group, Model A looks like this:

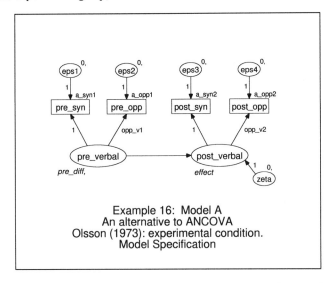

Example 16: Model A
An alternative to ANCOVA
Olsson (1973): experimental condition.
Model Specification

In each group, Model A specifies that **pre_syn** and **pre_opp** are indicators of a single latent variable called **pre_verbal**, and that **post_syn** and **post_opp** are indicators of another latent variable called **post_verbal**. The latent variable **pre_verbal** is interpreted as verbal ability at the beginning of the study, and **post_verbal** is interpreted as verbal ability at the conclusion of the study. This is Sörbom's *measurement* model.

The *structural* model specifies that **post_verbal** depends linearly on **pre_verbal**, although the slope and intercept of this regression is allowed to be different in the two groups.

The labels opp_v1 and opp_v2 for the regression weights and a_syn1, a_opp1, a_syn2 and a_opp2 for the intercepts of the measurement model set these parameters to the same values in the two groups. This is an assumption that could turn out to be wrong. In fact, one result of the upcoming analyses will be a test of this assumption. As Sörbom points out, some assumptions have to be made about the parameters of the measurement model in order to allow the groups to be compared with respect to the parameters of the structural model. The assumption that the measurement model has the same regression weights in both groups is plausible, and Sörbom showed that it is sufficient.

For the *control* subjects, the mean of **pre_verbal** and the intercept of **post_verbal** are fixed at zero (0). This establishes the control group as a reference condition for the group comparison—it is necessary to pick one such reference in order to make the factor mean structure(s) identifiable. For the *experimental* subjects, the mean and intercept parameters of the latent factors are allowed to be nonzero. The term *pre_diff* represents the difference in verbal ability prior to treatment (coaching), and the term *effect* represents the improvement of the experimental group relative to the control group.

The **Amos Graphics** file for this example is **ex16-a.amw**.

Note: Sörbom's model imposes no between-group constraints on the variance terms of the six latent exogenous variables. Thus, the four observed variables may show different unique variance components in the control and experimental conditions. The common variance components, given by the variance estimates of **pre_verbal** and **zeta**, may also be different. These assumptions will be investigated more closely in Models X, Y and Z, below.

Modeling in Amos Text

The **Amos Text** file for Model A is `ex16-a.ami`:

```
Example 16, Model A:
Sorbom's Alternative to Analysis of Covariance,
using a group-invariant measurement model.

$Mods=4
$Standardized
$Smc

$Group name = control
$Structure
      pre_syn  = (a_syn1) + (1)       pre_verbal  + (1) eps1
      pre_opp  = (a_opp1) + (opp_v1) pre_verbal  + (1) eps2
      post_syn = (a_syn2) + (1)       post_verbal + (1) eps3
      post_opp = (a_opp2) + (opp_v2) post_verbal + (1) eps4

      post_verbal = (0) + () pre_verbal + (1) zeta

$Include = olss_cnt.amd

$Next group

$Group name = experimental
$Structure
      pre_syn  = (a_syn1) + (1)       pre_verbal  + (1) eps1
      pre_opp  = (a_opp1) + (opp_v1) pre_verbal  + (1) eps2
      post_syn = (a_syn2) + (1)       post_verbal + (1) eps3
      post_opp = (a_opp2) + (opp_v2) post_verbal + (1) eps4

      post_verbal = (effect) + () pre_verbal + (1) zeta
$Mstructure
      pre_verbal (pre_diff)

$Include = olss_exp.amd
```

Results for Model A

Unfortunately, Model A cannot be accepted at any conventional significance level:

```
Chi-square =      34.775
Degrees of freedom =     6
Probability level =      0.000
```

The following message provides further evidence that Model A is wrong:

```
The following variances are negative

         zeta
       --------
         -2.868
This solution is not admissible.
```

The evidence against Model A, both from the chi-square statistic and from the fact that the solution is inadmissible, is convincing. We should see whether there is some modification to Model A that will allow it to fit the data while still permitting a meaningful comparison of the experimental and control groups. If you add the command $Mods=4 to the input file shown above, you will get a listing of modification indices that exceed 4. There will be a separate listing for the control group and for the experimental group. In the control group, no modification index exceeds 4, so the display for that group will be empty. Here is the modification index output from the experimental group:

```
Modification Indices
--------------------


Covariances:                              M.I.    Par Change
                                        --------- ----------
        eps2 <----------------> eps4    10.508      4.700
        eps2 <----------------> eps3     8.980     -4.021
        eps1 <----------------> eps4     8.339     -3.908
        eps1 <----------------> eps3     7.058      3.310


Variances:                                M.I.    Par Change
                                        --------- ----------


Regression Weights:                       M.I.    Par Change
                                        --------- ----------


Means:                                    M.I.    Par Change
                                        --------- ----------


Intercepts:                               M.I.    Par Change
                                        --------- ----------
```

Model B

The largest modification index obtained with Model A is for the covariance between **eps2** and **eps4** in the experimental group, indicating that the chi-square statistic will drop by at least 10.508 if **eps2** and **eps4** are allowed to have a nonzero covariance. The parameter change statistic of 4.700 indicates that the covariance estimate will be positive if set free. The term **eps2** represents unique variation of **pre_opp**, and **eps4** represents unique variation of **post_opp**, where the observed variables **pre_opp** and **post_opp** are obtained by administering the same test, *opposites*, on two different occasions. It is therefore reasonable to assume some positive correlation between **eps2** and **eps4**, on statistical as well as applied grounds.

Modeling in Amos Graphics

The next step is to consider the revised Model B, with unique terms **eps2** and **eps4** correlated in the experimental group. This can be done in **Amos Graphics** by adding a two-headed arrow between **eps2** and **eps4**, and estimating the covariance of these two terms in the experimental group but constraining it to zero in the control group. Be sure to leave the **All groups** check box of the **Parameter value** dialog empty, so that the constraint applies only to the control group:

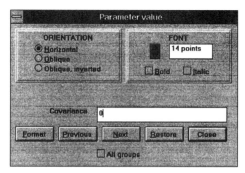

Model B for the *control* subjects is:

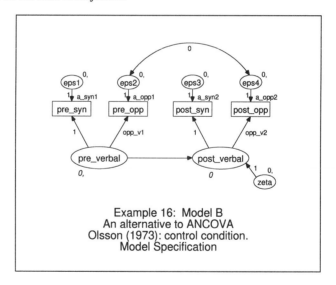

Example 16: Model B
An alternative to ANCOVA
Olsson (1973): control condition.
Model Specification

And for the *experimental* subjects:

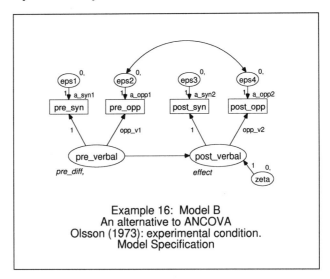

Example 16: Model B
An alternative to ANCOVA
Olsson (1973): experimental condition.
Model Specification

The **Amos Graphics** input file for this example is **ex16-b.amw**.

Modeling in Amos Text

To specify Model B in **Amos Text**, just add the line

```
eps2 <---> eps4
```

to the **$Structure** command for the experimental group. The full specification of Model B, from file **ex16-b.ami,** is:

```
Example 16, Model B:
Sorbom's Alternative to Analysis of Covariance,
correlated residuals in experimental group.

$Mods=4
$Standardized
$Smc

$Group name = control
$Structure
    pre_syn  = (a_syn1) + (1)       pre_verbal  + (1) eps1
    pre_opp  = (a_opp1) + (opp_v1) pre_verbal  + (1) eps2
    post_syn = (a_syn2) + (1)       post_verbal + (1) eps3
    post_opp = (a_opp2) + (opp_v2) post_verbal + (1) eps4

    post_verbal = (0) + () pre_verbal + (1) zeta

$Include = olss_cnt.amd

$Next group

$Group name = experimental
$Structure
    pre_syn  = (a_syn1) + (1)       pre_verbal  + (1) eps1
    pre_opp  = (a_opp1) + (opp_v1) pre_verbal  + (1) eps2
    post_syn = (a_syn2) + (1)       post_verbal + (1) eps3
    post_opp = (a_opp2) + (opp_v2) post_verbal + (1) eps4

    post_verbal = (effect) + () pre_verbal + (1) zeta

    eps2 <---> eps4
$Mstructure
    pre_verbal (pre_diff)

$Include = olss_exp.amd
```

Results for Model B

In moving from Model A to Model B, the chi-square statistic dropped by 17.712 (more than the promised 10.508) while the number of degrees of freedom dropped by just one:

```
Chi-square =      17.063
Degrees of freedom =    5
Probability level =     0.004
```

Model B is certainly an improvement over Model A, but still does not fit the data well. Furthermore, the variance of **zeta** in the *control* group has a negative estimate (not shown here), just as it had for Model A. These two facts argue strongly against Model B. There is room for improvement, however, because the modification indices (produced by $Mods=4) suggest further modifications of Model B. The listed modification indices for the control group are:

```
Modification Indices
. . . . . . . . . . . . . . . . . . .


Covariances:                                        M.I.    Par Change
                                                  ---------  ----------
          eps2 <----------------> eps4            4.727       2.141
          eps1 <----------------> eps4            4.086      -2.384
```

The remaining modification indices, including those for the experimental group, are all
less than four. The largest modification index (of 4.727) is for the covariance term
between **eps2** and **eps4** in the control group, suggesting that the unique terms for the
opposites test should be correlated not only in the experimental group, but in the control
group as well.

Model C

Model C is just like Model B, except that the terms **eps2** and **eps4** are correlated in both
control and experimental groups.

Modeling in Amos Graphics

To specify Model C, simply relax the covariance parameter between **eps2** and **eps4** in
the control group of Model B. Here is the view of the new control group structure, as
found in file **ex16-c.amw**:

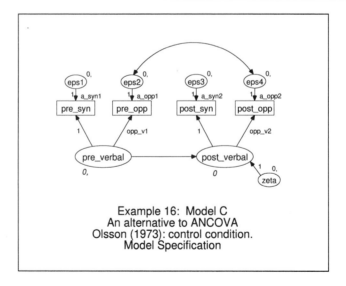

Example 16: Model C
An alternative to ANCOVA
Olsson (1973): control condition.
Model Specification

Modeling in Amos Text

The **Amos Text** input, from file **ex16-c.ami**, for Model C is:

```
Example 16, Model C:
Sorbom's Alternative to Analysis of Covariance,
correlated residuals in experimental and
control groups.

$Mods=4
$Standardized
$Smc

$Group name = control
$Structure
      pre_syn  = (a_syn1) + (1)       pre_verbal  + (1) eps1
      pre_opp  = (a_opp1) + (opp_v1)  pre_verbal  + (1) eps2
      post_syn = (a_syn2) + (1)       post_verbal + (1) eps3
      post_opp = (a_opp2) + (opp_v2)  post_verbal + (1) eps4

      post_verbal = (0) + () pre_verbal + (1) zeta

      eps2 <···> eps4

$Include = olss_cnt.amd

$Next group

$Group name = experimental
$Structure
      pre_syn  = (a_syn1) + (1)       pre_verbal  + (1) eps1
      pre_opp  = (a_opp1) + (opp_v1)  pre_verbal  + (1) eps2
      post_syn = (a_syn2) + (1)       post_verbal + (1) eps3
      post_opp = (a_opp2) + (opp_v2)  post_verbal + (1) eps4

      post_verbal = (effect) + () pre_verbal + (1) zeta

      eps2 <···> eps4
$Mstructure
      pre_verbal (pre_diff)

$Include = olss_exp.amd
```

Results for Model C

Finally, a model that fits:

```
Chi-square =      2.797
Degrees of freedom =    4
Probability level =     0.592
```

From the point of view of statistical goodness of fit, there is no reason to reject Model C.

Perhaps even more importantly, all the variance estimates are positive. Here are the parameter estimates for the 105 control subjects:

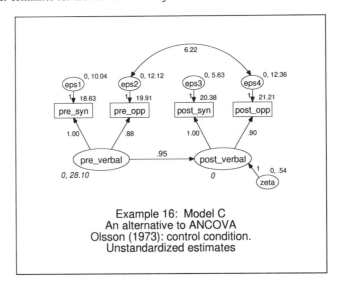

Example 16: Model C
An alternative to ANCOVA
Olsson (1973): control condition.
Unstandardized estimates

And here is a path diagram displaying the parameter estimates for the 108 experimental subjects:

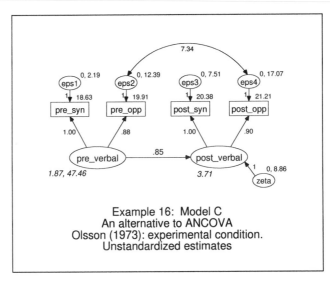

Example 16: Model C
An alternative to ANCOVA
Olsson (1973): experimental condition.
Unstandardized estimates

Most of these parameter estimates are of only incidental interest, although they should be inspected for whether they have *reasonable* values. We have already noted that the variance estimates are all positive. The path coefficients in the measurement model are likewise positive, which is reassuring—mixed positive and negative regression weights in the measurement model would have been difficult to interpret and would cast doubt on the model. The covariance between **eps2** and **eps4** is positive in both groups, as expected.

The primary concern of this analysis lies with the regression of **post_verbal** on **pre_verbal**. The intercept, fixed at zero in the control group, is estimated to be 3.71 in the experimental group. The regression weight is estimated at 0.95 in the control group and 0.85 in the experimental group. The regression weights for the two groups are close and might, in fact, be identical in the two populations. Because identical regression weights would allow a greatly simplified evaluation of the treatment, limiting the comparison of the two groups to a comparison of their intercepts, it is worthwhile to try such a model.

Model D

Model D specifies equal regression weights in the structural model. That is, Model D is just like Model C except that it specifies that the regression weight for predicting **post_verbal** from **pre_verbal** is the same for both groups.

Modeling in Amos Graphics

For the path diagram, we introduce one more parameter constrained to be equal in both groups: a common parameter for the path from **pre_verbal** to **post_verbal**, which will be named pre2post. The path diagram for the experimental subjects follows below. The diagram for the control subjects differs only in that the mean for **pre_verbal** and the intercept for **post_verbal** are both fixed at zero. The **Amos Graphics** input file is ex16-d.amw.

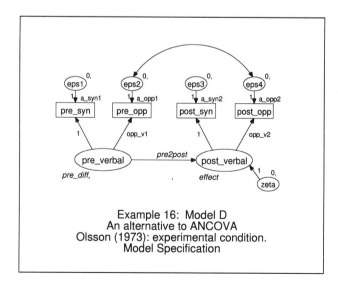

Example 16: Model D
An alternative to ANCOVA
Olsson (1973): experimental condition.
Model Specification

Modeling in Amos Text

The **Amos Text** input file `ex16-d.ami` implements Model B:

```
Example 16, Model D:
Sorbom's Alternative to Analysis of Covariance,
correlated residuals in experimental and
control groups, homogeneous regression
slopes.

$Mods=4
$Standardized
$Smc

$Group name = control
$Structure
     pre_syn  = (a_syn1) + (1)       pre_verbal  + (1) eps1
     pre_opp  = (a_opp1) + (opp_v1)  pre_verbal  + (1) eps2
     post_syn = (a_syn2) + (1)       post_verbal + (1) eps3
     post_opp = (a_opp2) + (opp_v2)  post_verbal + (1) eps4

     post_verbal = (0) + (pre2post) pre_verbal + (1) zeta

     eps2 <---> eps4

$Include = olss_cnt.amd

$Next group

$Group name = experimental
$Structure
     pre_syn  = (a_syn1) + (1)       pre_verbal  + (1) eps1
     pre_opp  = (a_opp1) + (opp_v1)  pre_verbal  + (1) eps2
     post_syn = (a_syn2) + (1)       post_verbal + (1) eps3
     post_opp = (a_opp2) + (opp_v2)  post_verbal + (1) eps4

     post_verbal = (effect) + (pre2post) pre_verbal + (1)
zeta

     eps2 <---> eps4
$Mstructure
     pre_verbal (pre_diff)

$Include = olss_exp.amd
```

The label `pre2post`, in parentheses, constrains the regression weights between the two latent variables to be equal in the two groups.

Results for Model D

Model D would be accepted at conventional significance levels:

```
Chi-square =       3.976
Degrees of freedom =     5
Probability level =      0.553
```

Testing Model D against Model C gives a chi-square value of $1.179 \, (= 3.976 - 2.797)$ with $1 \, (= 5 - 4)$ degree of freedom. Again, you would accept the hypothesis of equal regression weights.

With equal regression weights, the comparison of treated and untreated subjects can now focus on the difference between their intercepts. Here are the parameter estimates for the 105 control subjects:

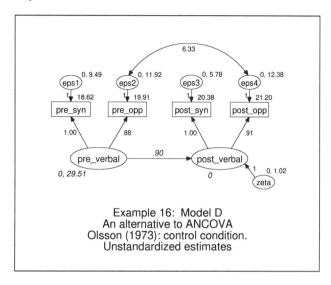

Example 16: Model D
An alternative to ANCOVA
Olsson (1973): control condition.
Unstandardized estimates

The estimates for the 108 experimental subjects are:

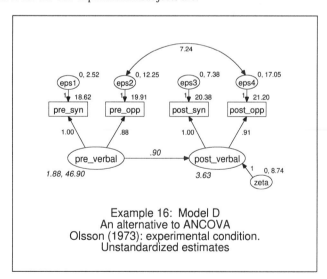

Example 16: Model D
An alternative to ANCOVA
Olsson (1973): experimental condition.
Unstandardized estimates

The parameter estimates look reasonable, so we will proceed to a discussion of the intercepts. The intercept (additive constant) for the experimental group is estimated as 3.627, with an associated critical ratio of 7.591. Thus, the intercept for the experimental group is significantly different from the intercept for the control group, which happens to be fixed at zero.

Model E

Another way of testing the difference in **post_verbal** intercepts is to repeat the Model D analysis with equality constraints added. Since the intercept for the control group is already fixed at zero, we need to add the requirement that the intercept be equal to zero in the experimental group as well. This restriction is used in Model E. The **Amos Text** input file, named **ex16-e.ami**, is:

```
Example 16, Model E:
Sorbom's Alternative to Analysis of Covariance,
correlated residuals in experimental and
control groups, homogeneous regression
slopes, but no treatment effect.

$Mods=4
$Standardized
$Smc

$Group name = control
$Structure
      pre_syn  = (a_syn1) + (1)       pre_verbal  + (1) eps1
      pre_opp  = (a_opp1) + (opp_v1) pre_verbal  + (1) eps2
      post_syn = (a_syn2) + (1)       post_verbal + (1) eps3
      post_opp = (a_opp2) + (opp_v2) post_verbal + (1) eps4

      post_verbal = (0) + (pre2post) pre_verbal + (1) zeta

      eps2 <---> eps4

$Include = olss_cnt.amd

$Next group

$Group name = experimental
$Structure
      pre_syn  = (a_syn1) + (1)       pre_verbal  + (1) eps1
      pre_opp  = (a_opp1) + (opp_v1) pre_verbal  + (1) eps2
      post_syn = (a_syn2) + (1)       post_verbal + (1) eps3
      post_opp = (a_opp2) + (opp_v2) post_verbal + (1) eps4

      post_verbal = (0) + (pre2post) pre_verbal + (1) zeta

      eps2 <---> eps4
$Mstructure
      pre_verbal (pre_diff)

$Include = olss_exp.amd
```

The **Amos Graphics** specification of Model E is just like that of Model D, except that the intercept in the regression of **post_verbal** on **pre_verbal** is fixed at 0 in *both* groups. The **Amos Graphics** input file is **ex16-e.amw** (not reproduced here).

Results for Model E

Model E has to be rejected:

```
Chi-square =     55.094
Degrees of freedom =    6
Probability level =    0.000
```

Comparing Model E against Model D yields a chi-square value of 51.018 (= 55.094 – 3.976) with 1 (= 6 – 5) degree of freedom. Model E has to be rejected in favor of Model

D. Because the fit of Model E is significantly worse than that of Model D, the hypothesis of equal intercepts again has to be rejected.

> *Translation*: The control and experimental groups differ at the time of the posttest in a way that cannot be accounted for by differences that existed at the time of the pretest. The experimenter thus attributes the difference at the time of the posttest to the intervening test coaching treatment.

Multiple model input

The previous five examples can be entered into a single file, using suitably modified parameter labels. The **Amos Text** multiple-model specification, from the file `ex16_a2e.ami`, is:

```
Example 16, Models A through E:
Sorbom's Alternative to Analysis of Covariance.

$Mods=4
$Standardized
$Smc

$Group name = control
$Structure
      pre_syn  = (a_syn1) + (1)       pre_verbal  + (1) eps1
      pre_opp  = (a_opp1) + (opp_v1) pre_verbal  + (1) eps2
      post_syn = (a_syn2) + (1)       post_verbal + (1) eps3
      post_opp = (a_opp2) + (opp_v2) post_verbal + (1) eps4

      post_verbal = (0) + (c_beta) pre_verbal + (1) zeta

      eps2 <---> eps4  (c_e2e4)

$Include = olss_cnt.amd

$Next group

$Group name = experimental
$Structure
      pre_syn  = (a_syn1) + (1)       pre_verbal  + (1) eps1
      pre_opp  = (a_opp1) + (opp_v1) pre_verbal  + (1) eps2
      post_syn = (a_syn2) + (1)       post_verbal + (1) eps3
      post_opp = (a_opp2) + (opp_v2) post_verbal + (1) eps4

      post_verbal = (effect) + (e_beta) pre_verbal + (1) zeta

      eps2 <---> eps4  (e_e2e4)
$Mstructure
      pre_verbal (pre_diff)

$Include = olss_exp.amd

$Model = Model_A
      c_e2e4 = 0
      e_e2e4 = 0
$Model = Model_B
      c_e2e4 = 0
$Model = Model_C
$Model = Model_D
      c_beta = e_beta
$Model = Model_E
      c_beta = e_beta
      effect = 0
```

The corresponding multiple-model specification for **Amos Graphics** is given in the file `ex16-a2e.amw` (not shown here).

This completes Sörbom's (1978) analysis of the Olsson data.

Comparison of Sörbom's method with the method of Example 9

Sörbom's alternative to analysis of covariance is more difficult to apply than the method of Example 9. If you are trying to choose between the two methods, you should realize that Sörbom's method is not just different from the method of Example 9, but superior in the sense of being more general. That is, you can duplicate the method of Example 9 by using Sörbom's method with suitable parameter constraints.

The remainder of this example presents three additional models called X, Y and Ż. Comparisons among these new models will allow us to duplicate the results of Example 9. However, we will also find evidence that the method used in Example 9 was inappropriate. The purpose of this fairly complicated exercise is to call attention to the limitations of Example 9's alternative to an analysis of covariance, and to show that some of the assumptions of that method can be tested and relaxed in Sörbom's approach.

Model X

First, consider a new Model X, say, which requires that the variances and covariances of the observed variables are the same for the control and experimental conditions. The means of the observed variables may differ between the two populations. Model X does not specify any linear dependencies among the variables. The assumptions of Model X are rather basic, and the model may not appear interesting at all. However, the subsequent Models Y and Z *are* interesting, and we will want to know how well they fit the data, compared to Model X.

Modeling in Amos Text

The **Amos Text** specification of Model X, from file **ex16-x.ami**, is:

```
Example 16, Model X:
Group-invariant covariance structure.

$Mods=4
$Standardized
$Smc

$Group name = control
$Structure
        pre_syn (v_s1)
        pre_opp (v_o1)
        post_syn (v_s2)
        post_opp (v_o2)
        pre_opp <--> pre_syn (c_s1o1)
        post_opp <--> pre_opp (c_o1o2)
        post_syn <--> post_opp (c_s2o2)
        pre_syn <--> post_syn (c_s1s2)
        post_opp <--> pre_syn (c_s1o2)
        post_syn <--> pre_opp (c_s2o1)

$Include = olss_cnt.amd

$Next group

$Group name = experimental
$Structure
        pre_syn (v_s1)
        pre_opp (v_o1)
        post_syn (v_s2)
        post_opp (v_o2)
        pre_opp <--> pre_syn (c_s1o1)
        post_opp <--> pre_opp (c_o1o2)
        post_syn <--> post_opp (c_s2o2)
        pre_syn <--> post_syn (c_s1s2)
        post_opp <--> pre_syn (c_s1o2)
        post_syn <--> pre_opp (c_s2o1)

$Include = olss_exp.amd
```

The **$Mstructure** command is not used in this file, because Model X does not impose any assumptions on the population means. No intercepts are used either, since the model contains no regression equations. Model X simply requires estimating the population variances and covariances under the assumption that they are group-invariant, and Amos will compute fit statistics for this hypothesis. Thus, Amos does not need to estimate the means of the four observed variables.

Modeling in Amos Graphics

Because there are no intercepts or means to estimate, the **Means** button can be released. The **Amos Graphics** file for Model X is **ex16-x.amw**, with the group-invariant path diagram:

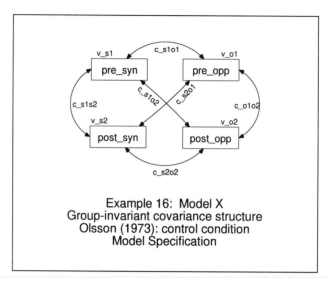

Example 16: Model X
Group-invariant covariance structure
Olsson (1973): control condition
Model Specification

Results for Model X

Model X has to be rejected at nearly any level of significance.

```
Chi-square =      29.145
Degrees of freedom =   10
Probability level =     0.001
```

The analyses that follow (Models Y and Z) are actually inappropriate now that we are satisfied that Model X is inappropriate. We will carry out the analyses as an exercise in order to demonstrate that they yield the same results as obtained in Example 9.

Model Y

Consider a model that is just like Model D above, but with the following additional constraints:

- Verbal ability at the pretest (**pre_verbal**) has the same variance in the control and experimental groups.

- The variances of **eps1**, **eps2**, **eps3**, **eps4** and **zeta** are the same for both groups.

- The covariance between **eps2** and **eps4** is the same for both groups.

Apart from the correlation between **eps2** and **eps4**, Model D required that **eps1**, **eps2**, **eps3**, **eps4** and **zeta** be uncorrelated among themselves and with every other exogenous variable, so these new requirements amount to requiring that the variances and covariances of *all exogenous* variables be the same for both groups. Altogether, then, the new model imposes two kinds of constraints:

Model D requirements: All regression weights and intercepts are the same for both groups, except possibly for the intercept used in predicting **post_verbal** from **pre_verbal**.

Additional Model Y requirements: The variances and covariances of the exogenous variables are the same for both groups.

As it turns out, these are the same assumptions that were made in Model B of Example 9. The difference is that, here, the assumptions are made explicit and can be tested. We skip the **Amos Graphics** input for Model Y which can be found in the file **ex16-y.amw**. The **Amos Text** input file (**ex16-y.ami**) for Model Y follows:

```
Example 16, Model Y:
Sorbom's Alternative to Analysis of Covariance,
homogeneous regression slopes, homogeneous
variances and covariances of all exogenous
variables, and group-invariant intercepts for
the observed variables (i.e., Model B of
Example 9 written as a two-group problem).

$Mods=4
$Standardized
$Smc

$Group name = control
$Structure
    pre_syn  = (a_syn1) + (1)        pre_verbal  + (1) eps1
    pre_opp  = (a_opp1) + (opp_v1) pre_verbal  + (1) eps2
    post_syn = (a_syn2) + (1)        post_verbal + (1) eps3
    post_opp = (a_opp2) + (opp_v2) post_verbal + (1) eps4

    post_verbal = (0) + (pre2post) pre_verbal + (1) zeta

    eps2 <---> eps4 (c_e2e4)
    pre_verbal (v_v1)
    zeta       (v_z)
    eps1       (v_e1)
    eps2       (v_e2)
    eps3       (v_e3)
    eps4       (v_e4)

$Include = olss_cnt.amd

$Next group

$Group name = experimental
$Structure
    pre_syn  = (a_syn1) + (1)        pre_verbal  + (1) eps1
    pre_opp  = (a_opp1) + (opp_v1) pre_verbal  + (1) eps2
    post_syn = (a_syn2) + (1)        post_verbal + (1) eps3
    post_opp = (a_opp2) + (opp_v2) post_verbal + (1) eps4

    post_verbal = (effect) + (pre2post) pre_verbal + (1) zeta

    eps2 <---> eps4 (c_e2e4)
    pre_verbal (v_v1)
    zeta       (v_z)
    eps1       (v_e1)
    eps2       (v_e2)
    eps3       (v_e3)
    eps4       (v_e4)
$Mstructure
    pre_verbal (pre_diff)

$Include = olss_exp.amd
```

Results for Model Y

Model Y has to be rejected:

```
Chi-square =      31.816
Degrees of freedom =   12
Probability level =     0.001
```

This is a good reason for being dissatisfied with the analysis of Example 9, since it depended upon Model Y (which, in Example 9, was called Model B) being correct. If you look back at Example 9, you will see that we accepted Model B there ($\chi^2 = 2.684$, $df = 2$, $p = .261$). So how can we say that the same model has to be rejected here ($\chi^2 = 31.816$, $df = 1$, $p = .001$)? The answer is that, while the null hypothesis is the same in both cases (Model B in Example 9 and Model Y in the present example), the alternative hypotheses are different. In Example 9, the alternative against which Model B is tested includes the assumption that the variances and covariances of the observed variables are the same for both values of the **treatment** variable (also stated in the Technical Note near the end of Example 1). In other words, the test of Model B carried out in Example 9 implicitly assumed homogeneity of variances and covariances for the control and experimental populations. This is the very assumption that is made explicit in Model X of the present example.

Model Y is a restricted version of Model X. It can be shown that the assumptions of Model Y (equal regression weights for the two populations, and equal variances and covariances of the exogenous variables) imply the assumptions of Model X (equal covariances for the observed variables). Models X and Y are therefore *nested* models, and it is possible to carry out a *conditional* test of Model Y given that Model X is true. Of course, it will only make sense to do that test if Model X really were true, and we have already concluded it is not. Nevertheless, let's continue the exercise by testing Model Y against Model X. The difference in chi-square values is 2.671 (*i.e.*, 31.816 − 29.145) with 2 (= 12 − 10) degrees of freedom. These figures are identical (within rounding error) to those of Example 9, Model B. The difference is that, in Example 9 we assumed that the test was appropriate. Now we are quite sure (because we rejected Model X) that it is not.

If you have any doubts that the current Model Y is the same as Model B of Example 9, you should compare the parameter estimates from the two analyses. Here are the Model Y parameter estimates for the 108 experimental subjects. See if you can match up these estimates displayed here with the unstandardized (or *raw*) parameter estimates obtained by Model B of Example 9.

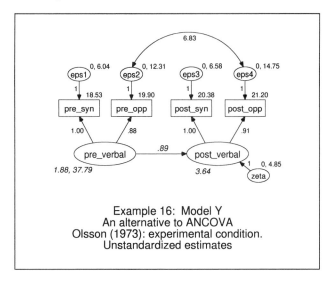

Example 16: Model Y
An alternative to ANCOVA
Olsson (1973): experimental condition.
Unstandardized estimates

Model Z

Finally, construct a new model (Model Z) by adding to Model Y the requirement that the intercept in the equation for predicting **post_verbal** from **pre_verbal** be the same in both populations. This model is equivalent to Model C of Example 9. The **Amos Graphics** model specification for the experimental condition, from file **ex16-z.amw**, follows below (the **Amos Text** input file, **ex16-z.ami**, is not shown):

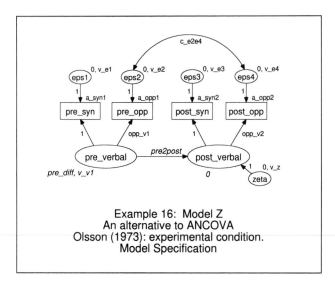

Example 16: Model Z
An alternative to ANCOVA
Olsson (1973): experimental condition.
Model Specification

Results for Model Z

This model has to be rejected.

```
Chi-square =      84.280
Degrees of freedom =   13
Probability level =     0.000
```

Model Z also has to be rejected when compared to Model Y (χ^2-*difference* = 84.280 − 31.816 = 52.464, *df* = 13 -12 = 1). Within rounding error, this is the same difference in chi-square values and degrees of freedom as in Example 9, when Model C was compared to Model B.

Example 17: Missing data

Purpose

This example demonstrates the use of full information factor analysis when there are missing data.

Introduction

It often happens that anticipated data values fail to materialize. Perhaps a subject fails to participate in part of a study. Or maybe a person filling out a questionnaire skips a couple of questions. A study may find that some people have not told you their age, some have not reported their income, others did not show up on the day you measured reaction times, and so on. For one reason or another, the dataset may have gaps.

One standard method for dealing with incomplete data is to eliminate from the analysis any observation for which some data value is missing. This is often called *listwise* deletion. That is, for example, if a person fails to report his income, you would eliminate that person from your study and proceed with a conventional analysis based on complete data, but with a reduced sample size. This method is unsatisfactory as it requires discarding the information contained in the responses that the person did give. If missing values are common, this method may require discarding the bulk of a sample.

Another standard approach, called *pairwise* deletion, is to calculate each sample moment separately, excluding an observation from the calculation only when it is missing a value that is needed for the computation of that particular moment. For example, in calculating the sample mean income you would exclude all people whose incomes you do not know. Similarly, in computing the sample covariance between age and income you would exclude all observations where income is missing, plus all records without age information.

A third approach is data *imputation*, replacing the missing values with some kind of guess, and then proceeding with a conventional analysis appropriate for complete data. For example, you might compute the mean income of the persons who reported their income, and then attribute that income to all persons who did not report their income. Beale and Little (1975) discuss methods for data imputation, which are implemented in many statistical packages.

Amos does not use any of these methods. Even in the presence of missing data, it computes full information maximum likelihood estimates (Anderson, 1957). For this reason, whenever you have missing data, you may prefer to use Amos to do a conventional analysis, such as a simple regression analysis (as in Example 4) or to estimate means only (as in Example 13).

It should be mentioned that there is one kind of missing data that Amos cannot deal with. (Neither can any other general approach to missing data, such as the three mentioned above.) Sometimes the very fact that a value is missing conveys information. It could be, for example, that people with very high incomes tend (more than others) not to answer questions about income. Failure to respond may thus convey probabilistic information about a person's income level, beyond all the information already given in the observed data. In such a case, Amos's approach to missing data is not applicable.

Amos assumes that data values that are missing are *missing at random*. It is not always easy to know whether this assumption is valid or what it means in practice (Rubin, 1976). On the other hand, if the *missing at random* condition is satisfied, Amos provides estimates that are efficient and consistent. By contrast, the selection methods mentioned previously do not provide efficient estimates, and provide consistent estimates only under the stronger condition that the data are *missing completely at random* (Little and Rubin, 1989).

The data

For this example we have modified the Holzinger and Swineford (1939) data used in Example 8. The original data set (in the file **grnt_fem.amd**) contains the scores of 73 girls on six tests, for a total of 438 data values. Each one of the 438 data values was marked as missing with probability 0.30. The result is contained in the file **grant_x.amd**, where a data value of - 1 indicates missing data:

```
! Holzinger and Swineford (1939) Grant-White sample.
! Intelligence factor study. Raw data of 73 female
! students from the Grant-White high school, Chicago.
!
! This version simulates missing data.
! Each of the 438 data values was replaced, with
! probability 0.30, by the missing data code '-1'.
! The sample proportion of 'missing' values is 0.27.

$Input variables
    visperc      ! Visual perception score
    cubes        ! Test of spatial visualization
    lozenges     ! Test of spatial orientation
    paragraph    ! Paragraph comprehension score
    sentence     ! Sentence completion score
    wordmean     ! Word meaning test score

$Sample size =   73
$Missing = -1
$Raw data
    33.  -1.  17.   8.  17.  10.
    30.  -1.  20.  -1.  -1.  18.
    -1.  33.  36.  -1.  25.  41.
                  ...              (67 similar lines omitted here).
    35.  -1.  10.   9.  13.  11.
    18.  24.  13.  -1.  16.   7.
    28.  22.  15.  -1.  23.  30.
```

The command **$Missing = –1** in the data file instructs Amos that the value ‑1 is a special code for missing data, and that it does not refer to a test score of ‑1.

Approximately 27% of the data in **grant_x.amd** are missing. Complete data are available for only seven cases. This is an example of how, under listwise deletion of missing values, the remaining sample size can become too small to estimate even simple multivariate models. With the full information approach, however, Amos can use all observed data values to estimate models with many parameters, including saturated models.

Model A

Before attempting to fit a nontrivial model to the data in **grant_x.amd**, it can be useful to first obtain estimates of means, variances and covariances of the six tests. Model A simply specifies these first and second moments.

Modeling in Amos Graphics

For six observed variables, Model A requires that a total of $6 \cdot (6 - 1) / 2 = 15$ covariance paths appear in the path diagram — one two-headed arrow for each pair of observed variables. The trick is to arrange all variable objects, covariance paths and parameter values, so that the diagram will be readable.

Amos Graphics provides a number of graphical design tools for producing a readable path diagram — especially helpful in this case are the **Move**, **Shape** and various **Align ...** buttons, plus the **Move parameters** command found in the Edit menu. Also, parameter values may be distinguished more easily from others if they are oriented parallel to their respective covariance paths; to do so, select the *Oblique* button in the **Parameter constraints** dialog box for that parameter.

The **Amos Graphics** input file, `ex17-a.amw`, arranges the six observed variable objects in a circle:

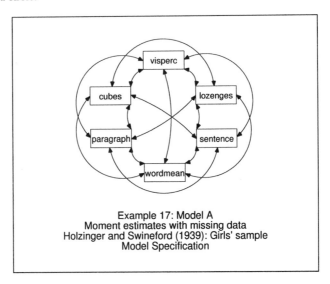

Example 17: Model A
Moment estimates with missing data
Holzinger and Swineford (1939): Girls' sample
Model Specification

A further, small step is required with the analysis of missing data: the **Means** button must be pressed when calculating the model estimates, even though you might not be interested in these estimates for the particular problem. If you forget to press the **Means** button, then the model estimation phase will quickly terminate with an error message.

> *Note*: In this problem, the data file, `grant_x.amd`, already identifies the missing data code via the command **$Missing = -1**. As an alternative, this **$Missing** command could also have been placed in the **$** command section for this problem.

Modeling in Amos Text

The following **Amos Text** input file will obtain the moment estimates:

```
Example 17, Model A:
Full-information estimates of means, variances,
and covariances in the presence of missing data.

Uses the grant_x.amd dataset, i.e., Holzinger and
Swineford (1939) psychological test data of 73
female students of the Grant-White high school,
with 27 percent of the values randomly missing.

$Standardized
$Smc
$All implied moments
$Sample moments

$Mstructure
      visperc ()
      cubes ()
      lozenges ()
      wordmean ()
      paragraph ()
      sentence ()

$Include = grant_x.amd
```

This is the same input file you would use with complete data. This input file does not specifically request estimates for variances and covariances, but that is not necessary. Whenever **Amos Text** estimates means, it also estimates variances and covariances.

> *Note*: When the calculations of the model estimates involve missing data, the **Amos Text** input file must also ask for *mean* estimates. The input of Model A implies such mean-level terms by using an **$Mstructure** command. In other models, when it may be advantageous to specify a model in equation format with a **$Structure** command, the equations should contain intercept terms. These are the **Amos Text** equivalents of having the **Means** button pressed in **Amos Graphics**. If the mean and/or intercept terms were omitted, Amos Text would terminate with an error message, before attempting to calculate any parameter estimates.

Results for Model A

Amos Text output

Here are the parameter estimates obtained for Model A (*i.e.*, with no constraints on the means, variances and covariances). The estimates, the standard errors and the critical ratios are interpreted in the same way as in an analysis of complete data.

Means:	Estimate	S.E.	C.R.	Label
visperc	28.883	0.910	31.756	
cubes	25.154	0.540	46.592	
lozenges	14.962	1.101	13.591	
wordmean	18.263	1.061	17.211	
paragraph	10.976	0.466	23.572	
sentence	18.802	0.632	29.730	

Covariances:	Estimate	S.E.	C.R.	Label
visperc <---------> cubes	17.484	4.614	3.789	
visperc <------> lozenges	31.173	9.232	3.377	
cubes <--------> lozenges	17.036	5.459	3.121	
visperc <------> wordmean	14.665	8.314	1.764	
cubes <--------> wordmean	3.470	4.870	0.713	
lozenges <-----> wordmean	29.655	10.574	2.804	
visperc <-----> paragraph	8.453	3.705	2.281	
cubes <-------> paragraph	2.739	2.179	1.257	
lozenges <----> paragraph	9.287	4.596	2.021	
wordmean <----> paragraph	23.616	5.010	4.714	
visperc <------> sentence	14.382	5.114	2.813	
cubes <--------> sentence	1.678	2.929	0.573	
lozenges <-----> sentence	10.544	6.050	1.743	
wordmean <-----> sentence	29.577	6.650	4.447	
paragraph <----> sentence	13.470	2.945	4.574	

Variances:	Estimate	S.E.	C.R.	Label
visperc	49.584	9.398	5.276	
cubes	16.484	3.228	5.106	
lozenges	67.901	13.404	5.066	
wordmean	73.974	13.221	5.595	
paragraph	13.570	2.515	5.396	
sentence	25.007	4.629	5.402	

And the **$All implied moments** command shown in the **Amos Text** input file displays these estimates (but not their standard errors) in tabular form:

```
Implied (for all variables) Covariances

          sentence paragrap wordmean lozenges cubes    visperc
          -------- -------- -------- -------- -------- --------
sentence   25.007
paragraph  13.470   13.570
wordmean   29.577   23.616   73.974
lozenges   10.544    9.287   29.655   67.901
cubes       1.678    2.739    3.470   17.036   16.484
visperc    14.382    8.453   14.665   31.173   17.484   49.584


Implied (for all variables) Means

          sentence paragrap wordmean lozenges cubes    visperc
          -------- -------- -------- -------- -------- --------
           18.802   10.976   18.263   14.962   25.154   28.883
```

These parameter estimates, even the estimated means, are different from those computed under either pairwise or listwise deletion methods. For example, in the case of the visual perception test, **visperc**, scores are available for 53 examinees. The sample mean of these 53 **visperc** scores is 28.245. One might reasonably expect the Amos estimate of the mean visual perception score to be 28.245 rather than 28.883. However, this is a case where intuition is incorrect.

In an analysis with incomplete data, Amos does not display a chi-square statistic for testing goodness of fit. Instead, it displays the following information:

```
Function of log likelihood =    1363.586
Number of parameters =   27
```

The Number of parameters is just the number of parameters that were estimated (in this case, there are 6 means, 6 variances and 15 covariances). The Function of log likelihood does not have a simple interpretation. In general, the better a model fits the data, the smaller this statistic will be, but there is no absolute standard for deciding when the statistic is small enough to accept the model. In any case, the present model (Model A) is a trivial one that places no constraints on the means, variances and covariances, so there is no hypothesis to be tested anyway.

We will see shortly, however, that it is possible to use this statistic in much the same way as a chi-square statistic in comparing two or more nested models. Thus, the current value of this statistic, 1363.586, will become useful later as a baseline to compare the nontrivial Model B (below) which *does* impose constraints on implied moments. The upcoming model will not fit the data as well as the present one (because of the constraints on the moments), and so the Function of log likelihood will be larger than 1363.586. We will be interested in seeing how much larger.

Amos Graphics output

Here is the path diagram displaying the correlations (*i.e.*, standardized parameter estimates) among the six observed variables:

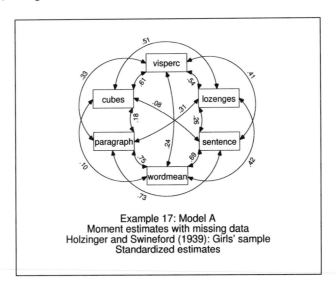

Example 17: Model A
Moment estimates with missing data
Holzinger and Swineford (1939): Girls' sample
Standardized estimates

Model B

We will now try to fit the common factor analysis model of Example 8 (shown below) to the Holzinger and Swineford data in file **grant_x.amd**. The difference from the analysis in Example 8 is that this time 27% of the data are missing.

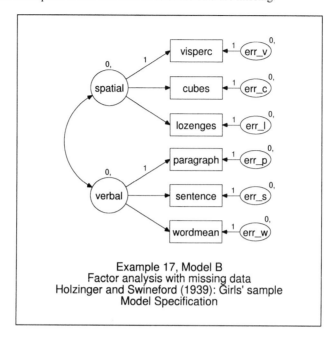

Example 17, Model B
Factor analysis with missing data
Holzinger and Swineford (1939): Girls' sample
Model Specification

Modeling in Amos Graphics

Since the path diagram is identical to the one used in Example 8, you can copy the file **ex08.amw,** and use it with two trivial adjustments. First, make sure that the **Means** button is pressed. Second, change the **$** command file for this analysis to include the new data file, **grant_x.amd**.

Modeling in Amos Text

Model B can be specified in **Amos Text** as shown in the file **ex17-b.ami**:

```
Example 17, Model B:
Full-information factor analysis in the presence
of missing data.

$Standardized
$Smc
$All implied moments
$Sample moments

$Structure
    visperc   = ( ) + (1)  spatial + (1) err_v
    cubes     = ( ) +       spatial + (1) err_c
    lozenges  = ( ) +       spatial + (1) err_l

    paragraph = ( ) + (1)  verbal  + (1) err_p
    sentence  = ( ) +       verbal  + (1) err_s
    wordmean  = ( ) +       verbal  + (1) err_w

$Include = grant_x.amd
```

This looks just like the **Amos Text** input file from Example 8, except that each of the six regression equations following the **$Structure** command contains a set of empty parentheses for the intercept term. When analyzing data with missing values you have to ask for an estimate of each additive constant except for those assumed to be zero. This is different from the analysis of complete data, where terms for the additive constants are not necessary unless the model specifies constraints among the intercepts.

> *Note*: As you know from the discussion of Model A above, you have to use the **$Mstructure** command to ask for an estimate of the mean of each exogenous variable (except for means assumed to be zero). In the present example, all of the exogenous variables are assumed to have means of zero in order to make the model identified. Thus, the **$Mstructure** command is not necessary here.

Results for Model B

Amos Text output

The parameter estimates, standard errors and critical ratios have the same interpretation as in an analysis of complete data:

```
Regression Weights:                        Estimate    S.E.      C.R.     Label
-------------------                        --------   -------   -------   -------

        visperc <-------- spatial           1.000
        cubes <---------- spatial           0.511     0.153     3.347
        lozenges <------- spatial           1.047     0.316     3.317
        paragraph <------ verbal            1.000
        sentence <------- verbal            1.259     0.194     6.505
        wordmean <------- verbal            2.140     0.326     6.572


Intercepts:                                Estimate    S.E.      C.R.     Label
-----------                                --------   -------   -------   -------

                        visperc            28.885     0.913    31.632
                          cubes            24.998     0.536    46.603
                       lozenges            15.153     1.133    13.372
                        wordmean           18.097     1.055    17.146
                       paragraph           10.987     0.468    23.495
                        sentence           18.864     0.636    29.646


Covariances:                               Estimate    S.E.      C.R.     Label
------------                               --------   -------   -------   -------

        spatial <--------> verbal           7.993     3.211     2.490


Variances:                                 Estimate    S.E.      C.R.     Label
----------                                 --------   -------   -------   -------

                        spatial            29.563    11.600     2.549
                         verbal            10.814     2.743     3.943
                          err_v            18.776     8.518     2.204
                          err_c             8.034     2.669     3.011
                          err_l            36.625    11.662     3.141
                          err_p             2.825     1.277     2.212
                          err_s             7.875     2.403     3.277
                          err_w            22.677     6.883     3.295
```

The fit of Model B to the data is summarized as follows:

```
Function of log likelihood =    1375.133
Number of parameters =   19
```

The Function of log likelihood is used to compare the fit among two or more nested models. Model B (with a fit statistic of 1375.133 and 19 parameters) is structurally nested within Model A (with a fit statistic of 1363.586 and 27 parameters). In a case like this, where a stronger model (B) is being compared to a weaker model (A), and where the stronger model is correct, you can say the following: The amount by which the Function of log likelihood increases when you switch from the weaker model to the stronger model is an observation on a *chi-square* random variable with degrees of freedom equal to the difference in the number of parameters of the two models. In the present example, Model B's Function of log likelihood exceeds that for Model A by 11.547 (= 1375.133 – 1363.586). At the same time, Model B requires estimating only 19 parameters while Model A requires estimating 27 parameters, for a difference of 8. In other words, if Model B is correct, 11.547 is an observation on a chi square variable with 8 degrees of freedom, which is not significant at the .05 level. That is, we accept (at the .05 level) the hypothesis that Model B is correct.

As the present example illustrates, in order to test a model with incomplete data, you have to compare its fit to that of another, alternative model. In this example, we wished to test Model B, and it was necessary also to fit Model A as a standard model of comparison. The alternative model has to meet two requirements. First, you have to be satisfied that it is correct. Model A certainly meets this criterion, since it places no constraints on the implied moments, and cannot be wrong. Second, it must be more general than the model you wish to test. Any model that can be obtained by removing some of the constraints on the parameters of the model under test will meet this second criterion. If you have trouble thinking up an alternative model, you can always use the saturated model that requires estimating all means, variances, and covariances without constraints.

Amos Graphics output

Here is the path diagram displaying the standardized estimates and the squared multiple correlations of the observed variables:

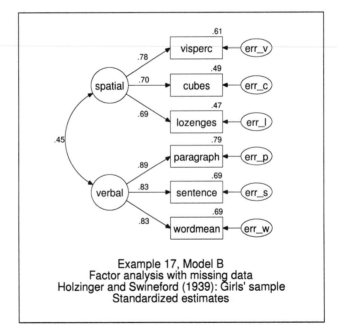

Example 17, Model B
Factor analysis with missing data
Holzinger and Swineford (1939): Girls' sample
Standardized estimates

These (standardized) parameter values can be compared to those obtained from the complete data in Example 8. Both sets of estimates are identical at the first decimal place. Considering the sizable percentage of missing data in **grant_x.amd**, and the small size (N = 73) this sample had to begin with, the match is about as close as can possibly be expected.

Example 18: More about missing data

Purpose

This example demonstrates the analysis of data in which some observations are missing *intentionally* by virtue of the measurement design. The purpose of including this additional demonstration is to call attention to study situations in which it may be advantageous to collect incomplete, instead of complete, data.

Introduction

Researchers do not ordinarily like missing data. One does not plan to have gaps in the data, and when they occur one does not ordinarily like that fact. Nevertheless, there are situations in which it can be desirable *not* to observe every variable on every occasion. Matthai (1951) and Lord (1955) describe designs in which certain data are intentionally missing. The basic principle employed in such designs is that, when it is impossible or too costly to obtain sufficient observations on a variable, estimates with improved accuracy can be obtained by taking additional observations on other, correlated, variables. Such designs can be highly useful, but, because of computational difficulties, they have not previously been employed except in very simple situations. This example describes only one of many possible designs in which some data are intentionally not collected. The method of analysis is the same as in Example 17.

The data

We have modified Attig's data (introduced in Example 1) by eliminating some of the data values and treating them as missing. The file **atty_mis.amd**, listed below, contains scores of Attig's 40 young subjects on the two vocabulary tests **vocabulary** and **vocab.short**:

```
! Subset of the Attig (1983) Space data.
! Vocabulary data of 40 young subjects.
!
! 30 subjects, picked at random, had their
! 'vocabulary' scores replaced with the
! missing data code '-1'.

$Input Variables
      vocab.short    ! Raw score on WAIS subset
      vocabulary     ! Raw score on WAIS
$Sample size = 40
$Missing = -1
$Raw data
    10      59
    12      66
     8      58
        ...    (4 similar lines omitted here)
     9      52
     8      60
     5      48
    13      -1
    12      -1
    14      -1
        ...    (24 similar lines omitted here)
    10      -1
     9      -1
    12      -1
```

The variable **vocabulary** is the raw score on the WAIS vocabulary test. **vocab.short** is the raw score on a small subset of the same test. In the file **atty_mis.amd**, the **vocabulary** scores were deleted for 30 randomly picked subjects, and a missing data code of −1 was substituted instead.

A second data file, **atto_mis.amd**, contains vocabulary test scores for the 40 old subjects, again with 30 randomly picked **vocabulary** scores marked as missing:

```
! Subset of the Attig (1983) Space data.
! Vocabulary data of 40 old subjects.
!
! 30 subjects, picked at random, had their
! 'vocabulary' scores replaced with the
! missing data code '-1'.

$Input Variables
      vocab.short    ! Raw score on WAIS subset
      vocabulary     ! Raw score on WAIS
$Sample size = 40
$Missing = -1
$Raw data !
     14        77
     14        77
     11        72
          . . .      (4 similar lines omitted here)
      6        47
      4        47
      0        40
     12        -1
     14        -1
     13        -1
          . . .      (24 similar lines omitted here)
     14        -1
     14        -1
     13        -1
```

Of course no sensible person deletes data that have already been collected. In order for this example to make sense, imagine that the data were obtained in the following situation:

The variable **vocabulary** is one of the best tests of vocabulary knowledge. It is highly reliable and valid, and it is the customary instrument for important diagnoses. Unfortunately it is also an expensive test. Maybe it takes a long time to give the test, or maybe it has to be administered on an individual basis or it has to be scored by a highly trained person. A second vocabulary test, **vocab.short,** is available but is not as good. However, it is short, inexpensive and easy to administer to a large number of people at once. The cheap test, **vocab.short,** is given to 40 young and 40 old subjects. Then, 10 randomly picked subjects in each group are asked to take the expensive test (**vocabulary**). The purpose of the research is to

- estimate the average **vocabulary** test score in the population of young subjects

- estimate the average **vocabulary** score in the population of old subjects

- test the hypothesis that the two populations have the same average **vocabulary** score.

There is no immediate research interest in similar statistics of the less reliable **vocab.short** scores. However, as will be demonstrated below, the **vocab.short** scores carry information that allows more efficient answers to the research questions about the **vocabulary** scores. This gain in efficiency can be surprisingly large.

Model A

The fact that the designer of the study, and not the test takers, randomly ignored 30 scores in each group does not affect the method of analysis. Model A estimates means, variances and covariances of the two vocabulary tests in both groups of subjects. The **$Crdiff** command is used to obtain the critical ratio statistic for the difference of young and old subjects' **vocabulary** scores.

Modeling in Amos Graphics

Model A can be specified in **Amos Graphics** as a two-group model, similar to Model A of Example 10:

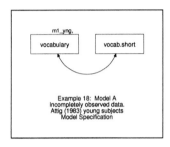

Example 18: Model A
Incompletely observed data.
Attig (1983) young subjects
Model Specification

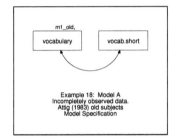

Example 18: Model A
Incompletely observed data.
Attig (1983) old subjects
Model Specification

Two objects for the exogenous observed variables **vocabulary** and **vocab.short** appear in each group, connected by a two-headed (covariance) path. Model A places no restrictions on its ten parameters (two means, two variances and one covariance term in each of two groups). There is one free parameter for each of the first and second moments—the model is saturated.

The **Amos Graphics** input file for Model A is **ex18-a.amw**. The **$** command section of each group contains an **$Include** command referencing the data files, **atty_mis.amd** and **atto_mis.amd**, respectively. These data files already contain the command **$Missing = -1**, so it does not have to be included in the **$** command section. However, because there are missing data, remember to keep the **Means** button pressed.

The **$Crdiff** command, even though it appears only in the **$** command section of the group of young subjects, applies to all model parameters in both groups. The output from the **$Crdiff** command is a ten-by-ten lower-half matrix of 45 critical ratios for the differences between any two parameter estimates. Parameter labels, if supplied, are used as row and column headings of the output matrix. Because Model A focuses on the difference in group means of the **vocabulary** test, we are using the labels m1_yng and m1_old for the two parameters. These unique labels make it obvious where the critical value for the group difference appears in the matrix.

Modeling in Amos Text

The **Amos Text** input file **ex18-a.ami** requests estimates of means, variances and covariances of both vocabulary tests in both groups of subjects:

```
Example 18:  Model A
Incompletely observed data.
Verbal subtests of Attig's (1983) data
of old and young subjects.

In each group, 30 observations of the
vocabulary test are missing.

$Crdiff

$Group name = young_subjects
$Mstructure
     vocabulary (m1_yng)
     vocab.short ()

$Include = atty_mis.amd

$Next group

$Group name = old_subjects
$Mstructure
     vocabulary (m1_old)
     vocab.short ()

$Include = atto_mis.amd
```

The **$Crdiff** command is included because we are interested in seeing the critical ratio for the difference between the mean **vocabulary** scores for young and old subjects. The parameter labels m1_yng and m1_old are supplied to identify this critical ratio in the matrix produced by the **$Crdiff** command.

Output from Model A

Amos Graphics output

Here are the two path diagrams containing the means, variances, and covariances for the young and old subjects, respectively:

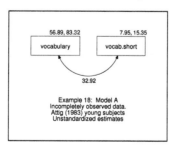

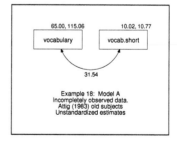

Amos Text output

The parameter estimates and standard errors for the young subjects are:

Means:		Estimate	S.E.	C.R.	Label
	vocabulary	56.891	1.765	32.232	m1_yng
	vocab.short	7.950	0.627	12.673	par-3
Covariances:		Estimate	S.E.	C.R.	Label
vocabulary <----> vocab.short		32.916	8.694	3.786	par-6
Variances:		Estimate	S.E.	C.R.	Label
	vocabulary	83.320	25.639	3.250	par-5
	vocab.short	15.347	3.476	4.416	par-7

And for the old subjects:

Means:		Estimate	S.E.	C.R.	Label
	vocabulary	65.001	2.167	29.992	m1_old
	vocab.short	10.025	0.526	19.073	par-4
Covariances:		Estimate	S.E.	C.R.	Label
vocabulary <----> vocab.short		31.545	8.725	3.616	par-9
Variances:		Estimate	S.E.	C.R.	Label
	vocabulary	115.063	37.463	3.071	par-8
	vocab.short	10.774	2.440	4.416	par-10

The estimates for the mean of **vocabulary** are 56.891 in the young population and 65.001 in the old population. Notice that these are not the same as the sample means that would have been obtained from the 10 young and 10 old subjects who took the **vocabulary** test. The respective sample means of 58.5 and 62 are good estimates of the population means (the best that can be had from two samples of size 10), but the Amos estimates (56.891 and 65.001) use information contained in the **vocab.short** scores, and are more efficient.

How much more accurate are the mean estimates that include the information of the **vocab.short** scores? Some idea can be obtained by looking at estimated standard errors. For the young subjects the standard error for 56.891 shown above is about 1.765 whereas the standard error of the sample mean, 58.5, is about 2.21. For the old subjects the standard error for 65.001 is about 2.167 while the standard error of the sample mean, 62, is about 4.21. Although the standard errors just mentioned are only approximations, they still provide a reasonable basis for comparison. In the case of the young subjects, using the information contained in the **vocab.short** scores reduces the standard error of the estimated **vocabulary** mean by about 21%. In the case of the old subjects, the standard error was reduced by about 49%.

Another way to evaluate the additional information due to the **vocab.short** scores is by evaluating the sample size requirements. Suppose you did not use the information in the **vocab.short** scores, how many more young examinees would have to take the **vocabulary** test to reduce the standard error of its mean by 21%? Likewise, how many more old examinees would have to take the **vocabulary** test to reduce the standard error of its mean by 49%? The answer is that, because the standard error of the mean is inversely proportional to the square root of the sample size, it would require about 1.6 times as many young subjects and about 3.8 times as many old subjects. That is, it would require about 16 young subjects and 38 old subjects taking the **vocabulary** test, instead of 10 young and 10 old subjects taking both tests, and 30 young and 30 old subjects taking the short test alone. Of course this calculation treats the estimated standard errors as though they were exact standard errors, and so it gives only a rough idea of how much is gained by using scores on the **vocab.short** test.

We would now like to test how likely it is that the young and old populations have different mean **vocabulary** scores. The estimated mean difference is 8.11 (65.001 − 56.891). An approximate critical ratio statistic for this difference is produced by the **$Crdiff** command:

```
Critical Ratios for Differences between Parameters

          m1_yng   m1_old   par-3    par-4    par-5    par-6    par-7
       --- ------  -------- -------- -------- -------- -------- --------
m1_yng    0.000
m1_old    2.901    0.000
par-3   -36.269  -25.286    0.000
par-4   -25.448  -30.012    2.535    0.000
par-5     1.028    0.712    2.939    2.858    0.000
par-6    -2.702   -3.581    2.864    2.628   -2.806    0.000
par-7   -10.658  -12.123    2.095    1.514   -2.877   -2.934    0.000
par-8     1.551    1.334    2.859    2.803    0.699    2.136    2.650
par-9    -2.847   -3.722    2.697    2.462   -1.912   -0.111    1.725
par-10  -15.314  -16.616    1.121    0.300   -2.817   -2.452   -1.077

          par-8    par-9    par-10
       -------- -------- --------
par-8     0.000
par-9    -2.804    0.000
par-10   -2.884   -3.023    0.000
```

The first two rows and columns, labeled m1_yng and m1_old, refer to the group means of the **vocabulary** test. The critical ratio for the mean difference is 2.901, according to which the means differ significantly at the .05 level: the older population scores higher on the long test than the younger population.

Another test of equal **vocabulary** group means can be obtained by re-estimating the model with equality constraints imposed on these means. We will do that next, but first note the Function of log likelihood for Model A:

```
Function of log likelihood =    429.963
Number of parameters =   10
```

Model B

Model B adds the constraint that **vocabulary** has the same mean in the young and old populations.

Modeling in Amos Graphics

The group means of the **vocabulary** test can be constrained either by using the same parameter label in both groups or by equating the two parameter labels m1_yng and m1_old of Model A in a **$Model** command section. The Amos Graphics input file **ex18-b.amw** uses the latter approach, adding the two statements

```
$Model=Model_A
$Model=Model_B
    m1_yng = m1_old
```

to the **$** command section of the sample of young subjects. An advantage of using a multi-model format is that Amos will compute the χ^2 statistic and p value for the model comparison.

Modeling in Amos Text

The **Amos Text** input file of Model B, **ex18-b.ami**, uses the *same* parameter label (mn_vocab) for the two group means of the **vocabulary** test:

```
Example 18:  Model B
Incompletely observed data.
Verbal subtests of Attig's (1983) data
of old and young subjects.

In each group, 30 observations of the
vocabulary test are missing.

$Crdiff

$Group name = young_subjects
$Mstructure
        vocabulary (mn_vocab)
        vocab.short ()

$Include = atty_mis.amd

$Next group

$Group name = old_subjects
$Mstructure
        vocabulary (mn_vocab)
        vocab.short ()

$Include = atto_mis.amd
```

Output from Model B

The following portion of the output reports the fit of Model B:

```
Function of log likelihood =    437.813
Number of parameters =    9
```

The difference in fit measures between Models B and A is 7.85 (= 437.813 − 429.963), and the difference in the number of parameters estimated is 1 (= 10 − 9). If Model B is correct (*i.e.,* if the young and old populations have the same mean **vocabulary** score), then 7.85 is an observation on a random variable that has a chi-square distribution with one degree of freedom. Since values larger than 3.84 are significant at the .05 level when there is one degree of freedom, Model B is rejected in favor of Model A—concluding that younger and older subjects differ in their mean **vocabulary** scores.

Example 19: Bootstrapping

Purpose

This example demonstrates how to obtain robust standard error estimates by the bootstrap method.

Introduction

Bootstrapping (Efron, 1982) is a versatile method for evaluating the empirical sampling distribution of parameter estimates. In particular, bootstrapping can be used to obtain empirical standard error estimates of the model parameters, in addition to the regular standard error estimates that are part of the usual Amos output when maximum likelihood or generalized least squares estimation is employed. To calculate these latter standard errors, Amos uses formulas that depend on the normal-theory assumptions described in the Technical Note on page 322.

Bootstrapping is a completely different approach to the problem of estimating standard errors. Why would you want another approach? To begin with, Amos does not have formulas for all the standard errors you might want, such as standard errors for squared multiple correlations. Lack of an explicit formula for standard errors is never a problem with bootstrapping, however. Bootstrapping can be used to generate an approximate standard error for many statistics that Amos computes, regardless of whether a formula for the standard error is known. Even when Amos has formulas for standard errors, these formulas are only good under the assumptions of multivariate normality and when the correct model is employed. In contrast, approximate standard errors computed by bootstrapping do not suffer from these limitations.

Bootstrapping has its own shortcomings, however. For one thing, it requires fairly large samples. It is also expensive computationally (fortunately, high-speed personal computers have made bootstrapping a much less time-consuming proposition). For readers who are new to bootstrapping, we recommend the *Scientific American* article by Diaconis and Efron (1983).

The present example demonstrates bootstrapping with a factor analysis model but, of course, bootstrapping can be used with any model. Incidentally, Amos's bootstrapping capability can be beneficial not only with complex estimation problems but also with simple ones like that of Example 1.

The data

The Holzinger and Swineford (1939) data, introduced and described in Example 8, will be used for this example. The data are contained in the file **grnt_fem.amd**.

A factor analysis model

Modeling in Amos Text

The following input file is the same as the one in Example 8, except for the first two **$** commands, which are new:

```
Example 19:
Bootstrapping

Holzinger and Swineford (1939) Grant-White sample.
Intelligence factor study. Raw data of 73 female
students from the Grant-White high school, Chicago.
Standard errors for all parameter estimates, including
squared multiple correlations, are obtained by
bootstrapping.

$Bootstrap = 500
$Specran

$Standardized
$Smc

$Structure
    visperc   = (1) spatial + (1) err_v
    cubes     =     spatial + (1) err_c
    lozenges  =     spatial + (1) err_l

    paragraph = (1) verbal  + (1) err_p
    sentence  =     verbal  + (1) err_s
    wordmean  =     verbal  + (1) err_w

$Include = grnt_fem.amd
```

The command **$Bootstrap = 500** requests 500 bootstrap replications for computing the bootstrapped standard errors.

The command **$Specran** picks a "special" pseudo-random number generator for bootstrap sampling which is portable but has the disadvantage of otherwise not being very good. That is, if you use **$Specran** in your input file you will get the same bootstrapping results on every computer. The **$Specran** command is used in this example so that readers can duplicate the results *exactly* on their own computer system. Normally, because **$Specran** does not deliver really good random numbers, it should not be used.

Note: Another command, **$Seed = <*number*>**, can be used to supply an initial seed value for the random number generator. Different seed values must be supplied with two or more Amos sessions, if these are supposed to generate independent sets of bootstrap samples. Conversely, in order to draw the exact same set of samples in each of several Amos sessions, the same seed number must be given each time. Currently, because the present example requires only one sample, the **$Seed** command is left at its default value.

Modeling in Amos Graphics

The path diagram for this model is the same one used in Example 8:

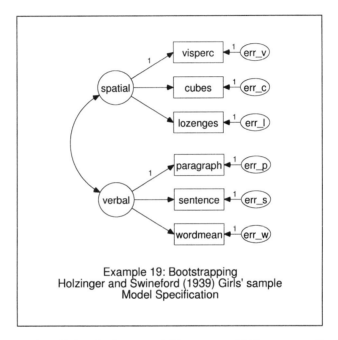

Example 19: Bootstrapping
Holzinger and Swineford (1939) Girls' sample
Model Specification

 Two lines must be added to the **$** command file to request 500 bootstrap replications and invoke the "special" portable random number generator:

```
$Bootstrap=500
$Specran
```

The input file for this example is **ex19.amw**. None of the added features illustrated in this example are displayed in the path diagram—the bootstrap output will be strictly text-based.

Speed of the analysis

The speed at which Amos can perform bootstrap simulation varies greatly, depending on how large a sample is used to begin with, and how quickly the model can be refitted to each bootstrap sample. Several components contribute to computing speed, particularly the speed of floating point calculations supported by the computer hardware, whether the 16- or 32-bit version of Amos is used, how many parameters there are in the model, and how well these are defined. 500 bootstrap replications might take a long time on some systems, and run very quickly on others. The current example goes very quickly on the current (1994) crop of high-end personal computers: Computation times for the 500 bootstrap replications range between 31 and 100 seconds on 66 MHz 486/DX and 60 MHz Pentium systems.

Just in case, Amos reports the progress of the bootstrap operations in its standard report window:

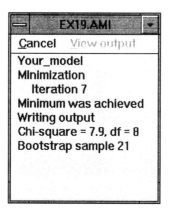

The line **Bootstrap sample...** counts the number of bootstraps performed so far. If you feel the pace is going too slowly, you can select **Cancel**, and stop the bootstrapping process.

Results of the analysis

The model fit is, of course, the same as in Example 8:

```
Chi-square =       7.853
Degrees of freedom =     8
Probability level =     0.448
```

The unstandardized parameter estimates are also the same as in Example 8. However, now the focus is on the standard error estimates computed by normal-theory maximum likelihood, and on comparing them to standard errors obtained by bootstrapping. Here, again, are the maximum likelihood estimates of parameters and their standard errors:

```
Regression Weights:                          Estimate     S.E.      C.R.     Label
...............                              ........   .......   .......   .......

        visperc <········· spatial            1.000
        cubes <··········· spatial            0.610      0.143     4.250
        lozenges <······· spatial             1.198      0.272     4.405
        paragraph <······· verbal             1.000
        sentence <········· verbal            1.334      0.160     8.322
        wordmean <········· verbal            2.234      0.263     8.482


Standardized Regression Weights:             Estimate
...............................              ........

        visperc <········· spatial            0.703
        cubes <··········· spatial            0.654
        lozenges <······· spatial             0.736
        paragraph <······· verbal             0.880
        sentence <········· verbal            0.827
        wordmean <········· verbal            0.841


Covariances:                                 Estimate     S.E.      C.R.     Label
...........                                  ........   .......   .......   .......

        spatial <·········> verbal            7.315      2.571     2.846


Correlations:                                Estimate
.............                                ........

        spatial <·········> verbal            0.487


Variances:                                   Estimate     S.E.      C.R.     Label
..........                                   ........   .......   .......   .......

                          spatial           23.302      8.123     2.868
                           verbal            9.682      2.159     4.485
                            err_v           23.873      5.986     3.988
                            err_c           11.602      2.584     4.490
                            err_l           28.275      7.892     3.583
                            err_p            2.834      0.868     3.263
                            err_s            7.967      1.869     4.263
                            err_w           19.925      4.951     4.024


Squared Multiple Correlations:               Estimate
.............................               ........

                          wordmean           0.708
                          sentence           0.684
                          paragraph          0.774
                          lozenges           0.542
                             cubes           0.428
                           visperc           0.494
```

The bootstrap output begins with summary diagnostics of the resampling process. For interpreting any bootstrap standard errors or confidence intervals, it is important to know whether there were bootstrap samples for which model estimates could not be computed and, if so, how many such aberrant cases were encountered. This information is reported concisely in the lines:

```
  0 bootstrap samples were unused because of a singular covariance matrix.
  0 bootstrap samples were unused because a solution was not found.
500 usable bootstrap samples were obtained.
```

If you are bootstrapping from a small or not continuously distributed sample, it is conceivable that one or more of your bootstrapped samples had singular covariance matrices. Similarly, Amos may not be able to find a solution for some of the bootstrap samples, at least not within the limits of the minimization algorithm (*cf.*, **$Iterations**,

---

$Crit1, and **$Crit2** commands). Had such samples occurred, Amos would have reported them here, but would have left them out of any subsequent standard error calculations and bootstrap distribution graphs. If the message reports several problematic samples, then bootstrapping should perhaps not be performed for that particular problem.

The bootstrap estimates of the standard errors are:

```
Bootstrap Standard Errors
-------------------------


                                             S.E.                      S.E.
Regression Weights:              S.E.        S.E.      Mean    Bias     Bias
-------------------              -----       -----     -----   -----    -----

    visperc <-------- spatial    0.000       0.000     1.000   0.000    0.000
    cubes <---------- spatial    0.133       0.004     0.616   0.006    0.006
    lozenges <------- spatial    0.443       0.014     1.259   0.061    0.020
    paragraph <------ verbal     0.000       0.000     1.000   0.000    0.000
    sentence <------- verbal     0.159       0.005     1.343   0.009    0.007
    wordmean <------- verbal     0.263       0.008     2.253   0.019    0.012


                                             S.E.                      S.E.
Standardized (Beta) Weights:     S.E.        S.E.      Mean    Bias     Bias
---------------------------      -----       -----     -----   -----    -----

    visperc <-------- spatial    0.128       0.004     0.703   0.000    0.006
    cubes <---------- spatial    0.100       0.003     0.644  -0.009    0.004
    lozenges <------- spatial    0.121       0.004     0.731  -0.005    0.005
    paragraph <------ verbal     0.047       0.001     0.878  -0.002    0.002
    sentence <------- verbal     0.043       0.001     0.825  -0.002    0.002
    wordmean <------- verbal     0.052       0.002     0.841   0.000    0.002


                                             S.E.                      S.E.
Covariances:                     S.E.        S.E.      Mean    Bias     Bias
------------                     -----       -----     -----   -----    -----

    spatial <--------> verbal    2.638       0.083     7.386   0.071    0.118


                                             S.E.                      S.E.
Correlations:                    S.E.        S.E.      Mean    Bias     Bias
-------------                    -----       -----     -----   -----    -----

    spatial <--------> verbal    0.124       0.004     0.499   0.012    0.006


                                             S.E.                      S.E.
Variances:                       S.E.        S.E.      Mean    Bias     Bias
----------                       -----       -----     -----   -----    -----

                    spatial      9.455       0.299    23.810   0.508    0.423
                    verbal       2.119       0.067     9.611  -0.072    0.095
                    err_v        8.847       0.280    22.676  -1.197    0.396
                    err_c        3.262       0.103    11.409  -0.192    0.146
                    err_l       10.371       0.328    26.883  -1.393    0.464
                    err_p        0.850       0.027     2.736  -0.098    0.038
                    err_s        1.356       0.043     7.734  -0.233    0.061
                    err_w        5.559       0.176    19.270  -0.656    0.249


                                             S.E.                      S.E.
Squared Multiple Correlations:   S.E.        S.E.      Mean    Bias     Bias
-----------------------------    -----       -----     -----   -----    -----

                    wordmean     0.086       0.003     0.710   0.002    0.004
                    sentence     0.070       0.002     0.682  -0.002    0.003
                    paragraph    0.080       0.003     0.773  -0.001    0.004
                    lozenges     0.178       0.006     0.549   0.008    0.008
                    cubes        0.125       0.004     0.425  -0.002    0.006
                    visperc      0.182       0.006     0.510   0.016    0.008
```

The first column, labeled S.E., gives the bootstrapped estimate of the standard error, which is simply the standard deviation of the parameter estimates computed across the 500 bootstrap samples. This figure should be compared to the approximate standard error estimates obtained by maximum likelihood. The second column, labeled S.E. (S.E.), gives the approximate standard error of the bootstrap standard error estimate itself. As you can see, these entries are small throughout the second column, as they should be.

The column labeled Mean represents the average parameter estimate computed across bootstrap samples. This bootstrap mean is not necessarily identical to the original estimate. On the contrary, it can turn out being quite different. The fourth column, labeled Bias, gives the difference between the bootstrap mean and original estimate. If the average estimate of the bootstrapped samples is higher than the original estimate, then Bias will be positive. The last column, labeled S.E. (Bias), gives the approximate standard error of the bias estimate.

Computational formulas for these statistics are documented in the section entitled **Text output** in the *Amos Reference Guide*, and in Amos's on line Help facility.

In the present example, many of the bootstrap standard errors are quite close to the approximate standard errors obtained originally by maximum likelihood. The three exceptions from this rule are associated with the two spatial tests **lozenges** and **visperc**. The bootstrap standard error of the regression weight of **lozenges** on the **spatial** factor is 0.443, which is 60 percent larger than the maximum likelihood approximation. Similarly, the respective bootstrap standard errors for the residual variance terms for **visperc** and **lozenges** are 48 and 31 percent larger than the standard errors obtained by the maximum-likelihood method. The latter two parameter estimates are also significantly biased. In conclusion, the distribution of parameter estimates associated with the **spatial** common factor appears wider than expected under normal distribution assumptions.

We will not attempt to resolve why the bootstrap and normal-theory standard errors are different in this example. One promising next step would probably involve studying the joint and marginal distribution statistics of the three spatial tests. It could be that there are outliers in the data, or that there is a considerable amount of censoring in some of the tests, or that the distributions might simply be rather skewed. In any case, bootstrap simulations are a powerful tool to diagnose the presence of distribution problems in the data and to gauge their effects on the parameter estimates.

> *Note*: Because the **$Standardized** and **$Smc** commands were included in the input file, the bootstrap procedure produces standard errors and bias estimates for the standardized path coefficients, factor correlations, and squared multiple correlations. Amos does not provide normal-theory standard errors for these estimates. Yet, as the example demonstrates, it is easy to obtain empirical interval estimates for these parameters by bootstrapping.

Example 20: Bootstrapping for model comparison

Purpose

This example demonstrates the use of the bootstrap for model comparison. The problem addressed by this method is not that of evaluating an individual model in absolute terms, but of choosing among two or more competing models. Browne (1982) and Stine (1989) suggested the possibility of using bootstrapping for model selection in analysis of moment structures. Linhart and Zucchini (1986) described a general schema for bootstrapping and model selection that is appropriate for a large class of models, including structural modeling. The Linhart and Zucchini approach is employed here.

The bootstrap approach to model comparison can be summarized as follows:

1. Generate several bootstrap samples by sampling with replacement from the original sample. In other words: the *original sample* serves as the *population* for purposes of bootstrap sampling.

2. Fit every competing model to every bootstrap sample. After each analysis, calculate the discrepancy between the implied moments from the bootstrap sample and the sample moments from the bootstrap population.

3. For each model, calculate the average (across bootstrap samples) of the discrepancies from step 2.

4. Choose the model whose average discrepancy (from step 3) is smallest.

The data

The present example uses the combined male and female data from the Grant-White high school sample of the Holzinger and Swineford (1939) study, previously discussed in Examples 8, 12, 15, 17 and 19. The same six psychological tests are used. The 145 combined observations are given in the file `grant.amd`.

Five models

Five measurement models are applied to the six psychological tests. *Model 1* is an unrestricted factor analysis model with one factor:

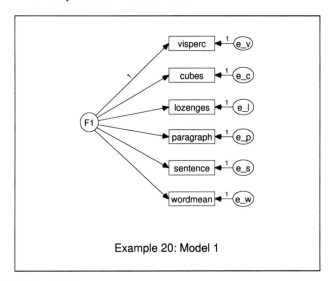

Example 20: Model 1

Model 2 is an unrestricted factor analysis with two factors. Note that the two zero constraints in the model are not restrictions, but fix the factors at some arbitrary orientation so that the model becomes identified (Anderson, 1984; Bollen and Jöreskog, 1985; Jöreskog, 1979):

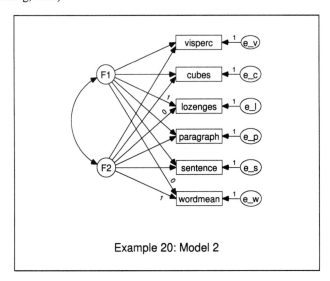

Example 20: Model 2

Model 2R is a restricted factor analysis model with two factors, in which the first three tests depend upon only one of the factors while the remaining three tests depend only upon the other factor:

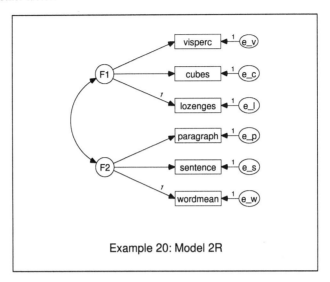

Example 20: Model 2R

The remaining two models provide the customary points of reference for comparing the fit of the previous models to the sample data. The *saturated model* simply restates the covariance structure:

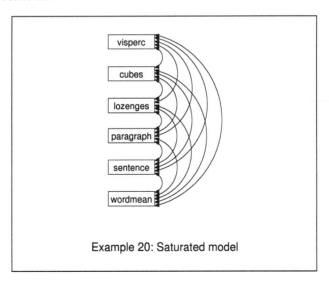

Example 20: Saturated model

And the *independence model* assumes that the six variables are uncorrelated:

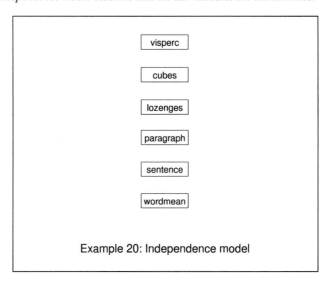

Example 20: Independence model

You would not ordinarily fit the saturated and independence models separately, since Amos automatically reports fit measures for those two models in the course of every analysis. However, it is necessary to specify explicitly the saturated and independence models in order to get bootstrap results for those models.

Five separate bootstrap analyses are performed, one for each model. For each of the five analyses, the following lines are given in the **$** command section:

```
$Seed = 3
$Iterations = 40
$Bootstrap = 1000
$Include = grant.amd
```

The **Amos Graphics** input files for the five models are called **ex20-1.amw, ex20-2.amw, ex20-2r.amw, ex20-sat.amw,** and **ex20-ind.amw.** The **Amos Text** input files use the same names but with the extension **.ami**.

Text output

From the analysis of Model 1, the following message indicates that it was not necessary to discard any bootstrap samples. All 1000 bootstrap samples were used:

```
0 bootstrap samples were unused because of a singular covariance matrix.
0 bootstrap samples were unused because a solution was not found.
1000 usable bootstrap samples were obtained.
```

For each of the five models and for each of the 1000 bootstrap samples, the bootstrap simulation shows by how much the implied sample moments differ from the population moments. The following output shows the distribution of

$$C_{ML}(\hat{\alpha}_b, \mathbf{a}) = C_{KL}(\hat{\alpha}_b, \mathbf{a}) - C_{KL}(\mathbf{a}, \mathbf{a}), \quad b = 1, \ldots, 1000,$$

where $\mathbf{a}$ contains the moments from the original sample of 145 Grant-White students (*i.e.*, the moment of the bootstrap population) and $\hat{\alpha}_b$ contains the implied moments obtained from fitting the model to the *b-th* bootstrap sample. $C_{ML}(\hat{\alpha}_b, \mathbf{a})$ here is a measure of how much the population moments differ from the moments estimated from the *b-th* bootstrap sample using Model 1:

```
                            --------+--------------------
                             48.268|**
                             52.091|********
                             55.913|*************
      ML discrepancy         59.735|*******************
      (implied vs pop)       63.557|*****************
                             67.379|************
                             71.202|********
         N = 1000            75.024|******
      Mean = 64.162          78.846|***
      S. e. = 0.292          82.668|*
                             86.490|**
                             90.313|**
                             94.135|*
                             97.957|*
                            101.779|*
                            --------+--------------------
```

The average of $C_{ML}(\hat{\alpha}_b, \mathbf{a})$ over the 1000 bootstrap samples is 64.162 with a standard error of .292. Similar histograms, along with means and standard errors, are displayed for the other four models, but are not reproduced here. The average discrepancies for the five competing models are shown in Table 20.1 along with values of the BCC, AIC, and CAIC criteria.

Model	Failures	Mean discrepancy	BCC	AIC	CAIC
1	0	64.16 (.29)	68.17	66.94	114.66
2	19	29.14 (.35)	36.81	35.07	102.68
2R	0	26.57 (.30)	30.97	29.64	81.34
Sat.	0	32.05 (.37)	44.15	42.00	125.51
Indep.	0	334.32 (.24)	333.93	333.32	357.18

Table 20.1: Fit Measures for Five Competing Models (Standard Errors in Parentheses)

The *failures* column in Table 20.1 indicates that the likelihood function of Model 2 could not be maximized for 19 of the 1000 bootstrap samples. Nineteen additional bootstrap samples were generated for Model 2 in order to bring the total number of bootstrap samples to the target of 1000. The 19 samples where Model 2 could not be fitted successfully caused no problem with the other four models. Consequently, 981 bootstrap samples were common to all five models.

No attempt was made to find out why Model 2 estimates could not be computed for 19 bootstrap samples. As a rule, algorithms for analysis of moment structures tend to fail for models that fit the sample poorly. Conversely, if there were some other way to successfully estimate Model 2 from these 19 samples, say with hand-picked start values or a superior algorithm, it would likely have resulted in relatively large discrepancies. According to this line of reasoning, disregarding any bootstrap samples with estimation failure will likely lead to a downwards bias of the mean discrepancy for this model. Thus, estimation failures during bootstrapping would be of concern primarily when they occur for the model with the lowest mean discrepancy.

In this example, the lowest mean discrepancy (26.57) occurs for Model 2R, confirming the model choice based on the BCC, AIC, and CAIC criteria. The differences among the mean discrepancies are large compared to their standard errors. Since all models were fit to the same bootstrap samples (except for samples where Model 2 was not successfully fitted) one would expect to find positive correlations across bootstrap samples between discrepancies for similar models. Unfortunately, Amos does not report those correlations. Calculating the correlations by hand showed that they are quite close to one, so that standard errors for the differences between means in Table 20.1 are on the whole even smaller than the standard errors of the means.

Summary

Bootstrapping can be a practical aid in model selection for analysis of moment structures. The Linhart and Zucchini (1986) approach uses the expected discrepancy between implied and population moments as the basis for model comparisons. The method is conceptually simple and easy to apply. It does not employ any arbitrary "magic number" such as a significance level. Of course, the theoretical appropriateness of competing models and the reasonableness of their associated parameter estimates are not taken into account by the bootstrap procedure, and need to be given appropriate weight at some other stage in the model evaluation process.

Example 21: Bootstrapping to compare estimation methods

Purpose

This example shows how bootstrapping can be used to choose among competing estimation criteria.

Introduction

The discrepancy between the population moments and the moments implied by a model depends not only on the model, but also on the estimation method. The technique used in Example 20 to compare models with respect to their ability to recover population moments can be adapted to the comparison of estimation methods. This capability is particularly needed in choosing among estimation methods that are known to be optimal only asymptotically, and whose relative merits in finite samples would be expected to depend on the model, the sample size and the population distribution. The principal obstacle to carrying out this program for comparing estimation methods is that it requires a prior decision about how to measure the discrepancy between the population moments and the moments implied by the model. There appears to be no way to make this decision without favoring some estimation criteria over others. Of course, if every choice of population discrepancy leads to the same conclusion, questions about which is the appropriate population discrepancy can be considered academic. The present example presents such a clear-cut case.

The data

The Holzinger-Swineford (1939) data from Example 20 (in file `grant.amd`) are used in the present example.

The model

The present example estimates the parameters of Model 2R from Example 20 by four alternative methods: Asymptotically distribution-free (ADF), maximum likelihood (ML), generalized least squares (GLS), and unweighted least squares (ULS). To compare the four estimation methods, Amos needs to be run four times. In each of the four analyses the factor specification for Model 2R is the same, and can be entered either in **Amos Graphics** or **Amos Text**.

Amos **$** commands are used to specify the estimation method and bootstrap parameters. To evaluate the *asymptotically distribution-free* (ADF) estimation method using the same 1000 bootstrap samples that were used in Example 20, the following **$** commands are entered:

```
$Adf
$Bootml
$Bootadf
$Bootgls
$Bootuls

$Seed = 3
$Iterations = 40
$Bootstrap = 1000
$Include = grant.amd
```

The **$Adf** command specifies that ADF estimation should be used to fit the model to each bootstrap sample. The commands **$Bootml, $Bootadf, $Bootgls** and **$Bootuls** specify that C_{ML}, C_{ADF}, C_{GLS}, and C_{ULS} should each be used to measure the discrepancy between the sample moments in the original sample and the implied moments from each bootstrap sample.

To evaluate the ML, GLS, and ULS estimation methods, repeat the analysis three times, replacing the **$Adf** command with **$Ml, $Gls,** and **$Uls** in turn. The **Amos Graphics** input files for this problem are **ex21-adf.amw, ex21-ml.amw, ex21-gls.amw** and **ex21-uls.amw**, respectively. The **Amos Text** files use the same naming convention, but with the extension **.ami**.

Text output

In the first of the four analyses, using ADF (**$Adf**) estimation, the **$Bootadf** command produces the following histogram output:

```
--------+--------------------
          7.359|*
         10.817|********
         14.274|****************
ADF discrepancy    17.732|********************
(implied vs pop)   21.189|*******************
         24.647|*************
         28.104|********
  N = 1000    31.562|****
  Mean = 20.601  35.019|**
  S. e. = 0.218  38.477|**
         41.934|*
         45.392|*
         48.850|*
         52.307|*
         55.765|*
--------+--------------------
```

This portion of the output shows the distribution of the population discrepancy $C_{\text{ADF}}(\hat{\alpha}_b, \mathbf{a})$ across 1000 bootstrap samples, where $\hat{\alpha}_b$ contains the implied moments obtained by minimizing $C_{\text{ADF}}(\hat{\alpha}_b, \mathbf{a}_b)$, *i.e.*, the sample discrepancy. The average of $C_{\text{ADF}}(\hat{\alpha}_b, \mathbf{a})$ across 1000 bootstrap samples is 20.601, with a standard error of 0.218.

Similarly, the **$Bootml**, **$Bootgls** and **$Bootuls** commands produce the following histograms:

```
                          --------+-------------------
                   11.272|****
                   22.691|********************
                   34.110|********************
ML discrepancy     45.530|***********
(implied vs pop)   56.949|*****
                   68.368|***
                   79.787|**
    N = 1000       91.207|*
  Mean = 36.860   102.626|*
  S. e. = 0.571   114.045|*
                  125.464|*
                  136.884|
                  148.303|
                  159.722|
                  171.142|*
                          --------+-------------------


                          --------+-------------------
                    7.248|**
                   11.076|********
                   14.904|***************
GLS discrepancy    18.733|********************
(implied vs pop)   22.561|**************
                   26.389|***********
                   30.217|*******
    N = 1000       34.046|****
  Mean = 21.827    37.874|**
  S. e. = 0.263    41.702|***
                   45.530|*
                   49.359|*
                   53.187|*
                   57.015|*
                   60.844|*
                          --------+-------------------


                          --------+-------------------
                  5079.897|******
                 30811.807|********************
                 56543.716|********
ULS discrepancy  82275.625|****
(implied vs pop) 108007.534|**
                 133739.443|*
                 159471.352|*
    N = 1000     185203.261|*
  Mean = 43686.444 210935.170|
  S. e. = 1011.591 236667.079|*
                 262398.988|
                 288130.897|
                 313862.806|
                 339594.715|
                 365326.624|*
                          --------+-------------------
```

The four distributions just reported are summarized in the first row of Table 21.1. The remaining three rows show the results of estimation by minimizing C_{ML}, C_{GLS} and C_{ULS}, respectively.

		Population discrepancy for evaluation: $C(\hat{\alpha}_b, \mathbf{a})$			
		C_{ADF}	C_{ML}	C_{GLS}	C_{ULS}
Sample	C_{ADF}	20.60 (.22)	36.86 (.57)	21.83 (.26)	43686 (1012)
discrepancy	C_{ML}	19.19 (.20)	26.57 (.30)	18.96 (.22)	34760 (758)
for estimation	C_{GLS}	19.45 (.20)	31.45 (.40)	19.03 (.21)	37021 (830)
$C(\hat{\alpha}_b, \mathbf{a}_b)$	C_{ULS}	24.89 (.35)	31.78 (.43)	24.16 (.33)	35343 (793)

Table 21.1: Mean of $C(\hat{\alpha}_b, \mathbf{a})$ across 1000 Bootstrap Samples (Standard Errors in Parentheses)

The first column, labeled C_{ADF}, shows the relative performance of the four estimation methods according to the population discrepancy, C_{ADF}. Since 19.19 is the smallest mean discrepancy in the C_{ADF} column, C_{ML} is the best estimation method according to the C_{ADF} criterion. Similarly, examining the C_{ML} column of Table 21.1 shows that C_{ML} is the best estimation method according to the C_{ML} criterion.

Although the four columns of the table disagree on the exact ordering of the four estimation methods, ML is in all cases the method with the lowest mean discrepancy. The difference between ML estimation and GLS estimation is slight in some cases. Unsurprisingly, ULS estimation performed badly according to all of the population discrepancies employed. More interesting is the poor performance of ADF estimation, indicating that ADF estimation is unsuited to this combination of model, population and sample size.

Appendices

Appendix A: Notation

q = the number of parameters.

γ = the vector of parameters (of order q).

G = the number of groups.

$N^{(g)}$ = the number of observations in group g.

$N = \sum_{g=1}^{G} N^{(g)}$, the total number of observations in all groups combined.

$p^{(g)}$ = the number of observed variables in group g.

$p*^{(g)}$ = the number of sample moments in group g. When means and intercepts are explicit model parameters, the relevant sample moments are means, variances and covariances, so that $p*^{(g)} = p^{(g)}\left(p^{(g)} + 3\right)\big/2$. Otherwise, only sample variances and covariances are counted so that $p*^{(g)} = p^{(g)}\left(p^{(g)} + 1\right)\big/2$.

$p = \sum_{g=1}^{G} p*^{(g)}$, the number of sample moments in all groups combined.

$d = p - q$, the number of degrees of freedom for testing the model.

$x_{ir}^{(g)}$ = the r-th observation on the i-th variable in group g.

$\mathbf{x}_i^{(g)}$ = the r-th observation in group g.

$\mathbf{S}^{(g)}$ = the sample covariance matrix for group g.

$\Sigma^{(g)}(\gamma)$ = the covariance matrix for group g, according to the model.

$\mu^{(g)}(\gamma)$ = the mean vector for group g, according to the model.

$\Sigma_0^{(g)}$ = the population covariance matrix for group g.

$\mu_0^{(g)}$ = the population mean vector for group g.

$\mathbf{s}^{(g)} = \mathrm{vec}\left(\mathbf{S}^{(g)}\right)$, the $p*^{(g)}$ distinct elements of $\mathbf{S}^{(g)}$ arranged in a single column vector.

$\sigma^{(g)}(\gamma) = \mathrm{vec}\left(\Sigma^{(g)}(\gamma)\right)$.

r = the nonnegative integer specified by the **$chicorrect** command. By default $r = G$. When **$emulisrel6** is used, $r = G$, and cannot be changed by using **$chicorrect**.

$n = N - r$.

$\mathbf{a}$ = the vector of order p containing the sample moments for all groups. That is, $\mathbf{a}$ contains the elements of $\mathbf{S}^{(1)}, \dots, \mathbf{S}^{(G)}$, and also (if means and intercepts are explicit model parameters) $\overline{\mathbf{x}}^{(1)}, \dots, \overline{\mathbf{x}}^{(G)}$.

α_0 = the vector of order p containing the population moments for all groups. That is, α_0 contains the elements of $\Sigma_0^{(1)}, \dots, \Sigma_0^{(G)}$, and also (if means and intercepts are explicit model parameters) $\mu_0^{(1)}, \dots, \mu_0^{(G)}$. The ordering of the elements of $\alpha(\gamma)$ must match the ordering of the elements of $\mathbf{a}$.

$\alpha(\gamma)$ = the vector of order p containing the population moments for all groups according to the model. That is, $\alpha(\gamma)$ contains the elements of $\Sigma^{(1)}(\gamma), \dots, \Sigma^{(G)}(\gamma)$, and also (if means and intercepts are explicit model parameters) $\mu^{(1)}(\gamma), \dots, \mu^{(G)}(\gamma)$. The ordering of the elements of $\alpha(\gamma)$ must match the ordering of the elements of $\mathbf{a}$.

$F\left(\alpha(\gamma), \mathbf{a}\right)$ = the function (of γ) that is minimized in fitting the model to the sample.

$\hat{\gamma}$ = the value of γ that minimizes $F\left(\alpha(\gamma), \mathbf{a}\right)$

$\hat{\Sigma}^{(g)} = \Sigma^{(g)}(\hat{\gamma})$

$\hat{\mu}^{(g)} = \mu^{(g)}(\hat{\gamma})$

$\hat{\alpha} = \alpha(\hat{\gamma})$

Appendix B: Discrepancy functions

Amos minimizes discrepancy functions (Browne, 1982, 1984) of the form,

$$(D1) \qquad C(\alpha, \mathbf{a}) = [N - r] \left(\frac{\sum_{g=1}^{G} N^{(g)} f\left(\mu^{(g)}, \Sigma^{(g)}; \ \bar{\mathbf{x}}^{(g)}, \mathbf{S}^{(g)}\right)}{N} \right) = [N - r] F(\alpha, \mathbf{a}).$$

Different discrepancy functions are obtained by changing the way f is defined. If means and intercepts are unconstrained and do not appear as explicit model parameters, $\bar{\mathbf{x}}^{(g)}$ and $\mu^{(g)}$ will be omitted and f will be written $f\left(\Sigma^{(g)}; \ \mathbf{S}^{(g)}\right)$.

The discrepancy functions C_{KL} and F_{KL} are obtained by taking f to be

$$f_{KL}\left(\mu^{(g)}, \Sigma^{(g)}; \bar{\mathbf{x}}^{(g)}, \mathbf{S}^{(g)}\right) = \log\left|\Sigma^{(g)}\right| + \mathrm{tr}\left(\mathbf{S}^{(g)} \Sigma^{(g)^{-1}}\right) + \left(\bar{\mathbf{x}}^{(g)} - \mu^{(g)}\right)' \Sigma^{(g)^{-1}} \left(\bar{\mathbf{x}}^{(g)} - \mu^{(g)}\right).$$

Except for an additive constant that depends only on the sample size, f_{KL} is -2 times the Kullback-Leibler information quantity (Kullback and Leibler, 1951). Strictly speaking, C_{KL} and F_{KL} do not qualify as discrepancy functions according to Browne's definition since $F_{KL}(\mathbf{a}, \mathbf{a}) \neq 0$.

For *maximum likelihood* estimation (**$ml**), C_{ML} and F_{ML} are obtained by taking f to be

$$
\begin{aligned}
f_{ML}\left(\mu^{(g)}, \Sigma^{(g)}; \bar{\mathbf{x}}^{(g)}, \mathbf{S}^{(g)}\right) &= f_{KL}\left(\mu^{(g)}, \Sigma^{(g)}; \bar{\mathbf{x}}^{(g)}, \mathbf{S}^{(g)}\right) - f_{KL}\left(\bar{\mathbf{x}}^{(g)}, \mathbf{S}^{(g)}; \bar{\mathbf{x}}^{(g)}, \mathbf{S}^{(g)}\right) \\
&= \log\left|\Sigma^{(g)}\right| + \operatorname{tr}\left(\mathbf{S}^{(g)}\Sigma^{(g)^{-1}}\right) - \log\left|\mathbf{S}^{(g)}\right| - p^{(g)} + \left(\bar{\mathbf{x}}^{(g)} - \mu^{(g)}\right)' \Sigma^{(g)^{-1}}\left(\bar{\mathbf{x}}^{(g)} - \mu^{(g)}\right).
\end{aligned}
$$
(D2)

For *generalized least squares* estimation (**$gls**), C_{GLS} and F_{GLS} are obtained by taking f to be

$$
f_{GLS}\left(\Sigma^{(g)};\ \mathbf{S}^{(g)}\right) = \tfrac{1}{2}\operatorname{tr}\left[\mathbf{S}^{(g)^{-1}}\left(\mathbf{S}^{(g)} - \Sigma^{(g)}\right)\right]^2 .
$$
(D3)

For *asymptotically distribution-free* estimation (**$adf**), C_{ADF} and F_{ADF} are obtained by taking f to be

$$
f_{ADF}\left(\Sigma^{(g)}; \mathbf{S}^{(g)}\right) = \sum_{g=1}^{G}\left[\mathbf{s}^{(g)} - \sigma^{(g)}(\gamma)\right]' \mathbf{U}^{(g)^{-1}}\left[\mathbf{s}^{(g)} - \sigma^{(g)}(\gamma)\right],
$$
(D4)

where the elements of $\mathbf{U}^{(g)}$ are given by Browne (1984, Equations 3.1–3.4):

$$
\bar{x}_i^{(g)} = \frac{1}{N_g}\sum_{r=1}^{N_g} x_{ir}^{(g)},
$$

$$
w_{ij}^{(g)} = \frac{1}{N_g}\sum_{r=1}^{N_g}\left(x_{ir}^{(g)} - \bar{x}_i^{(g)}\right)\left(x_{jr}^{(g)} - \bar{x}_j^{(g)}\right),
$$

$$
w_{ij,kl}^{(g)} = \frac{1}{N_g}\sum_{r=1}^{N_g}\left(x_{ir}^{(g)} - \bar{x}_i^{(g)}\right)\left(x_{jr}^{(g)} - \bar{x}_j^{(g)}\right)\left(x_{kr}^{(g)} - \bar{x}_k^{(g)}\right)\left(x_{lr}^{(g)} - \bar{x}_l^{(g)}\right),
$$

$$
\left[\mathbf{U}^{(g)}\right]_{ij,kl} = w_{ij,kl}^{(g)} - w_{ij}^{(g)}w_{kl}^{(g)} .
$$

For *'scale free' least squares* estimation (**$sls**), C_{SLS} and F_{SLS} are obtained by taking f to be

$$
f_{SLS}\left(\Sigma^{(g)};\ \mathbf{S}^{(g)}\right) = \tfrac{1}{2}\operatorname{tr}\left[\mathbf{D}^{(g)^{-1}}\left(\mathbf{S}^{(g)} - \Sigma^{(g)}\right)\right]^2 ,
$$
(D5)

where $\mathbf{D}^{(g)} = \mathrm{diag}\!\left(\mathbf{S}^{(g)}\right)$.

For *unweighted least squares* estimation (**$uls**), C_{ULS} and F_{ULS} are obtained by taking f to be

(D6) $\qquad f_{ULS}\!\left(\Sigma^{(g)};\ \mathbf{S}^{(g)}\right) = \tfrac{1}{2}\ \mathrm{tr}\!\left[\mathbf{S}^{(g)} - \Sigma^{(g)}\right]^{2}.$

The **$emulisrel6** command can be used to replace (D1) with

(D1a) $\qquad C = \displaystyle\sum_{g=1}^{G}\left(N^{(g)} - 1\right)F^{(g)}.$

F is then calculated as $F = C/(N - G)$.

When $G = 1$ and $r = 1$, (D1) and (D1a) are equivalent, giving

$$C = \left(N^{(1)} - 1\right)F^{(1)} = (N-1)F.$$

For maximum likelihood, asymptotically distribution-free, and generalized least squares estimation, both (D1) and (D1a) have a chi-square distribution for correctly specified models under appropriate distributional assumptions. Asymptotically, (D1) and (D1a) are equivalent. However, both formulas can exhibit some inconsistencies in finite samples. Suppose you have two independent samples and a model for each. Furthermore, suppose that you analyze the two samples simultaneously, but that, in doing so, you impose no constraints requiring any parameter in one model to equal any parameter in the other model. Then if you minimize (D1a), the parameter estimates obtained from the simultaneous analysis of both groups will be the same as from separate analyses of each group alone. Furthermore, the discrepancy function (D1a) obtained from the simultaneous analysis will be the sum of the discrepancy functions from the two separate analyses. Formula (D1) does not have this property when r is nonzero. Using formula (D1) to do a simultaneous analysis of the two groups will give the same parameter estimates as two separate analyses, but the discrepancy function from the simultaneous analysis will not be the sum of the individual discrepancy functions.

On the other hand, suppose you have a single sample to which you have fitted some model using Amos. Now suppose that you arbitrarily split the sample into two groups of unequal size and perform a simultaneous analysis of both groups, employing the original model for both groups, and constraining each parameter in the first group to be equal to the corresponding parameter in the second group. If you have minimized (D1) in both analyses, you will get the same results in both. However, if you use (D1a) in both analyses, the two analyses will produce different estimates and a different minimum value for F.

All of the inconsistencies just pointed out can be avoided by using (D1) with the choice $r = 0$, so that (D1) becomes

$$C = \sum_{g=1}^{G} N^{(g)} F^{(g)} = NF.$$

Appendix C: Measures of fit

Model evaluation is one of the most unsettled and difficult issues connected with structural modeling. Bollen and Long (1993), MacCallum (1990), Mulaik, et al. (1989), and Steiger (1990) present a variety of viewpoints and recommendations on this topic. Dozens of statistics, besides the value of the discrepancy function at its minimum, have been proposed as measures of the merit of a model. Amos calculates most of them.

Fit measures are reported for each model specified by a **$model** command and for two additional models called the "saturated" model and the "independence" model. In the *saturated model* no constraints are placed on the population moments. The saturated model is the most general model possible. It is a vacuous model in the sense that it is guaranteed to fit any set of data perfectly. Any Amos model is a constrained version of the saturated model. The *independence model* goes to the opposite extreme. In the independence model, the observed variables are assumed to be uncorrelated with each other. When means are being estimated or constrained, the means of all observed variables are fixed at zero. The independence model is so severely and implausibly constrained that you would expect it to provide a poor fit to any interesting set of data. It frequently happens that each one of the models that you have specified can be so constrained as to be equivalent to the independence model. If this is the case, the saturated model and the independence model can be viewed as two extremes between which your proposed models lie.

For every estimation method except maximum likelihood, Amos also reports fit measures for a *zero model*, in which every parameter is fixed at zero.

Measures of parsimony

Models with relatively few parameters (and relatively many degrees of freedom) are sometimes said to be high in parsimony, or simplicity. Models with many parameters (and few degrees of freedom) are said to be complex, or lacking in parsimony. This use of the terms, simplicity and complexity, does not always conform to everyday usage. For example, the saturated model would be called complex while a model with an elaborate pattern of linear dependencies but with highly constrained parameter values would be called simple.

While one can inquire into the grounds for preferring simple, parsimonious models (e.g., Mulaik, et al., 1989), there does not appear to be any disagreement that parsimonious models are preferable to complex ones. When it comes to parameters, all other things being equal, less is more. At the same time, well fitting models are preferable to poorly fitting ones. Many fit measures represent an attempt to balance these two conflicting objectives—simplicity and goodness of fit.

> "In the final analysis, it may be, in a sense, impossible to define one *best* way to combine measures of complexity and measures of badness-of-fit in a single numerical index, because the precise nature of the *best* numerical tradeoff between complexity and fit is, to some extent, a matter of personal taste. The choice of a model is a classic problem in the two-dimensional analysis of preference." (Steiger, 1990, p. 179)

NPAR

NPAR is the number of distinct parameters (q) being estimated. Two regression weights, say, that are required to be equal to each other count as one parameter, not two.

Note: Use the **\npar** text macro to display the number of parameters in the output path diagram.

DF

DF is the number of degrees of freedom for testing the model:

$$df = d = p - q.$$

where p is the number of sample moments and q is the number of distinct parameters. Rigdon (1994) gives a detailed explanation of the calculation and interpretation of degrees of freedom.

Note: Use the **\df** text macro to display the model degrees of freedom in the output path diagram.

PRATIO

The parsimony ratio (James, Mulaik and Brett, 1982; Mulaik, et al., 1989; Mulaik, et al., 1989) expresses the number of constraints in the model being evaluated as a fraction of the number of constraints in the independence model:

$$\mathbf{PRATIO} = \frac{d}{d_i},$$

where d is the degrees of freedom of the model being evaluated and d_i is the degrees of freedom of the independence model. The parsimony ratio is used in the calculation of **PNFI** and **PCFI** (see Parsimony adjusted measures on page 567).

Note: Use the **\pratio** text macro to display the value of the parsimony ratio in the output path diagram.

The minimum sample discrepancy function

CMIN

CMIN is the minimum value, $\hat{C}$, of the discrepancy, C (see Appendix B).

Note: Use the **\cmin** text macro to display the minimum value $\hat{C}$ of the discrepancy function C in the output path diagram.

P

P is the probability of getting as large a discrepancy as occurred with the present sample (under appropriate distributional assumptions and assuming a correctly specified model). That is, **P** is a "*p* value" for testing the hypothesis that the model fits perfectly in the population.

One approach to model selection employs statistical hypothesis testing to eliminate from consideration those models that are inconsistent with the available data. Hypothesis testing is a widely accepted procedure and there is a lot of experience in its use. However, its unsuitability as a device for model selection was pointed out early in the development of analysis of moment structures (Jöreskog, 1969). It is generally acknowledged that most models are useful approximations that do not fit perfectly in the population. In other words, the null hypothesis of perfect fit is not credible to begin with and will in the end be accepted only if the sample is not allowed to get too big.

If you encounter resistance to the foregoing view of the role of hypothesis testing in model fitting, the following quotations may come in handy. The first two quotes predate the development of structural modeling, and refer to other model fitting problems.

> "The power of the test to detect an underlying disagreement between theory and data is controlled largely by the size of the sample. With a small sample an alternative hypothesis which departs violently from the null hypothesis may still have a small probability of yielding a significant value of χ^2. In a very large sample, small and unimportant departures from the null hypothesis are almost certain to be detected." (Cochran, 1952)

> "If the sample is *small* then the χ^2 test will show that the data are '*not* significantly different from' quite a wide range of very different theories, while if the sample is *large*, the χ^2 test will show that the data are *significantly* different from those expected on a given theory even though the difference may be so very slight as to be negligible or unimportant on other criteria." (Gulliksen and Tukey, 1958, pp. 95–96)

> "Such a hypothesis [of perfect fit] may be quite unrealistic in most empirical work with test data. If a sufficiently large sample were obtained this χ^2 statistic would,

no doubt, indicate that any such non-trivial hypothesis is statistically untenable."
(Jöreskog , 1969, p. 200)

"... in very large samples virtually all models that one might consider would have to be rejected as statistically untenable .... In effect, a *non*significant chi-square value is desired, and one attempts to infer the validity of the hypothesis of no difference between model and data. Such logic is well-known in various statistical guises as attempting to prove the null hypothesis. This procedure cannot generally be justified, since the chi-square variate v can be made small by simply reducing sample size." (Bentler and Bonett, 1980, p. 591)

"Our opinion ... is that this null hypothesis [of perfect fit] is implausible and that it does not help much to know whether or not the statistical test has been able to detect that it is false." (Browne and Mels, 1992, p. 78).

See **PCLOSE** on page 559.

Note: Use the \p text macro for displaying this p value in the output path diagram.

CMIN/DF

CMIN/DF is the minimum discrepancy, $\hat{C}$, (see Appendix B) divided by its degrees of freedom:

$$\frac{\hat{C}}{d}.$$

Several writers have suggested the use of this ratio as a measure of fit. For every estimation criterion except for **$uls** and **$sls**, the ratio should be close to one for correct models. The trouble is that it isn't clear how far from one you should let the ratio get before concluding that a model is unsatisfactory.

Rules of thumb:

"...Wheaton et al. (1977) suggest that the researcher also compute a *relative* chi-square (χ^2/df) .... They suggest a ratio of approximately five or less 'as beginning to be reasonable.' In our experience, however, χ^2 to degrees of freedom ratios in the range of 2 to 1 or 3 to 1 are indicative of an acceptable fit between the hypothetical model and the sample data." (Carmines and McIver, 1981, page 80)

"... different researchers have recommended using ratios as low as 2 or as high as 5 to indicate a reasonable fit." (Marsh and Hocevar, 1985).

"... it seems clear that a χ^2/df ratio > 2.00 represents an inadequate fit." (Byrne, 1989, p. 55).

Note: Use the \cmindf text macro to display the value of **CMIN/DF** in the output path diagram.

FMIN

FMIN is the minimum value, $\hat{F}$, of the discrepancy, F (see Appendix B).

Note: Use the **\fmin** text macro to display the minimum value $\hat{F}$ of the discrepancy function F in the output path diagram.

Measures based on the population discrepancy

Steiger and Lind (1980) introduced the use of the population discrepancy function as a measure of model adequacy. The population discrepancy function, F_0, is the value of the discrepancy function obtained by fitting a model to the population moments rather than to sample moments. That is,

$$F_0 = \min_\gamma \left[F(\alpha(\gamma), \ \alpha_0) \right]$$

in contrast to

$$\hat{F} = \min_\gamma \left[F(\alpha(\gamma), \ \mathbf{a}) \right].$$

Steiger, Shapiro and Browne (1985) showed that under certain conditions $\hat{C} = n\hat{F}$ has a noncentral chi-square distribution with d degrees of freedom and noncentrality parameter $\delta = C = nF$. The Steiger-Lind approach to model evaluation centers around the estimation of F_0 and related quantities.

This section of the Users' Guide relies mainly on Steiger and Lind (1980) and Steiger, Shapiro and Browne (1985). The notation is primarily that of Browne and Mels (1992).

NCP

$NCP = \max(\hat{C} - d, \ 0)$ is an estimate of the noncentrality parameter, $\delta = C_0 = nF_0$.

The columns labeled **LO 90** and **HI 90** contain the lower limit (δ_L) and upper limit (δ_U) of a 90% confidence interval, on δ. δ_L is obtained by solving

$$\Phi\left(\hat{C} \middle| \delta, \ d\right) = .95$$

for δ, and δ_U is obtained by solving

$$\Phi\left(\hat{C} | \delta, \ d\right) = .05$$

for δ, where $\Phi(x|\delta, d)$ is the distribution function of the noncentral chi-squared distribution with noncentrality parameter δ and d degrees of freedom.

Note: Use the **\ncp** text macro to display the value of the non-centrality parameter estimate in the path diagram, **\ncplo** to display the lower 90% confidence limit, and **\ncphi** for the upper 90% confidence limit.

F0

$$FO = \hat{F}_0 = \max\left(\frac{\hat{C} - d}{n}, 0\right) = \frac{NCP}{n} \text{ is an estimate of } \frac{\delta}{n} = F_0, \text{ the population discrepancy.}$$

The columns labeled **LO 90** and **HI 90** contain the lower limit and upper limit of a 90% confidence interval on F_0:

$$\text{LO 90} = \sqrt{\frac{\delta_L}{n}}$$

$$\text{HI 90} = \sqrt{\frac{\delta_U}{n}} \; .$$

Note: Use the **\f0** text macro to display the value of $\hat{F}_0$ in the output path diagram, **\f0lo** to display its lower 90% confidence estimate, and **\f0hi** to display the upper 90% confidence estimate.

RMSEA

F_0 incorporates no penalty for model complexity and will tend to favor models with many parameters. In comparing two nested models, F_0 will never favor the simpler model. Steiger and Lind (1980) suggested compensating for the effect of model complexity by dividing F_0 by the number of degrees of freedom for testing the model. Taking the square root of the resulting ratio gives the population "root mean square error of approximation", called **RMS** by Steiger and Lind, and **RMSEA** by Browne and Cudeck (1993).

$$\text{population RMSEA} = \sqrt{\frac{F_0}{d}}$$

$$\text{estimated RMSEA} = \sqrt{\frac{\hat{F}_0}{d}}$$

The columns labeled **LO 90** and **HI 90** contain the lower limit and upper limit of a 90% confidence interval on the population value of **RMSEA**. The limits are given by

$$\text{LO 90} = \sqrt{\frac{\delta_L/n}{d}}$$

$$\text{HI 90} = \sqrt{\frac{\delta_U/n}{d}}$$

Rule of thumb:

> "Practical experience has made us feel that a value of the RMSEA of about .05 or less would indicate a close fit of the model in relation to the degrees of freedom. This figure is based on subjective judgment. It cannot be regarded as infallible or correct, but it is more reasonable than the requirement of exact fit with the RMSEA = 0.0. We are also of the opinion that a value of about 0.08 or less for the RMSEA would indicate a reasonable error of approximation and would not want to employ a model with a RMSEA greater than 0.1." (Browne and Cudeck, 1993)

Note: Use the **\rmsea** text macro to display the estimated root mean square error of approximation in the output path diagram, **\rmsealo** for its lower 90% confidence estimate and **\rmseahi** for its upper 90% confidence estimate.

PCLOSE

$\text{PCLOSE} = 1 - \Phi\!\left(\hat{C} \mid .05^2 nd, d\right)$ is a "*p* value" for testing the null hypothesis that the population **RMSEA** is no greater than .05:

$$H_0: \text{RMSEA} \leq .05 \quad.$$

By contrast, the "*p* value" in the **P** column (see **P** on page 554) is for testing the hypothesis that the population **RMSEA** is zero:

$$H_0: \text{RMSEA} = 0 \quad.$$

Based on their experience with **RMSEA**, Browne and Cudeck (1993) suggest that a **RMSEA** of .05 or less indicates a "close fit". Employing this definition of "close fit", **PCLOSE** gives a test of close fit while **P** gives a test of exact fit.

Note: Use the **\pclose** text macro to display the "*p* value" for close fit of the population **RMSEA** in the output path diagram.

Information-theoretic measures

Amos reports several statistics of the form $\hat{C} + kq$ or $\hat{F} + kq$, where k is some positive constant.

Each of these statistics creates a composite measure of badness of fit ($\hat{C}$ or $\hat{F}$) and complexity (q) by forming a weighted sum of the two. Simple models that fit well receive low scores according to such a criterion. Complicated, poorly fitting models get high scores. The constant k determines the relative penalties to be attached to badness of fit and to complexity.

The statistics described in this section are intended for model comparisons and not for the evaluation of an isolated model.

All of these statistics were developed for use with maximum likelihood estimation. Amos reports them for **$gls** and **$adf** estimation as well, although it is not clear that their use is appropriate there.

AIC

The Akaike information criterion (Akaike 1973, 1987) is given by

$$\text{AIC} = \hat{C} + 2q \ .$$

See also **ECVI** on page 561.

Note: Use the **\aic** text macro to display the value of the Akaike information criterion in the output path diagram.

BCC

The Browne-Cudeck (1989) criterion is given by,

$$\text{BCC} = \hat{C} + 2q \frac{\displaystyle\sum_{g=1}^{G} b^{(g)} \frac{p^{(g)}\left(p^{(g)} + 3\right)}{N^{(g)} - p^{(g)} - 2}}{\displaystyle\sum_{g=1}^{G} p^{(g)}\left(p^{(g)} + 3\right)}$$

where $b^{(g)} = N^{(g)} - 1$ if the **$emulisrel6** command has been used, or $b^{(g)} = n\dfrac{N^{(g)}}{N}$ if it has not.

BCC imposes a slightly greater penalty for model complexity than does **AIC**.

BCC is the only measure in this section that was developed specifically for analysis of moment structures. Browne and Cudeck provided some empirical evidence suggesting that **BCC** may be superior to more generally applicable measures. Arbuckle (in preparation) gives an alternative justification for **BCC** and derives the above formula for multiple groups.

See also **MECVI** on page 562.

Note: Use the **\bcc** text macro to display the value of the Browne-Cudeck criterion in the output path diagram.

BIC

The Bayes information criterion (Schwarz, 1978; Raftery, 1993) is given by the formula,

$$\text{BIC} = \hat{C} + q \, \ln\left(N^{(1)} p^{(1)}\right).$$

In comparison to the **AIC**, **BCC** and **CAIC**, the **BIC** assigns a greater penalty to model complexity, and so has a greater tendency to pick parsimonious models. The **BIC** is reported only for the case of a single group where means and intercepts are not explicit model parameters.

Note: Use the **\bic** text macro to display the value of the Bayes information criterion in the output path diagram.

CAIC

Bozdogan's (1987) **CAIC** (consistent **AIC**) is given by the formula,

$$\text{CAIC} = \hat{C} + q\left(\ln N^{(1)} + 1\right).$$

CAIC assigns a greater penalty to model complexity than either **AIC** or **BCC**, but not as great a penalty as does **BIC**. **CAIC** is reported only for the case of a single group where means and intercepts are not explicit model parameters.

Note: Use the **\caic** text macro to display the value of the consistent **AIC** statistic in the output path diagram.

ECVI

Except for a constant scale factor, **ECVI** is the same as **AIC**:

$$\text{ECVI} = \frac{1}{n}(\text{AIC}) = \hat{F} + \frac{2q}{n}.$$

The columns labeled **LO 90** and **HI 90** give the lower limit and upper limit of a 90% confidence interval on the population **ECVI**:

$$\text{LO 90} = \frac{\delta_L + d + 2q}{n},$$

$$\text{HI 90} = \frac{\delta_U + d + 2q}{n}.$$

See also **AIC** on page 560.

Note: Use the **\ecvi** text macro to display the value of the expected cross-validation index in the output path diagram, **\ecvilo** to display its lower 90% confidence estimate, and **\ecvihi** for its upper 90% confidence estimate.

MECVI

Except for a scale factor, **MECVI** is identical to **BCC**:

$$\mathbf{MECVI} = \frac{1}{n}(\mathbf{BCC}) = \hat{F} + 2q \frac{\displaystyle\sum_{g=1}^{G} a^{(g)} \frac{p^{(g)}\left(p^{(g)}+3\right)}{N^{(g)} - p^{(g)} - 2}}{\displaystyle\sum_{g=1}^{G} p^{(g)}\left(p^{(g)}+3\right)},$$

where $a^{(g)} = \dfrac{N^{(g)} - 1}{N - G}$ if the **\$emulisrel6** command has been used, or $a^{(g)} = \dfrac{N^{(g)}}{N}$ if it has not.

See also BCC on page 560.

Note: Use the **\mecvi** text macro to display the modified **ECVI** statistic in the output path diagram.

Comparisons to a baseline model

Several fit measures encourage you to reflect on the fact that, no matter how badly your model fits, things could always be worse.

Bentler and Bonett (1980) and Tucker and Lewis (1973) suggested fitting the independence model or some other very badly fitting "baseline" model as an exercise to see how large the discrepancy function becomes. The object of the exercise is to put the fit of your own model(s) into some perspective. If none of your models fit very well, it may cheer you up to see a *really* bad model. For example, as the following output shows, Model A from Example 6 has a rather large discrepancy ($\hat{C}$ = 71.47) in relation to its degrees of freedom. On the other hand, 71.544 does not look so bad compared to 2131.790 (the discrepancy for the independence model).

Model	NPAR	CMIN	DF	P	CMIN/DF
A	15	71.544	6	0.000	11.924
B	16	6.383	5	0.271	1.277
Saturated model	21	0.000	0		
Independence model	6	2131.790	15	0.000	142.119

This things-could-be-worse philosophy of model evaluation is incorporated into a number of fit measures. All of the measures tend to range between zero and one, with values close to one indicating a good fit. Only **NFI** (described below) is guaranteed to be between zero and one, with one indicating a perfect fit. (**CFI** is also guaranteed to be between zero and one, but this is because values bigger than one are reported as one, while values less than zero are reported as zero.)

The independence model is only one example of a model that can be chosen as the baseline model, although it is the one most often used, and the one that Amos uses. Sobel and Bohrnstedt (1985) contend that the choice of the independence model as a baseline model is often inappropriate. They suggest alternatives, as did Bentler and Bonett (1980), and give some examples to demonstrate the sensitivity of **NFI** to the choice of baseline model.

NFI

The Bentler-Bonett (1980) normed fit index (**NFI**), or Δ_1 in the notation of Bollen (1989) can be written

$$\text{NFI} = \Delta_1 = 1 - \frac{\hat{C}}{\hat{C}_b} = 1 - \frac{\hat{F}}{\hat{F}_b},$$

where $\hat{C} = n\hat{F}$ is the minimum discrepancy of the model being evaluated and $\hat{C}_b = n\hat{F}_b$ is the minimum discrepancy of the baseline model.

In Example 6 the independence model can be obtained by adding constraints to any of the other models. Any model can be obtained by constraining the saturated model. So Model A, for instance, with $\chi^2 = 71.544$, is unambiguously "in between" the perfectly fitting saturated model ($\chi^2 = 0$) and the independence model $\chi^2 = 2131.790$).

```
            Model  NPAR      CMIN   DF          P    CMIN/DF
    .............  ....   .......   ..   ........  .........
                A    15    71.544    6      0.000     11.924
                B    16     6.383    5      0.271      1.277
  Saturated model    21     0.000    0
Independence model    6  2131.790   15      0.000    142.119
```

Looked at in this way, the fit of Model A is a lot closer to the fit of the saturated model than it is to the fit of the independence model. In fact you might say that Model A has a discrepancy that is 96.6% of the way between the (terribly fitting) independence model and the (perfectly fitting) saturated model:

$$\text{NFI} = \frac{2131.790 - 71.54}{2131.790} = 1 - \frac{71.54}{2131.790} = .966.$$

Rule of thumb:

> "Since the scale of the fit indices is not necessarily easy to interpret (e.g., the indices are not squared multiple correlations), experience will be required to establish values of the indices that are associated with various degrees of meaningfulness of results. In our experience, models with overall fit indices of less than .9 can usually be improved substantially. These indices, and the general hierarchical comparisons described previously, are best understood by examples." (Bentler and Bonett, 1980, p. 600, referring to both the **NFI** and the **TLI**)

Note: Use the **\nfi** text macro to display the normed fit index value in the output path diagram.

RFI

Bollen's (1986) relative fit index (**RFI**) is given by

$$\text{RFI} = \rho_1 = 1 - \frac{\hat{C}/d}{\hat{C}_b/d_b} = 1 - \frac{\hat{F}/d}{\hat{F}_b/d_b},$$

where $\hat{C}$ and d are the discrepancy and the degrees of freedom for the model being evaluated, and $\hat{C}_b$ and d_b are the discrepancy and the degrees of freedom for the baseline model.

The **RFI** is obtained from the **NFI** by substituting F/d for F.

RFI values close to 1 indicate a very good fit.

Note: Use the **\rfi** text macro to display the relative fit index value in the output path diagram.

IFI

Bollen's (1989) incremental fit index (**IFI**) is given by

$$\text{IFI} = \Delta_2 = \frac{\hat{C}_b - \hat{C}}{\hat{C}_b - d},$$

where $\hat{C}$ and d are the discrepancy and the degrees of freedom for the model being evaluated, and $\hat{C}_b$ and d_b are the discrepancy and the degrees of freedom for the baseline model.

IFI values close to 1 indicate a very good fit.

Note: Use the \ifi text macro to display the incremental fit index value in the output path diagram.

TLI

The Tucker-Lewis coefficient (ρ_2 in the notation of Bollen, 1989) was discussed by Bentler and Bonett (1980) in the context of analysis of moment structures, and is also known as the Bentler-Bonett non-normed fit index (**NNFI**).

$$\text{TLI} = \rho_2 = \frac{\dfrac{\hat{C}_b}{d_b} - \dfrac{\hat{C}}{d}}{\dfrac{\hat{C}_b}{d_b} - 1},$$

The typical range for **TLI** lies between zero and one, but it is not limited to that range. **TLI** values close to 1 indicate a very good fit.

Note: Use the \tli text macro to display the value of the Tucker-Lewis index in the output path diagram.

CFI

The comparative fit index (**CFI**; Bentler, 1990) is given by.

$$\text{CFI} = 1 - \frac{\max\left(\hat{C} - d,\ 0\right)}{\max\left(\hat{C}_b - d_b,\ 0\right)} = \frac{\text{NCP}}{\text{NCP}_b},$$

where $\hat{C}$, d, and **NCP** are the discrepancy, the degrees of freedom and the noncentrality parameter estimate for the model being evaluated, and $\hat{C}_b$, d_b and NCP_b are the discrepancy, the degrees of freedom and the noncentrality parameter estimate for the baseline model.

The **CFI** is identical to McDonald and Marsh's (1990) relative noncentrality index (**RNI**),

$$RNI = 1 - \frac{\hat{C} - d}{\hat{C}_b - d_b},$$

except that the **CFI** is truncated to fall in the range from 0 to 1. **CFI** values close to 1 indicate a very good fit.

Note: Use the \cfi text macro to display the value of the comparative fit index in the output path diagram.

Parsimony adjusted measures

James, et al. (1982) suggested multiplying the **NFI** by a "parsimony index" so as to take into account the number of degrees of freedom for testing both the model being evaluated and the baseline model. Mulaik (1989) suggested applying the same adjustment to the **GFI**. Amos also applies a parsimony adjustment to the **CFI**.

See also **PGFI** on page 569.

PNFI

The **PNFI** is the result of applying James, et al.'s (1982) parsimony adjustment to the **NFI**:

$$\text{PNFI} = (\text{NFI})(\text{PRATIO}) = \text{NFI}\,\frac{d}{d_b},$$

where d is the degrees of freedom for the model being evaluated, and d_b is the degrees of freedom for the baseline model.

Note: Use the **\pnfi** text macro to display the value of the parsimonious normed fit index in the output path diagram.

PCFI

The **PCFI** is the result of applying James, et al.'s (1982) parsimony adjustment to the **CFI**:

$$\text{PCFI} = (\text{CFI})(\text{PRATIO}) = \text{CFI}\,\frac{d}{d_b}$$

where d is the degrees of freedom for the model being evaluated, and d_b is the degrees of freedom for the baseline model.

Note: Use the **\pcfi** text macro to display the value of the parsimonious comparative fit index in the output path diagram.

GFI and related measures

GFI

The **GFI** (goodness of fit index) was devised by Jöreskog and Sörbom (1984) for **$ml** and **$uls** estimation, and generalized to other estimation criteria by Tanaka and Huba (1985). The **GFI** is given by

$$\text{GFI} = 1 - \frac{\hat{F}}{\hat{F}_b}$$

where $\hat{F}$ is the minimum value of the discrepancy function defined in Appendix B and $\hat{F}_b$ is obtained by evaluating F with $\Sigma^{(g)} = \mathbf{0}$, $g = 1, 2,...,G$. An exception has to be made for maximum likelihood estimation, since (D2) in Appendix B is not defined for $\Sigma^{(g)} = \mathbf{0}$. For the purpose of computing **GFI** in the case of maximum likelihood estimation, $f\left(\Sigma^{(g)};\ \mathbf{S}^{(g)}\right)$ in Appendix B is calculated as

$$f\left(\Sigma^{(g)};\ \mathbf{S}^{(g)}\right) = \tfrac{1}{2}\ \text{tr}\left[\mathbf{K}^{(g)}{}^{-1}\left(\mathbf{S}^{(g)} - \Sigma^{(g)}\right)\right]^2$$

with $\mathbf{K}^{(g)} = \Sigma^{(g)}(\hat{\gamma}_{ML})$, where $\hat{\gamma}_{ML}$ is the maximum likelihood estimate of γ. **GFI** is always between zero (0) and unity (1), where unity indicates a perfect fit.

Note: Use the **\gfi** text macro to display the value of the goodness-of-fit index in the output path diagram.

AGFI

The **AGFI** (adjusted goodness of fit index) takes into account the degrees of freedom available for testing the model. It is given by

$$\text{AGFI} = 1 - (1 - \text{GFI})\frac{d_b}{d},$$

where

$$d_b = \sum_{g=1}^{G} p^{*(g)}.$$

The **AGFI** is bounded above by one, which indicates a perfect fit. It is not, however, bounded below by zero, as the **GFI** is.

Note: Use the **\agfi** text macro to display the value of the adjusted GFI in the output path diagram.

PGFI

The **PGFI** (parsimony goodness of fit index), suggested by Mulaik, et al. (1989), is a modification of the **GFI** that takes into account the degrees of freedom available for testing the model:

$$PGFI = GFI \frac{d}{d_b},$$

where d is the degrees of freedom for the model being evaluated, and

$$d_b = \sum_{g=1}^{G} p^{*(g)}$$

is the degrees of freedom for the baseline zero model.

Note: Use the **\pgfi** text macro to display the value of the parsimonious GFI in the output path diagram.

Miscellaneous measures

HI 90

See **LO 90** on page 570.

HOELTER

Hoelter's (1983) "critical N" is the largest sample size for which one would accept the hypothesis that a model is correct. Hoelter does not specify a significance level to be used in determining the critical N, although he uses .05 in his examples. Amos reports a critical N for significance levels of .05 and .01. Here are the critical N's displayed by Amos for each of the models in Example 6.

```
                         HOELTER       HOELTER
              Model         .05           .01
          . . . . . . . .  . . . . . . .  . . . . . . .
                  A          164           219
                  B         1615          2201
   Independence model         11            14
```

Model A, for instance, would have been accepted at the .05 level if the sample moments had been exactly as they were found to be in the Wheaton study, but with a sample size of 164. With a sample size of 165, Model A would have been rejected. Hoelter argues that a critical N of 200 or better indicates a satisfactory fit. In an analysis of multiple groups, he suggests a threshold of 200 times the number of groups. Presumably this threshold is to be used in conjunction with a significance level of .05. This standard eliminates Model A and the independence model in Example 6. Model B is satisfactory according to the Hoelter criterion. I am not myself convinced by Hoelter's arguments in favor of the 200 standard. Unfortunately, the use of critical N as a practical aid to model selection requires some such standard. Bollen and Liang (1988) report some studies of the critical N statistic.

Note: Use the **\hfive** text macro to display Hoelter's critical N in the output path diagram for $\alpha = 0.05$, or the **\hone** text macro for $\alpha = 0.01$.

LO 90

Amos reports a 90% confidence interval for the population value of several statistics. The upper and lower boundaries are given in columns labeled **HI 90** and **LO 90**.

RMR

The **RMR** (root mean square residual) is the square root of the average squared amount by which the sample variances and covariances differ from their estimates obtained under the assumption your model is correct:

$$\text{RMR} = \sqrt{\sum_{g=1}^{G}\left\{\sum_{i=1}^{p_g}\sum_{j=1}^{j\leq i}\left(\hat{s}_{ij}^{(g)} - \sigma_{ij}^{(g)}\right)^2\right\} \Bigg/ \sum_{g=1}^{G} p *^{(g)}} \ .$$

The smaller the **RMR** is, the better. An **RMR** of zero indicates a perfect fit.

The following output from Example 6 shows that, according to the **RMR**, Model A is the best among the models considered except for the saturated model:

```
           Model        RMR        GFI       AGFI       PGFI
. . . . . . . . . . . . . . . . . . . . . . . . . . . . . . . . . . . . .
               A        0.284      0.975      0.913      0.279
               B        0.758      0.998      0.990      0.238
   Saturated model      0.000      1.000
Independence model     12.356      0.494      0.292      0.353
```

Note: Use the **\rmr** text macro to display the value of the root mean square residual in the output path diagram.

Selected list of fit measures

If you want to focus on a few fit measures, you might consider the implicit recommendation of Browne and Mels (1992), who elect to report only the following fit measures:

CMIN on page 554

P on page 554

FMIN on page 556

F0 on page 558, with 90% confidence interval

PCLOSE on page 559

RMSEA on page 558, with 90% confidence interval

ECVI on page 561, with 90% confidence interval

For the case of maximum likelihood estimation, Browne and Cudeck (1989, 1992) suggest substituting **MECVI** (page 562) for **ECVI**.

Appendix D: Numerical diagnosis of nonidentifiability

In order to decide whether a parameter is identified, or whether an entire model is identified, Amos examines the rank of the matrix of approximate second derivatives, and of some related matrices. The method used is similar to that of McDonald and Krane (1977). There are objections to this approach in principle (Bentler and Weeks, 1980; McDonald, 1982). There are also practical problems in determining the rank of a matrix in borderline cases. Because of these difficulties, you should judge the identifiability of a model on *a priori* grounds if you can. With complex models, this may be impossible, so that you will have to rely on Amos's numerical determination. Fortunately, Amos is pretty good at assessing identifiability in practice.

References

Bibliography

Akaike, H. (1973). Information theory and an extension of the maximum likelihood principle. In Petrov, B. N., & Csaki, F. (Eds.), *Proceedings of the 2nd International Symposium on Information Theory*. Budapest: Akademiai Kiado, 267–281.

Akaike, H. (1987). Factor analysis and AIC. *Psychometrika, 52*, 317–332.

Anderson, T. W. (1957). Maximum likelihood estimates for a multivariate normal distribution when some observations are missing. *Journal of the American Statistical Association, 52*, 200–203.

Anderson, T.W. (1984). *An introduction to multivariate statistical analysis*. New York: Wiley.

Arbuckle, J. L. (in preparation). Bootstrapping and model selection for analysis of moment structures.

Arbuckle, J.L. (1996) Full information estimation in the presence of incomplete data. In G.A. Marcoulides and R.E. Schumacker (1996) Advanced structural equation modeling: issues and techniques. Mahwah, NJ: Lawrence Erlbaum Associates

Arbuckle, J. L. (1994a). Advantages of model-based analysis of missing data over pairwise deletion. Presented at the RMD Conference on Causal Modeling, West Lafayette, Indiana.

Arbuckle, J. L. (1994b). A permutation test for analysis of covariance structures. Presented at the annual meeting of the Psychometric Society, University of Illinois, Champaign, Illinois.

Attig, M. S. (1983). The processing of spatial information by adults. Presented at the annual meeting of The Gerontological Society, San Francisco.

Beale, E. M. L., & Little, R. J. A. (1975). Missing values in multivariate analysis. *Journal of the Royal Statistical Society Series B, 37*, 129–145.

Bentler, P. M. (1980). Multivariate analysis with latent variables: Causal modeling. *Annual Review of Psychology, 31*, 419–456.

Bentler, P. M. (1985). *Theory and Implementation of EQS: A Structural Equations Program*. Los Angeles: BMDP Statistical Software.

Bentler, P. (1990). Comparative fit indexes in structural models. *Psychological Bulletin, 107*, 238–246

Bentler, P. M., & Bonett, D. G. (1980). Significance tests and goodness of fit in the analysis of covariance structures. *Psychological Bulletin, 88*, 588–606.

Bentler, P. M., & Chou, C. (1987). Practical issues in structural modeling. *Sociological Methods and Research, 16*, 78–117.

Bentler, P. M., & Freeman, E. H. (1983). Tests for stability in linear structural equation systems. *Psychometrika, 48*, 143–145.

Bentler, P. M., & Weeks, D. G. (1980). Linear structural equations with latent variables. *Psychometrika, 45*, 289–308.

Bentler, P. M., & Woodward, J. A. (1979). Nonexperimental evaluation research: Contributions of causal modeling. In Datta, L., & Perloff, R. (Eds.), *Improving Evaluations*. Beverly Hills: Sage.

Bollen, K. A. (1986). Sample size and Bentler and Bonett's nonnormed fit index. *Psychometrika, 51*, 375–377.

Bollen, K. A. (1987). Outliers and improper solutions: A confirmatory factor analysis example. *Sociological Methods and Research, 15*, 375–384.

Bollen, K. A. (1989). *Structural equations with latent variables*. New York: Wiley.

Bollen, K. A. (1989). A new incremental fit index for general structural equation models. *Sociological Methods and Research, 17*, 303–316.

Bollen, K.A. & Jöreskog, K.G. (1985). Uniqueness does not imply identification: A note on confirmatory factor analysis. *Sociological Methods and Research*, 14, 155–163.

Bollen, K. A., & Liang, J. (1988). Some properties of Hoelter's CN. *Sociological Methods and Research, 16*, 492–503.

Bollen, K. A., & Long, J. S. (Eds.) (1993). *Testing structural equation models*. Newbury Park, California: Sage.

Bollen, K. A., & Stine, R. A. (1992). Bootstrapping goodness-of-fit measures in structural equation models. *Sociological Methods and Research, 21*, 205–229.

Boomsma, A. (1987). The robustness of maximum likelihood estimation in structural equation models. In Cuttance, P., & Ecob, R. (Eds.) *Structural Modeling by Example: Applications in Educational, Sociological, and Behavioral Research*. Cambridge University Press, 160–188.

Botha, J. D., Shapiro, A., & Steiger, J. H. (1988). Uniform indices-of-fit for factor analysis models. *Multivariate Behavioral Research, 23*, 443–450.

Bozdogan, H. (1987). Model selection and Akaike's information criterion (AIC): The general theory and its analytical extensions. *Psychometrika, 52*, 345–370.

Browne, M. W. (1982). Covariance structures. In Hawkins, D. M. (Ed.) *Topics in applied multivariate analysis*. Cambridge: Cambridge University Press, 72–141.

Browne, M. W. (1984). Asymptotically distribution-free methods for the analysis of covariance structures. *British Journal of Mathematical and Statistical Psychology, 37*, 62–83.

Browne, M. W., & Cudeck, R. (1989). Single sample cross-validation indices for covariance structures. *Multivariate Behavioral Research, 24*, 445–455.

Browne, M. W., & Cudeck, R. (1993). Alternative ways of assessing model fit. In Bollen, K. A., & Long, J. S. (Eds.) *Testing structural equation models*. Newbury Park, California: Sage, 136–162.

Browne, M. W., & Mels, G. (1992). RAMONA User's Guide. The Ohio State University, Columbus, Ohio.

Byrne, B. M. (1989). *A primer of LISREL: Basic applications and progamming for confirmatory factor analytic models*. New York: Springer-Verlag.

Carmines, E. G., & McIver, J. P. (1981). Analyzing models with unobserved variables. In Bohrnstedt, G. W., & Borgatta, E. F. (Eds.) *Social measurement: Current issues*. Beverly Hills: Sage.

Cliff, N. (1973). Scaling. *Annual Review of Psychology*, *24*, 473–506.

Cliff, N. (1983). Some cautions concerning the application of causal modeling methods. *Multivariate Behavioral Research*, *18*, 115–126.

Cochran, W. G. (1952). The χ^2 test of goodness of fit. *Annals of Mathematical Statistics*, *23*, 315–345.

Cook, T. D., & Campbell, D. T. (1979). *Quasi-experimentation: Design and analysis issues for field settings*. Chicago: Rand McNally.

Cudeck, R., & Browne, M. W. (1983). Cross-validation of covariance structures. *Multivariate Behavioral Research*, *18*, 147–167.

Davis, W.R. (1993). The FC1 rule of identification for confirmatory factor analysis: A general sufficient condition. *Sociological Methods and Research*, *21*, 403–437.

Diaconis, P., & Efron, B. (1983). Computer-intensive methods in statistics. *Scientific American*, *248*, 116–130.

Dolker, M., Halperin, S., & Divgi, D. R. (1982). Problems with bootstrapping Pearson correlations in very small samples. *Psychometrika*, *47*, 529–530.

Draper, N. R., & Smith, H. (1981). *Applied regression analysis. (2nd Ed.)* New York: Wiley.

Edgington, E. S. (1987). *Randomization Tests* (Second edition). New York: Marcel Dekker.

Efron, B. (1979). Bootstrap methods: Another look at the jackknife. *Annals of Statistics*, *7*, 1–26.

Efron, B. (1982). *The jackknife, the bootstrap and other resampling plans*. (SIAM Monograph #38) Philadelphia: Society for Industrial and Applied Mathematics.

Efron, B. (1987). Better bootstrap confidence intervals. *Journal of the American Statistical Association*, *82*, 171–185.

Efron, B., & Gong, G. (1983). A leisurely look at the bootstrap, the jackknife, and cross-validation. *American Statistician*, *37*, 36–48.

Efron, B., & Tibshirani, R. J. (1993). *An introduction to the bootstrap*. New York: Chapman and Hall.

Felson, R. B., & Bohrnstedt, G. W. (1979). "Are the good beautiful or the beautiful good?" The relationship between children's perceptions of ability and perceptions of physical attractiveness. *Social Psychology Quarterly*, *42*, 386–392.

Fox, J. (1980). Effect analysis in structural equation models. *Sociological Methods and Research*, *9*, 3–28.

Gulliksen, H., & Tukey, J. W. (1958). Reliability for the law of comparative judgment. *Psychometrika*, *23*, 95–110.

Hamilton, L. C. (1990). *Statistics with Stata*. Pacific Grove, California: Brooks/Cole.

Hayduk, L. A. *Structural equation modeling with LISREL*. (1987). Baltimore: Johns Hopkins University Press.

Hoelter, J. W. (1983). The analysis of covariance structures: Goodness-of-fit indices. *Sociological Methods and Research*, *11*, 325–344.

Holzinger, K. J., & Swineford, F. A. (1939). A study in factor analysis: The stability of a bi-factor solution. *Supplementary Educational Monographs*, No. 48. Chicago: University of Chicago, Dept. of Education.

Hubert, L. J., & Golledge, R. G. (1981). A heuristic method for the comparison of related structures. *Journal of Mathematical Psychology*, *23*, 214–226.

Huitema, B.E. (1980). *The analysis of covariance and alternatives*. New York: Wiley.

James, L. R., Mulaik, S. A., & Brett, J. M. (1982). *Causal analysis: Assumptions, models and data*. Beverly Hills: Sage.

Jöreskog, K. G. (1967). Some contributions to maximum likelihood factor analysis. *Psychometrika*, *32*, 443–482.

Jöreskog, K. G. (1969). A general approach to confirmatory maximum likelihood factor analysis. *Psychometrika*, *34*, 183–202.

Jöreskog, K. G (1971). Simultaneous factor analysis in several populations. *Psychometrika*, *36*, 409–426.

Jöreskog, K.G. (1979). A general approach to confirmatory maximum likelihood factor analysis with addendum.. In Jöreskog, K.G. & Sörbom, D. [Eds.] *Advances in factor analysis and structural equation models*. Cambridge, MA: Abt Books, 21–43.

Jöreskog, K. G., & Sörbom, D. (1984). *LISREL-VI user's guide* (3rd ed.). Mooresville, Indiana: Scientific Software.

Jöreskog, K. G., & Sörbom, D. (1989). *LISREL-7 user's reference guide*. Mooresville, Indiana: Scientific Software.

Kaplan, D. (1989). Model modification in covariance structure analysis: Application of the expected parameter change statistic. *Multivariate Behavioral Research*, *24*, 285–305.

Kendall, M. G., & Stuart, A. (1973). *The advanced theory of statistics* (vol. 2, 3rd edition). New York: Hafner.

Kullback, S., & Leibler, R. A. (1951). On information and sufficiency. *Annals of Mathematical Statistics*, *22*, 79–86.

Lee, S., & Hershberger, S. (1990). A simple rule for generating equivalent models in covariance structure modeling. *Multivariate Behavioral Research, 25*, 313–334.

Linhart, H., & Zucchini, W. (1986). *Model selection*. New York: Wiley.

Little, R.J.A. & Rubin, D.B. (1989). The analysis of social science data with missing values. *Sociological Methods and Research, 18*, 292–326.

Loehlin, J. C. (1992). *Latent variable models: An introduction to factor, path, and structural analysis* (2nd edition). Hillsdale, New Jersey: Erlbaum.

Lord, F. M. (1955). Estimation of parameters from incomplete data. *Journal of the American Statistical Association, 50*, 870–876.

MacCallum, R. (1986). Specification searches in covariance structure modeling. *Psychological Bulletin, 100*, 107–120.

MacCallum, R. C. (1990). The need for alternative measures of fit in covariance structure modeling. *Multivariate Behavioral Research, 25*, 157–162.

MacCallum, R.C., Roznowski, M. & Necowitz, L.B. (1992). Model modifications in covariance structure analysis: The problem of capitalization on chance. *Psychological Bulletin, 111*, 490–504.

MacCallum, R.C., Wegener, D.T., Uchino, B.N., & Fabrigar, L.R. (1993). The problem of equivalent models in applications of covariance structure analysis. *Psychological Bulletin, 114*, 185–199.

Manly, B. F. J. (1991). *Randomization and Monte Carlo Methods in Biology*. London: Chapman and Hall.

Mantel, N. (1967). The detection of disease clustering and a generalized regression approach. *Cancer Research, 27*, 209–220.

Mantel, N., & Valand, R. S. (1970). A technique of nonparametric multivariate analysis. *Biometrics, 26*, 47–558.

Mardia, K. V. (1970). Measures of multivariate skewness and kurtosis with applications. *Biometrika, 57*, 519–530.

Mardia, K. V. (1974). Applications of some measures of multivariate skewness and kurtosis in testing normality and robustness studies. *Sankhya*, Series B, *36*, 115–128.

Marsh, H. W., & Hocevar, D. (1985). Application of confirmatory factor analysis to the study of self-concept: First- and higher-order factor models and their invariance across groups. *Psychological Bulletin, 97*, 562–582.

Matthai, A. (1951). Estimation of parameters from incomplete data with application to design of sample surveys. *Sankhya, 11*, 145–152.

McDonald, R. P. (1978). A simple comprehensive model for the analysis of covariance structures. *British Journal of Mathematical and Statistical Psychology, 31*, 59–72.

McDonald, R. P (1982). A note on the investigation of local and global identifiability. *Psychometrika, 47*, 101–103.

McDonald, R. P. (1989). An index of goodness-of-fit based on noncentrality. *Journal of Classification, 6*, 97–103.

McDonald, R. P., & Krane, W. R. (1977). A note on local identifiability and degrees of freedom in the asymptotic likelihood ratio test. *British Journal of Mathematical and Statistical Psychology*, *30*, 198–203.

McDonald, R. P., & Krane, W. R. (1979). A Monte-Carlo study of local identifiability and degrees of freedom in the asymptotic likelihood ratio test. *British Journal of Mathematical and Statistical Psychology*, *32*, 121–132.

Mulaik, S. A. (1990). An analysis of the conditions under which the estimation of parameters inflates goodness of fit indices as measures of model validity. Paper presented at the Annual Meeting, Psychometric Society, Princeton, NJ, June 28–30, 1990.

Mulaik, S. A., James, L. R., Van Alstine, J., Bennett, N., Lind, S., & Stilwell, C. D. (1989). Evaluation of goodness-of-fit indices for structural equation models. *Psychological Bulletin*, *105*, 430–445.

Olsson, S. (1973). *An experimental study of the effects of training on test scores and factor structure*. Uppsala, Sweden: University of Uppsala, Department of Education.

Raftery, A. E. (1993). Bayesian model selection in structural equation models. In Bollen, K. A., & Long, J. S. (Eds.) *Testing structural equation models*. Newbury Park, California: Sage, 163–180.

Rigdon, E. E. (1994). Calculating degrees of freedom for a structural equation model. *Structural Equation Modeling*, *1*, 274–278.

Rigdon, E. E. (1994). Demonstrating the effects of unmodeled random measurement error. *Structural Equation Modeling*, *1*, 375–380.

Rock, D. A., Werts, C. E., Linn, R. L., & Jöreskog, K. G. (1977). A maximum likelihood solution to the errors in variables and errors in equations model. *Journal of Multivariate Behavioral Research*, *12*, 187–197.

Rubin, D. E. (1976). Inference and missing data. *Biometrika*, *63*, 581–592.

Runyon, R. P., & Haber, A. (1980). *Fundamentals of behavioral statistics*, 4th ed. Reading, Mass.: Addison-Wesley.

Saris, W. E, Satorra, A., & Sörbom, D (1987). The detection and correction of specification errors in structural equation models. In Clogg, C. C. (Ed.). *Sociological methodology 1987*. San Francisco: Jossey-Bass.

Schwarz, G. (1978). Estimating the dimension of a model. *The Annals of Statistics*, *6*, 461–464.

Sobel, M. E., & Bohrnstedt, G. W. (1985). Use of null models in evaluating the fit of covariance structure models. In Tuma, N. B (Ed.) *Sociological methodology 1985*. San Francisco: Jossey-Bass, 152–178.

Sörbom, D. (1974). A general method for studying differences in factor means and factor structure between groups. *British Journal of Mathematical and Statistical Psychology*, *27*, 229–239.

Sörbom, D. (1978). An alternative to the methodology for analysis of covariance. *Psychometrika*, *43*, 381–396.

Steiger, J. H. (1989). *EzPATH: Causal modeling*. Evanston, Illinois: Systat.

Steiger, J. H. (1990). Structural model evaluation and modification: An interval estimation approach. *Multivariate Behavioral Research, 25*, 173–180.

Steiger, J. H., Shapiro, A., & Browne, M. W. (1985). On the multivariate asymptotic distribution of sequential chi-square statistics. *Psychometrika, 50*, 253–263.

Stelzl, I. (1986). Changing a causal hypothesis without changing the fit: Some rules for generating equivalent path models. *Multivariate Behavioral Research, 21*, 309–331.

Stine, R. (1989). An introduction to bootstrap methods: Examples and ideas. *Sociological Methods and Research, 18*, 243–291.

Swain, A. J. (1975). Analysis of parametric structures for variance matrices. Unpublished Ph.D. thesis, University of Adelaide.

Tanaka, J. S., & Huba, G. J. (1985). A fit index for covariance structure models under arbitrary GLS estimation. *British Journal of Mathematical and Statistical Psychology, 38*, 197–201.

Tanaka, J. S., & Huba, G. J. (1989). A general coefficient of determination for covariance structure models under arbitrary GLS estimation. *British Journal of Mathematical and Statistical Psychology, 42*, 233–239.

Tucker, L. R and Lewis, C. (1973). A reliability coefficient for maximum likelihood factor analysis. *Psychometrika, 38*, 1–10.

Warren, R. D., White, J. K., & Fuller, W. A. (1974). An errors-in-variables analysis of managerial role performance. *Journal of the American Statistical Association, 69*, 886–893.

Wheaton, B. (1987). Assessment of fit in overidentified models with latent variables. *Sociological Methods and Research, 16*, 118–154.

Wheaton, B., Muthén, B., Alwin, D. F., & Summers, G. F. (1977). Assessing reliability and stability in panel models. In Heise, D. R. (Ed.) *Sociological methodology 1977.* San Francisco: Jossey-Bass, 84–136.

Wichman, B. A., & Hill, I. D. (1982). An efficient and portable pseudo-random number generator. Algorithm AS 183. *Applied Statistics, 31*, 188–190.

Winer, B.J. (1971). *Statistical principles in experimental design.* New York: McGraw-Hill.

Wothke, W. (1993). Nonpositive definite matrices in structural modeling. In Bollen, K A., & Long, J. S. (Eds.), *Testing structural equation models* (pp. 256–293). Newbury Park, California: Sage.

Index

Binary data file (data input), 3, 12, 26, 27, 50–57
Blank lines, 175, 198, 310
Blank spaces, 175, 310
Bohrnstedt, G. W., ii, 387–389, 427–430, 435, 439, 563, 579–582
Bollen, K. A., 2, 6, 183, 184, 240, 279, 294, 303, 351, 397, 532, 551, 563, 565, 570, 578, 579, 582, 583
Bonett, D. G., 555, 563–565, 578
Boomsma, A., 252, 578
Bootadf ($ command), 182
Bootbs ($ command), 183
Bootfactor ($ command), 185
Bootgls ($ command), 187
Bootml ($ command), 188
Bootnormal ($ command), 189
Bootsls ($ command), 190
Bootstrap
  asymptotically distribution-free discrepancy. *See* $bootadf
  bias-corrected confidence intervals, 199
  Bollen and Stine test of model fit. *See* $bootbs
  confidence interval
    bias-corrected. *See* $confidencebc
    percentile-corrected. *See* $confidencepc
  generalized least-squares discrepancy. *See* $bootgls
  maximum likelihood discrepancy. *See* $bootml
  normal distribution. *See* $bootnormal
  number of samples. *See* $bootstrap
  parametric, 189. *See* $bootnormal
  percentile-corrected confidence intervals, 201
  population, 531, 535
  sample, 122, 182–195, 280, 283, 284, 297, 298, 525–531, 534–541
  scale-free least squares discrepancy. *See* $bootsls
  seed for random numbers. *See* $seed
  standard errors. *See* $bootstrap
  technical output. *See* $bootverify
  unweighted least squares discrepancy. *See* $bootuls
Bootstrap ($ command), 191

Bootuls ($ command), 194
Bootverify ($ command), 195
Botha, J. D., 578
Bozdogan, H., 578
Brett, J. M., 553, 580
Brief ($ command), 196
Browne, M. W., 6, 113, 197, 281, 531, 547, 548, 555–561, 572, 578, 579, 583
Browne-Cudeck criterion (BCC), 560
Byrne, B. M., 555, 579

C

CAIC (fit measure), 561
Calculate Estimates (graphics tool), 122
Campbell, D. T., 403, 579
Carmines, E. G., 555, 579
Case of characters in $ commands, 178
Causal
  model, 1, 577–579, 582
  relation, 1, 577–579, 582
CFI (comparative fit index), 565
Change printer settings (graphics tool), 60
Change screen colors (graphics tool), 152
Change the page layout (graphics tool), 146
Change the shape of objects (graphics tool), 78
Character
  dollar sign $, 126, 175, 310, 311, 314, 315, 320
  exclamation point, 176, 310
  semicolon, 176
  space, 175, 310
  tab, 176, 204, 205, 224, 249
Characteristic value, 285, 287, 296
Characters, special, 175
Chicorrect ($ command), 197
Chi-square
  distribution, 184, 292, 329, 331, 365, 412, 521, 549, 557
  fit statistic, 134, 184, 233, 279, 289, 292–294, 328–331, 336, 363, 365, 372, 373, 376, 378, 384, 407, 408, 412, 446, 451, 453, 458, 480, 483, 505, 583

Choose miscellaneous options (graphics tool), 159
Choose the width of lines (graphics tool), 157
Choose typefaces (graphics tool), 121
Chou, C., 252, 578
Cliff, N., 579
CMIN (fit measure), 554, 555
Cochran, W. G., 554, 579
Collinearity diagnostic
  condition number, 285
Comment, 176, 310, 452
Comments in $ command, 176, 310, 452
comparative Fit index (CFI), 565
Comparison of models, ii, 288, 292, 367, 383, 384, 457, 458, 473, 474, 520, 531, 536, 560
Compress ($ command), 198
Condition number of sample moments, 285
Confidence intervals
  bias-corrected, 199
  percentile-corrected, 201
Confidence limits, 570
confidencebc ($ command), 199
confidencepc ($ command), 201
CONFIG.AMD file, 13, 14, 120, 129, 218, 219
Configuration files, 13, 14, 120, 129, 218, 219
Confirmatory factor analysis, 578, 579, 581
Consistent estimate, 500
Constraint
  across groups, 434
  equality, 228, 229, 260, 328, 376, 382, 397, 434, 490, 519
  value, 324, 369, 452
Cook, T. D., 403, 579
Copy a diagram to the clipboard (graphics tool), 64
Corest ($ command), 203
Correlations
  implied by model. *See* $impliedmoments
Correlations ($ command), 204
Covariance

sample, 134, 186, 205, 237, 250, 251, 259, 270, 273, 285–287, 294, 295, 304, 318, 321, 328, 346, 352, 419, 451, 463, 499, 545
Covariance structure, 134, 344, 421, 450–452, 458, 493, 533, 578–583
Covariances
  implied by model. *See* $impliedmoments
  not positive definite. *See* $nonpositive
  of estimates. *See* $covest
  sample. *See* $covariances, $samplemoments
Covariances ($ command), 205
Covest ($ command), 206
Crdiff ($ command), 207
Crit1 ($ command), 208
Crit2 ($ command), 209
Cudeck, R., 113, 558–561, 572, 578, 579

D

Data input
  ASCII data, 26, 50
  database formats, 3, 12, 26, 27, 50–57
    dBase III and IV, 3, 50
    Foxpro (2.0 and 2.5), 3, 50
    MS Access (1 and 2), 3, 50
    multiple groups, 55, 56
    SPSS SAV file, 3, 26, 27, 52
  original Amos format, 26, 50
    $correlations, 204
    $covariances, 205
    $include, 218
    $inputvariables, 220
    $means, 224
    $missing, 226
    $rawdata, 249
    $samplesize, 252
    $standarddeviations, 258
  text data, 26, 50
Data sets
  attg_old.amd, 413, 415, 419–423, 449, 452, 456, 457
  attg_yng.amd, 309–311, 314–316, 325, 335, 413–416, 421, 423, 449, 452, 456, 457
  dbf format, 3, 50

Incomplete data analysis by full information maximum likelihood, 1, 384, 499–501, 505, 510, 577, 581

Incremental fit index (IFI), 565

Independence model, 298, 384, 534, 551, 553, 563, 564, 570, 571

Indirect effect, 268, 299, 386

Information criteria. *See* AIC, BCC, BIC, CAIC, ECVI, MECVI

Information-theoretic measures of fit, 560

Initial values, 136, 138, 185, 192, 234, 265

Input data. *See* $correlations, $covariances, $means, $rawdata, $samplesize, $standarddeviations

Input line length of $ commands, 175

Inputvariables ($ command), 220

Installation, i, 7, 8
  AMOS environment variable, 11
  Directory permissions, 10
  File permissions, 10
  IBM OS/2 2.11, 7
  IBM OS/2 Warp, 7, 12, 13
  Marking files execute-only, 10, 13
  Marking files/directories read-only, 10, 13, 14
  Multi-user system, i, 10, 13
  Required disk space, 8
  Required memory, 8
  SoftWindows 3.0, 7
  SoftWindows 95, 7
  TEMP environment variable, 14
  Uninstalling Amos, i, 13
  Win32s patch, 7–12
  Windows 3.0, 7
  Windows 3.1, 7–13
  Windows 95, 7–13
  Windows NT, 7–10, 13

Installation instructions, i, 7–11

Iterations ($ command), 221

J

James, L. R., 553, 567, 580, 582

Jöreskog, K. G., 6, 228–232, 246, 296, 305, 367, 368, 371–373, 397, 401, 441, 532, 554, 555, 568, 578, 580, 582

K

Kaplan, D., 233, 580

Kendall, M. G., 214, 580

Krane, W. R., 397, 573, 582

Kullback, S., 547, 580

Kurtosis. *See* $normalitycheck

L

Latent variable, 2, 3, 6, 17, 22, 65, 75–77, 96, 99–102, 134, 147–150, 252, 344, 357, 367, 397, 406, 475, 478, 488, 577, 578, 581, 583

Lee, S., 247, 581

Leibler, R. A., 547, 580

Lewis, C., 114, 563, 565, 583

Liang, J., 570, 578

Linelength ($ command), 222

Lines
  blank, 175, 198, 310

Linhart, H., 531, 536, 581

Link objects (graphics tool), 69

Linn, R. L., 582

Lisrel. *See* $chicorrect, $emulisrel6 *and* Appendix B

Listwise deletion of missing data, 499, 501, 505

Little, R. J. A., 499, 500, 577, 581

LO 90 (confidence limit), 570

Loehlin, J. C., 581

Long, J. S., 294, 551, 578, 579, 582, 583

Longitudinal study, 367

Lord, F. M., 513, 581

M

MacCallum, R. C., 247, 376, 551, 581

Macros (text macros), 112, 158, 330, 331, 436, 552–571

Manly, B. F. J., 581

MANOVA, 449, 458

Mantel, N., 581

Mardia, K. V., 581

Marsh, H. W., 555, 581

Matthai, A., 513, 581

Maxdecimalplaces ($ command), 223

Maximum likelihood

bootstrapped distribution of discrepancy function. *See* $bootml *and* Example 21

covariance estimates. *See* $covariances, $(no)unbiased, $(no)useunbiased

fit function. *See* $ml

Monte Carlo simulation. *See* $bootnormal

standard deviation estimates. *See* $standarddeviations, $(no)unbiased, $(no)useunbiased

McDonald, R. P., 281, 397, 565, 573, 581, 582

McIver, J. P., 555, 579

Mean
  implied by model, 181, 217, 250, 290, 291, 294
  residual, 294, 297
  sample, 2, 134, 189, 224, 250, 251, 284, 294, 295, 318, 339, 340, 352, 367, 387, 450–453, 462, 463, 475, 476, 499, 505, 518

Mean level model, 2, 4, 118, 134, 138, 197, 224, 226, 234, 284, 285, 293, 449–452, 455, 460–464, 467–470, 473, 494, 500–503, 507, 516, 545–547, 561, 582

Mean-level model
  Default for identification, 134, 462

Means ($ command), 224

Means and intercept model, 2, 4, 118, 134, 138, 197, 224, 226, 234, 284, 285, 293, 449–452, 455, 460–462, 464, 467–470, 473, 494, 500–503, 507, 516, 545–547, 561, 582

Means modeling, 2, 4, 118, 134, 138, 197, 224, 226, 234, 284, 285, 293, 449–452, 455, 460–464, 467–470, 473, 494, 500–503, 507, 516, 545–547, 561, 582

Measurement error, 340, 351, 354, 368, 375, 401, 403, 582

Measurement model, 354–358, 385, 470, 478, 479, 486, 532

Measures of fit, ii, 298, 551, 581

MECVI (fit measure), 562

Mels, G., 555, 557, 572, 579

Memory requirements, 8

Menu
  Align|Horizontal, 85
  Align|Parameter font attributes, 91
  Align|Parameter position, 90
  Align|Pen width, 93
  Align|Size, 89
  Align|Vertical, 86
  Align|Width, 88
  Diagram|Draw Covariance, 98
  Diagram|Draw Path, 97
  Diagram|Redraw Diagram, 108
  Diagram|Scroll, 107
  Diagram|Zoom, 103
  Diagram|Zoom In, 104
  Diagram|Zoom Out, 105
  Diagram|Zoom Page, 106
  Edit|Copy (to clipboard), 64
  Edit|Deselect All, 68
  Edit|Duplicate, 72
  Edit|Erase, 73
  Edit|Fit to page, 81
  Edit|Link, 69
  Edit|Move, 71
  Edit|Move Parameters, 74
  Edit|Redo, 63
  Edit|Reflect, 75
  Edit|Rotate, 77
  Edit|Select, 65
  Edit|Select All, 67
  Edit|Shape of object, 78
  Edit|Space horizontally, 79
  Edit|Space vertically, 80
  Edit|Touch up, 82
  Edit|Undo, 62
  File|Exit, 61
  File|New, 45
  File|Open..., 46
  File|Print..., 58
  File|Printer Setup..., 60
  File|Retrieve backup..., 47
  File|Save, 48
  File|Save as..., 49
  Global|Colors..., 152
  Global|Decimal Places..., 158
  Global|Miscellaneous..., 159
  Global|Outline, 154
  Global|Page Layout..., 146
  Global|Pen width..., 157
  Global|Shapes|Golden, 156

implied by model. *See*
$allimpliedmoments,
$impliedmoments
of sample. *See* $samplemoments; *also*
$covariances, $correlations,
$means, $standarddeviations
residual. *See* $residualmoments
Monte Carlo simulation, 189, 581
Move objects (graphics tool), 71
Move parameters (graphics tool), 74
Move tools (graphics tool), 165
Mstructure ($ command), 234
Mulaik, S. A., 551–553, 567, 569, 580,
582
Multi-group analysis, 413–415, 423,
433
Multi-user system, i, 10, 13
Multivariate analysis of variance, 449,
458
Muthén, B., 583

N

Name variables (graphics tool), 109
NCP (noncentrality parameter), 557
Necowitz, L.B., 376, 581
Nextgroup ($ command), 235
NFI (normed fit index), 563
NNFI (non-normed fit index), 565
Noallimpliedmoments ($ command),
236
Nonidentifiability, ii
Nonidentified model, 230, 271, 286,
303, 304, 346, 355, 371, 397
Non-normed fit index (NNFI), 565
Nonpositive ($ command), 237
Nonrecursive model, ii, 232, 296, 299,
349, 387, 388, 394, 429, 434, 435
Normal distribution
diagnostics. *See* $normalitycheck
estimation methods based on. *See* $ml,
$gls
Monte Carlo simulation. *See*
$bootnormal
requirements. *See* Distribution
assumptions for Amos models
Normalitycheck ($ command), 238
Normed fit index (NFI), 563
notation, 545

Nouseunbiased ($ command), 236
NPAR (number of parameters), 552
Number of
decimal places reported
in list output
See $maxdecimalplaces,
$mindecimalplaces,
$significantfigures
in path diagram, parameter
estimates
See Menu: Text|Parameter
Format…
in path diagram, text macros
See Menu: Global|Decimalplaces…
groups. *See* $nextgroup *and*
Menu:
Model-Fit|Groups/Models…
observations. *See* $samplesize
variables. *See* $inputvariables,
$ovariablecount, $uvariablecount,
$variablecount
Numerical diagnosis of
nonidentifiability, ii, 573

O

Observed ($ command), 241
Observed variable, ii, 17–20, 35, 95, 96,
110, 128, 134, 155, 156, 181, 205,
213, 217, 238–248, 286–291, 311–
313, 316, 333, 334, 339–342, 344,
349, 351, 354, 355, 360, 368, 385,
386, 389, 392, 396–439, 468–470,
479, 480, 493, 496, 497, 501, 502,
506, 510, 516, 545, 551
olss_all.amd (data set), 404, 406, 410,
411
olss_cnt.amd (data set), 476, 479, 483,
485, 488–493, 496
olss_exp.amd (data set), 475, 479, 483,
485, 488–493, 496
Olsson, S., 404–407, 410, 411, 475–
477, 491, 582
Operating system
IBM OS/2 2.11 with WIN-OS/2, 7
IBM OS/2 Warp with WIN-OS/2, 7,
12, 13
Windows 3.0, 7
Windows 3.1, 7, 8, 11–13

T

wheaton.amd (data set), 229, 230, 367, 370, 379, 382

White, J. K., 339, 352, 459–462, 583

Wichman, B. A., 257, 583

Win32s, 7, 8, 11, 12

Windows 3.0, 7

Windows 3.1, 7–13

Windows 95, 7–13

Windows dialect
  Insignia Solutions SoftWindows 3.x, 7
  Insignia Solutions SoftWindows 95, 7
  MS-Windows 3.0, 7
  MS-Windows 3.1, 7, 8, 11–13
  MS-Windows 95, 7–13
  MS-Windows NT, 7–10, 13
  Win32s patch, 7, 8, 11, 12
  WIN-OS/2 (IBM OS/2 2.11), 7

WIN-OS/2 (IBM OS/2 Warp), 7, 12, 13

Windows NT, 7–10, 13

Winer, B.J., 433, 583

Woodward, J. A., 403, 578

Worked examples, i, 10, 14, 369, 382

Wothke, W., 6, 237, 304, 583

Z

Zero model, 551, 569

Zoom in (graphics tool), 104

Zoom in on a selected area (graphics tool), 103

Zoom out (graphics tool), 105

Zoom to view a full page (graphics tool), 106

Zucchini, W., 531, 536, 581